EduCart

LET'S MAKE LEARNING INTERESTING

MW01714045

SAMPLE QUESTION PAPERS

SCIENCE

CBSE CLASS 10

(For February 2020 Exam)

Based on **20th September** 2019 CBSE Announced Sample Paper

EduCart
London | Agra | Noida
e-mail : quickreply@educart.net

EduCart
LET'S MAKE LEARNING INTERESTING

EduCart uses latest design and content trends through our R&D office in London to provide high quality children books from Nursery to Class 10 that are sold pan-India.

HEAD OFFICE
28/115, Jyoti Block
Sanjay Place
Agra, U.P. 282002

R&D OFFICE
5 Biddulph Mansions
Elgin Avenue
London, UK W9 1HZ

BRANCH OFFICE
#106, Tower 6
Lotus Panache
Noida, U.P 201304

CONTACT HERE | quickreply@educart.net
Award Winning Customer Support (We reply super fast)

BUY BOOK HERE | www.educart.net
All our latest books available at Cash On Delivery here.

Edition
Latest Edition

eduCart ***contributes Rupee One*** *on every book purchased by you to the* ***Friends of Tribals Society*** *Organization for better education of tribal children.*

Hello!

Friends, CBSE has made significant changes in the exam pattern for the upcoming February 2020 Class 10 Boards. And so have we, in this year's edition! New objective section is included based on the CBSE latest sample paper. Also revised and added are CBSE experts recommended questions in each sample paper.

This year, we have exclusively partnered with CBSE topper to provide latest CBSE Board paper solutions along with topper's unique tips. Continuing from an exemplary success of last year, EduCart has also roped in CBSE expert veterans and best-in-class teachers pan India, to prepare a TOP X^{th} Class Sample Papers series.

Let's start.

Reviews

S C BODH
To: quickreply@educart.net

Sample question paper mathematics CBSE class 10 is very helpful as it has easy solutions for questions. I used your sample for students providing me this book as specimen copy...

Received on Dec 09, 2018

★★★★★ **Helpful**

By Tribeni P. on Jan 11, 2019

The book is awesome. As a 10th student I recommend this for all the students who are appearing for board exam 2019.

5★ **15 awesome sample papers and good quality**

Books in good quality, book has 15 sample papers with solutions and focus and key points and toppers suggestions.

By Sahil on Feb 25, 2019

★★★★★ **Thank you!!!!**

By Rajvi Saxena on Apr 04, 2019

OMG! your sample papers ware so bullseye. I saw a lot of familiar questions in the board paper. Just wanted to say thanks!!

★★★★★ **It's a good book**

By Ram Chandra on Feb 16, 2019

Very good book for Examination.

Mahatmaji Technical
Published on Dec 3, 2018

CBSE Sample Paper Best Book- Educart 2019 Sample Papers

4.7M Subscribers

Excellent

By Rohit Raj on Jan 01, 2019

Your toppers tips and solved papers were very useful for practice, thank you educart.

★★★★★ **Best sample papers for class 10**

By Fazil on Oct 19, 2018

Best sample paper for cbse class 10 mathematics. Same difficulty level as asked in board exams. Practicing in this sample paper book would definitely increase your confidence level.

5★ **Loved it for the good sample papers**

It's a nice book for class 10. 85-95 percentage, we can easily score through educart.I suggest this for board exam.

By Ajay on Oct 10, 2018

SHWETA CHAUHAN
To: quickreply@educart.net

After a long time, I got a sample containing good explanation and accurate answers. I have recommended your sample paper to my students.

Received on Nov 30, 2018

Contents

(Self-assessment papers' solution are on our website)

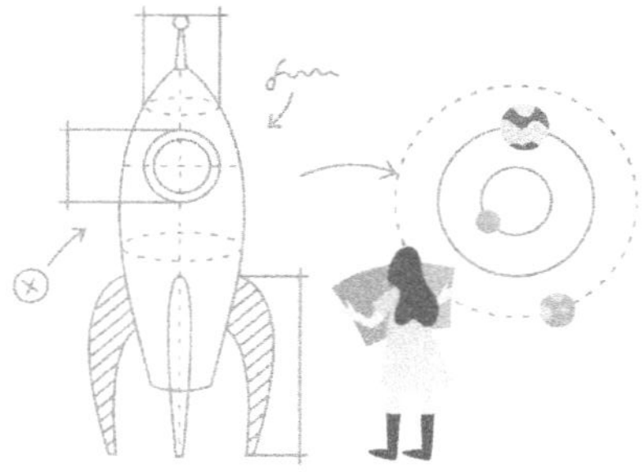

Question Paper Design

Typology of Questions	Objective type (1 Mark) 25% marks	Short Answer (3 Marks) 37.5% marks	Long Answer (5 Marks) 37.5% marks
Remembering: Exhibit memory of previously learned material by recalling facts, terms, basic concepts, and answers.	7Q	2Q	1Q
Understanding: Demonstrate understanding of facts and ideas by organizing, comparing, translating, interpreting, giving descriptions, and stating main ideas	4Q	2Q	2Q
Applying: Solve problems to new situations by applying acquired knowledge, facts, techniques and rules in a different way.	4Q	1Q	2Q
Analyzing and Evaluating: Examine and break information into parts by identifying motives or causes. Make inferences and find evidence to support generalizations Present and defend opinions by making judgments about information, validity of ideas, or quality of work based on a set of criteria.	5Q	2Q	1Q
Creating: Compile information together in a different way by combining elements in a new pattern or proposing alternative solutions.	-	3Q	-
Total	**20Q (20 marks)**	**10Q (30 marks)**	**6Q (30 marks)**

Note: All questions would be compulsory. However, an internal choice is provided in each section.

Syllabus

COURSE STRUCTURE CLASS-X

Units	Unit Name	Marks
I	Chemical Substances-Nature and Behaviour	25
II	World of Living	23
III	Natural Phenomena	12
IV	Effects of Current	13
V	Natural Resources	07
	TOTAL	**80**

Theme : Materials (55 Periods)

Unit I: Chemical Substances - Nature and Behaviour

Chemical reactions: Chemical equation, Balanced chemical equation, implications of a balanced chemical equation, types of chemical reactions: combination, decomposition, displacement, double displacement, precipitation, neutralization, oxidation and reduction.

Acids, bases and salts: Their definitions in terms of furnishing of H^+ and OH^- ions, General properties, examples and uses, concept of pH scale (Definition relating to logarithm not required), importance of pH in everyday life; preparation and uses of Sodium Hydroxide, Bleaching powder, Baking soda, Washing soda and Plaster of Paris.

Metals and nonmetals: Properties of metals and non-metals; Reactivity series; Formation and properties of ionic compounds; Basic metallurgical processes; Corrosion and its prevention.

Carbon compounds: Covalent bonding in carbon compounds. Versatile nature of carbon. Homologous series. Nomenclature of carbon compounds containing functional groups (halogens, alcohol, ketones, aldehydes, alkanes and alkynes), difference between saturated hydrocarbons and unsaturated hydrocarbons. Chemical properties of carbon compounds (combustion, oxidation, addition and substitution reaction). Ethanol and Ethanoic acid (only properties and uses), soaps and detergents.

Periodic classification of elements: Need for classification, early attempts at classification of elements (Dobereiner's Triads, Newland's Law of Octaves, Mendeleev's Periodic Table), Modern periodic table, gradation in properties, valency, atomic number, metallic and non-metallic properties.

Theme: The World of the Living (50 Periods)

Unit II: World of Living

Life processes: 'Living Being'. Basic concept of nutrition, respiration, transport and excretion in plants and animals.

Control and co-ordination in animals and plants: Tropic movements in plants; Introduction of plant hormones; Control and co-ordination in animals: Nervous system; Voluntary, involuntary and reflex action; Chemical co-ordination: animal hormones.

Reproduction: Reproduction in animals and plants (asexual and sexual) reproductive health-need and methods of family planning. Safe sex vs HIV/AIDS. Child bearing and women's health.

Heredity and Evolution: Heredity; Mendel's contribution- Laws for inheritance of traits: Sex determination: brief introduction; Basic concepts of evolution.

Theme : Natural Phenomena (23 Periods)

Unit III: Natural Phenomena

Reflection of light by curved surfaces; Images formed by spherical mirrors, centre of curvature, principal axis, principal focus, focal length, mirror formula (Derivation not required), magnification.

Refraction; Laws of refraction, refractive index.

Refraction of light by spherical lens; Image formed by spherical lenses; Lens formula (Derivation not required); Magnification. Power of a lens.

Functioning of a lens in human eye, defects of vision and their corrections, applications of spherical mirrors and lenses.

Refraction of light through a prism, dispersion of light, scattering of light, applications in daily life.

Theme: How Things Work (32 Periods)

Unit IV: Effects of Current

Electric current, potential difference and electric current. Ohm's law; Resistance, Resistivity, Factors on which the resistance of a conductor depends. Series combination of resistors, parallel combination of resistors and its applications in daily life. Heating effect of electric current and its applications in daily life. Electric power, Interrelation between P, V, I and R.

Magnetic effects of current: Magnetic field, field lines, field due to a current carrying conductor, field due to current carrying coil or solenoid; Force on current carrying conductor, Fleming's Left Hand Rule, Electric Motor, Electromagnetic induction.

Induced potential difference, Induced current. Fleming's Right Hand Rule, Electric Generator, Direct current. Alternating current: frequency of AC. Advantage of AC over DC. Domestic electric circuits.

Theme: Natural Resources (20 Periods)

Unit V: Natural Resources

Sources of energy: Different forms of energy, conventional and non-conventional sources of energy: Fossil fuels, solar energy; biogas; wind, water and tidal energy; Nuclear energy. Renewable versus non-renewable sources of Energy.

Our environment: Eco-system, Environmental problems, Ozone depletion, waste production and their solutions. Biodegradable and non-biodegradable substances.

Management of natural resources: Conservation and judicious use of natural resources. Forest and wild life; Coal and Petroleum conservation. Examples of people's participation for conservation of natural resources. Big dams: advantages and limitations; alternatives, if any. Water harvesting. Sustainability of natural resources.

CBSE Notification

केन्द्रीय माध्यमिक शिक्षा बोर्ड
CENTRAL BOARD OF SECONDARY EDUCATION

150 YEARS OF CELEBRATING THE MAHATMA

F.1001/CBSE/Dir(Acad)/2019 **March 6, 2019**
Circular No. Acad-11/2019

All Heads of CBSE affiliated schools

Subject: Strengthening Assessment and Evaluation Practices of the Board.

As we focus our attention on 'what our students are learning' alongwith 'the skill sets they are acquiring', it becomes imperative to strengthen current Assessment and Evaluation Practices and align them to the future requirements of the learners. The Board has always stressed that its students must acquire the skills of critical thinking, problem solving, analyzing information, collaboration, effective communication, developing curiosity and imagination as part of the learning process. You are also aware that the Board continues to make small changes in the assessment and evaluation practices almost every year to eventually reach the goal of achieving the aforementioned skills for all its students.

Report card of the National Assessment Survey (2017-18) has indicated that the performance of CBSE class X students in Mathematics, Science, Social Science, English and Modern Indian Language is 52%, 51%, 53%, 58% and 62% respectively. Although this competency-based survey places the CBSE students above the national average, it indicates that there is ample scope for improvement in their performance.

Further, the decision by MHRD to participate in PISA (Programme for International Student Assessment) in 2021, has given even more impetus to the requirement of aligning the Board's assessment system to future requirements. It may also be mentioned here, that since the Board has made it mandatory for all its affiliated schools to adopt the Learning Outcomes vide circular dated 18.01.2019, it is a necessity now that 'assessment of learning' must be augmented with 'assessment as learning' and 'assessment for learning'.

In view of above, countrywide consultations were held with CBSE stake holders including teachers, students, heads of Institutions and experts in the field to suggest ways to strengthen the Assessment and Evaluation Practices of the Board. It was agreed upon that the School Based / Internal Assessment needs to be strengthened by incorporating more diverse strategies. Further, there is need of exposing the students to different types and formats of questions in the year end/ Board examination, so that a large range of learning outcomes can be assessed. Based on this, following few changes are proposed in the Assessment and Examination practices for the year 2019-20 onwards. As the next academic session (2019-20) is going to start from April 2019 onwards, hence a summary view of the proposed changes in Internal Assessment and Year End/ Board Examinations are hereby informed in advance.

Classes IX-X

	Existing	Proposed
Maximum marks per subject :	100 marks	No Change
Types of assessment	▪ Internal Assessment ▪ Year End/Board Examination ▪ School Based Assessment of Co-scholastic Areas (Art Education, Health and Physical Education including Work Experience , Discipline)	No Change
Marks distribution	Internal Assessment : Year End/Board Exams 20 : 80	No Change

Internal Assessment

	Existing		Proposed	
	Periodic Test		**Periodic Assessment**	
	Periodic Test (Pen Paper Test)	10 marks	**Pen Paper Test**	5 marks
Components of Internal Assessment			**Multiple Assessment** strategies to be used. (quizzes, oral test, concept map, exit cards, visual expression etc.)	5 marks
	Notebook (Class work)		**Portfolio** (Classwork plus peer assessment, self-assessment, achievements of student in the subject, reflections, narrations, journals, etc)	5 marks
	Subject enrichment consisting of aspects like Practical work for Science; Labwork for Mathematics; Map work & Project Work for Social Science and Listening and Speaking skills for languages, etc.	5 marks	**Subject enrichment** ▪ Social Science Project Work ▪ No changes in other subjects	5 marks

Board Examination/ Year-end Examination

Board Examination	**Existing**	**Proposed**	
Marks	Marks 80	No change	
Duration	3 hours	No change	
Internal Choice	33%	No change	
COMPONENTS OF BOARD EXAMINATION PAPER	SHORT ANSWER/LONG ANSWER (OBJECTIVE AS WELL AS SUBJECTIVE)	OBJECTIVE TYPE INCLUDING MULTIPLE CHOICE QUESTIONS	20 MARKS (THIS IS ALREADY INCORPORATED IN 2019 BOARD EXAMS IN MANY SUBJECTS)
		Subjective – number of questions will be reduced to enable student to have enough time to give analytical and creative responses.	60 marks

School Based Assessment of Co-scholastic Areas (Work Experience, Art Education, Health & Physical Education Discipline)

Assessment of Co-scholastic areas	**Existing**	**Proposed**
	▪ Internally Assessed ▪ On a 5-point scale	No change

It may be noted that the changes introduced in 2019 Board Exams – that is, 33% internal options and section wise format – shall continue henceforth for all subjects. The details of the Year End-Board Examination/ Internal Assessment/School Based Assessment for the academic year 2019-20, shall be reflected in the Curriculum document to be published by the Board. The curriculum document shall be made available to all the schools by April 2019. This circular is being issued in advance to enable schools to prepare for implementing the few proposed changes from next academic session (2019-20) onwards.

Schools are also hereby informed that the Board is preparing detailed guidelines on how Art can be integrated with the teaching learning process at all levels. This is a part of the Board's thrust on innovative pedagogy, that will go a long way in achieving the process of 'assessment as learning'. These guidelines are being issued separately.

(Dr. Joseph Emmanuel)
Director (Academics)

2019 CBSE Topper Tips

Friends, on request of the EduCart team, followed below are some points I've prepared for you to keep in mind whilst attempting the Class 10 Board Exams:

Cross-check The Paper

Verify the question paper for any missing or unordered pages so that you don't panic later on or attempt questions in the wrong order.

Use the first 15 minutes effectively

There is 33% internal choice this time in each section. You get good 15 minutes in the beginning to read the question paper. Use this time to mark the questions with choice, the one you are more confident in attempting, to avoid confusion and save time while writing the exam.

Prioritise your Sections Order

Decide which Section would you want to attempt first and which Section at last. Always attempt the easy questions first. This way your confidence will grow and you will be mentally ready to take on the more challenging questions.

Mark the tough ones

Try to mark the questions you definitely don't know the answer to, and remember to leave space to come back to answering them at the end.

Select your options wisely

In some of the objective questions, you will get multiple choices. Do not rush into choosing a particular choice. If unable to find the answer; use the rule of elimination to reach the most appropriate answer.

Write neat and clean

Write your answer in a clean and legible handwriting. Draw a line after each answer to indicate end of that answer and beginning of new answers. Start new sections from a new page.

Answers Structure Has To Be Right

- Underline value points for all answers.
- Follow word counts to save on time.
- Explain lengthy answers with examples and diagrams.
- Always draw diagrams with pencil with a proper labeling in block letters.
- Recheck for all logics and calculations in case of numerical.
- Try to write most of the answers in bullet points and make the important points highlighted/underlined.

FAQs

1. What is the best way to practice from this book to score good marks?

In order to crack the board exam, this book is custom made to start with Topper Tips and CBSE markers basic points. This includes an explanation of how to smartly structure your 3 hours during the paper. Once, you have read the basics, you should start with practice of CBSE latest sample paper that is introduced recently. This will give you an accurate flavour of the type of questions that will come in the February 2020 exam.

Topper's section is next where the last 2 years topper's solutions are given to learn how a toper scores full marks in all types of questions. Then you start with our most likely 10 solved sample papers (strictly based on the upcoming board exam), where you time yourself to complete each paper and cross-check your performance with solutions.

Lastly, the unsolved papers help you practice without the temptation of looking at the back and fine-tune your preparation. These are 15 solid papers that if done well will fully prepare you to do well in the board exam.

2. What's the best way to know about any exam relevant CBSE announcements or CBSE official Sample Paper release?

Although you can find everything on CBSE's official website www.cbseacademic.nic.in, it's a bit unstructured and information is hard to find. However, our team is always in sync with CBSE, so just e-mail us your query on quickreply@educart.net.

3. What is the Pass Marks Cut-off and Criteria?

In order to be declared as having passed the examination, a candidate has to obtain a grade higher than E (*i.e.* atleast 33% marks) in all the five subjects of external examination in the main or at the compartmental examinations. In case of a subject involving practical work, a candidate has to obtain 33% marks in theory and 33% marks in practical separately in addition to 33% marks in aggregate in order to qualify in that subject.

4. What is the process of applying for a recheck of Marks in a particular subject?

Any student has the right to do so within a week from date of declaration of CBSE board exam result. The whole process of verification of marks is done online.

Steps to apply for verification/rechecking of the answer sheet, are as follows:

Apply for rechecking of marks on the CBSE's website www.cbse.nic.in by filling in your details and paying ₹ 500 per subject online (only)

The result of verification of marks will be uploaded on the website automatically.

Overall, the verification will be restricted to checking whether all the answers have been checked, there has been no mistake in totalling of marks for each question and the marks have been transferred correctly on the title page of the answer book. A candidate may also apply for obtaining a copy of the evaluated answer book(s) at a later stage if not satisfied with the evaluation.

5. What are the provisions for providing alternate Questions to candidates with Disabilities in the context of Class X examination?

Alternative type questions are provided in lieu of questions having visual inputs for disabled candidates in the subjects of English Communicative and Social Science. Separate question papers with enlarged font size are provided in the subjects of Mathematics and Science.

(Note: For categories of disabilities for which alternate question paper/enlarged font size question paper is permissible please refer to the CBSE website www.cbse.nic.in).

6. What criteria does CBSE use in awarding of Grades at the end of Class X?

For awarding the grades the Board puts all the passed students in rank order and awards grades as follows:

A-1	Top 1/8th of the passed candidates
A-2	Next 1/8th of the passed candidates
B-1	Next 1/8th of the passed candidates
B-2	Next 1/8th of the passed candidates
C-1	Next 1/8th of the passed candidates
C-2	Next 1/8th of the passed candidates
D-1	Next 1/8th of the passed candidates
D-2	Next 1/8th of the passed candidates
E	Failed candidates

Time Management

Divide the 3 hours such that you mentally allocate a particular time to each Section beforehand and can revise all the answers. So you can finish the paper within a manageable time limit. With input from the experts in this field, we have collated a fair breakdown of time that should be spent on each section:

Section	Section-wise Questions	Time To Be Spent (Per Question)	Section-wise Total Time
A	20Q (20 marks)	1.5 minutes	20 x 1.5 = **30 minutes**
B	10Q (30 marks)	7 minutes	10 x 7 = **70 minutes**
C	6Q (30 marks)	11 minutes	6 x 11 = **66 minutes**
Revision Time: **14 minutes**			

CBSE SAMPLE PAPER

20th September 2019

SCIENCE

Note: This recently uploaded CBSE sample paper is provided by EduCart to know the exact exam pattern. It will have the CBSE marking scheme after the paper for reference as provided to us by CBSE.

Time Allowed: 3 Hours | *Maximum Marks: 80*

General Instructions:

i. The question paper comprises three sections – A, B and C. Attempt all the sections.
ii. All questions are compulsory.
iii. Internal choice is given in each section.
iv. All questions in Section A are one-mark questions comprising MCQ, VSA type and assertion-reason type questions. They are to be answered in one word or in one sentence.
v. All questions in Section B are three-mark, short-answer type questions. These are to be answered in about 50 - 60 words each.
vi. All questions in Section C are five-mark, long-answer type questions. These are to be answered in about 80 - 90 words each.
vii. This question paper consists of a total of 30 questions.

SECTION - A

1. Define catenation. **1**

2. How does valency of an element vary across a period? **1**

3. **Answer question numbers 3(a) - 3(d) on the basis of your understanding of the following paragraph and the related studied concepts.**

Renewable energy sources such as wind energy are vital for the Indian economy, not only from the point of view of supply, but also from the perspective of environmental and social benefits. India is the world's fifth largest wind-power producer and the largest windmill facilities in India are installed in Tamil Nadu. Muppandal is a small village of Tamil Nadu and one of the most important sites of wind-farm in the state. It uses wind from the Arabian Sea to produce renewable energy. The suitability of Muppandal as a site for wind farms stems from its geographical location as it has access to the seasonal monsoon winds.

The electrical generators used on wind turbines in sites like Muppandal, produce an output AC of 240 V and a frequency of 50 Hz even when the wind speed is fluctuating. A transformer may be required to increase or decrease the voltage so it is compatible with the end usage, distribution or transmission voltage, depending on the type of interconnection.

(a) State the principle behind electric generator. 1

(b) The output frequency of wind turbine is 50 Hz. What is meant by this statement? 1

(c) Why do you think Muppandal is at an advantageous position for this project? 1

(d) Based on the data represented in the graph below, which of the two cities A or B would be an ideal location for establishing a wind-farm and why? 1

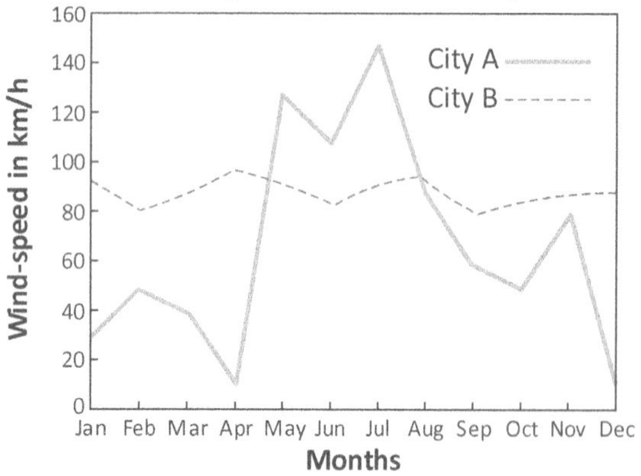

4. Question numbers 4(a) - 4(d) are based on the two tables given below. Study these tables related to blood sugar levels and answer the questions that follow. Table A (Blood glucose chart)

	Mean Blood Glucose Level (mg/dL)
Doctor's advice needed	380
	350
	315
	280
	250
	215
Good	180
	150
Excellent	115
	80
	50

Table B (Blood Report of Patient X and Y)

Time of check	**Blood Glucose ranges (mg/dL)**	
	Patient X	Patient Y
Before breakfast (Fasting)	< 100	70 - 130
Before lunch, supper and snack	< 110	70 - 130
Two hours after meals	< 140	< 180
Bedtime	< 120	90 - 15

(a) Refer to Table B showing the blood report of the levels of glucose of patients X and Y.

Infer the disease which can be diagnosed from the given data. 1

(b) Identify the hormone whose level in the blood is responsible for the above disease. 1

(c) Which one of the following diets would you recommended to the affected patient?

(i) High sugar and low fat diet. **(ii)** Low sugar and high protein diet.

(iii) High Fat and low fiber diet. **(iv)** Low sugar and high fiber diet. 1

(d) Refer to the Table A and suggest the value of the mean blood glucose level beyond which doctor's advice is necessary:

(i) 180 mg/dL **(ii)** 115 mg/dL

(iii) 50 mg/dL **(iv)** 80 mg/dL 1

5. When we enter a dark room coming from outside, immediately the things inside the room do not appear clear to our eyes. This is because:

(i) pupils do not open at all in the dark. **(ii)** pupils take time to adjust.

(iii) light travels slower in a dark room. **(iv)** pupils open very quickly in the dark.

OR

The phenomena of light responsible for the working of the human eye is

(i) reflection **(ii)** refraction

(iii) power of accommodation **(iv)** persistence of vision 1

6. When a 4V battery is connected across an unknown resistor there is a current of 100 mA in the circuit. The value of the resistance of the resister is:

(i) 4 Ω **(ii)** 40 Ω

(iii) 400 Ω **(iv)** 0.4 Ω 1

7. Unit of electric power may also be expressed as:

(i) volt-ampere **(ii)** kilowatt-hour

(iii) watt-second **(iv)** joule-second. 1

8. It was found that water from a river was contaminated with Coliform bacteria. Which one of the following pollutant might have got mixed with the water?

(i) Fertilizer run off **(ii)** Industrial waste

(iii) Pesticides **(iv)** Human faecal matter

OR

Which one of the following stakeholders of forests causes the maximum damage to forest?

(i) People who live in or around the forest

(ii) The forest department of the government

(iii) The wildlife and native enthusiasts

(iv) The industrialists 1

9. Which one of the following green house gases is a contributor due to incomplete combustion of coal and petroleum?

(i) Oxides of nitrogen **(ii)** Methane

(iii) Carbon monoxide **(iv)** Carbon dioxide 1

10. Which of the following reactions is an endothermic reaction?

(i) Burning of coal.

(ii) Decomposition of vegetable matter into compost.

(iii) Process of respiration.

(iv) Decomposition of calcium carbonate to form quick lime and carbon dioxide. 1

11. Identify the basic salt from the following salts:

(i) Na_2CO_3 **(ii)** NH_4Cl

(iii) $NaNO_3$ **(iv)** KCl 1

12. The positions of four elements A, B, C and D in the modern periodic table are shown below. Which element is most likely to form an acidic oxide?

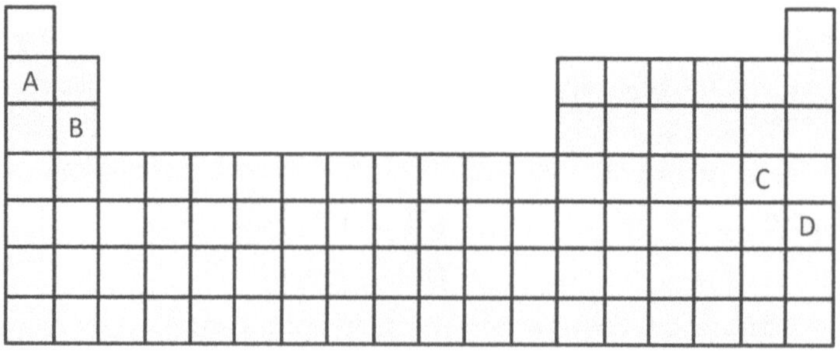

(i) A **(ii)** B

(iii) C **(iv)** D

OR

Elements P, Q, R and S have atomic numbers 11, 15, 17 and 18 respectively. Which of them are reactive non-metals?

(i) P and Q **(ii)** P and R

(iii) Q and R **(iv)** R and S 1

For question numbers 13 and 14, two statements are given-one labeled Assertion (A) and the other labeled Reason (R). Select the correct answer to these questions from the codes (i), (ii), (iii) and (iv) as given below:

(i) Both A and R are true and R is correct explanation of the assertion.

(ii) Both A and R are true but R is not the correct explanation of the assertion.

(iii) A is true but R is false.

(iv) A is false but R is true.

13. **Assertion:** Following are the structural isomers of butane.

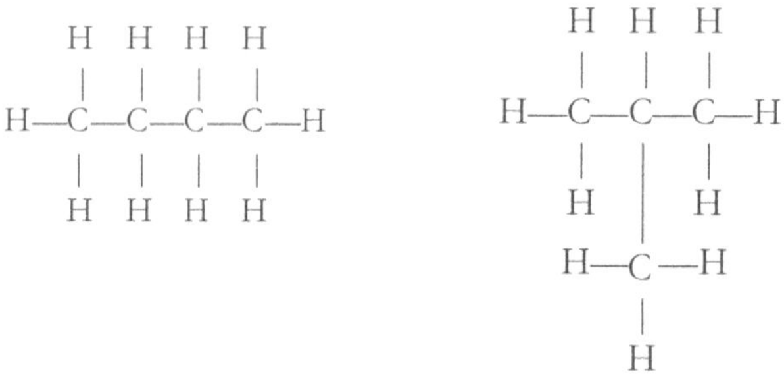

Reason: Structural isomers have the same molecular formula but they differ in their structures. 1

14. **Assertion:** A fuse wire is always connected in parallel with the mainline.

Reason: If a current larger than the specified value flows through the circuit, fuse wire melts. 1

SECTION - B

15. **(i)** Write two observations when lead nitrate is heated in a test tube.

(ii) Name the type of reaction.

(iii) Write a balanced chemical equation to represent the above reaction. 3

16. A compound 'X' of sodium is used as an antacid and it decomposes on strong heating.

(i) Name the compound 'X' and give its chemical formula.

(ii) Write a balanced chemical equation to represent the decomposition of 'X'.

(iii) Give one use of compound 'X' besides an antacid.

OR

You are provided with 90 mL of distilled water and 10 mL of concentrated sulphuric acid to prepare dilute sulphuric acid.

(i) What is the correct way of preparing dilute sulphuric acid? Give reason.

(ii) How will the concentration of H_3O^+ ions change on dilution? **3**

17. Two elements X and Y have atomic numbers 12 and 16 respectively. To which period of the modern periodic table do these two elements belong? What type of bond will be formed between them and why? Also give the chemical formula of the compound formed. **3**

18. **(i)** Create a terrestrial food chain depicting four trophic levels.

(ii) Why do we not find food chains of more than four trophic levels in nature?

OR

How will you create an artificial aquatic ecosystem, which is self-sustainable? **3**

19. Explain the processes of aerobic respiration in mitochondria of a cell and anaerobic respiration in yeast and muscle with the help of word equations. **3**

20. In a pea plant, the trait of flowers bearing purple colour (PP) is dominant over white colour (pp). Explain the inheritance pattern of F1 and F2 generations with the help of a cross following the rules of inheritance of traits. State the visible characters of F1and F2 progenies. **3**

21. Explain giving reasons the bending of the shoot tip of a plant towards light source coming from one side of the plant. **3**

22. It is desired to obtain an erect image of an object, using concave mirror of focal length of 12 cm.

(i) What should be the range of the object distance in the above case?

(ii) Will the image be smaller or larger than the object? Draw a ray diagram to show the formation of image in this case.

(iii) Where will the image of this object be, if it is placed 24 cm in front of the mirror? **3**

23. Suppose your parents have constructed a two room house and you want that in the living room there should be a provision of one electric bulb, one electric fan, a refrigerator and a plug point for appliances of power up to 2 kilowatt. Draw a circuit diagram showing electric fuse and earthing as safety devices. **3**

24. In the figure given below, a narrow beam of white light is shown to pass through a triangular glass prism. After passing through the prism, it produces a spectrum XY on the screen.

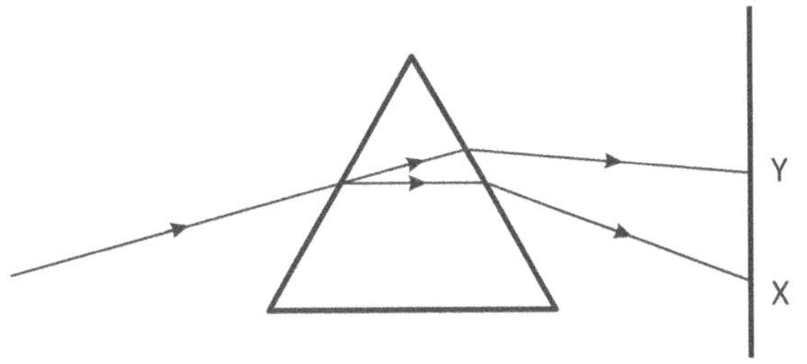

(i) Name the phenomenon.

(ii) State the colours seen at X and Y.

(iii) Why do different colours of white light bend at different angles through a prism?

OR

(i) What is visible spectrum?

(ii) Why is red used as the stopping light at traffic signals?

(iii) Two triangular glass prisms are kept together connected through their rectangular side. A light beam is passed through one side of the combination. Will there be any dispersion? Justify your answer. **3**

SECTION - C

25. Metal X is found in nature as its sulphide XS. It is used in the galvanisation of iron articles. Identify the metal X. How will you convert this sulphide ore into the metal? Explain with equations.

OR

State the reason for the following:

(i) Aluminium oxide is called an amphoteric oxide.

(ii) An iron strip dipped in a blue copper sulphate solution turns the blue solution pale green.

(iii) Hydrogen gas is not evolved when most metals react with nitric acid.

(iv) Calcium does not occur in free state in nature.

(v) Sodium or potassium metals are kept immersed under kerosene. **5**

26. The formulae of four organic compounds are given below:

A	B	C	D
C_2H_4	CH_3COOH	C_2H_5OH	C_2H_6

(i) Which one of these compounds A, B, C or D is a saturated hydrocarbon?

(ii) Identify the organic acid and give its structural formula.

(iii) Which of the above compounds when heated at 443K in the presence of concentrated H_2SO_4 forms ethene as the major product? What is the role played by concentrated H_2SO_4 in this reaction? Also write the chemical equation involved.

(iv) Give a chemical equation when B and C react with each other in presence of concentrated H_2SO_4. Name the major product formed and mention one of its important use. **5**

27.

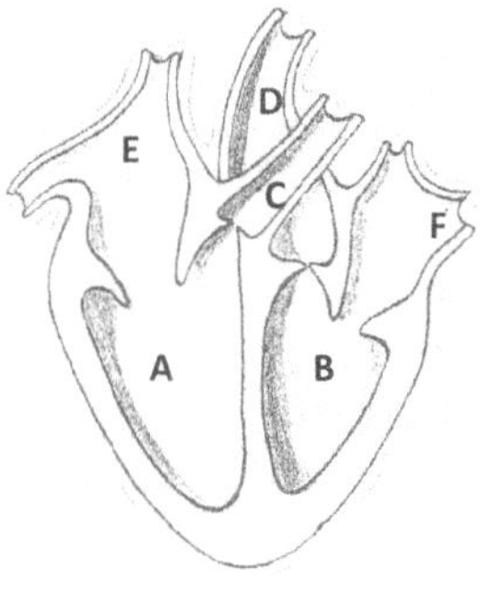

(i) Identify any two parts from the above diagram which carry oxygenated and deoxygenated blood.

(ii) Explain the process of double circulation with the help of a flow chart. **5**

28. **(i)** Describe the various steps involved in the process of binary fission with the help of a diagram.

(ii) Why do multicellular organisms use complex way of reproduction? **5**

OR

(i) Describe the role of prostate gland, seminal vesicle and testes in the human male reproductive system.

(ii) How is the surgical removal of unwanted pregnancies misused?

(iii) Explain the role of oral contraceptive pills in preventing conception. **5**

29. **(i)** Consider a conductor of resistance 'R', length 'L', thickness'd' and resistivity 'ρ'. Now this conductor is cut into four equal parts. What will be the new resistivity of each of these parts? Why?

(ii) Find the resistance if all of these parts are connected in:

(a) Parallel **(b)** Series

(iii) Out of the combinations of resistors mentioned above in the previous part, for a given voltage which combination will consume more power and why? **5**

30. **(i)** A lens produces a magnification of -0.5. Is this a converging or diverging lens? If the focal length of the lens is 6 cm, draw a ray diagram showing the image formation in this case.

(ii) A girl was playing with a thin beam of light from a laser torch by directing it from different directions on a convex lens held vertically. She was surprised to see that in a particular direction, the beam of light continues to move along the same direction after passing through the lens. State the reason for her observation. Draw a ray diagram to support your answer.

OR

(i) On entering in a medium from air, the speed of light becomes half of its value in air. Find the refractive index of that medium with respect to air?

(ii) A glass slab made of a material of refractive index n_1 is kept in a medium of refractive index n_2.

A light ray is incident on the slab. Draw the path of the rays of light emerging from the glass slab, if (i) $n_1 > n_2$ (ii) $n_1 = n_2$ (iii) $n_1 < n_2$. **5**

MARKING SCHEME

20th September 2019

Note: This is the marking scheme provided by CBSE of the 20th September 2019 Sample Paper. EduCart has not done any editing on it. Our fully solved sample paper start later in the book.

SECTION - A

1. The property of self-linking of atoms of an element through covalent bonds in order to form straight chain, branched chains or cyclic chains of different sizes is called catenation. **1**

2. The valency of an element first increases and then decreases across a period. **1**

3. **(a)** The principle behind electric generator is Electromagnetic Induction—the phenomenon of producing current in a coil by changing the magnetic field associated with it. **1**

   (b) The polarity of the output alternating current changes every 1/100 seconds.

   Alternately: In 1 second the output (AC) completes 50 cycles. **1**

   (c) The suitability of Muppandal as a site for wind farms stems from its geographical location as it has access to the seasonal monsoon winds. **1**

   (d) City A **½**

   It is more suitable for a wind-farm as there is consistently high wind-speed in that city throughout the year. **½**

4. **(a)** Diabetes **1**

   (b) Insulin **1**

   (c) **(iv)** low sugar high fibre diet **1**

   (d) **(i)** 180mg/dL **1**

5. **(ii)** pupils take time to adjust

   OR

   (ii) refraction **1**

6. **(ii)** 40 Ω.

   V = IR, V = 4V, I = 100,

   mA = 0.1 A

   Hence $R = \frac{V}{I} = \frac{4}{0.1}\ \Omega$

   $= 40\ \Omega$. **1**

7. **(i)** volt-ampere

   Power = Voltage × Current. **1**

8. **(iv)** Human faecal matter

   OR

   (iv) The Industrialist **1**

9. **(iii)** Carbon monoxide **1**

10. **(iv)** Decomposition of calcium carbonate to form quick lime and carbon dioxide. **1**

11. **(i)** Na_2CO_3 **1**

12. **(iii)** C

    OR

    (iii) Q and R **1**

13. **(i)** Both assertion and reason are true and reason is the correct explanation of assertion. **1**

14. **(iv)** Assertion is false but reason is true. **1**

15. **(i)** It turns yellow due to formation of lead oxide and Reddish brown fumes evolve. ½ + ½

(ii) Thermal decomposition reaction. **1**

(iii) $2Pb(NO_3)_2 \xrightarrow{\text{Heat}} 2PbO + 4NO_2 + O_2$ **1**

16. **(i)** Sodium bicarbonate/Sodium hydrogen carbonate/baking soda and its formula is $NaHCO_3$ ½ + ½

(ii) $2NaHCO_3 \xrightarrow{\text{Heat}} Na_2CO_3 + CO_2 + H_2O$ **1**

(iii) It is used in fire extinguisher and for baking. (any one) **1**

OR

(i) Add 10 mL of concentrated sulphuric acid slowly to 90 mL of water with constant stirring. **1**

Dilution of acid is a highly exothermic process. If water is added to concentrated sulphuric acid, heat generated causes the mixture to splash leading to burns and the glass container can break. **1**

(ii) Decreases per unit volume. **1**

17. Electronic configuration of

X: 2,8,2, Y: 2,8,6 ½ + ½

Both X and Y belong to 3rd period. ½

Ionic bond will be formed. ½

Reason: X will lose 2 electrons and Y will gain 2 electrons to complete their octet and become stable. **1**

Formula is XY ½

18. **(i)** The various steps in a food chain at which the transfer of food(or energy) takes place are called trophic levels. In a food chain, each step representing an organism forms a trophic level. **1**

The four trophic levels are:

(a) Autotrophs are at the primary level which fix the sunlight and produce their own food,

(b) Primary consumers or herbivores come at the second level

(c) Secondary consumers or small carnivores come at the third level and

(d) Tertiary consumers or the large carnivores come at the last level

The above is an example of food chain.

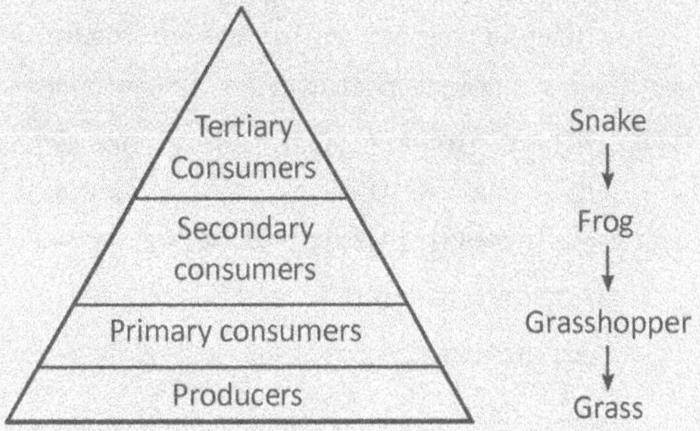

2

(ii) According to the 10% law, the amount of energy available will not be sufficient for the survival of the organism in the 5th trophic level. **1**

OR

- Large jar filled with water, oxygen, food and aquatic plants and animals.
- Oxygen/oxygen pump.
- Fish food.
- Aquatic plants/Producers provide O_2 during photosynthesis.
- Aquatic animals/Consumers release CO_2 for the process of photo-synthesis.
- Decomposers are also important for natural cleaning of the aquarium. **3**

19.

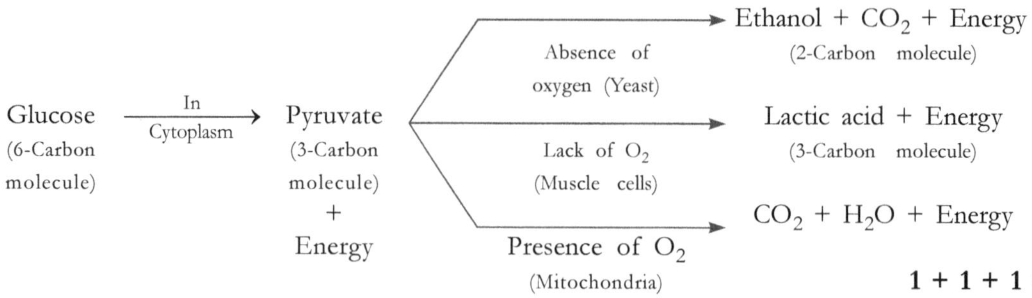

1 + 1 + 1 = 3

20. Let purple trait be represented by: PP

White trait be : pp

parental	PP × pp	
	↓	
F1	Pp × Pp	(Selfing)
F2	↓	
Gametes	P	p
P	PP	Pp
p	Pp	pp

½ + ½

Visible characters of F1 progeny all flowers are purple coloured and in F2 progenies 3 are purple coloured and 1 is white coloured flower. **½ + 1 + ½**

21. When growing plant shoot tip detects light a hormone called auxin is synthesised in the shoot tip which is sensitive to light. **1**

Auxin diffuses towards the shady side of the stem. **½**

It stimulates the growth of cells on the shady side of the plant which causes bending of the plant to the other side. **1**

This gives the appearance that the stem of the plant bends in the direction of light. **½**

22. **(i)** Range of distance should be 0 cm to < 12 cm. **½**

(ii) The image will larger than the object.

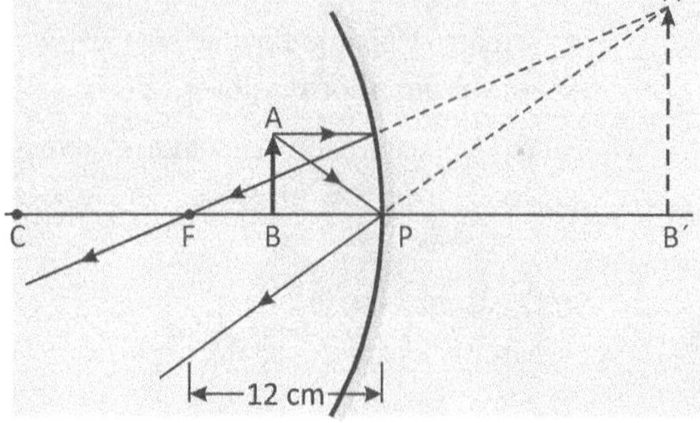

(0.5 mark to be deducted if no arrows marked or wrongly marked arrows) **1½**

(iii) Image will be at 24cm in front of the mirror or the image is formed at C. **1**

23.

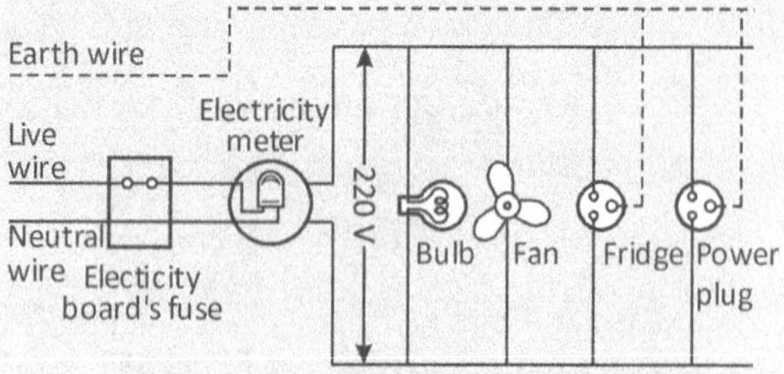

(i) Four components should be labelled. **1**

(ii) All of them should be in parallel and there should be a fuse for safety. **½ + ½**

(iii) Live and earth wires should be there. **1**

(0.5 mark to be deducted if all parts of the diagram are not labeled)

24. **(i)** The phenomenon is called dispersion. **1**

(ii) X — Violet Y — Red **½ + ½**

(iii) Different colours of white light bend through different angles with respect to the incident beam of light due to difference in speed of light of different wavelengths. **1**

OR

(i) Visible spectrum is the band of coloured components of a white light beam. **1**

(ii) Red light is scattered the least by air molecules and has longer wavelength. It travels the longest distance. **1**

(iii) The given setup will behave like a glass slab, resulting in recombination of the seven colours to produce white light. **1**

SECTION - C

25. Metal X is Zinc **1**

The sulphide ore is first heated strongly in supply of oxygen and changed into its oxide. This process is called roasting. **1**

$2ZnS + 3O_2 \xrightarrow{\text{Heat}} 2ZnO + 2SO_2$ **1**

Zinc oxide is then reduced to zinc metal by heating it with carbon. This process is called reduction. **1**

$2ZnO + C \xrightarrow{\text{Heat}} 2Zn + CO_2$ **1**

OR

(i) As it reacts with both acids as well as bases to form salts. **1**

(ii) Iron being more reactive than copper displaces copper from copper sulphate to form green ferrous sulphate solution. **1**

(iii) Nitric acid is a strong oxidising agent. Hydrogen gas produced gets oxidised to H_2O. **1**

(iv) Calcium is a very reactive metal. It reacts with the chemicals in surroundings and occurs in combined state. **1**

(v) Sodium and potassium are highly reactive metals and react vigorously with oxygen in air and may even catch fire. They do not react with kerosene. **1**

26. **(i)** D is a saturated hydrocarbon ½

(ii) B is an organic acid. ½

Structural formula

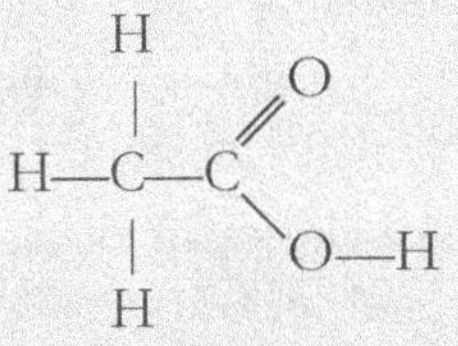

½

(iii) C is the compound. ½

It acts as a dehydrating agent and removes a water molecule from ethanol. ½

$C_2H_5OH \xrightarrow{\text{hot conc. } H_2SO_4} C_2H_4 + H_2O$ **1**

(iv) $CH_3COOH + C_2H_5OH \xrightarrow{\text{conc. } H_2SO_4} CH_3COOC_2H_5 + H_2O$ **1**

Major product is Ester and it is used in making perfumes/flavouring agents. ½

27. **(i)** Oxygenated : B/D/F [B = left ventricle/D = aorta/F = left auricle/pulmonary vein]

Deoxygenated: A/C/E [A = right ventricle/C = pulmonary artery/E = right auricle/vena cava]

(any two) ½ + ½ + ½ + ½

(ii)

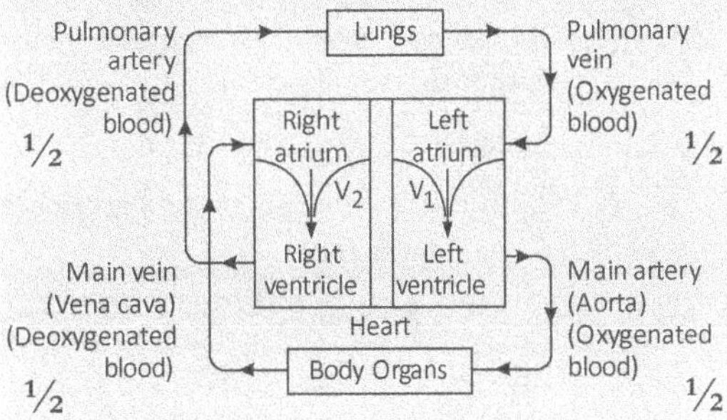

(1 mark should be deducted if the arrows are not correctly marked) **3**

28. **(i)** Binary fission

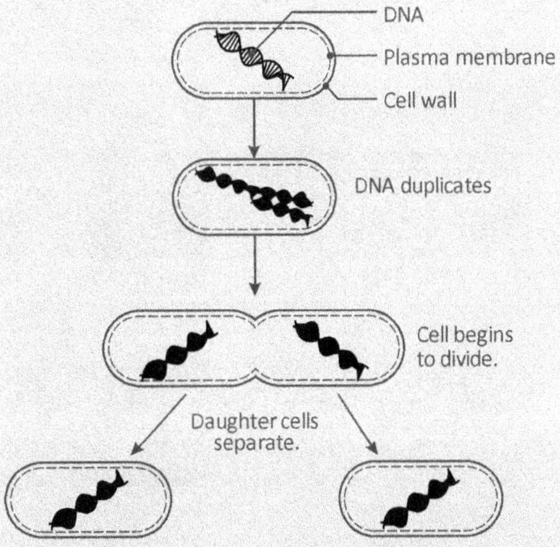

3

(ii) Multicellular organisms cannot reproduce by cell because they are not simple random collection of cells. In them, specialized cells are organized as tissues which are organized into organs. Cell-by-cell division would be impractical. Multicellular organisms, therefore, require to use more complex ways of reproduction. **2**

OR

(i) Prostate glands and seminal vesicle : add their secretions so that the sperms are in a fluid and it makes their transport easier and also provides nutrition. Testes secrete testosterone which brings about changes in the appearances in the boys at the time of puberty. **3**

(ii) Female foeticides/illegal sex selected abortion of female foeticide. **1**

(iii) Interfere in release of egg and eggs are not released. **1**

29. **(i)** Resistivity will not change as it depends on the nature of the material of the conductor. **1**

(ii) The length of each part becomes L/4. ρ, A constant.

$$R = \rho L/A.$$ ½

Resistance of each part

$$R_{part} = (\rho L/4)/A = R/4.$$ ½

(a) In parallel the

$$\frac{1}{R_{eqv}} = \frac{1}{R_{part}} + \frac{1}{R_{part}} + \frac{1}{R_{part}} + \frac{1}{R_{part}}$$

$$= \frac{4}{R_{part}} = \frac{16}{R}$$

$$\Rightarrow \quad R_{eqv} = \frac{R}{16}\Omega$$ ½

(b) In series the

$$R_{eqv} = \frac{R}{4} + \frac{R}{4} + \frac{R}{4} + \frac{R}{4} = R\Omega$$ **1**

(iii) $$P = \frac{V^2}{R}.$$ **1**

If R_{eqv} is less, power consumed will be more. ½

In the given case, R_{eqv} is lesser in the parallel and power consumed will be more. ½

30. **(i)** The image will be real and inverted, since the magnification has negative value. **1**

The lens that can produce a real and inverted image is a converging/convex lens. **1**

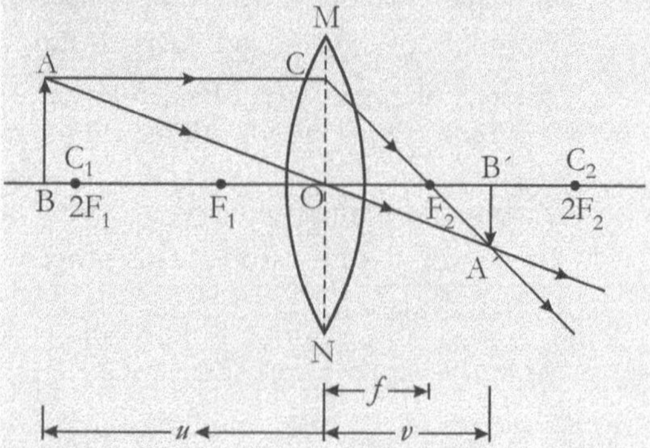

2

(1/2 *mark should be deducted if the arrows are not correctly marked*)

In the figure $OF_1 = OF_2 = 6$ cm.

(Marks will be deducted if arrows are not shown)

(ii) The girl must have directed the ray of light along the direction of the optical centre of the lens because the ray of light passes straight through the optical centre of the lens. **1**

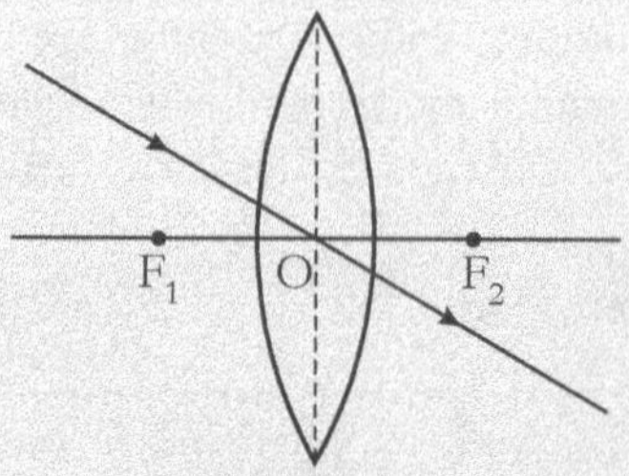

1

OR

(i) Refractive Index of a medium (μ) = Velocity of light in vacuum/Velocity of light in the medium.

Let the velocity of light in vacuum be v_1 and velocity of light in the medium be v_2.

$$\frac{v_1}{2} = v_2.$$ ½

Hence $$\mu = \frac{v_1}{v_2}$$

$$= \frac{v_1}{\left(\frac{v_1}{v_2}\right)}$$

$$= 2$$ **1**

(ii) (a) The ray moves towards the normal. **½**

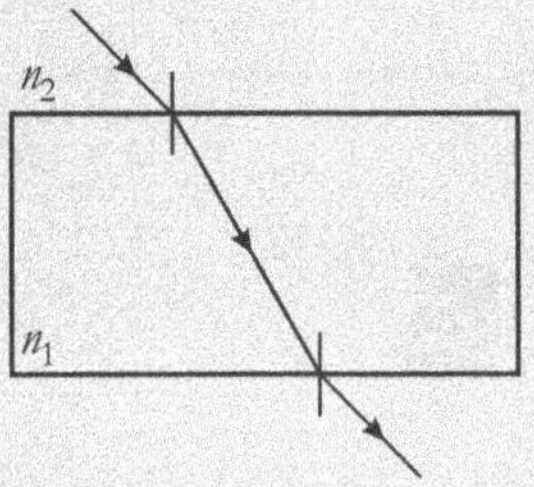

1

(b) The ray moves undeviated.

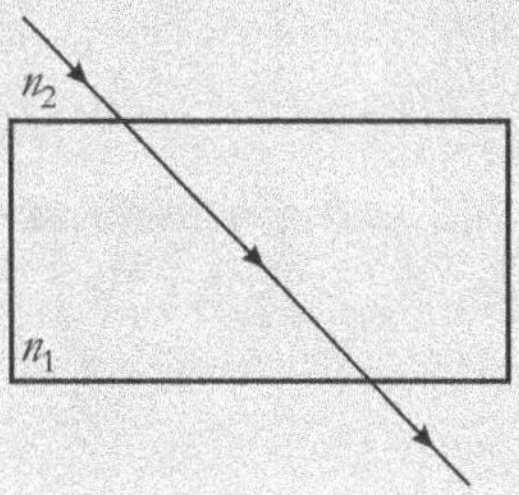

1

(c) The ray moves away from the normal.

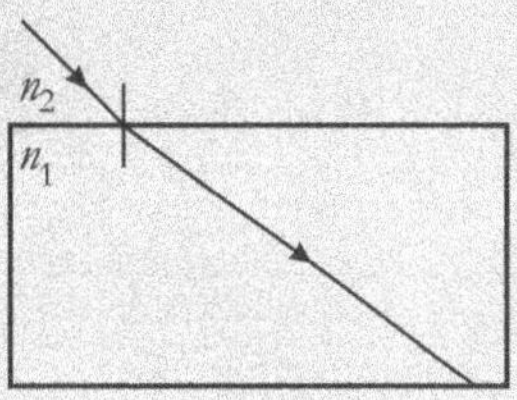

1

CBSE BOARD EXAM

13th March 2019, Class 10

Time Allowed: 3 Hours *Maximum Marks: 80*

SCIENCE

Note: Exam format for February 2020 exams is different to this paper. However, this is the latest CBSE paper and very relevant for practice. EduCart has exclusively worked with CBSE 2019 Topper this year to provide solution to Set 1 and unique questions of Set 2 and 3.

General Instructions:

i. The question paper comprises three sections, A, B and C. You are to attempt all the sections.
ii. All questions are compulsory.
iii. All questions of Section-A, B and C are to be attempted separately.
iv. There is an internal choice in six questions of one mark each, three questions of three marks each and two questions of five mark each.
v. Question numbers **1** to **10** in Section-A are **1** mark question. They are to be answered in one word or in one sentence.
vi. Question numbers **11** to **20** in Section-A are **1** mark multiple choice questions. The answers need to be selected from the given options.
vii. Question numbers **21** to **30** in Section-B are **3** marks questions. These are to be answered in about 50 words each.
viii. Question numbers **31** to **36** in Section-C are **5** marks questions. These are to be answered in 70 words each.

SET - 1

SECTION - A

1. Name two industries based on forest produce. 1

2. Why are the heating elements of electric toasters and electric irons made of an alloy rather than a pure metal? 1

SECTION - B

3. Write the molecular formula of ethene and draw its electron dot structure. 2

4. Give reasons:

   a. Platinum, gold and silver are used to make jewellery.

   b. Metals like sodium and potassium are stored under oil. 2

OR

Silver articles becomes black when kept in open for some time, whereas copper vessels lose their shiny brown surfaces and gain a green coat when kept in open. Name the substance present in air with which these metals react and write the name of the products formed. 2

5. The absolute refractive index of Ruby is 1.7. Find the speed of light in Ruby. The speed of light in vacuum is 3×108 m/s. 2

SECTION - C

6. On heating blue coloured powder of copper (II) nitrate in a boiling tube, black copper oxide, O_2 and a brown gas X is formed.

   i. identify the type of reaction and the gas X.

   ii. Write balanced chemical equation of aqueous solution of the gas X.

   iii. Write the pH range of aqueous solution of the gas X. 3

7. i. While diluting an acid, why is it recommended that the acid should be added to water and not water to the acid?

   ii. Dry hydrogen chloride gas does not change the colour of dry litmus paper. Why? 3

OR

How is sodium hydroxide manufactured in industries? Name the process. In this process a gas X is formed as by-product. This gas reacts with lime water to give a compound Y, which is used as a bleaching agent in the chemical industry, Identify X and Y and write the chemical equation of the reactions involved. 3

8. What are amphoteric oxides? Give an example. Write balanced chemical equations to justify your answer. 3

9. What is a homologous series of carbon compounds? Give an example and list its three characteristics. 3

10. List in tabular form three distinguishing features between autotrophic nutrition and heterotrophic nutrition. 3

11. What is transpiration? List its two functions. 3

OR

   i. What is translocation? Why is it essential for plants?

   ii. Where do the substances in plants reach as a result of translocation? 3

12. What is carpel? Write the function of its various parts. 3

13. A student holding a mirror in his hand, directed the reflecting surface of the mirror towards the Sun. He then directed the reflected light on to a sheet of paper held close to the mirror.

   i. What should he do to burn the paper?

   ii. Which type of mirror does he have?

   iii. Will he be able to determine the approximate value of focal length of this mirror from this activity? Give reason and draw ray diagram to justify your answer in this case. 3

OR

A 10 cm tall object is placed perpendicular to the principal axis of a convex lens of focal length 12 cm. The distance of the object from the lens is 18 cm. Find the nature, position and size of the image formed. 3

14. What are solar cells? Explain the structure of solar panel. List two principal advantages associated with solar cells. **3**

15. Write the essential function performed by ozone at the higher levels of the Earth's atmosphere? How is it produced? Name the synthetic chemicals mainly responsible for the drop of amount of ozone in the atmosphere. How can the use of these chemicals be reduced? **3**

SECTION - D

16. **i.** List any three observations which posed a challenge to Mendeleev's Periodic Law.
ii. How does the metallic character of elements vary on moving from
a. Left to right in a period
b. From top to bottom in a group of the Modern Periodic Table? Give reason for your answer. **5**

OR

The electrons in the atoms of four elements A, B, C and D are distributed in three shells having 1, 3, 5 and 7 electrons respectively in their outermost shells. Write the group numbers in which these elements are placed in the Modern Periodic Table. Write the electronic configuration of the atoms of B and D and the molecular formula of the compound formed when B and D combine. **5**

17. **i.** Why is the use of iodized salt advisable? Name the disease caused due to deficiency of iodine in our diet and state its one symptom
ii. How do nerve impulses travel in the body? Explain. **5**

OR

What is hydrotropism? Design an experiment to demonstrate this phenomenon. **5**

18. **i.** What are homologous structures? Give an example.
ii. "The sex of a newborn child is a matter of chance and none of the parents may be considered responsible for it." Justify this statement with the help of a flow chart showing sex determination in human beings. **5**

19. When do we consider a person to be myopic or hypermetropic? List two causes of hypermetropia. **5**

20. **a.** How will you infer with the help of an experiment that same current flows through every part of a circuit containing three resistors in series connected to a battery?
b. Consider the given circuit and find the current flowing in the circuit and potential difference across the 15 Ω resistor when the circuit is closed. **5**

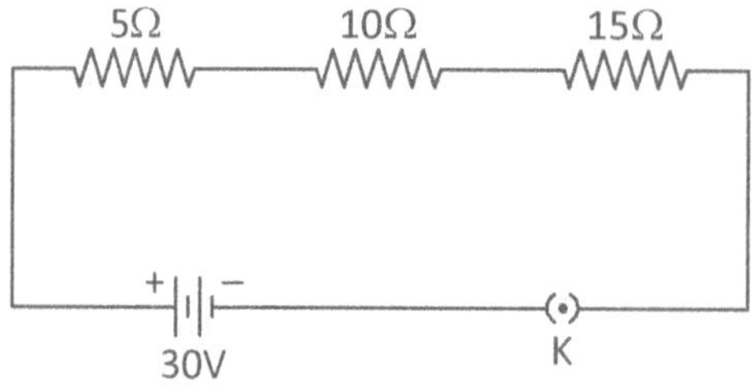

OR

a. Three resistors R_1, R_2 and R_3 are connected in parallel and the combination is connected to a battery, ammeter, voltmeter and key. Draw suitable circuit diagram and obtain an expression for the equivalent resistance of the combination of the resistors.

b. Calculate the equivalent resistance of the following network: 5

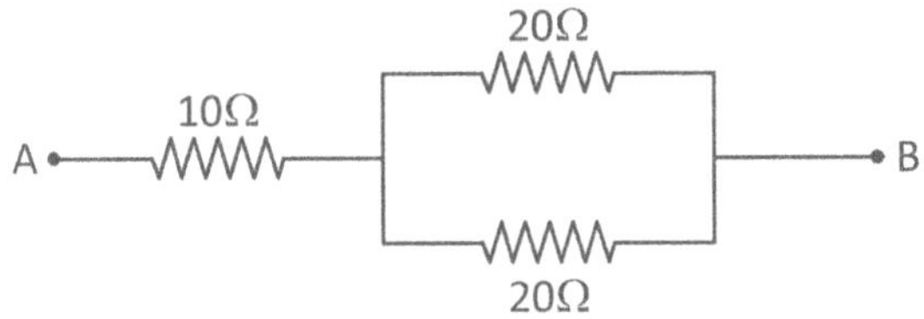

21. Draw the pattern of magnetic field lines produced around a current carrying straight conductor passing perpendicularly through a horizontal cardboard. State and apply right hand thumb rule to mark the direction of the field lines. How will the strength of the magnetic field change when the point where magnetic field is to be determined is moved away from the straight conductor? Give reason to justify your answer. 5

SECTION - E

22. A teacher provided acetic acid, water, lemon juice, aqueous solution of sodium hydrogen carbonate and sodium hydroxide to students in the school laboratory to determine the pH values of these substances using pH papers. One of the students reported the pH values of the given substances as 3, 12, 4, 8 and 14 respectively. Which one of these values is not correct? Write its correct value stating the reason. 2

OR

What would a student report nearly after 30 minutes of placing duly cleaned strips of aluminium, copper, iron and zinc in freshly prepared iron sulphate solution taken in four beakers?

23. What is observed when a pinch of sodium hydrogen carbonate is added to 2 mL of acetic acid taken in a test tube? Write chemical equation for the reaction involved in thise case. 2

24. List in proper sequence four steps of obtaining germinating dicot seeds. 2

OR

After examining a prepared slide under the high power of a compound microscope, a student concludes that the given slide shows the various stage of binary fission in a unicellular organism. Write two observations on the basis of which such a conclusion may be drawn. 2

25. List four precautions which a student should observe while preparing a temporary mount of a leaf peel to show stomata in his school laboratory. 2

26. Draw the path of a ray of light when it enters one of the faces of a glass slab at a angle of nearly 45°. Label on it: **i.** angle of refraction. **ii.** angle of emergence and **iii.** lateral displacement. 2

OR

A Student traces the path of a ray of light through a glass prism as shown in the diagram but leaves it incomplete and unlabelled. Redraw and complete the diagram. Also label on it $\angle i$, $\angle e$, $\angle r$ and $\angle D$.

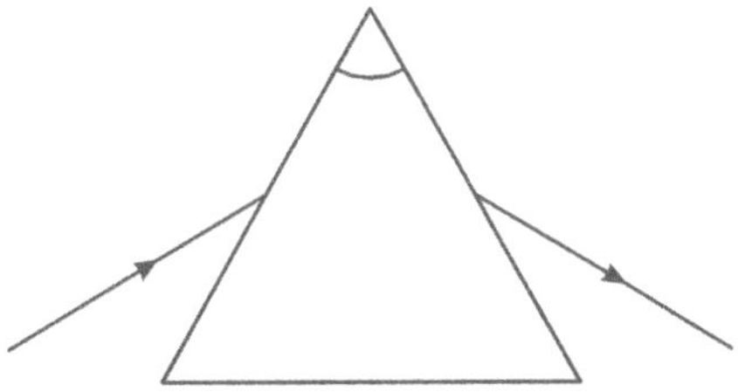

27. The current flowing through a resistor connected in a circuit and the potential difference develop across its ends are as shown in the diagram by milliammeter and voltmeter reading respectively.

i. What are the least counts of these meters?

ii. What is the resistance of the resistor? 2

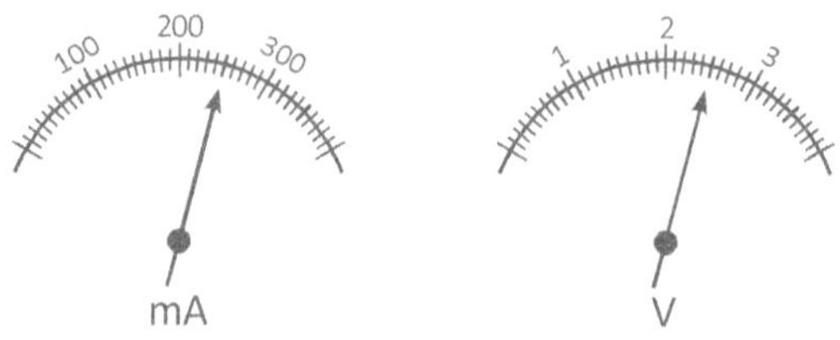

SET - 2

(questions that are different)

SECTION - A

1. Write two advantages associated with water harvesting at the community level.
2. Should the resistance of a voltmeter be low or high? Give reason.

SECTION - B

3. Draw electron dot structure of carbon dioxide and write the nature of bonding between carbon and oxygen in its molecule.

OR

List two properties of carbon which lead to the huge number of carbon compounds we see around us, giving reason for each.

4. Give reason:

   a. Carbonate and sulphide ores are usually converted into oxides during the process of extraction.

   b. Aluminium is a highly reactive metal; still it is widely used in making cooking utensils.

5. The power of a lens is +5 diopters. What is the nature and focal length of this lens? At what distance from this lens should an object be placed so as to get its inverted image of the same size?

SECTION - C

6. List two types of the transport system in human beings and write the functions of any one of these.
7. Distinguish between pollination and fertilisation. Mention the site and the product of fertilisation in a flower.
8. List three environmental consequences of using fossil fuels. Suggest three steps to minimise the pollution caused by various energy sources.
9. Which compounds are called: **i.** alkanes, **ii.** alkenes and **iii.** alkynes? C_4H_{10} belongs to which of these? Draw two structural isomers of this compound.

SECTION - D

10. a. What are dominant and recessive traits?

    b. "Is it possible that a trait is inherited but may not be expressed in the next generation?" Give a suitable example to justify this statement.

11. a. What is scattering of light? Explain how the colour of the scattered light depends on the size of the scattering particles.

    b. Explain the reddish appearance of the Sun at sunrise or sunset. Why does it not appear red at noon?

SET - 3

(questions that are different)

SECTION - A

1. Why does the cord of an electric oven not glow while its heating element does?
2. Although coal and petroleum are produced by the degradation of biomass, yet we need to conserve these resources. Why?

SECTION - B

3. What is atmospheric refraction? List two phenomena which can be explained on the basis of atmospheric refraction
4. Name a metal of medium reactivity and write three main steps in the extraction of this metal from its sulphide ore.
5. List two chemical properties on the basis of which ethanol and ethanoic acid may be differentiated and explain how.

OR

Unsaturated hydrocarbons contain multiple bonds between two carbon atoms and these compounds show addition reactions. Out of saturated and unsaturated carbon compounds, which compounds are more reactive? Write a test to distinguish ethane from ethene.

SECTION - C

6. What happens to a beam of white light when it gets refracted through a glass prism? Which colour deviates the most and the least after refraction through a prism? What is likely to happen if a second identical prism is placed in an inverted position with respect to the first prism? Justify your answer.

OR

A student needs spectacles of power – 0·5 D for the correction of his vision.

   i. Name the defect in vision the student is suffering from.

   ii. Find the nature and focal length of the corrective lens.

   iii. List two causes of this defect.

7. Define a food chain. Design a terrestrial food chain of four trophic levels. If a pollutant enters at the producer level, the organisms of which trophic level will have the maximum concentration of the pollutant in their bodies? What is this phenomenon called?

8. During the reaction of some metals with dilute hydrochloric acid, the ollowing observations were made by a student:

  a. Silver does not show any change.

  b. Some bubbles of a gas are seen when lead is reacted with the acid.

  c. The reaction of sodium is found to be highly explosive.

  d. The temperature of the reaction mixture rises when aluminium is added to the acid.

  Explain these observations giving appropriate reason.

9. Given below are the steps for the extraction of copper from its ore. Write the chemical equation of the reactions involved in each case.

  i. Roasting of copper (I) sulphide

  ii. Reduction of copper (I) oxide from copper (I) sulphide

  iii. Electrolytic refining

10. a. Budding, fragmentation and regeneration, all are considered as asexual mode of reproduction. Why?

  b. With the help of neat diagrams, explain the process of regeneration in *Planaria.*

SECTION - D

11. A 6 cm tall object is placed perpendicular to the principal axis of a concave mirror of focal length 30 cm. The distance of the object from the mirror is 45 cm. Use mirror formula to determine the position, nature and size of the image formed. Also draw labelled ray diagram to show the image formation in this case.

OR

An object 6 cm in size is placed at 50 cm in front of a convex lens of focal length 30 cm. At what distance from the lens should a screen be placed in order to obtain a sharp image of the object? Find the nature and size of the image. Also draw labelled ray diagram to show the image formation in this case.

12. What is sexual reproduction? Explain how this mode of reproduction gives rise to more viable variations than asexual reproduction. How does this affect the evolution?

TOPPER SOLUTION

13th March 2019, Class 10 Board Exam

Solved by CBSE Topper

Note: These are exclusively handwritten solutions by CBSE 2019 Topper in partnership with EduCart. The solutions cover all Sets (Set 1, 2 and 3) as well as internal choice questions. These solutions will immensely help you to model your answers for the upcoming February 2020 Board Exams.

Section-A

1. The two industries based on forest products are:
(i) Wood industry
(ii) Paper manufacturing industry.
(iii) Medicine Industry

2. The heating elements of electric toasters and electric irons are made of an alloy rather than a pure metal because they have high resistivity rather than its constituting metals.

Section-B

3. Molecular formula of ethane is C_2H_4
Electron dot structure of ethane $CH_2 = CH_2$

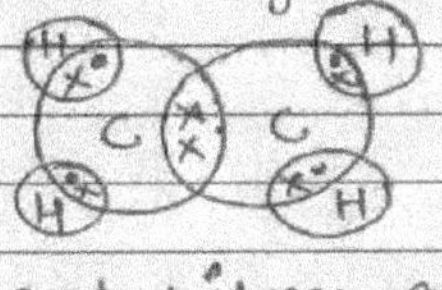

4. (i) Platinum, gold, and silver are used to make jewellery because Platinum, gold and silver are highly malleable, highly ~~reactive metal so they~~ ductile, lustrous and less reactive.
(ii) Sodium and potassium are highly reactive metal so they are stored under oil to protect from reaction with air.

OR

4. Silver reacts with sulphur in air. The product formed is silver sulphiod.
copper reacts with moisture & carbon dioxide in air. The product formed is copper carbonate.

We know that,

$$\mu = \frac{\text{Speed of light in vacuum}}{\text{speed of light in ruby}}$$

$$\text{Speed of light in ruby} = \frac{\text{speed of light in vacuum}}{\text{speed of light in ruby}} = \frac{3 \times 10^8}{1.7}$$

$$= 1.76 \times 10 \text{ m/s}$$

Section – C

6. (i) This is a thermal decomposition reaction.
The gas X is NO_2 or (nitrogen oxide)

(ii) $2Cu(NO_3)_2 \xrightarrow{\text{Heat}} 2CuO + O_2 + 4NO_2$

(iii) The aqueous solution of the gas is acidic because it is an oxide of a non-metal, so its pH range would be in between 0 to 7.

7. (i) Dilution of concentrated acid is an exothermic process. If water is added to a concentrated acid, the heat generated may cause the mixture to splash out and cause burns. When the acid is added to water slowly with constant stirring, the mixture will not splash out and the excess heat is absorbed by water.

(ii) Dry HCl does not contain free H+ ions in absence of water, so it will not change the colour of dry litmus paper.

OR

7. Sodium hydroxide is manufactured in industries by passing electricity through brine solution (an aqueous solution of sodium chloride) which decomposes to give chlorine and sodium hydroxide. The process is termed as the chlor-alkali process. the term chlor for chlorine and alkali for sodium hydroxide. Chlorine gas is given off at the anode and hydrogen gas is given off at the cathode. Sodium hydroxide solution is formed near the cathode.
The reaction that takes place is as follows :

$2NaCl(aq) + 2H_2O(l) \longrightarrow 2NaOH(aq) + Cl_2(g) + H_2(g)$

Sodium Chloride → Sodium hydroxide

Gas X formed is chlorine gas : Cl_2

$Ca(OH)_2(aq) + Cl_2(g) \longrightarrow Ca(OCl)Cl(s) + H_2O(g)$

Slaked lime → Bleaching (Y) powder

Gas X formed is chlorine gas : Cl_2

Compound Y is bleaching powder : $CaOCl_2$

8. Amphoteric oxides : Oxides of metals which have both ~~sides~~ acidic as well as basic behaviour are known as amphoteric oxides. Such metallic oxides reacts with acids as well as base to produce salt and water.

Examples of Amphoteric oxides are ~~ati~~ aluminium oxide and zinc oxides.

$Al_2O_3 + 6HCl \longrightarrow 2AlCl_3 + 3H_2O$

$Al_2O_3 + 2NaOH \longrightarrow 2NaAlO_2 + H_2O$

9. The homologous series is a series of carbon (organic) compounds which belong to the same family (i.e. possess same functional group) and show simiiliar chemical properties. The members of this series are called homologue and differ from each other by the member of CH_2 units in the main carbon chain. For example, methane, ethane, propane, butane etc. are all part of the alkane homologus series. The general formula of this series is $C_nH_{2n}+2$.

Methane CH_4 Ethane CH_3CH_3

Propane $CH_3CH_2CH_3$ Butane $CH_3CH_2CH_2CH_3$

It can be noticed that there is a difference of $-CH_2$ unit between each successive compound.

Characteristics of Homologous Series :

(i) All the members of series can be represented by the same general formula. e.g. General formula for ~~alkine~~ alkane series is C_nH_{2n+2}.

(ii) The members in any particular family have almost identical chemical properties. Their physical properties such as melting point, boiling point, density etc, show a regular gradation with the increase in the molecular mass.

(iii) The members of particular series can be prepared almost by the indentical methods.

10.

	Autotrophic Nutrition	Heterotrophic Nutrition
1.	They can prepare their own food.	They cannot prepare their own food.
2.	They require raw materials like CO_2, H_2O in the presence of sunlight and chlorophyll to prepare their food	They depend on other plants & animals for their food.
3.	They store the food in the form of starch.	They store the food in the form of glycogen.

11. Transpiration: The loss of water in the form of water vapour from the aerial parts of the plants (leaves, stems) is known as transpiration.

Functions:

(i) It helps in the absorption and upward movement of water and mineral dissolved in it from roots to the leaves.

(ii) It also helps in temperature regulation or cooling of plants.

OR

11. a. Translocation is defined as the process of movement of materials from leaves to all other parts of the plant body. Leaves of the plants perform photosynthesis and produce carbohydrates (sugar) which are translocated to the ~~non~~ non-photosynthetic parts (roots, flowers, fruits) of the plant through special tissues called phloem.

During photosynthesis, the formed carbohydrates (food to glucose) from leaves are transported to non-photosynthetic parts of plants like roots, stem tissues & other developing organs. This transport is carried out by the process of translocation. Therefore, translocation is essential in plants to carry out long distance transport between leaves and other plant parts.

b. As a result of translocation, food is transported to root, fruit, stem and all other growing organs of plants.

12. Female reproductive organ of the plants is known as Carpel. It has 3 important parts:

Ovary

- Swollen part at the bottom of a carpel is called ovary.
- The ovary makes ovules and stores them.
- Ovules contain the female gametes of the plants called ovum or egg.

Style

- Tube like structure that connects the ovary & stigmo.
- Passage for the growth of pollen tube.

Stigma

- Top part of the carpel.
- Stigma is for receiving the pollen grains from the anther of the stamen (during pollination).
- It is sticky so that pollen can stick to it.

13. a. To burn the paper student should move the mirror in such a way that paper is positioned at the focus of the mirror.

b. Student has converging type of mirror that is concave mirror

c. Yes, distance between mirror and focal point gives approximate focal length. He can measure the approximate value of focal length from this activity as paper will burn when it will be kept at focus of the mirror, as shown is figure.

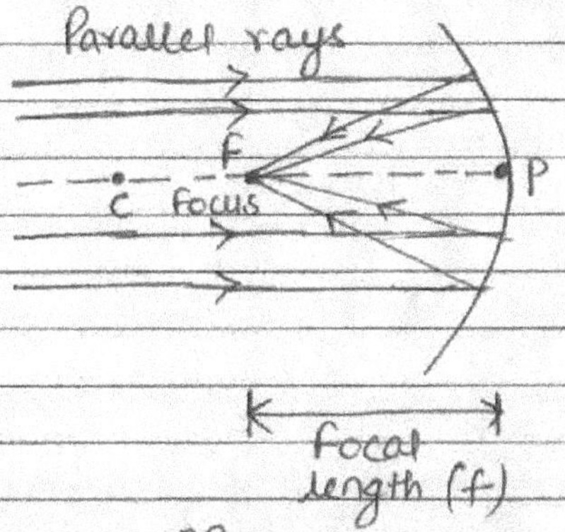

OR

13. Height of object, h = 10 cm; focal length, f = 12 cm; distance of object, u = −18 cm

Using lens formula

$$\frac{1}{f} = \left(\frac{1}{v}\right) - \left(\frac{1}{u}\right)$$

$$\frac{1}{f} + \frac{1}{u} = \frac{1}{-v}$$

$$\frac{1}{12} + \frac{1}{-18} = \frac{1}{v}$$

$$\frac{3-2}{36} = \frac{1}{v}$$

$$\frac{1}{36} = \frac{1}{v}$$

$V = 36$ cm

$m = \frac{V}{u}$

and, $m = \frac{\text{height of image}}{\text{height of object}}$

$\frac{V}{u} = \frac{\text{height of image}}{\text{height of object}}$

$\frac{36}{-18} = \frac{\text{height of image}}{10}$

-20 = height of image

This negative sign show that the object is inverted.

Nature of image : Real and inverted.

14. Solar cell : A device that converts solar energy directly into electrical energy. A large number of solar cells are combined in an arrangement called solar cell panel that can deliver enough electricity for practical use. The solar cell panels are mounted on specially designed inclined roof tops so that more solar energy is incident over it.

A typical cell develops a voltage of 0.5-1 V and can produce about 0.7 W of electricity.

Advantage of solar cell :

- They have no moving parts, require little maintenance and work quite satisfactorily without the use of any focusing device.
- They can be set up in remote and inaccessible hamlets or very sparsely inhabited areas in which laying of a power transmission line may be expensive and not commercially viable.

15. Ozone is a molecule formed by three atoms of oxygen. Oxygen is essential for all life processes whereas ozone is a deadly poison. At the higher levels of the atmosphere, it sheilds the surface of the earth from radiation (ultravoilet radiation) of the sun. which is highly dangerous to organisms as it can cause skin cancer.

The UV radiations split apart some molecular oxygen (O_2) into free oxygen (O) which then combine with the molecular oxygen (O_2) to form ozone. (O_3).

$$O_2 \longrightarrow O + O$$

$$O + O_2 \longrightarrow O_3 \text{ (ozone.)}$$

Chlorofluorocarbon (CFCs) a synthetic chemical which is used as refrigerants and fire extinguisher has been linked for sharp

drop of ozone in the atmosphere.
Methods to reduce CFC emission:

- Reduce the use of CFCs by minimizing the leakage through air conditioners and refrigerators.
- Use of CFCs is being restricted and replaced by more eco-friendly refrigerents under a UNEP (United Nations Environment Programme) initiative agreed upon in 1986.

Section-D

16. (i) Limitations of Mendeleev's classfication.

- No fixed position could be assigned to hydrogen in the ~~public~~ periodic table.
- Isotopes discovered long after Mendeleev's periodic classification of elements imparted a challange to Mendeleev's periodic law.
- The atomic masses of elements did not increase in a steady manner while going from one element to other which made it difficult to predict the number of elements that could be discovered between two elements.

(ii) a. Metallic character decreases on moving from left to right in a period. This is because tendancy to lose electron decreases due to increase in nuclear charge.

b. Metallic character increases on moving from top to bottom in a group. This is due to increase in the number of shells. i.e. size of attom increases and thus tendancy to lose electron increases

OR

16.

Element	No. of valence electrons	Electronic configuration	Group No.
A	1	2, 8, 1	1
B	3	2, 8, 3	13
C	5	2, 8, 5	15
D	7	2, 8, 7	17

Molecular formula of compound formed by B and D will be BD_3.

17. (i) Iodised salt is advisable because it is an essential element for the synthesis of thyroxine hormone. Iodine stimulates the thyroid gland to produce thyroxine hormone. It regulates carbohydrates, fat, and protein metabolism in our body. Deficiency of this hormone results in the enlargement of the thyroid gland. This can lead to goitre, a dicease characterized by swallen neck. Therefore, iodized salt is advised for

normal functioning of the thyroid gland.
Disease is goitre.
Symptom is swollen neck.

(ii) All information from our environment is detected by the specialised tips of some nerve cells. This information, acquired at the end of the dendritic tip of the nerve cell sets off a chemical reaction that creates an electrical impulse. This impulse travels from the ~~dendritic~~ dendrite to the cell body and then along the axon to its end. At the end of the axon, the electrical impulse sets off the release of some chemicals. These chemicals cross the gap, or synapse, and start a similar electrical impulse in a dendrite of the next neuron. This a general scheme of how nervous impulses ~~in a dendrite of the next neuron~~ travel in the body. A similar synapse finally allows delivery of such impulses from neurons to other cells, such as muscles cells or gland.

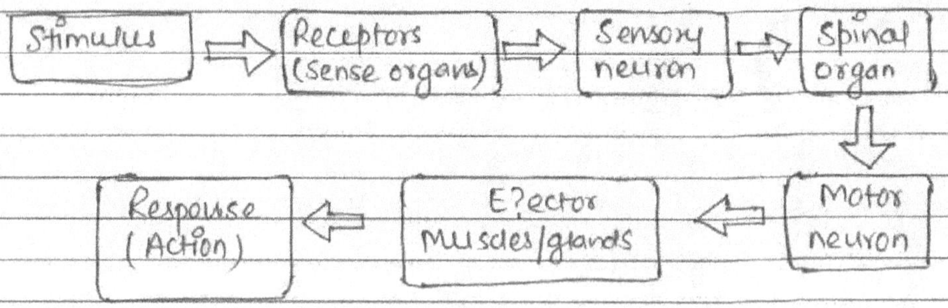

OR

17. Hydrotropism : The movement/response of part of plant (root) towards water.

Experiments to demonstrate hydrotropism :

Aim : To demonstrate hydrotropism

Material Required : Bean seeds, a deep container, sand and a porous flower pot.

Experiment :

Fill the container with sand. Make a pit on one side of the container and insert seeds on this side. Make a pit on other side of the container and insert the porous pot on the other side. Fill the pourous pot with water. Now keep aside the entire set up for a week.

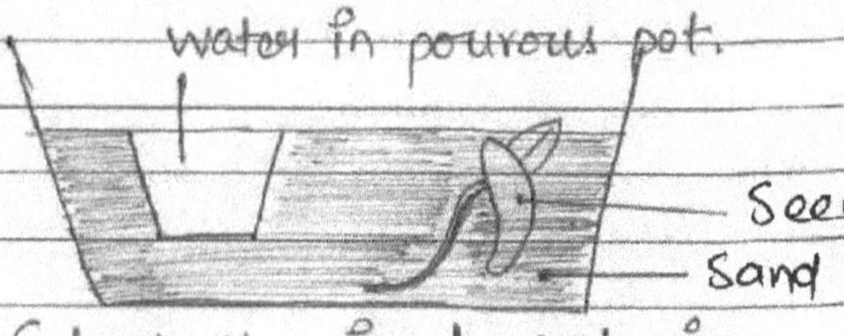

Set up showing hydrotropism

observation : After a week, when seeds are taken out, it is observed that the roots of the germinating seeds will grow in the direction of porous pot.

Result : It confirms that plant ~~grow~~ shows hydrotopism as the roots bend towards the porous pot of water. This experiment demonstrates the phenomenon of hydrotropism in roots.

18. a. Homologous structures are those structures which are similiar in origin but different in functions. e.g. the arm of the human, the wing of the bird.

b. "The sex of the newborn child is a matter of chance and none of the parents may be considered responsible for it."

Females have a perfect pair of sex chromosome, XX

Males have mismatched pair of sex chromosome, XY

There is an equal probability of fertilization of ovum with the sperm carrying either X or Y chromosomes. In case the ovum fertilizes with sperm carrying X chromosomes, the zygote develop into a female (XX) child. Fertization of ovum with Y-chromosome carrying sperm result into male (XY) child.

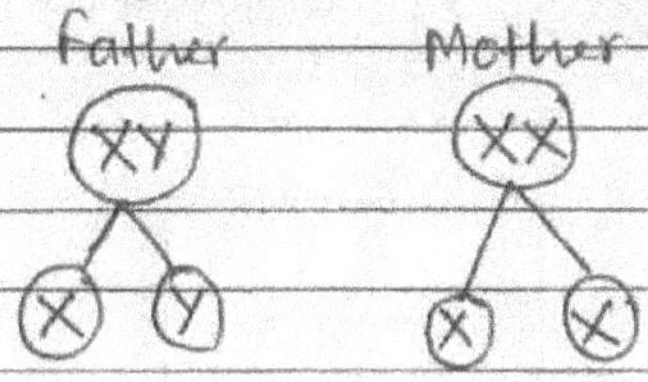

Female gamete → / Male gametes ↓	X	X
Y	XY	XY
X	XX	XX

XY, XY → Male child

XX, XX → Female child

19. Myopic : This term is used to define short-sightedness. Light from a distant object forms an image before it reaches the retina. A myopic person has clear vision when looking at objects close to them but distant objects will appear blurred.

Hypermetropia : It means long sightedness and the images of a nearby object is formed behind the retina. A hypermetropia person may have blurred vision when looking at objects close to them and clearer when looking at objects in the distance.

Cause of hypermetropia : This defect arises because :

(i) the focal length of the eye lens is too long.

(ii) the eyeball has become too small.

This defect can be corrected by using a convex lens of appropriate power. Eye-glasses with converging lenses provide the focusing power required for forming the image on the retina.

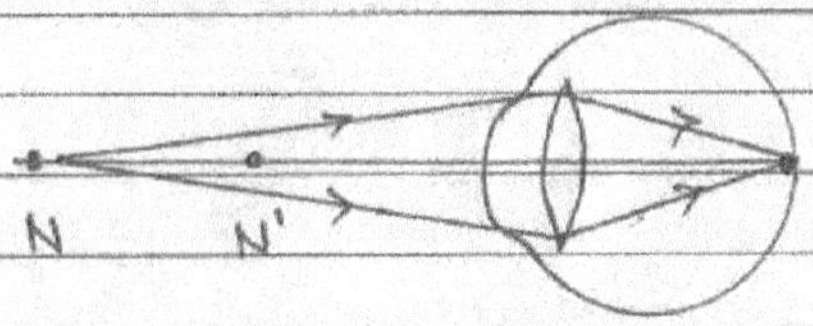

a. Near point of Hypermetropic eye

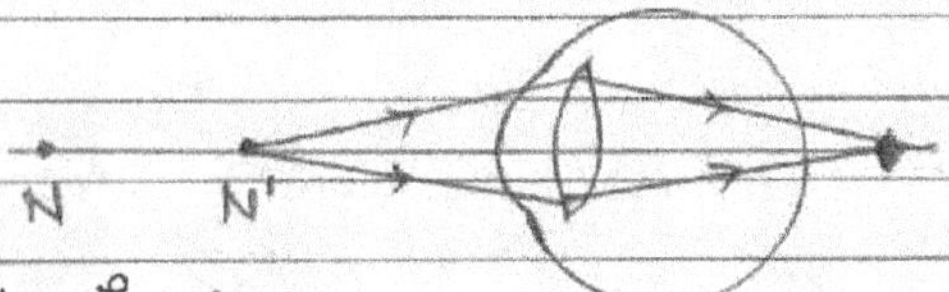

b. Hypermetropic eye

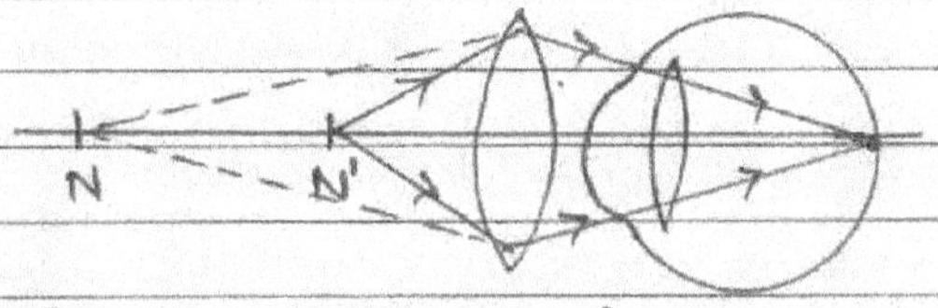

c. Correction of hypermetropic eye.

20. (a) When two or more resistors are joined end to end, they are said to be connected in series combination. The combined resistance of any number of resistances connected in series is equal to the sum of the individual resistances.

- connect an ammeter in the circuit and three voltmeters across each resistance as shown in figure.

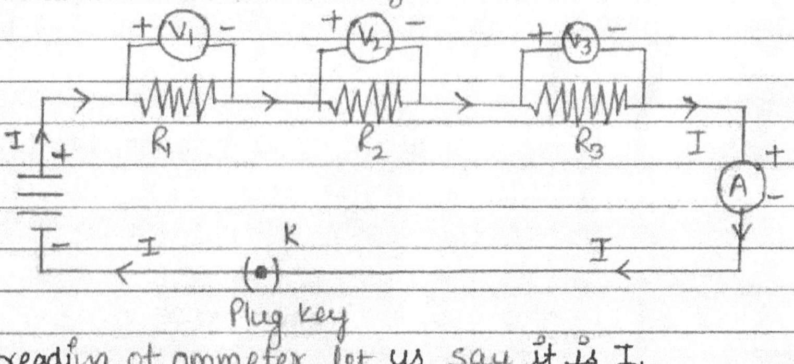

- Note the reading of ammeter let us say it is I.
- Note the reading of voltmeters let us say they are V_1, V_2 and V_3 respectively across R_1, R_2 and R_3.
- Change the position of ammeter to anywhere in between the resistors and note the ammeter reading each time

The ammeter reading will remain same everytime. Therefore when resistors are connected in series same current flows through all resistors, when it is connected to a battery.

(b) $R = R_1 + R_2 + R_3$

$R_{eq} = 5 + 10 + 15 = 30$ ohm

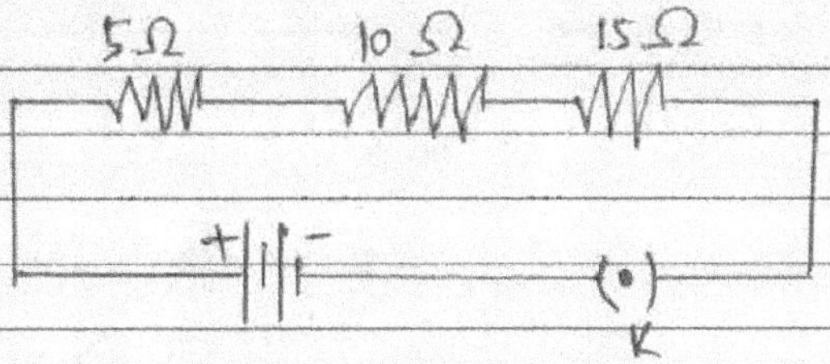

Also by Ohm's law

$$V = IR$$

$$I = \frac{V}{R} = \frac{30}{30} = 1 \text{ ampere}$$

Now as all resistors are in series so current in all will be same
So, Potential difference across 15 ohm resistors = 1 A X 15 ohm
= 15 volt.

OR

20. a. Three resistors R_1, R_2, R_3 are connected in parallel and the combination is connected to a battery, ammeter, voltmeter and key.

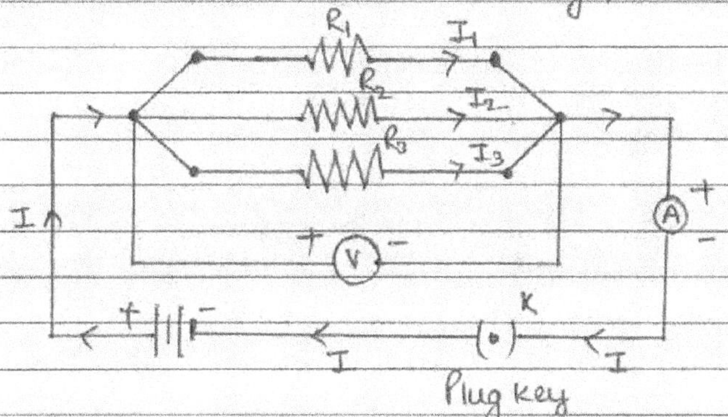

Total current = Sum of the curren flowing through each resistor

$$I = I_1 + I_2 + I_3$$

We know that, $V = IR$ or $I = \frac{V}{R}$

Therefore $I_1 = \frac{V}{R_1}$, $I_2 = \frac{V}{R_2}$ and $I_3 = \frac{V}{R_3}$

$$I = I_1 + I_2 + I_3$$

$$\frac{V}{R} = \frac{V}{R_1} + \frac{V}{R_2} + \frac{V}{R_3}$$

Thus we can say that the reciprocal of the equivalent resistant of the circuit is the sum of the reciprocals of all the individual resistances.

b. for the given circuit

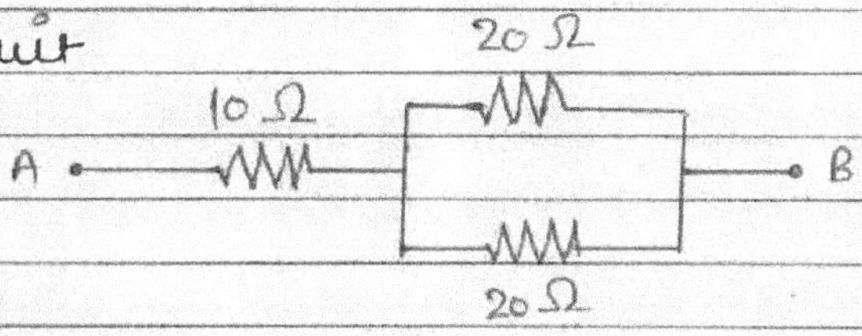

Let $R_1 = R_2 = 20$ ohm and $R_3 = 10$ ohm
Since, R_1 and R_2 resistors in parallel, so the net resistance

$$\frac{1}{R_4} = \frac{1}{R_1} + \frac{1}{R_2}$$
$$= \frac{1}{20} + \frac{1}{20}$$
$$= \frac{1}{10} \text{ ohm}$$

This gives, $R_4 = 10$ ohm
and $R_3 = 10$ ohm

Now R_3 and R_4 are in series, so
Net resistance $R = R_3 + R_4 = 20\ \Omega$

21. Magnetic feild lines produced around a current carrying straight conductor passing perpendicular through a horizontal cardboard.

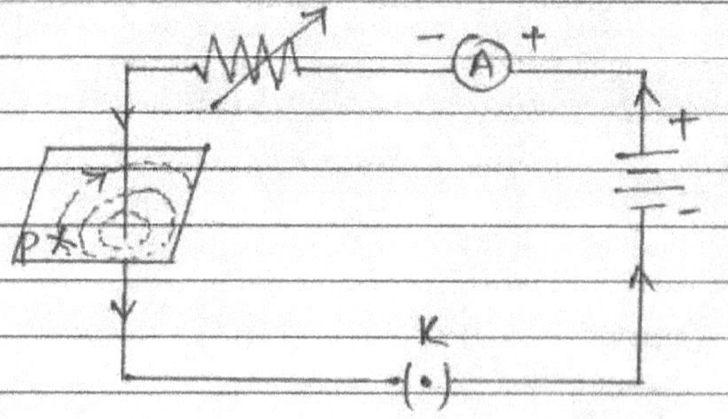

Right hand thumb rule: If we hold the current carrying conductor in the right hand such that the thumb points in the direction of current. then the fingers encircle the wire in the direction of magnetic lines of force.
The strength of the magnetic field will ~~be~~ reduce when the point where magnetic field is to be determined is moved away from the straight conductor as there is inverse relation between field strength and distance from current carrying conductor.

~~Section E~~

~~22.~~

Section-E

22.

Given Substance	Given pH	
Acentic acid	3	Correct
Water	12	Incorrect
Lemon juice	4	Correct
$NaHCO_3$	8	Correct
NaOH	14	Correct

The pH value of water given is incorrect. Its correct value is 7. It is neutral in nature.

OR

22. Case 1: $3FeSO_4(aq) + 2Al \longrightarrow Al_2(SO_4)_3(aq) + 3Fe(s)$

In this case light green solution of ferrous sulphate turns into colourless due to the displacement of Fe by Al.

Case 2: $FeSO_4 + Cu \longrightarrow$ No reaction

Because copper is less reactive than iron.

Case 3: $FeSO_4 + Fe \longrightarrow$ No reaction

Case 4: $FeSO_4(aq) + Zn \longrightarrow ZnSO_4(aq) + Fe$

Zinc is more reactive than iron so light green colour of solution turns into colourless.

23. When Sodium hydrogen carbonate is added to acetric acid, colourless and odourless carbon dioxide (CO_2) gas is evolved with brisk effervescence.

$NaHCO_3 + CH_3COOH \longrightarrow CH_3COONa + H_2O + CO_2$

Sodium hydrogen carbonatte	Acetic acid	Sodium acetate	Water	Carbon dioxide

24. Four steps of obtaining germinating dicot seeds are:

(i) Soaking of seeds
(ii) Emergence of radicle
(iii) Splitting of cotyledons
(iv) Emergence of plumule

OR

24. Two observations should be :
(i) Elongation of nucleus
(ii) Constriction appears due to the division of the cytoplasm.

25. Precautions :
(i) Cut the peel to a proper size and avoid folding it.
(ii) Always place the peel at the centre of the slide and hold the slide at the edges.
(iii) Do not overstrain or under strain the peel.
(iv) Remove access stain and glycerin with a blotting paper.
(v) Place cover slip carefully to avoid the air bubbles.

26.

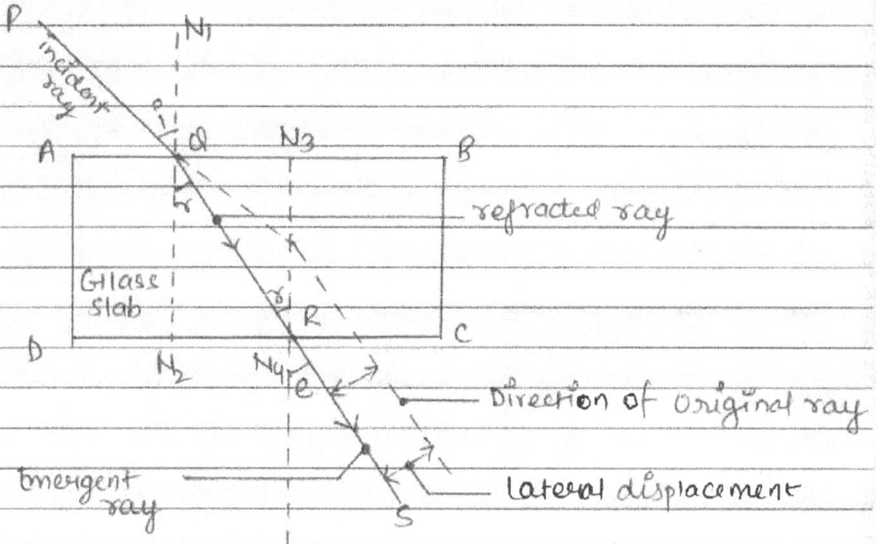

incident angle = ∠i refractive angle = ∠r
emergent angle = ∠e

OR

26.

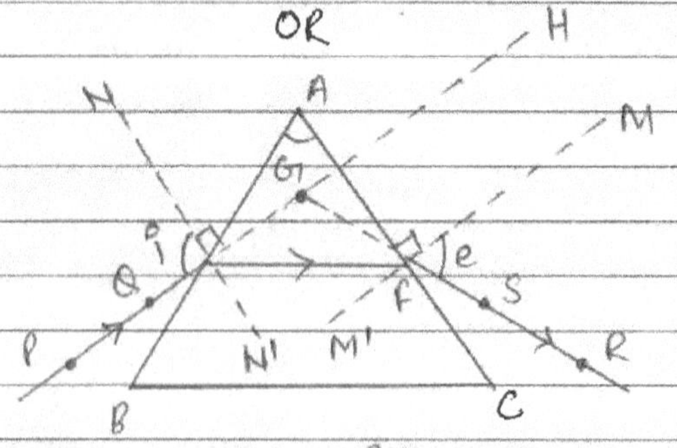

PE = incident ray EF = Refracted ray FS = Emergant ray
A = Angle of prism ∠i = Angle of incidence ∠r = Angle of refraction
∠e = Angle of emergence ∠D = Angle of deviation

27. a. Least count of ammeter $= \frac{100}{10} = 10$ mA

least count of voltmeter $= \frac{1}{10} = 0.1$ V

b. Reading of ammeter $= 200 + 5 \times 10$
$= 250$ mA $= 0.25$ A

Reading of voltmeter $= 2 + 4 \times 0.1 = 2.4$ V

$$R = \frac{V}{I} = \frac{2.4}{0.25} = 9.6 \text{ ohm}$$

Set-2

Section-A

1. Two advantage associated with water harvesting at the community level are:
(a) Overexploitation of water resources will be reduced and underground water table will ~~be~~ increase.
(b) Help to recharge the natural wells and provides moisture for vegetation over a wide area.

2. A voltmeter is always connected in parallel across a device to measure the voltage across it. If the voltmeter has low resistance, then the current will split and flow through the voltmeter also, thus changing the amount of current going through the element between two points thereby giving incorrect or undesired results across the device. Hence, it has a high resistance so that negligible current flows through it.

Section-B

3. Electron dot structure of CO_2 is

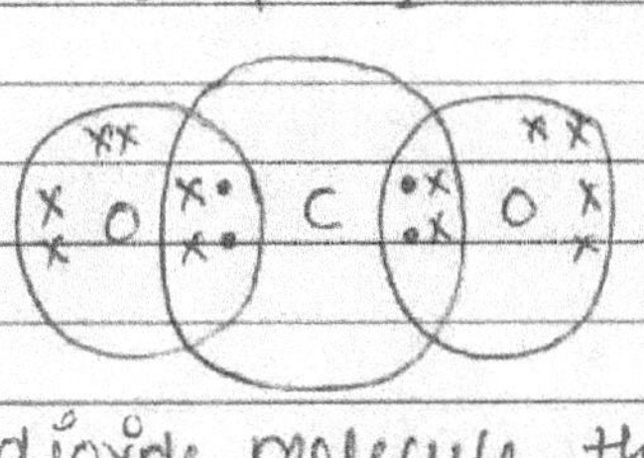

Thus, in carbon dioxide molecule, the carbon atom is linked to two oxygen atoms on both sides by two shared pairs of electrons resulting in double bonds on either side. Both carbon and oxygen atoms complete their octet as a result of electron sharing.

OR

3. The two features of carbon that give rise to a large number of carbon compounds or organic compounds are as follows :

(i) Catenation : Carbon has the ~~eqt~~ unique ability to form bonds with other atoms of carbon, giving rise to large molecules. This property is called catenation. These compounds may have long chains of carbon, branched chains of carbon or even carbon atoms arranged in rings.

(ii) Tetravalency : Since carbon has a valency of four, it is ~~simple~~ capable of bonding with four other ~~carbons~~. atoms of carbon. or atoms of some other mono-valent element. Compounds of carbon are formed with oxygen, hydrogen, nitrogen, sulphur, chlorine and many other elements.

4. (a) It is easier to obtain a metal from its oxide as compared to its sulphides and carbonates. Therefore, prior to reduction, the metal sulphides and carbonates are usually converted into metal oxides during the process of extraction.

(b) Aluminium is good conductor of heat. When exposed to air, the metal changes into its oxide called aluminium oxide Al_2O_3. It gets deposited over the surface of the metal and forms ~~of~~ a protective coating on the surface. Due to the presence of this layer, the metal becomes unreactive and can be used in making cooking utensils.

5. As the power is positive, therefore the lens is a convex lens.

$$P = \frac{1}{f}$$

$$5 = \frac{1}{f}$$

$$f = \frac{1}{5}$$

$$f = 0.2 \text{ m or } 20 \text{ cm}$$

Inverted image of same size will be obtained when object is placed at 2f, which is double of focal length So,

$$V = 20 \times 2 = 40 \text{ cm}$$

object must be placed at a distance of 40 cm from lens or at C to obtain an inverted image of same size.

Section-C

6\. The two types of transport system is human beings are:
(i) Blood circulatory system.
(ii) Lymphatic system / lymph or tissue fluid.

Functions of blood circulatory system are:
(i) Transport of oxygen: It helps in the transport of blood from heart to other parts of the body and also carying oxygen throughout the body.
(ii) Transport of disgested food: Along with carrying blood and oxygen it is also responsible for carrying the nutrients and minerals which are absorbed from the food that is digested in our body and also the hormones secreted in our body.
(iii) Transport of carbon dioxide
(iv) Transport of nitrogeneous waste.
(V) Transport of salts.

7\.

Pollination	Fertilization
Pollination refers to the transfer of pollen grains from anther to stigma	Fertilization refers to the fusion of male and female gamets.
Pollination is a physical process.	Fertilization is cellular, genetic, biochemical process.
Pollination can be achieved by various agents such as wind, insect etc.	Fertilization is assisted by the plant itsely.

Site of fertilization in a flower is ovary or ovule.
The product of fertilization in a flower is zygote.

10\. Environmetal consequences of using fossil fuels are:
(a) Burning of fossil fuels causes air pollution.
(b) On burning they produce acidic gases like CO_2, SO_2, SO_3, NO_2. These gases such as SO_2, SO_3 and NO_2 causes acid rains. which affects our water and soil resources.
(c) Excess of CO_2 gas contributes to the global warming due to its greenhouse effect.

Steps to minimize the pollution:

(a) Use of alternate source of energy and promoting eco-friendly substances.

(b) Use of various devices to reduce emission of harmful gases and implementing strong pollution control act against which causes punishment.

(c) By increasing efficiency of combustion process.

(d) Saving non-renewal fuels and using air and sun-light as a energy resource in our daily life.

14. (i) Alkanes are saturated compounds that consist of only single bond. Their general formula is C_nH_{2n+2}

(ii) Alkanes are unsaturated compounds that consists of double bond. Their general formula is C_nH_{2n}.

(iii) Alkynes are unsaturated compounds that consists of triple bond. Their general formula is ~~C_nH_{2n+2}~~ C_nH_{2n-2}

Since C_4H_{10} follows the general formula C_nH_{2n-2} therefore it is an alkane.

The following structures show the structural isomers of butane.

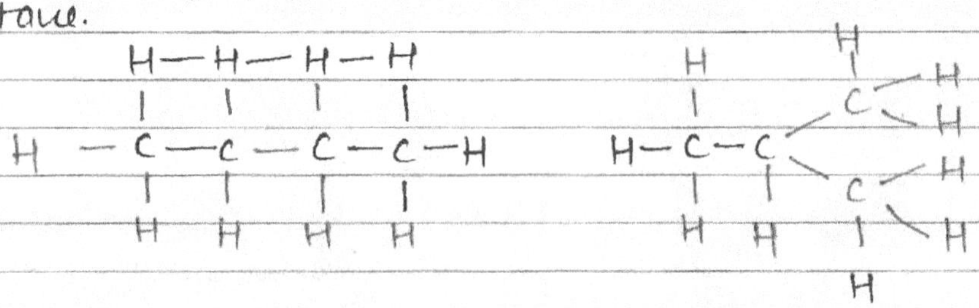

We see that both theese structures have the same formula C_4H_{10}.

Section-D

16. (a) The trait which express itsey in F_1 (first) generation after crossing contrasting (opposite) traits is known as dominant character (trait). For example 'Tall' is a dominant trait of pea plants

The trait which is not expressed in F_1 (first) generation after crossing contrasting (opposite) trait is known as recessive trait. For example 'Dwarf' is a recessive trait of pea plant.

(b) Yes it is possible that a trait is inherited but may not be expressed in the next generation cross pollinated tall pea plants with short (dwarf) pea plants.

Tall Dwarf Tall Tall Tall Tall

Self-pollinated the tall plants (F_1 generation ones):

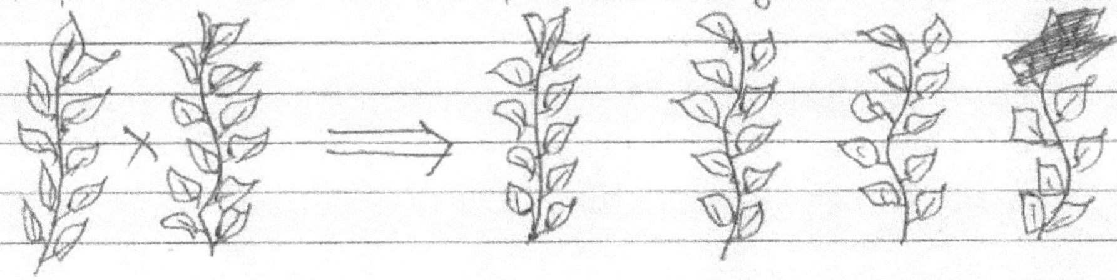

Tall Tall Tall Tall Tall Dwarf

(TT) (tt)
⇓ ⇓
(T) (T) (t) (t)

Cross pollination in pure plants	t	t
T	Tt (tall)	Tt (Tall)
T	Tt (tall)	Tt (tall)

⇒ All F1 are tall

(Tt) (Tt)
⇓ ⇓
(T) (t) (T) (t)

Self Pollination in F1 (Tt)	T	t
T	TT (Tall)	Tt (tall)
t	Tt (tall)	tt (dwarf)

⇒ 75% F2 are tall and 25% are dwarf

20. (a) Scattering is the phenomenon by which a beam of light is redirected in many different directions when it inteacts with a particle in the atmosphere. When sunlight strikes molecules in our atmosphere, the light is redirected in many directions.

The size of scattering particles do affect the color of the scattered particles.

- Very fine particles having sizes, less than the wave-length of the visible light mainly scatter blue light of shorter wavelength of the visible spectrum.

- Colors with longer wavelength i.e red is scattered be particles of relatively larger size.
- particles which are very large like raindrops, dust and ice particles scatter white light.

(b) During sunrise and sunset, sun is near horizon. Sunlight travels longer distance. Most of blue light scatter away by particles. Lights of longer wavelength reaches our eye so sun appears reddish. At noon, sun is directly overhead so sunlight travels lesser distance. Less amount of blue light is scattered giving white appearance to sun.

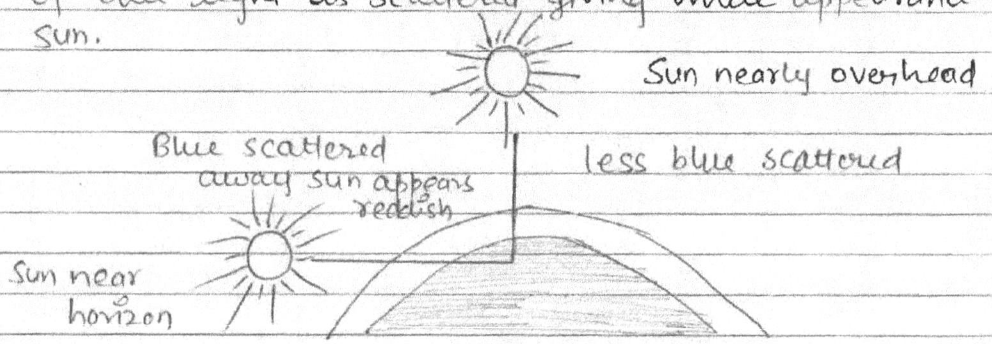

Set-3

Section-A

1. Cord is made ~~of~~ up of copper wire whereas heating element is made up of alloy which has very high resistance. So when current flows through the heating element, it becomes too hot and glows red. But the resistance of cord which is usually of copper or aluminium is very low, so it does not glow.

2. Although coal and petroleum are produced by the degradation of biomas, yet we need to converse these resources. This is because they are non-renewable and their formation takes millions of years and thus they may get exhausted in the future if we continue to use them at such a large scale.

Section-B

3. Refraction of light due to variation in optical density of earth is known as atmospheric refraction.

Two phenomenon which can be explained on the basis of atmospheric refraction :-

(i) Twinkling of Stars
(ii) Advance sunrise & delayed Sunset

4. Aluminium, Zinc, Iron, lead are the metals of medium reactivity.
Steps invovled in the extraction of this metal from its sulphide ore are:
(i) Concentration of ore enrichment
↓
(ii) Roasting | conversion of sulphide into oxide on heating in air.
↓
(iii) Reduction of metallic oxide to metal
↓
(iv) Purification of metal.

5. Chemical properties on the basis of which ethanol and ethanoic acid may be differentiated are:
- Eathenol does not react with metal carbonates while, ethanoic acid reacts with metal carbonates to form salt water and carbon dioxide. for example:

$$2CH_3COOH + Na_2CO_3 \longrightarrow 2CH_3COONa + CO_2 + H_2O$$

- Ethenol does not react with NaOH while, ethanoic acid reacts with NaOH to form sodium ethanoate and water. for example:

$$CH_3COOH + NaOH \longrightarrow CH_3COONa + H_2O$$

OR

Out of saturated and unsaturated carbon compounds, Unsaturated compounds are more reactive.

Test to distinguish ethane from ethene is Bromine water test:

If we react ethane with bromine water no reaction takes place. Thus, decolorization of reddish brown colour of bromine water does not take place. While if we react ~~above~~

ethone with bromine water. 1,2-dibromo ethane is formed and reddish brown colour of bromine water disappears. Reaction involved is shown as follows :

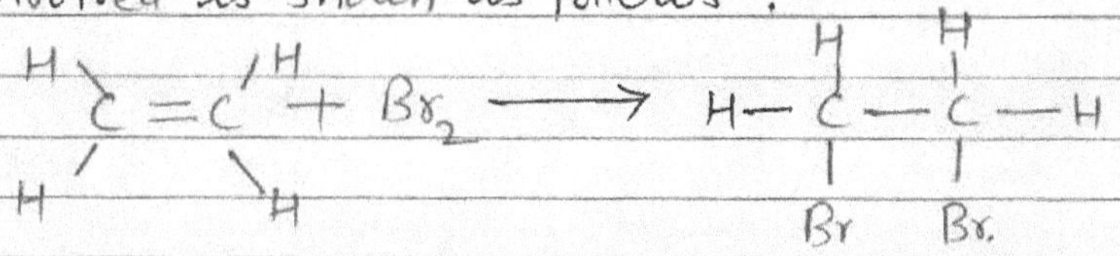

ethone 1,2 dibromoethane

Section-C

6. The white light splits into seven colours when it ~~goes~~ gets refracted through the glass prism (VIBGYOR). This phenominon of splitting of white light into its constituent seven colors on passing through a glass prism is called dispersion of light.

The colour that deviates most - Violet

The colour thate deviates least - Red

If a second identical prism is placed in an inverted position with respect to the first prism then it recombines all seven colours and gives a white light. This is because the refraction produced by the second prism is equal to and opposite to that produced by the first prism so the colours will disappear and again white light will be obtained.

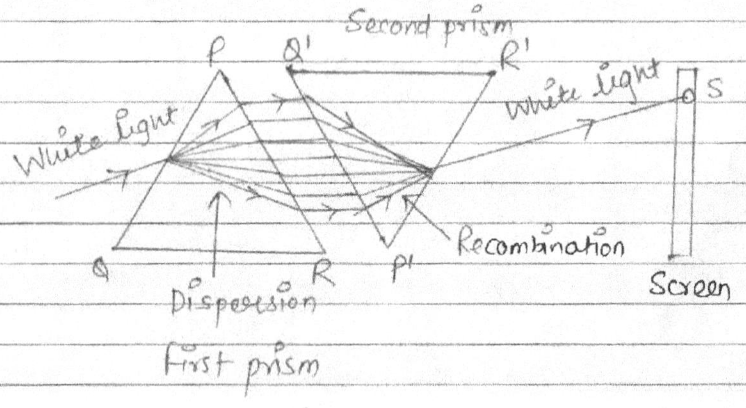

OR

6. (i) The student is suffering from Myopia.

(ii) focal length $= \frac{1}{P}$

$f = -\frac{1}{0.5}$

$f = -2m$

i.e focal length = −200 cm

As the focal length of the lens is negative, therefore nature of the lens is diverging i.e. it is a concave lens.

(iii) The two causes of this defect are :
(a) excessive curvature of the eye lens.
(b) elongation of eye ball.

7. Chain of organisms formed as a result of eating or being eaten by organisms or a series of organisms feeding on one another is called chain.
The four trophic levels are :
(a) Autotrophs are at the primary level which fix the sunlight and produce their own food,
(b) Primary consumers or herbivores come at the second level.
(c) Secondary consumers or small carnivores come at the third level and
(d) Tertiary consumers or the large carnivores come at the last level.

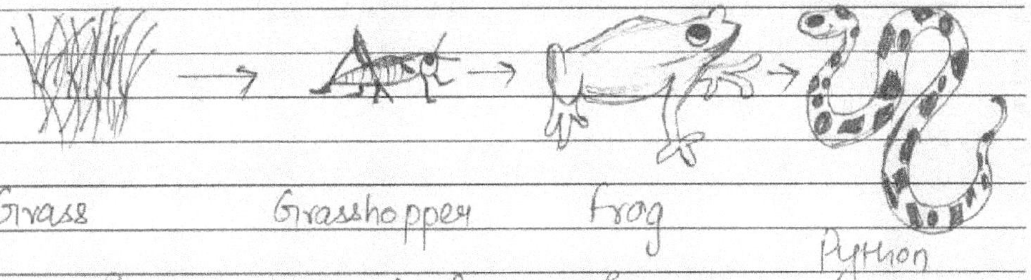

The above is an example of food chain.

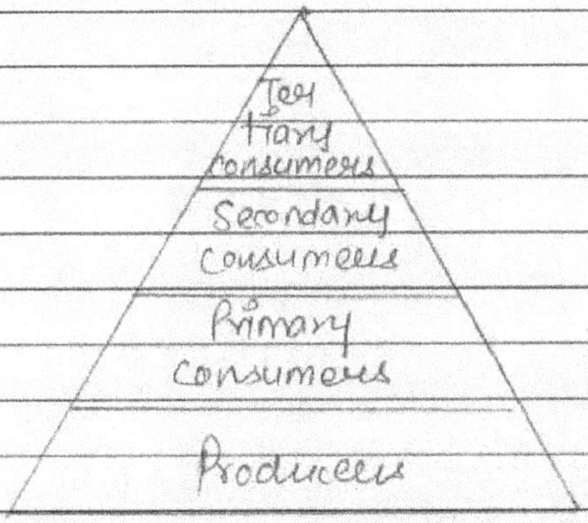

Snake
↓
Frog
↓
Grasshopper
↓
Grass

If a pollutant enters at the producer level, the organisms of tertiary trophic level will have the maximum concentration of the pollutant in their bodies.
This phenomenon is called Biological magnification or Bio-magnification.

9. (a) Silver is placed below Hydrogen in reactivity series and is among least reactive metal. So silver does not show any change because silver is less reactive than hydrogen It cannot displace hydrogen from dilute hydrochloric acid.

(b) When lead (Pb) reacts with acid bubbles are seen due to formation of hydrogen gas. This is because lead lies above hydrogen in reactivity series and thus displaces hydrogen from the acid. Rate of reaction is slow here.

$$\underset{\text{Lead}}{Pb(s)} + \underset{\text{hydrochloric acid}}{2HCl(aq)} \longrightarrow \underset{\text{Lead chloride}}{PbCl_2(s)} + \underset{\text{hydrgen}}{H_2(g)} \uparrow$$

(c) Sodium is higly reactive metal. It reacts with hydrochloric acid vigorously and explosively forming hydrogen gas along with the release of large amount of heat.

(d) The reaction between aluminium and hydrochloric acid is exothermic. Thus, temperature of the reaction mixture rises.

10. (i) Roasting of copper (I) Sulphide

$$2Cu_2S + 3O_2 \longrightarrow 2Cu_2O + 2SO_2$$

(ii) Reduction of copper (I) oxide from copper (I) Sulphide

$$2Cu_2O + Cu_2S \longrightarrow 6Cu + SO_2$$

(iii) Electrolytic refining

At Anode : $Cu \rightarrow Cu^{2+} + 2e^-$

At cathode : $Cu^{2+} + 2e^- \rightarrow Cu$

15. (a) Budding, fragmentation and regeneration are considered as asexual types of reproduction because all of them involve only one parent and gametes are not involved in reproduction. Organisms are formed as a result of mitotic divison and progeny (organism) are similiar in their genetic makeup and no variations.

(b) Planaria can be cut into any number of pieces and each piece grows through specialized cells. into a complete organism.

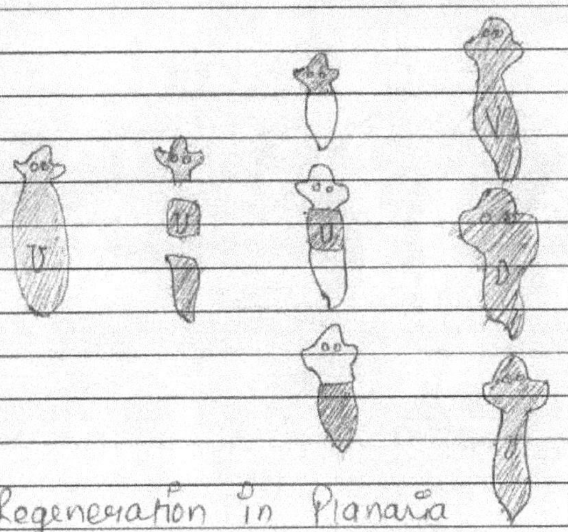

Regeneration in Planaria

Section-D

16. Given : Height of object = 6 cm

$f = -30$ cm

$u = -45$ cm

$v = ?$

nature = ?

Height of image = ?

by using mirror formula

$$\frac{1}{f} = \frac{1}{v} + \frac{1}{u}$$

$$\frac{1}{v} = \frac{1}{f} - \frac{1}{u}$$

$$\frac{1}{v} = -\frac{1}{30} - \frac{1}{-45} \Rightarrow -\frac{1}{30} + \frac{1}{45} = -\frac{1}{90}$$

image will be formed at a distance of 90 cm from the pole of mirror.

size of image

$$m = \frac{h_i}{h_o} = \frac{-v}{u} = -\frac{90}{45} = -2$$

$$h_i = -2 \times 6 = -12 \text{ cm}$$

Image formed will be real, inverted and enlarged.

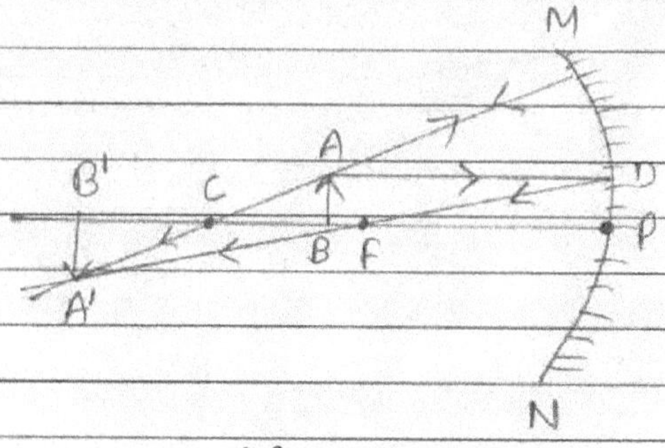

OR

16. Given Height of object = +6 cm
Object distance = −50 cm
focal length = +30 cm

Lens formula : $\frac{1}{f} = \frac{1}{v} - \frac{1}{u}$

$\frac{1}{v} = \frac{1}{f} + \frac{1}{u} = \frac{1}{v} = \frac{1}{30} - \frac{1}{50} = \frac{5-3}{150} = \frac{2}{150}$

Image distance $v = \frac{150}{2} = +75$ cm

$m = \frac{h_i}{h_o} = \frac{v}{u}$

$\frac{h_i}{6} = \frac{75}{-50}$

$h_i = \frac{-75 \times 6}{50} = -9$ cm

Hence image formed is real, inverted and enlarged.

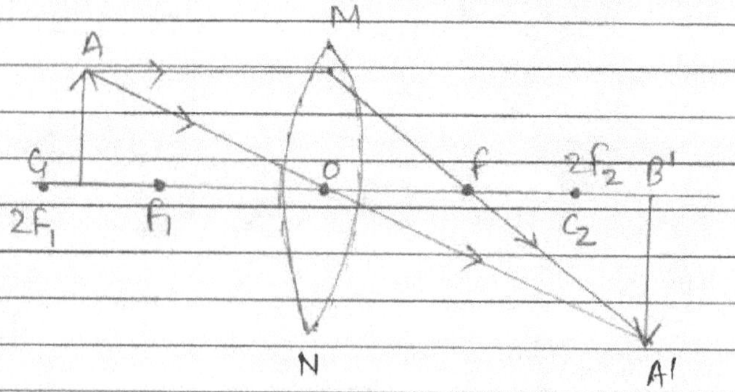

(d)

20. When male and female organisms are involved in producing young ones or when gametes from two organisms of opposite sex fuse to produce young ones, the process is known as sexual reproduction.

During sexual reproduction, at the time of gemete formation meiotic cell division takes place. During meiosis crossing over between fragments of homologous chromosomes occurs which brings about new gene combinations to be transfferred to new generations.
Crossing over ~~to~~ is the fundamental cause of origin of variations in sexually reproducing organisms. Asexual reproduction does not involve meiosis and crossing over because of one parent lineage. Hence, only minute variations may occur in them due to mutation. The variations caused by crossing over in sexually reproducing organisms are subjected to the selection process. Natural selection selects those variations which have more adaptive value and guide them towards evolution of new species. In this way sexual reproduction gives rise to more viable variation for evolution. More variations helps in the process of evolution. Helpful variations accumulate over time and produce new species and result in evolution.

TOPPER SOLUTION

16th March 2018, Class 10

SCIENCE

Note: This CBSE provided topper answer sheet (solutions) is specially added for your understanding of how to ideally model your answer. Exam format for February 2020 exams is significantly different to this CBSE paper.

Time Allowed: 3 Hours | *Maximum Marks: 80*

General Instructions:

i. The question paper comprises two Sections, A and B. You are to attempt both the sections.
ii. All questions are compulsory.
iii. All questions of Section A and Section B are to be attempted separately.
iv. There is an internal choice in three questions of three marks each, two questions of five marks each in Section A and in one question of two marks in Section B.
v. Question numbers 1 and 2 in Section A are one-mark questions. They are to be answered in one word or in one sentence.
vi. Question numbers 3 to 5 in Section A are two-marks questions. These are to be answered in about 30 words each.
vii. Question numbers 6 to 15 in Section A are three-marks questions. These are to be answered in about 50 words each.
viii. Question numbers 16 to 21 in Section A are five-marks questions. These are to be answered in about 70 words each.
ix. Question numbers 22 to 27 in Section B are based on practical skills. Each question is a two-marks question. These are to be answered in brief.

SECTION - A

1. A Mendelian experiment consisted of breeding pea plants bearing violet flowers with pea plants bearing white flowers. What will be the result in F1 progeny? **1**

Sol. As violet colour of flowers is dominant,
Genotype of white flowers :- 'vv'
Genotype of violet flowers :- 'VV'

Genotype of F_1 progeny :- 'Vv'
According to law of dominance, colour of flowers in F_1 progeny will be violet.

2. Write the energy conversion that takes place in a hydropower plant. **1**

Sol. Potential energy of water stored in reservoir ⟶ Kinetic energy of flowing water ⟶ Mechanical (Kinetic) energy of turbine axle ⟶ Electrical energy (converted in generator)

3. A compound 'X' on heating with excess conc. sulphuric acid at 443 K gives an unsaturated compound 'Y'. 'X' also reacts with sodium metal to evolve a colourless gas 'Z'. Identify 'X', 'Y' and 'Z'. Write the equation of the chemical reaction of formation of 'Y' and also write the role of sulphuric acid in the reaction. **2**

Sol. X – Ethanol [C_2H_5OH]
Y – Ethene [C_2H_4]
Z – Hydrogen [H_2]

$$\underset{(X)}{C_2H_5OH} \xrightarrow[443K]{Conc.\ H_2SO_4} \underset{(Y)}{C_2H_4} + H_2O$$

Sulphuric acid (conc. H_2SO_4) acts as a dehydrating agent and removes a molecule of water from 'ethanol' to give unsaturated compound 'ethene'.

4. **a.** Name one gustatory receptor and one olfactory receptor present in human beings.

b. Write *a* and *b* in the given flow chart of neuron through which information travels as an electrical impulse.

Dendrite ⟶ *a* ⟶ b ⟶ End point of Neuron **2**

Sol. Gustatory receptor present in tongue to detect taste.
Olfactory receptor present in nose to detect smell.

Dendrite ⟶ Cyton/Cell body ⟶ Axon ⟶ End pt of neuron

5. If the image formed by a spherical mirror for all positions of the object placed in front of it is always erect and diminished, what type of mirror is it? Draw a labelled ray diagram to support your answer. **2**

Sol. Convex mirror always form erect and diminished object.

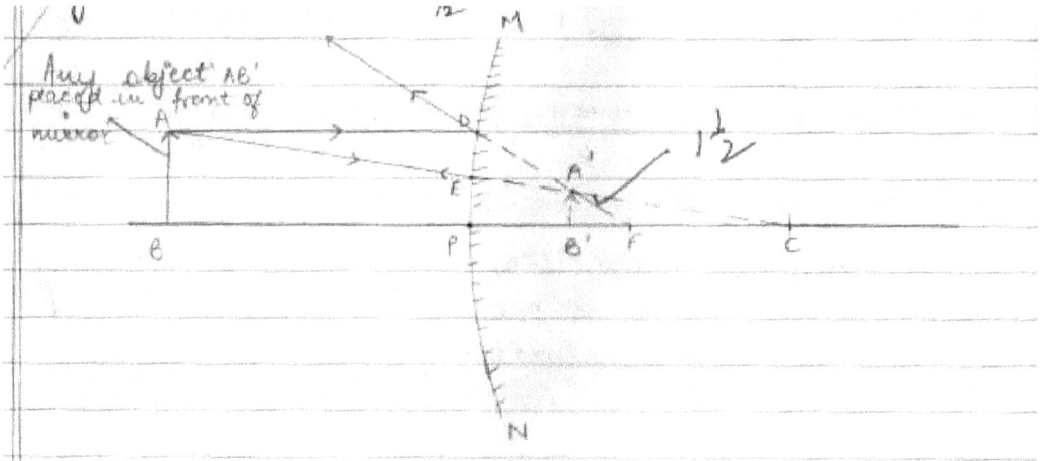

A' B' — virtual & erect img. formed between pole & focus of convex mirror

6. Decomposition reactions require energy either in the form of heat or light or electricity for breaking down the reactants. Write one equation each for decomposition reactions where energy is supplied in the form of heat, light and electricity. **3**

Sol. (i) Thermal decomposition reaction

$2FeSO_4(s) \xrightarrow{\Delta} Fe_2O_3(s) + SO_2(g) + SO_3(g)$

(green coloured crystals) (Iron(III) oxide brown coloured) (sulphur dioxide) (a suffocating smell)

⇒ Green coloured crystals change to brown coloured Fe_2O_3 along with gases like SO_2 & SO_3.

(ii) Photo decomposition reaction

$AgCl(s) \xrightarrow{Sunlight} Ag(s) + Cl_2(g)$

(White coloured) (Grey coloured)

(iii) Electrolytic decomposition reaction

$2H_2O(l) \xrightarrow{Electricity} 2H_2(g) + O_2(g)$

7. 2 mL of sodium hydroxide solution is added to a few pieces of granulated zinc metal taken in a test tube. When the contents are warmed, a gas evolves which is bubbled through a soap solution before testing. Write the equation of the chemical reaction involved and the test to detect the gas. Name the gas which will be evolved when the same metal reacts with dilute solution of a strong acid. **3**

OR

The pH of a salt used to make tasty and crispy pakoras is 14. Identify the salt and write a chemical equation for its formation. List its two uses. **3**

Sol. $NaOH\ (aq.) + Zn\ (s) \xrightarrow{\Delta} Na_2ZnO_2 + H_2(\uparrow)$
(sodium hydroxide solution) (sodium zincate)

Thus, in this reaction, hydrogen gas is evolved.

As the gas is passed through soap solution, bubbles filled with hydrogen gas come out. Bring a candle near the bubbles evolved, the bubble bursts & the gas inside it starts burning with a pop sound & extinguishes the candle. This tests the presence of H_2 gas in them.
Even if the zinc metal reacts with a solution of strong acid, hydrogen gas is produced / evolved.
[Eg. $Zn + 2HCl \rightarrow ZnCl_2 + H_2$]

8. **a.** Why are most carbon compounds poor conductors of electricity?

b. Write the name and structure of a saturated compound in which the carbon atoms are arranged in a ring. Give the number of single bonds present in this compound. **3**

Sol. **a.** Carbon compounds are covalently bonded and hence the bond is formed by sharing of electrons between two or more combining atoms. Due to this, they don't form any ions or electrically charged particles within the solution nor they give free electrons. As we know, conduction of electricity requires flow of free electrons in solids & ions in fluids, they don't conduct electricity.

b.

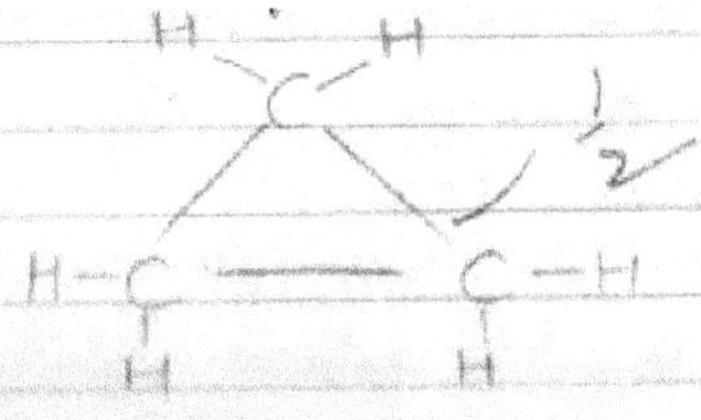

— Cyclopropane

Structure

9. Name the hormones secreted by the following endocrine glands and specify one function of each :

a. Thyroid **b.** Pituitary **c.** Pancreas **3**

Sol. a. Thyroid gland :- Thyroxine hormone
Thyroxine hormone helps in metabolism of carbohydrates, fats and proteins and is thus responsible for best balanced body growth

b. Pituitary gland :- Growth hormone
It regulates growth and development of body. However, its reduced secretion causes 'dwarfism' and excess secretion causes 'gigantism'.

c. Pancreas — Insulin
Insulin regulates the blood sugar level & brings back the excess sugar level to normal.

10. Write one main difference between asexual and sexual mode of reproduction. Which species is likely to have comparatively better chances of survival – the one reproducing asexually or the one reproducing sexually? Give reason to justify your answer. **3**

Sol. Asexual mode of reproduction is uniparental & thus, doesn't involve any fusion of gametes & hence, fertilization.

Sexual mode of reproduction is biparental & thus involves fusion of both male & female gametes.

Among the two, sexually reproducing species have a better chance of survival. This is because reproduction in such species require contribution of equal genetic material from both the parents. This results in various combinations for genes.

Hence, the process of creation of variations is increased manifold as compared to asexually reproducing organisms. Thus, accumulation of such variations for long time, may lead to evolution. Not only this, we also know that variations are helpful for continuation of species in case the 'niche' changes drastically due to factors not under our control like global warming, meteorite hits etc. Asexual reproduction involves slight variations & thus, will not be very beneficial to produce a variation adaptable to drastically changed n

11. State the laws of refraction of light. Explain the term 'absolute refractive index of a medium' and write an expression to relate it with the speed of light in vacuum. **3**

OR

What is meant by power of a lens? Write its SI unit. A student uses a lens of focal length 40 cm and another of –20 cm. Write the nature and power of each lens. **3**

Sol. Power of a lens is defined as the reciprocal of its focal length when expressed in metres. It tells us about its (lens') converging or diverging capacity for a beam of parallel rays or any other as well.

SI unit of power is Dioptre (D)

$$P = \frac{1}{f\text{(in metres)}}$$

Focal length of lens (f) = 40 cm

$= \frac{40}{100} = \frac{2}{5}$ m

As we know, $P = \frac{1}{f}$

$P = \frac{1}{\frac{2}{5}} = \frac{5}{2} = +2.5$ D

The lens is convex lens which is a converging lens (∵ f & P are +ve)

Focal length of lens (f) = –20 cm $= \frac{-20}{100} = \frac{-1}{5}$ m

As we know, $P = \frac{1}{f}$

$P = \frac{1}{-\frac{1}{5}} = -5$ D

Nature of lens :- Concave lens which is a diverging lens (∵ f & P are –ve)

12. Show how would you join three resistors, each of resistance 9Ω so that the equivalent resistance of the combination is (i) 13.5Ω, (ii) 6Ω? **3**

OR

a. Write Joule's law of heating.

b. Two lamps, one rated 100 W; 220 V, and the other 60 W; 220 V, are connected in parallel to electric mains supply. Find the current drawn by two bulbs from the line, if the supply voltage is 220 V. **3**

Sol. a. Let R be the resistor of 9 Ω.

For 13.5 Ω :-

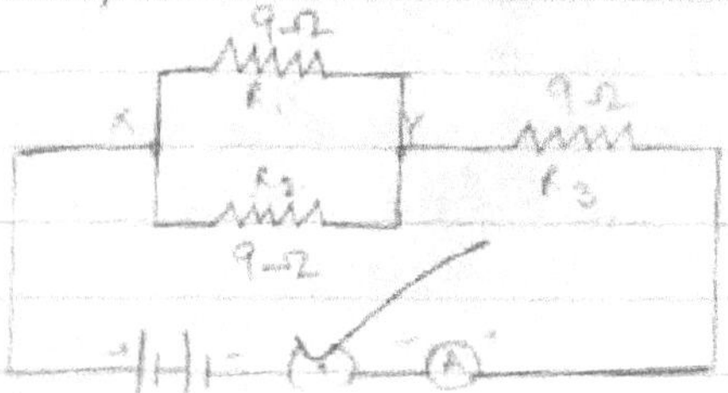

For parallel combination, $\frac{1}{R_p} = \frac{1}{R_1} + \frac{1}{R_2}$

$\frac{1}{R_p} = \frac{1}{9} + \frac{1}{9} = \frac{2}{9}$ ∴ $R_p = \frac{9}{2}$ Ω = 4.5 Ω

Resistance of total combination (R_T) $1\frac{1}{2}$

$R_p + R_3$ = 4.5 Ω + 9 Ω = 13.5 Ω.

b.

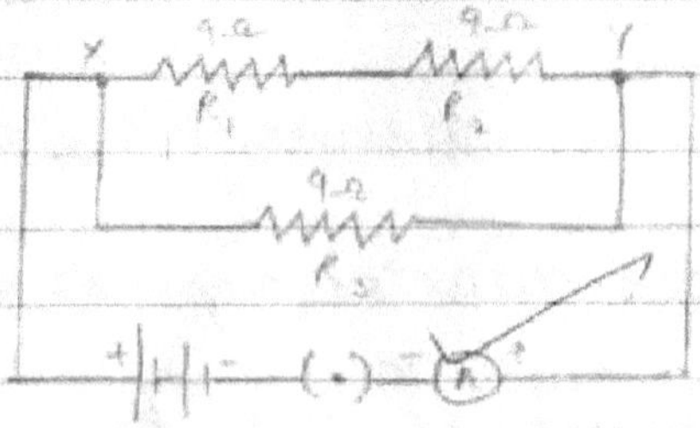

$R_s = R_1 + R_2 + R_3$ ...... [Law of combination of resistors in series]

$R_s = R_1 + R_2 = 9 + 9 = 18$ Ω

$\frac{1}{R_p} = \frac{1}{R_1} + \frac{1}{R_2}$ ...... [Law of combination of resistors in parallel]

$\frac{1}{R_p} = \frac{1}{R_s} + \frac{1}{R_3} = \frac{1}{18} + \frac{1}{9} = \frac{1+2}{18} = \frac{3}{18}$ Ω

$R_p = \frac{18}{3} = 6$ Ω $1\frac{1}{2}$

13. **a.** List the factors on which the resistance of a conductor in the shape of a wire depends.

b. Why are metals good conductors of electricity whereas glass is a bad conductor of electricity? Give reason.

c. Why are alloys commonly used in electrical heating devices? Give reason. **3**

Sol.

(a) Resistance of a conductor depends upon following factors :-

(i) It is directly proportional to length of conductor [$R \propto l$]

(ii) It is inversely proportional to area of cross section of conductor [$R \propto \frac{1}{A}$]

(iii) It depends upon nature of material of conductor

(iv) It depends upon temperature of conductor when it is being used.

(b) Metals are good conductors of electricity because of their lower resistivity. Metals have a resistivity of the order of 10^{-8} to 10^{-6} Ω m. Hence, they provide less opposition to the flow of electric charges through them & hence have higher conductivity.

Glass is a bad conductor of electricity as it has extremely high resistivity and hence provides great opposition to flow of free electrons/electric charges. Hence it is included in the group of insulators having resistivity of order of 10^{12} to 10^{17} Ω m.

(c) Alloys are used in electrical heating devices as:-

(i) They have higher resistivity than their constituent metals & thus a lot of heat energy is dissipated as charges flow through them.

(ii) They don't get oxidised or burnt at even high temperatures.

14. Students in a school listened to the news read in the morning assembly that the mountain of garbage in Delhi, suddenly exploded and various vehicles got buried under it. Several people were also injured and there was traffic jam all around. In the brain storming session the teacher also discussed this issue and asked the students to find out a solution to the problem of garbage. Finally they arrived at two main points—one is self management of the garbage we produce and the second is to generate less garbage at individual level.

a. Suggest two measures to manage the garbage we produce.

b. As an individual, what can we do to generate the least garbage? Give two points.

c. List two values the teacher instilled in his students in this episode. **3**

OR

a. Define excretion.

b. Name the basic filtration unit present in the kidney.

c. Draw excretory system in human beings and label the following organs of excretory system which perform following functions :

  i. form urine.

  ii. is a long tube which collects urine from kidney.

  iii. store urine until it is passed out.

d. Write one structural difference between the composition of artery and veins. **3**

Sol. (a) (i) For managing garbage, first we must segregate it into biodegrable & non biodegradable substances. Biodegradable substances like vegetable peels, domestic waste, animal excreta, cow dung etc. must be converted into manure. This not only helps in enriched growth of plants but also prevents dump of it in open, production of foul smell etc.

(ii) For non-biodegradable substances, we must further segregate as recyclable & non recyclable. All recyclable metals, plastic, glass must be sent to diff factories which after proper cleaning, process them in new products.

(iii) For rest over garbage, practices like filling it in landfills which can be converted into playground for children or incineration at places with proper management for it can be done.

(b) As an individual,

(i) We must follow the policy of 'reduce'. We should try to switch of lights when unnecessary for our resources & for garbage, try using same sheet of blank paper not used from other side, try making registers with utilising all the pages to reduce our demand for rough copies, reducing usage of plastic disposable cups.

(ii) We must follow the policy of 'reuse'. Using jam bottles, milk cartons, packaging boxes, ketchup bottles is a good way to use resources already once used.

(c) Teacher has instilled the values of 'environmental concern', 'eco friendliness', 'wise use of resources'.

15. What is a dam? Why do we seek to build large dams? While building large dams, which three main problems should particularly be addressed to maintain peace among local people? Mention them. **3**

Sol. → Dam is a structure made to obstruct the flow river for creating an impoundment or diverting the flow of water for one's own use.

→ Dams are built for storage of water for irrigation, electric generation, recreation, protection from drought or flood etc. $\frac{1}{2}+\frac{1}{2}$

Problems to be addressed to maintain peace among people :-

(i) They must be provided with full rehabilitation facilities. The ousters of Tawa Dam are still fighting for facilities promised to them in 1970.

(ii) They must be given required sum of money for once again creating necessary conditions for them. They should also be provided with equal land area that has been taken from them to construct a dam with a developmental approach.

(iii) Benefits of dam must be guaranteed to them and not only to rich urban areas & industries. $\frac{1}{2}$

(iv) Afforestation to reduce the damages due to large forests being cut & a shelter for wildlife which has been displaced.

16. **a.** Write the steps involved in the extraction of pure metals in the middle of the activity series from their carbonate ores.

b. How is copper extracted from its sulphide ore? Explain the various steps supported by chemical equations. Draw labelled diagram for the electrolytic refining of copper. **5**

Sol. (a) Extraction of pure metals from 'CO_3' ores :-

(i) Concentration of ore

→ Gangue or matrix must be removed from ore by processes taking in mind differences in physical & chemical properties of gangue & ore.

(ii) Calcination :-

→ The carbonate ores must be heated strongly in absence of air to convert them into metal oxides.

Eg. $ZnCO_3(s) \xrightarrow{\Delta} ZnO(s) + CO_2(\uparrow)$

(iii) Reduction by a more reactive metal or carbon :- $\frac{1}{2}$

$ZnO + C \longrightarrow Zn + CO$

This will happen as Carbon has higher affinity for ~~zinc~~ oxygen than zinc.

(iv) Finally, the obtained metal can be refined by electrolysis of their ~~salt~~ salt solution. $\frac{1}{2}$

(b) Copper glance [Cu_2S] is copper's sulphide ore. It is first roasted & then reduced by the remaining Cu_2S in tank.

$2Cu_2S(s) + 3O_2(g) \xrightarrow{\Delta} 2Cu_2O(s) + 2SO_2(g)$

[Copper (I) sulphide] [Copper (I) Oxide]

$2Cu_2O(s) + Cu_2S(s) \xrightarrow{\Delta} 6Cu(s) + SO_2(g)$ 2

This way, copper metal is extracted.

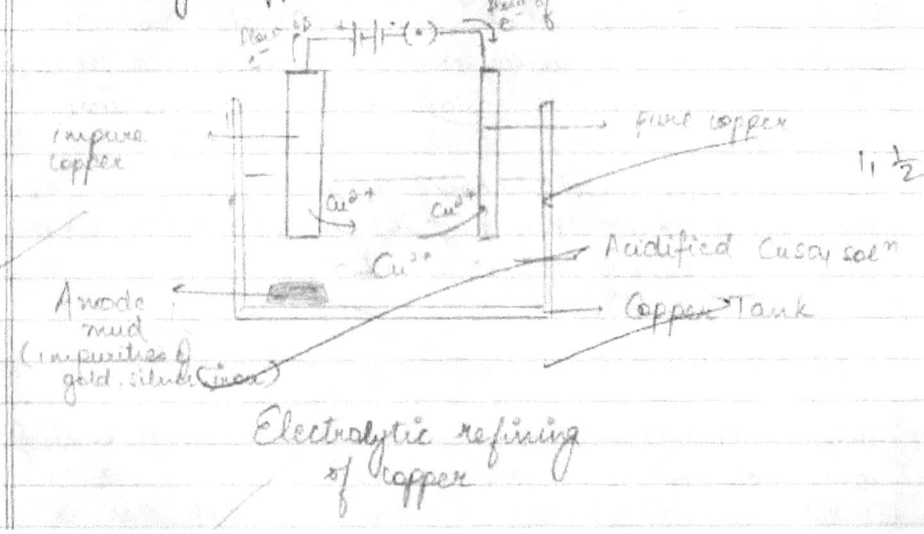

1, $\frac{1}{2}$

Electrolytic refining of copper

17. **a.** The modern periodic table has been evolved through the early attempts of Dobereiner, Newland and Mendeleev. List one advantage and one limitation of all the three attempts.

b. Name the scientist who first of all showed that atomic number of an element is a more fundamental property than its atomic mass.

c. State Modern periodic law. **5**

Sol. (i) Dobereiner's method of clasification

Advantage:- He, for the first time grouped metals on the basis of their similar chemical properties. He could find 3 Dobereiner's Triad which had a special

characteristic :-
When arranged in increasing atomic masses, the atomic mass of middle element was equal to average of atomic masses of other two ~~Tris~~

Li – 6.9 u
Na – 23 u
K – 39.1 u

½

→ This encouraged others to classify elements on basis of chemical properties and atomic masses.

Disadvantage: He could only place 9 such elements in 3 triads & thus wasn't efficient for a study of them. ½

(ii) Newland's Law of octaves – Classification of Newland

Advantage: He could place 56 elements known at that time in his classification & also for first time, studied periodic reccurrence of properties. In this classification, properties of every eight element resembled to that of first.

Disadvantage: His system worked only for lighter elements & properties matched only for elements till Calcium. Also, he placed some elements like Co & Ni even in same slot.

(iii) Mendeleev's classification

Advantage: He arranged elements on basis of increasing atomic masses & similar formulae for hydrides & oxides. He also left gaps in his tables which encouraged for discovery of new elements like eka-boron, eka-aluminium etc.

Disadvantage: He placed some elements with more atomic mass prior to ones having less atomic mass for similarity of properties but couldn't justify it. ½

Ex: He placed 'Te' (127.6u) before 'I' (126.9 u).

(b) Henry Moseley showed atomic no. as a more fundamental property. 1

(c) Modern Periodic Law states that "properties of elements are periodic function of their atomic no." 1

18. **a.** Mention any two components of blood.

b. Trace the movement of oxygenated blood in the body.

c. Write the function of valves present in between atria and ventricles.

d. Write one structural difference between the composition of artery and veins. **5**

OR

a. Define excretion.

b. Name the basic filtration unit present in the kidney.

c. Draw excretory system in human beings and label the following organs of excretory system which perform following functions :

i. form urine.

ii. is a long tube which collects urine from kidney.

iii. store urine until it is passed out. **5**

Sol. Excretion is the biological process of removal of harmful nitrogenous wastes like urea, uric acid etc. from our body which are produced as by product of chemical reactions taking inside our body.

(b) 'Nephron' is the basic filtration unit present in kid

c)

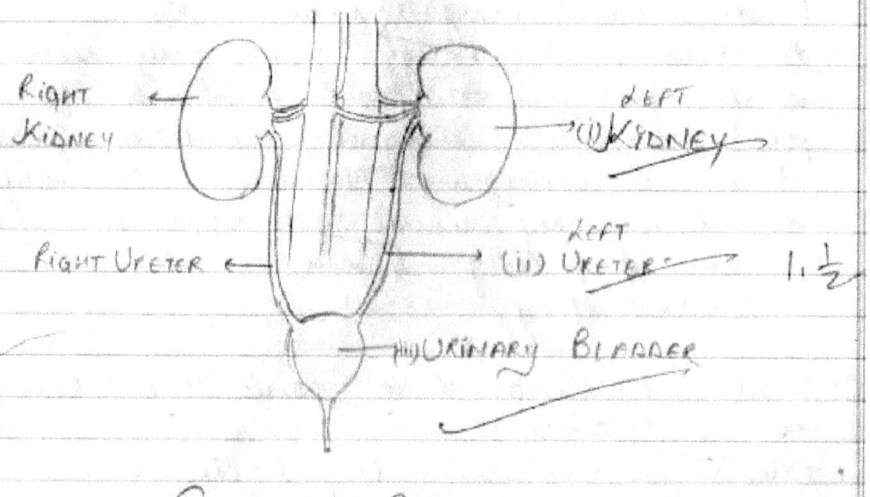

EXCRETORY SYSTEM IN HUMANS

19. **a.** Write the function of following parts in human female reproductive system :

i. Ovary **ii.** Oviduct **iii.** Uterus

b. Describe in brief the structure and function of placenta. **5**

Sol. (a)(i) Ovary has following functions :-

- It releases matured egg (female germ cell) once every month & thus, is responsible for produce & release (oogenesis & ovulation) of ovum.
- It secretes oestrogen & progesterone. Oestrogen controls secondary sexual characteristics in females at time of puberty & also promotes release & maturation of egg.

(ii) • Oviduct / Fallopian tube carries the released egg to the uterus.

• Oviduct is also the site of fertilization.

(iii) Uterus is a bag like structure where embryo is developed & implanted.
It helps the embryo to grow into foetus & also, develop a thick lining of blood vessels every month in order to receive a fertilized egg.
• Its rythmic contraction helps the baby to come out from mother's body (womb).

(b) Placenta is a disc shaped tissue embedded in uterine wall once implantation of embryo takes place. It has villi on the embryo's side & blood spaces on mother's side.
→ It helps in nourishment of child inside mother's womb. It also helps in exchange of nutrients, oxygen & waste products (released by embryo) between mother's & embryo's blood & thus, is responsible for maturation of embryo.

20. **a.** A student is unable to see clearly the words written on the black board placed at a distance of approximately 3 m from him. Name the defect of vision the boy is suffering from. State the possible causes of this defect and explain the method of correcting it.

b. Why do stars twinkle? Explain. **5**

OR

a. Write the function of each of the following parts of human eye :

i. Cornea **ii.** Iris

iii. Crystalline lens **iv.** Ciliary muscles

b. Why does the sun appear reddish early in the morning? Will this phenomenon be observed by an astronaut on the Moon? Give reason to justify your answer. **5**

Sol. (a)(i) Cornea is a thin transparent layer (membrane) on the outer bulge of eye. At cornea's outer surface, most of the refraction of light entering eye takes place.

(ii) Iris is a thick, dark, muscular diaphragm which controls the size of pupil by its contraction & relaxation & hence controls the amount of light entering the eye.

(iii) Crystalline lens is near a fibrous jelly like material which provides finer adjustment for focal length so that images for objects at all distances can be formed on retina.
When it becomes thin, focal length increases helpful to view far off objects & when becomes thick, helps to view nearby objects.

(iv) Ciliary muscles help in changing the shape of eye lens by their contraction & relaxation, helpful in changing curvature of eye lens & hence, its power.
When they contract, eye lens becomes thick & when they relax, it becomes thin.

1

(b) Sun is near the horizon early morning. Thus, the sun rays have to pass through thicker layers of atmosphere & have to travel larger distance before reaching observer's eyes. Thus, most of the lightrays of shorter wavelength like violet, blue etc are scattered by the smaller particles & hence, only reddish light rays reach our eyes.

1

On Moon, an astronaut won't see such phenomenon as their is no atmosphere & thus, no scattering particles for light to be scattered. Hence, it will be all dark on moon & reddish appearance of sun won't be possible.

21. **a.** State Fleming's left hand rule.

b. Write the principle of working of an electric motor.

c. Explain the function of the following parts of an electric motor:

i. Armature **ii.** Brushes **iii.** Split ring **5**

Sol. (a) Fleming's left Hand Rule states that if we stretch fore finger, middle finger & thumb of our left hand mutually perpendicular to each other, ~~then~~ such that our forefinger gives direction of magnetic field, middle finger gives the direction of current; then our thumb will give the direction of force experienced by conductor.

(b) Principle of electric motor :-
When a current carrying conductor is placed inside a magnetic field, it experiences a force due to the interaction of 2 magnetic fields - one of conductor carrying current & the already existing magnetic field.
Armature is the combination of current carrying coil wound on soft iron core.
This is attached to axle & rotates axle.

Brushes
Carbon brush provides conductivity. ½

Split ring
It acts as commutator & reverses direction of current ½

SECTION - B

22. A student added few pieces of aluminium metal to two test tubes A and B containing aqueous solutions of iron sulphate and copper sulphate. In the second part of her experiment, she added iron metal to another test tubes C and D containing aqueous solutions of aluminium sulphate and copper sulphate. In which test tube or test tubes will she observe colour change? On the basis of this experiment, state which one is the most reactive metal and why. 2

Sol. Test Tube A :-

$Al(s) + FeSO_4(aq) \longrightarrow Al_2(SO_4)_3(aq) + Fe(s)$
(green solⁿ) (colourless)

Test Tube B :-

$Al(s) + CuSO_4 \longrightarrow Al_2(SO_4)_3(aq) + Cu$
(blue solⁿ) (colourless)

Test Tube C :-

$Fe + Al_2(SO_4)_3 \longrightarrow$ No reaction

Test Tube D :-

$Fe(s) + CuSO_4(aq) \longrightarrow FeSO_4(aq) + Cu$
(blue solⁿ) (pale green solⁿ)

So, colour changed in Test Tube A, B, D. 1
Reactivity :- $Al > Fe > Cu$ ½, ½

23. What is observed when a solution of sodium sulphate is added to a solution of barium chloride taken in a test tube? Write equation for the chemical reaction involved and name the type of reaction in this case. **2**

Sol.

$Na_2SO_4(aq.) + BaCl_2(aq.) \longrightarrow BaSO_4(s) + 2NaCl(aq.)$
(white ppt.)

Rx^n :- Precipitation Rx^n / Double Displacement Rx^n ½

Observation - White coloured precipitate is formed ½

24. List the steps of preparation of temporary mount of a leaf peel to observe stomata. **2**

Sol.

(i) Take out a leaf peel from ventral side of leaf. ½
(ii) Place it on petridish after cutting its pieces. ½
(iii) Add some water & saffranin soln (stain) on petridish.
(iv) After some time, using brush, take out the peel & ½ place on the slide. Using blotting paper to drain excess stain.
(v) Add a drop of glycerine & carefully place a coverslip ½ to prevent air bubble.

25. Name the process by which an amoeba reproduces. Draw the various stages of its reproduction in a proper sequence. **2**

OR

A student is viewing under a microscope a permanent slide showing various stages of asexual reproduction by budding in yeast. Draw diagrams of what he observes. (in proper sequence) **2**

Sol.

Amoeba reproduces by binary fission. ½

Stages :-

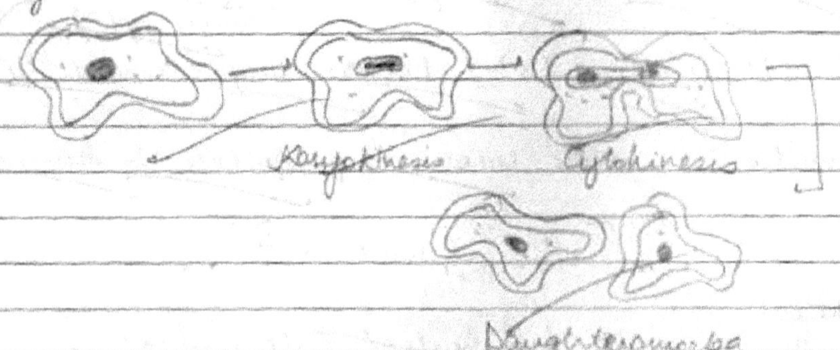

26. An object of height 4.0 cm is placed at a distance of 30 cm from the optical centre 'O' of a convex lens of focal length 20 cm. Draw a ray diagram to find the position and size of the image formed. Mark optical centre 'O' and principal focus 'F' on the diagram. Also find the approximate ratio of size of the image to the size of the object. **2**

Sol.

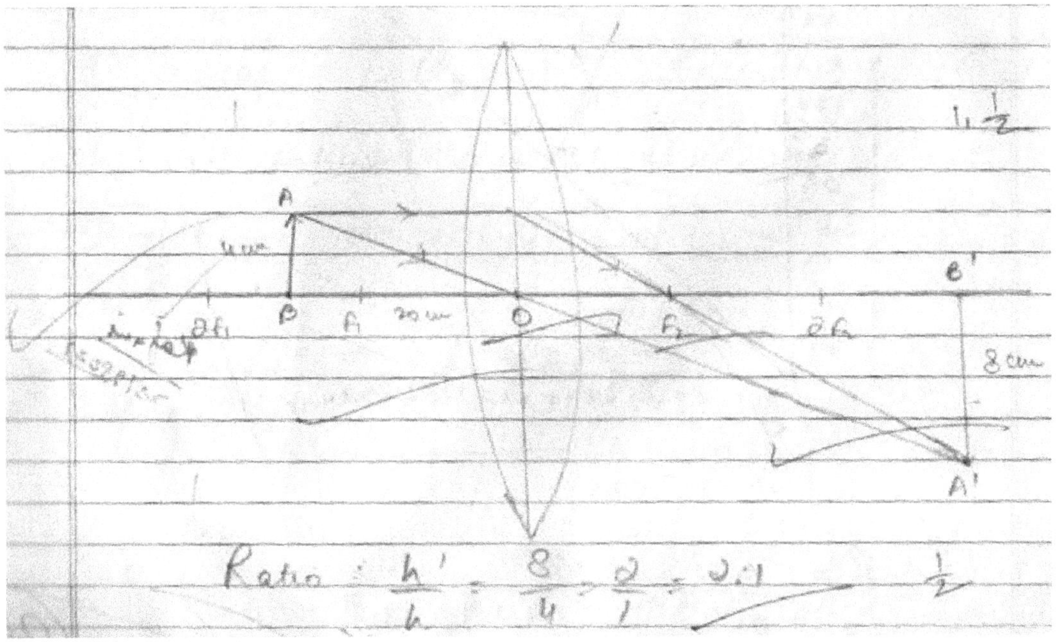

27. The values of current (I) flowing through a given resistor of resistance (R), for the corresponding values of potential difference (V) across the resistor are as given below :

V (volts)	0.5	1.0	1.5	2.0	2.5	3.0	4.0	5.0
I (amperes)	0.1	0.2	0.3	0.4	0.5	0.6	0.8	1.0

Plot a graph between current (I) and potential difference (V) and determine the resistance (R) of the resistor. **2**

Sol.

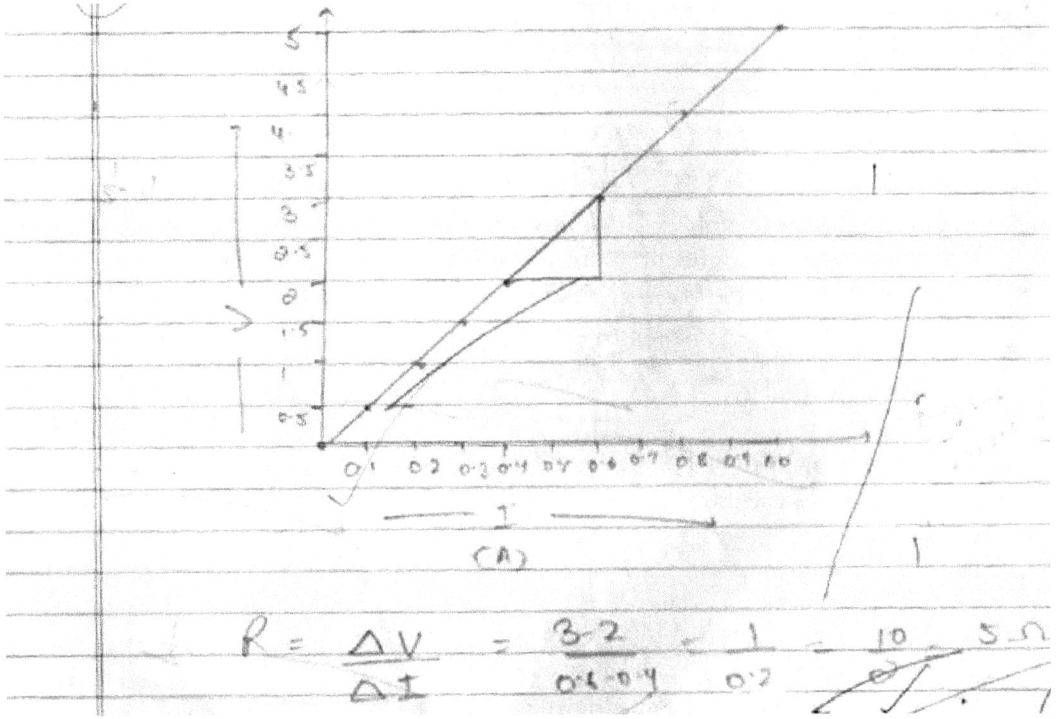

SAMPLE PAPER 1

CBSE - Class 10

SCIENCE

Time Allowed: 3 Hours | *Maximum Marks: 80*

General Instructions:

i. The question paper comprises three sections – A, B and C. Attempt all the sections.
ii. All questions are compulsory.
iii. Internal choice is given in each section.
iv. All questions in Section A are one-mark questions comprising MCQ, VSA type and assertion-reason type questions. They are to be answered in one word or in one sentence.
v. All questions in Section B are three-mark, short-answer type questions. These are to be answered in about 50 - 60 words each.
vi. All questions in Section C are five-mark, long-answer type questions. These are to be answered in about 80 - 90 words each.
vii. This question paper consists of a total of 30 questions.

SECTION - A

1. What is DNA? **1**

2. Molecular formula of a hydrocarbon is C_3H_8. Draw its complete structure and write its name. **1**

3. Answer question numbers 3(a)-3(d) on the basis of your understanding of the following paragraph and the related studied concepts.

India is lucky to receive solar energy for greater part of the year. It is estimated that during a year, India receives the energy equivalent to more than 5,000 trillion kWh. Under clear (cloudless) sky conditions, the daily average varies from 4 to 7 kWh/m^2. The solar energy reaching unit area at outer edge of the earth's atmosphere exposed perpendicularly to the rays of the Sun at an average distance between the Sun and earth is known as the solar constant. It is estimated to be approximately 1.4 kJ per second per square metre or 1.4 kW/m^2. Most of the sun's heat is absorbed in the atmosphere. Only a very small portion reaches the earth and it is this energy that can be harnessed for energy purposes. A black surface

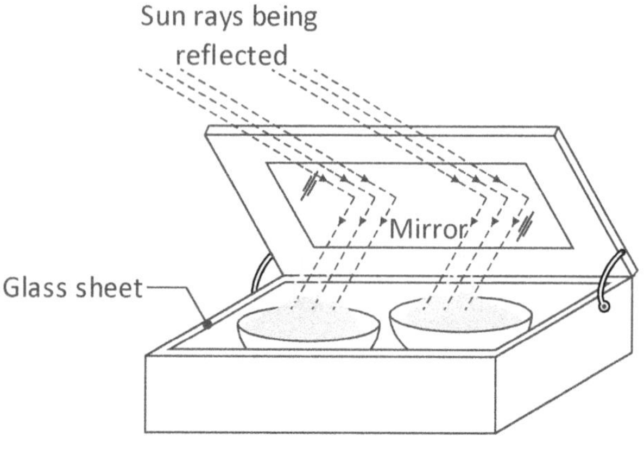

Fig. A Solar Cooker

absorbs more heat than a white surface. This property is used in Solar cookers, Solar water heaters and Solar cells.

3(a) What type of reaction occurs inside the sun that produces solar energy? **1**

3(b) Why is the solar cooker box covered with a glass sheet? **1**

3(c) What kind of mirror, concave, convex or plane, would be best suited for use in a solar cooker? Why? **1**

3(d) Name the semi-conductor material which is usually used for making solar cells. **1**

4. **Question numbers 4(a)-4(d) are based on table given below. Study this table and answer the questions that follow.**

Plaque is a deposit which collects around teeth. Following table shows the pH value of the plaque surrounding the teeth of a girl over a period of 4 hrs.

Time/h	pH
0.0	7.0
01.0	7.0
02.0	7.1
03.0	7.2
04.0	4.1

4(a) Which of the following is not the constituent of plaque?

(i) Acid **(ii)** Saliva

(iii) Bacteria **(iv)** Base **1**

4(b) State the time during the day, when the condition is most favorable for tooth decay as per the information given above

(i) 1 hr **(ii)** 2 hr

(iii) 4 hr **(iv)** 3 hr **1**

4(c) What substance is mixed with food in the mouth during chewing by the teeth? **1**

4(d) How can the formation of plaque be prevented? **1**

5. Three beakers labelled as A, B and C each containing 25 ml of water were taken. A small amount of NaOH, anhydrous $CuSO_4$ and NaCl were added to the beakers A, B and C respectively. It was observed that there was an increase in the temperature of the solutions contained in beakers A and B, whereas in case of beaker C, the temperature of the solution falls. Which one of the following statement(s) is (are) correct: **1**

(a) In beakers A and B, exothermic process has occurred

(b) In beakers A and B, endothermic process has occurred

(c) In beaker C exothermic process has occurred

(d) In beaker C endothermic process has occurred

(i) (a) only **(ii)** (b) only

(iii) (a) and (d) **(iv)** (b) and (c)

6. A light ray enters from medium A to medium B as shown in the figure. The refractive index of medium B relative to A will be: **1**

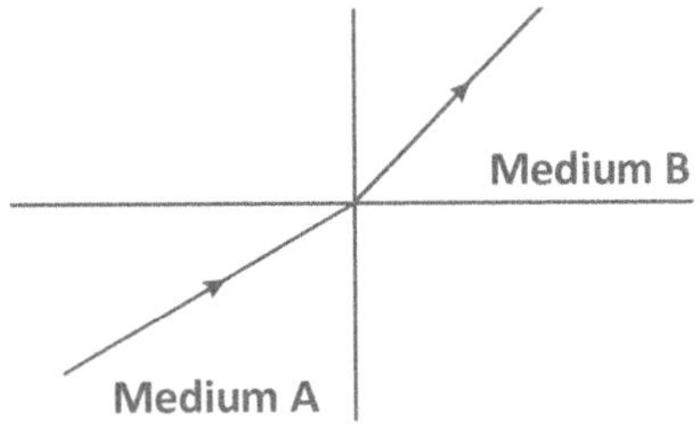

(i) Greater than unity
(ii) Less than unity
(iii) Equal to unity
(iv) Zero

7. Where would you locate the element with electronic configuration 2, 8 in the modern periodic table? **1**

(i) Group 8
(ii) Group 2
(iii) Group 18
(iv) Group 10

OR

An element which is an essential constituent of all organic compounds belongs to: **1**

(i) Group 1
(ii) Group 14
(iii) Group 15
(iv) Group 16

8. Aluminium is used for making cooking utensils. Which of the following properties of aluminium are responsible for the same: **1**

(a) Good thermal conductivity
(b) Good electrical conductivity
(c) Ductility
(d) High melting point

(i) (a) and (b)
(ii) (a) and (c)
(iii) (b) and (c)
(iv) (a) and (d)

9. Which of the following statement is incorrect: **1**

(i) For every hormone there is a gene
(ii) For every protein there is a gene
(iii) For production of every enzyme there is a gene
(iv) For every molecule of fat there is a gene

OR

Exchange of genetic material takes place in:

(i) Vegetative reproduction
(ii) Asexual reproduction
(iii) Sexual reproduction
(iv) Budding

10. Identify the circuit in which the electrical components have been properly connected. **1**

(i)
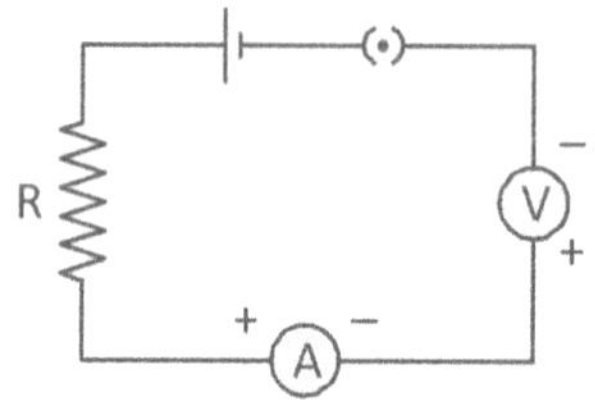

(ii)
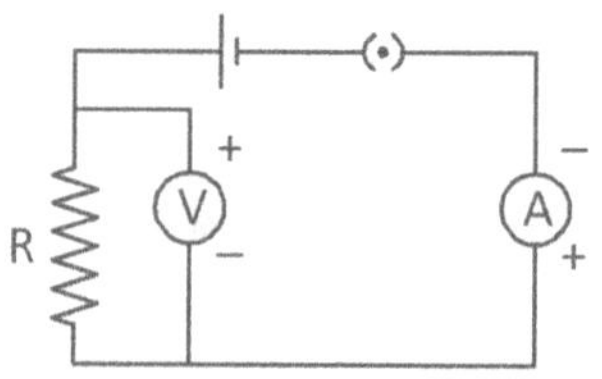

(iii)
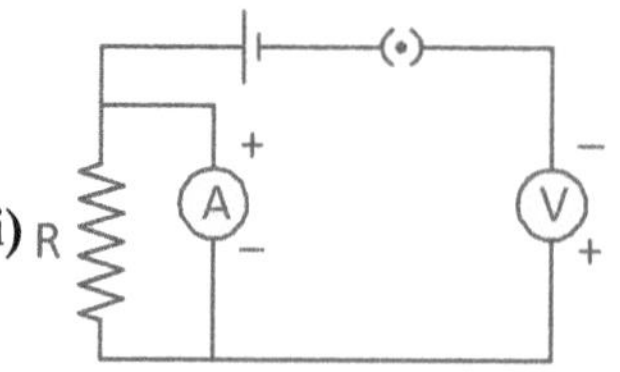

(iv)
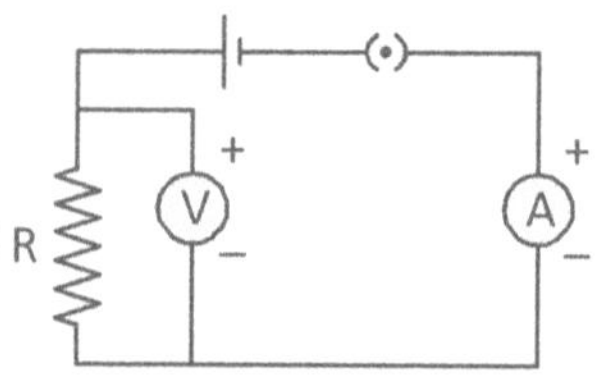

11. Commercial electric motors do not use: **1**

(i) An electromagnet to rotate the armature
(ii) Effectively large number of turns of conducting wire in the current carrying coil
(iii) A permanent magnet to rotate the armature
(iv) A soft iron core on which the coil is wound

12. The focal length of the eye lens increases when eye muscles: 1

(i) are relaxed and lens becomes thinner

(ii) contract and lens becomes thicker

(iii) are relaxed and lens becomes thicker

(iv) contract and lens becomes thinner

OR

Water in deep sea is bluish in colour due to: 1

(i) Absorption of light by the sea. (ii) Reflection of sky in water

(ii) Scattering of light (iv) Presence of plants in the sea.

For question numbers 13 and 14, two statements are given- one labeled Assertion (A) and the other labeled Reason (R). Select the correct answer to these questions from the codes (i), (ii), (iii) and (iv) as given below:

(i) Both A and R are true and R is correct explanation of the assertion.

(ii) Both A and R are true but R is not the correct explanation of the assertion.

(iii) A is true but R is false.

(iv) A is false but R is true.

13. **Assertion A** : Red colour is used in danger signals.

Reason R : The scattering of red is more as its wavelength is more. 1

14. **Assertion A** : Carbonic acid is weak acid

Reason R : It ionises completely in acqeous solution. 1

SECTION - B

15. Write the chemical equation of the reaction with an example in which the following changes has taken place:

(a) Change in colour

(b) Change in temperature

(c) Formation of precipitate 3

OR

Write an equation each for decomposition reaction(s) where energy is supplied in the form of heat, light or electricity. 3

16. Write the name given to the vertical columns and horizontal rows in the Modern Periodic Table. How does the metallic character of elements vary on moving down a vertical column? How does the sizeof atomic radius vary on moving left to right in a horizontal row? 3

17. Answer the following:

(a) What are autotrophs? Give one example of autotrophs.

(b) What are the conditions necessary for autotrophic nutrition? 3

OR

Why is diffusion insufficient to meet the oxygen requirements of multi-cellular organisms like humans? 3

18. The picture given below depicts the process of asexual reproduction in Plasmodium:

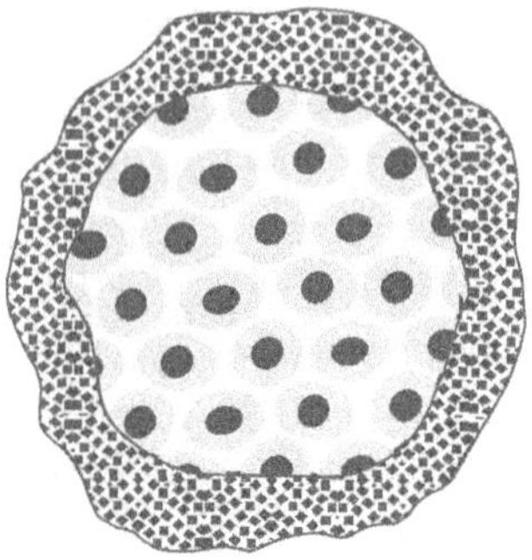

(a) Name the process depicted above and define it.

(b) What is meant by asexual reproduction? **3**

19. The power of lens is +2.0 D.

(a) Find the focal length of lens in meters.

(b) Name the kind of lens. Explain with the help of figure whether this lens would converge or diverge a beam of light. **3**

OR

"A convex lens of focal length 20 cm can produce a magnified virtual as well as real image." Is this a correct statement? If yes, where shall the object be placed in each case for obtaining these images? **3**

20. State reasons for the following:

(a) Non-metals cannot displace hydrogen from the acids

(b) Hydrogen is not a metal, yet it is placed in the activity series of metals

(c) Aluminium is more reactive than iron, yet its corrosion is less than that of iron **3**

21. Discuss the limitations of extracting energy from:

(a) Wind

(b) Water waves

(c) Sea/Ocean tides **3**

22. Answer the following questions:

(a) Why does a current carrying conductor, experiences a force when it is placed in a magnetic field?

(b) A circuit has a line of 5 A. How many lamps of rating 40W; 220V can simultaneously glow on this line safely? **3**

23. Suggest suitable mechanism(s) or plan for waste management in fertilizer industries. **3**

24. A man with blood group 'A' marries a woman with blood group 'O' and their daughter has blood group 'O'. Is this information enough to tell you which of the traits - blood group 'A' or 'O' is dominant? What criteria would you use to assess it? **3**

SECTION - C

25. Describe the following chemical properties of carbon compounds briefly and give one chemical reaction for each:

(a) Combustion **(b)** Addition **(c)** Substitution

(d) Esterification **(e)** Oxidation **5**

26. **(a)** Draw a neat diagram of human brain and label on it the following parts:

(i) Mid Brain | **(ii)** Pituitary gland

(iii) Cerebellum | **(iv)** Cerebrum

(b) Which is the main thinking part of the brain? **5**

27. Answer the following questions:

(a) What is the role of seminal vesicles and the prostate gland?

(b) What are the three categories of contraception methods? Write briefly about each. **5**

OR

What are the changes seen in girls at the time of puberty? Why does menstruation occur? **5**

28. Answer the following questions:

(a) Differentiate between roasting and calcination.

(b) Which of these two is used for sulphide ores and why?

(c) Write a chemical equation to illustrate the use of aluminium for joining cracked railway lines. **5**

OR

You are given a hammer, a battery, a bulb, wires and a switch.

(a) How would you use them to distinguish between samples of metals and non-metals?

(b) Assess the usefulness of these tests in distinguishing between metals and non-metals.

29. What is Tyndall effect? What are its causes? Name two phenomena observed in daily life which are based on Tyndall effect. **5**

OR

How does normal eye achieve accommodation? The given diagram shows the path of a ray of light through an equilateral prism. Answer the following questions:

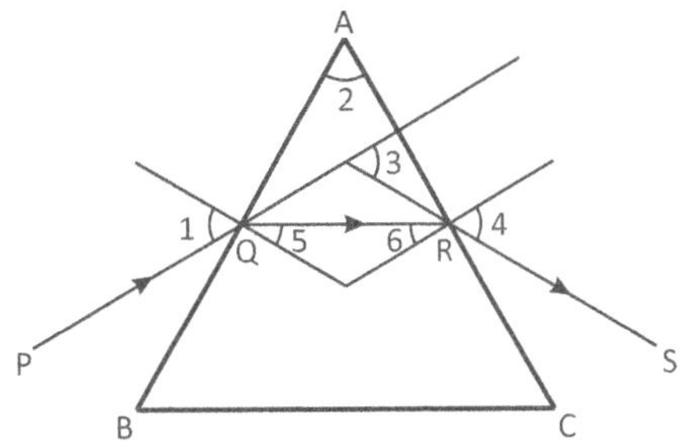

(a) Which is the refracted ray?

(b) Which is the emergent ray?

(c) What name is given to angle 1?

(d) What name is given to angle 3?

(e) What name is given to angle 5?

(f) What is the relation between angles 1, 2, 3 and 4?

30. State Ohm's law. How can this be verified experimentally? Does Ohm's law hold good under all conditions? Comment. **5**

SOLUTION

1

CBSE - Class 10

SECTION - A

1. DNA is the genetic material found in the chromosomes of the nucleus of the cell and that carries information for the inheritance of features from the parents to the off-springs (next generation). **1**

2. Molecular formula is C_3H_8
It is an Alkane and its name will be Propane. **½**
Complete structure is:

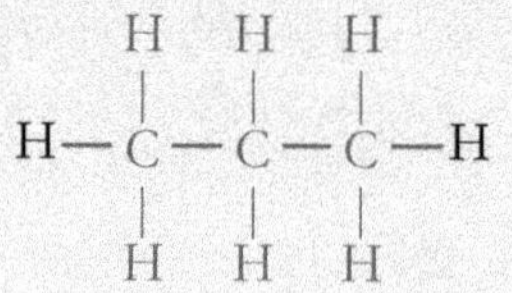

½

3. **(a)** Nuclear fusion **1**

3. **(b)** Solar cooker is covered with a glass sheet so as to trap the heat rays in the interior of the box of the cooker. **1**

3. **(c)** Concave and plane mirrors are used for making solar cooker because concave mirror converges a large amount of sun's rays at a point that is required for high heating and plane mirror reflects the rays of light in the form of a strong beam of sunlight on the top of the box that is required for moderate heating. **1**

3. **(d)** Silicon **1**

4. **(a) (iv)** Base

Explanation: As the three constituents of plaque other than food are acid, saliva and bacteria. **1**

(b) (iii) 4 hr.

Explanation: Time 4.0, lowest pH indicate the highest amount of acid produced by the bacteria. **1**

(c) Saliva **1**

(d) It can be prevented by brushing the teeth regularly with a basic toothpaste, as it neutralises the acids. **1**

5. **(iii)** (a) and (d) **1**

Explanation: For an exothermic reaction, heat releases during reaction so temperature increases whereas endothermic reactions proceed with absorption of heat which decrease the temperature of reaction.

6. **(i)** Greater than unity **1**

Explanation: Since ray of light bends towards the normal, when it goes from medium A to medium B, therefore, medium A is rarer and medium B is denser medium. Speed of light in rarer medium is greater than the speed of light in denser medium.
So refractive index of medium B with respect to medium A is greater than unity.

7. **(iii)** Group 18 **1**

Explanation: Element with electronic configuration 2, 8 will have an atomic number 10.
Thus, this element has completely filled sub shells and hence, it belongs to group 18 which is also known as noble gas group. Hence, we will place this element on the extreme

right side below the helium atom. This element is neon.

OR

(ii) Group 14 **1**

Explanation: Carbon is an essential element for all organic compounds and it belongs to group 14.

8. **(iv)** (a) and (d) **1**

Explanation: Some of the most common properties of Aluminium are good thermal conductivity, malleability, light weight and high melting point which make it useful for making cooking utensils.

9. **(iv)** For every molecule of fat there is a gene. **1**

Explanation: Fat biosynthesis occurs through metabolic reaction and fat molecules are not related to genes. On the other hand genes contain information for making proteins in a cell. The protein synthesized may be enzymes that catalyze biochemical reactions. The enzyme also controls the process of making hormones. This explains why a, b and c are correct.

OR

(iii) Sexual reproduction **1**

Explanation: Exchange of genetic material takes place in sexual reproduction as genes of two parents are involved. In asexual reproduction, no exchange of genetic material takes place as a single parent is involved. Budding and vegetative reproduction are types of asexual reproduction. So there is no exchange of genetic material.

10. **(ii)** **1**

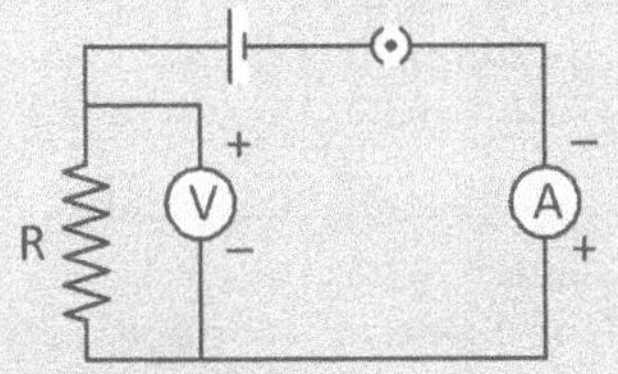

Explanation: Essential conditions necessary when electrical components are connected are:

- Voltmeter should be connected in parallel
- Ammeter is always connected in series
- Positive terminals of voltmeter and ammeter should be connected to positive terminal of the cell and their negative terminals should be joined to the negative terminal of the cell

Thus, the above conditions are satisfied in case (ii).

11. **(iii)** A permanent magnet to rotate the armature. **1**

Explanation: An electric motor is a device that converts electric energy into mechanical energy. An electric motor has an **electromagnet instead of permanent magnet** (as permanent magnet does not produce strong magnetic field). Large number of turns of the conducting wire in the current-carrying coil to produce stronger magnetic field. It also has a soft iron core on which the coil is wound also known as armature. Thus, commercial electric motors do not use permanent magnet to rotate the armature because permanent magnets are weak and do not produce strong magnetic field in the region

12. **(i)** are relaxed and lens becomes thinner. **1**

Explanation: The focal length of thin lens is greater than the focal length of thick glass.

OR

(iii) Scattering of light **1**

Explanation: The fine particles in water scatter mainly blue light having shortest wavelength.

13. **(iii)** A is true but R is false. **1**

Explanation: Red is used in danger signals as its scattering is less because of its large wavelength.

So, A is true but R is false.

14. **(iii)** A is true but R is false. **1**

Explanation: Carbonic acid does not completely ionizes in water.

So, A is true but R is false.

SECTION - B

15. Chemical Reactions with the following changes:

(a) Change in colour: Lead nitrate and potassium iodide solutions are colourless but on mixing the two, the precipitate of lead iodide formed is yellow in colour

$$\underset{\text{Lead Nitrate}}{Pb(NO_3)_2} + \underset{\text{Potassium iodide}}{2KI} \longrightarrow \underset{\text{Lead Iodide}}{PbI_2} + \underset{\text{Potassium Nitrate}}{2KNO_3}$$ 1

(b) Change in temperature: When zinc pieces react with sulphuric acid in a beaker or a flask, it is found to be warm. In this chemical reaction heat is evolved which is accompanied by rise in temperature

$$\underset{\text{Zinc}}{Zn} + \underset{\text{Sulphuric acid}}{H_2SO_4} \longrightarrow \underset{\text{Zinc Sulphate}}{ZnSO_4} + \underset{\text{Hydrogen gas}}{H_2} + \text{Heat}$$ 1

(c) Formation of precipitate: When silver nitrate solution is mixed with sodium chloride solution, a white precipitate of silver chloride is obtained

$$\underset{\text{Silver nitrate}}{AgNO_3} + \underset{\text{Sodium chloride}}{NaCl} \longrightarrow \underset{\substack{\text{Silver chloride}\\ \text{(ppt.)}}}{AgCl} + \underset{\text{Sodium nitrate}}{NaNO_3}$$ 1

OR

Decomposition reaction where energy is supplied in the form of heat:

Thermal decomposition of lead nitrate

$$\underset{\substack{\text{Lead nitrate}\\ \text{(White)}}}{2Pb(NO_3)_2} \xrightarrow{\text{Heat}} \underset{\substack{\text{Lead oxide}\\ \text{(Yellow)}}}{2PbO} + \underset{\substack{\text{Nitrogen dioxide}\\ \text{(Brown fumes)}}}{4NO_2} + O_2$$ 1

Decomposition reaction where energy is supplied in the form of electricity:

Electrolytic decomposition of molten sodium chloride

$$\underset{\text{Sodium chloride}}{2NaCl} \xrightarrow{\text{Electric current}} \underset{\text{Sodium metal}}{2Na} + Cl_2$$ 1

Decomposition reaction where energy is supplied in the form of light:

Photo - Decomposition reaction of Silver chloride

$$\underset{\substack{\text{Silver chloride}\\ \text{(White)}}}{2AgCl} \xrightarrow{\text{Sunlight}} \underset{\substack{\text{Silver}\\ \text{(Grey)}}}{2Ag} + Cl_2$$ 1

16. In the Modern Periodic Table, there are 18 vertical columns known as 'Groups' and 7 horizontal rows known as 'Periods'. 1

The metallic character increases as we move down the group. This is because the electrostatic attraction between the nucleus and the outer-most electron decreases due to increase in the distance between them as a new shell is added on moving down the group. So the valence electron can be easily lost by the element. 1

The size of atomic radius decreases on moving left to right in a horizontal row. When we move across a period, the number of electrons in the same shell increases leading to greater electrostatic attraction between the nucleus and the outer-most electron. This increased attraction pulls the outer-most electron closer to the nucleus, thereby decreasing the atomic size. 1

17. (a) Autotrophs: Those organisms which can make their own food from the inorganic substances present in the environment (carbon dioxide, water) are called autotrophs. ½

Example of autotrophs: All green plants. ½

(b) Conditions necessary for autotrophic nutrition are:

- Sun light
- Water
- Chlorophyll
- Carbon Dioxide (Air) 2

OR

Diffusion is insufficient to meet the oxygen requirements of multi-cellular organisms like humans because the volume of human body is so big that oxygen cannot diffuse into all internal cells so quickly. Since diffusion is a very slow process, it will take very long time to make oxygen available to all body cells. So to overcome this, multi-cellular organisms have specialized cells and tissues for performing various necessary functions of the body such as respiratory pigments present in blood take up the oxygen from the air in the lungs and carry it to all body cells. This helps the animals like humans to meet the sufficient oxygen requirement. **3**

18. **(a)** The process depicted in the given diagram is of Multiple Fission. **1**
Multiple fission can be defined as an asexual method of reproduction in organisms in which the parent organism splits to form many new organisms at the same time. **1**

(b) **Asexual reproduction:** The production of a new organism from a single parent without the involvement of sex cells or gametes is called asexual reproduction.
Example: Binary fission in Hydra. **1**

19. The power of lens is +2.0 D.

(a) We know that,

$$\text{Power} = \frac{1}{f}$$

So focal length of lens,

$$f = \frac{1}{P} = \frac{1}{2} = 0.5 \text{ m} = 50 \text{ cm}$$ **1**

(b) Since the power is positive, so the lens is convex lens. **1**
Convex lenses converge light rays (bring them together). **1**

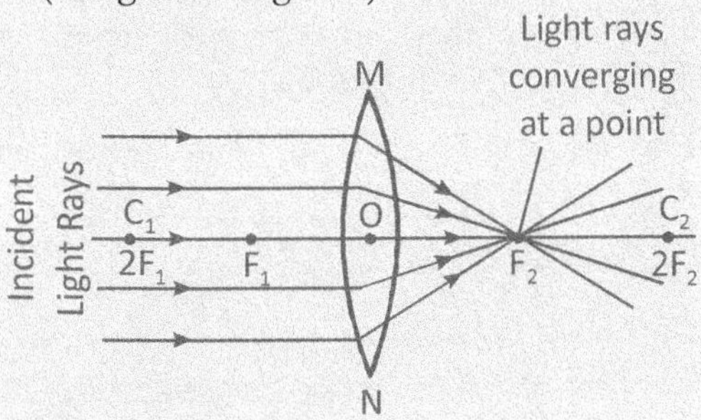

OR

Yes, the given statement is correct. The convex lens of focal length 20 cm can produce a magnified, virtual as well as real image. **1**
A convex lens of focal length 20 cm will produce a magnified virtual image if object is placed at a distance less than 20 cm from the lens. **1**
A convex lens of focal length 20 cm will produce a magnified real image if object is placed at a distance greater than 20 cm and less than 40 cm from the lens. **1**

20. **(a)** **Non-metals cannot displace hydrogen from the acids** because in order to displace hydrogen from acids, electrons must be supplied to the H^+ ions of the acids. Since a non-metal does not lose electrons readily being an electron acceptor, therefore they do not displace hydrogen from acids. **1**

(b) **Hydrogen is not a metal, yet it is placed in the activity series of metals** because like metals, hydrogen can lose electrons to form positive ions (H^+). **1**

(c) **Aluminium is more reactive than iron, yet its corrosion is less than that of iron** because Aluminium reacts with oxygen in the air to form a layer of oxide which protects the aluminium from further oxidation. On the other hand the oxides of iron (rust) tend to fall away, exposing the un-reacted iron to further oxidation. **1**

21. **(a)** **Limitations of extracting energy from the wind:** A windmill requires wind of speed more than 15 km/h to generate electricity from wind energy. Wind flowing with a sufficient speed is not available everywhere and all the time. Thus wind is not a dependable source of energy. **1**

(b) **Limitations of extracting energy from waves:** Very strong ocean waves are required in order to extract energy from waves. Wave energy would be commercially viable only at places where the waves are strong. These are not available all the time. **1**

(c) **Limitations of extracting energy from tides:** Very high tides are required in order to extract energy from the tides. There are very few sites suitable for harnessing tidal energy. The rise and fall of water during tides is not very large. So, large scale generation of electricity is not possible. 1

22. (a) **When a current-carrying conductor is placed in a magnetic field, the wire experiences a force** due to the interaction between the external magnetic field and the magnetic field produced by the moving charges in the wire.
The current carrying conductor generates it own magnetic field around it. This interacts with the external magnetic field. When two magnetic fields interact there will be attraction and repulsion between them based on the direction of the external magnetic field and the direction of the current in the conductor. That is why the conductor experiences a force. 1

(b) We know that,

$$I = \frac{P}{V} = \frac{40\text{ W}}{220\text{ V}} = \frac{2}{11} = 0.182\text{ A} \qquad 1$$

0.182 A or $\frac{2}{11}$ A is required by one lamp.
Current rating *i.e.*
maximum current = 5 A
No. of lamps

$$= \frac{\text{current rating}}{\text{current through one lamp}}$$

$$= \frac{5}{0.18} = 27\text{ lamps} \qquad 1$$

23. Fertilizer industries produce mainly two types of wastes: Gaseous and Effluents. Additionally they may release heat and fuel waste of coal which is being used as a source of energy.
1. **Gaseous wastes:** They are passed through wet scrubbers to dissolve the pollutant gases. Also polluting gases can be reduced by the use of catalytic converters which are fitted in chimneys in the industries. 1½
2. **Effluents:** Another second major waste in industries is the effluents obtained from industries. The effluents can be treated by various steps such as sedimentation, filtration and chlorination etc. After adopting these measures, the clean water can then be transferred to rivers as it will provide no harm to water bodies now. The sludge remained after the processes can be used as manure after decomposition. 1½

24. The given information is not enough to decide which blood group is dominant. 1
But universally, blood group A is dominant whereas blood group O is recessive. Here, father's Blood group has genotype AA or genotype AO, where as that of mother can be OA or OO.
For daughter to be born with blood group O, she must receive O type gene one each from father and mother. For this father blood group must have genotype AO and mother's blood group must have genotype OO. 2

SECTION - C

25. **Chemical properties of carbon compounds:**

(a) **Combustion:** The process of burning carbon and its compounds in excess of oxygen for the release of heat and light (energy) is known as combustion.

$$C + O_2 \longrightarrow CO_2 + \text{Heat} + \text{Light}$$

$$C_3H_8 + 5O_2 \longrightarrow 3CO_2 + 4H_2O + \text{Heat} + \text{Light} \qquad 1$$

(b) **Addition:** During addition reaction an unsaturated hydrocarbon adds hydrogen to the reaction in the presence of catalysts. Catalysts such as palladium or nickel increase the speed of reaction without being used up in that reaction to give saturated hydrocarbons.

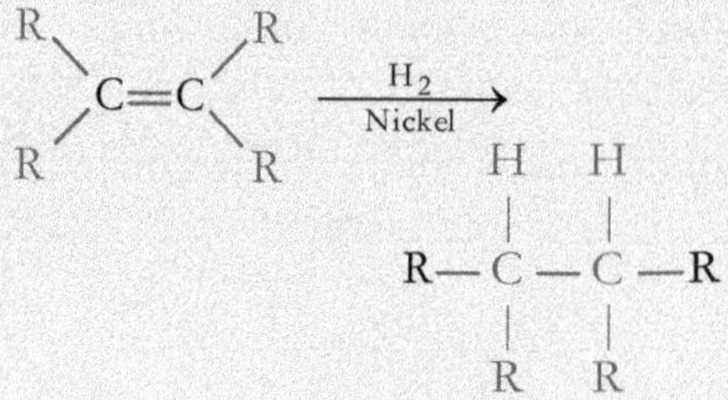

This reaction is extensively used in the hydrogenation of vegetable oils containing long unsaturated carbon chains using a nickel catalyst. **1**

(c) Substitution: A reaction in which one functional group or atom is replaced by another functional group or atom is called substitution reaction.

In the presence of sunlight addition of chlorine to hydrocarbons is a fast reaction that results in replacement of the hydrogen atoms one by one. This is an example of substitution reaction because chlorine replaces the hydrogen attached to the carbon atom in the hydrocarbon.

$$CH_4 + Cl_2 \xrightarrow{\text{Sunlight}} \underset{\text{Chloromethane}}{CH_3Cl} + HCl$$

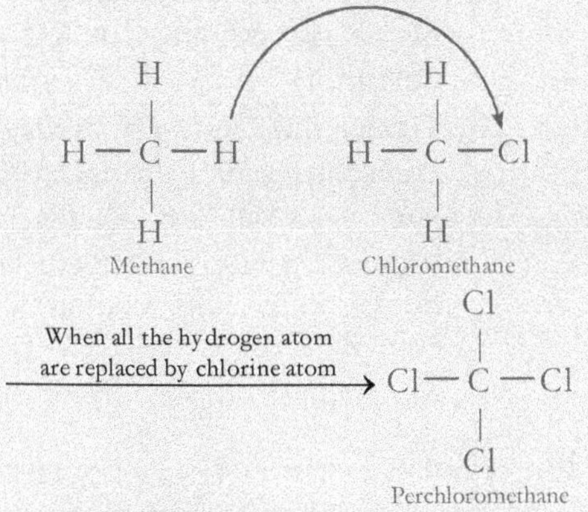

1

(d) Esterification: The reaction between an Acid and an Alcohol to produce ester as the product is called Esterification reaction. During this reaction a molecule of water is eliminated.

$$CH_3COOH + C_2H_5OH \xrightarrow{\text{Conc. } H_2SO_4} CH_3COOC_2H_5 + H_2O$$

In the above reaction, Ethanoic acid reacts with Ethyl alcohol to form an ester Ethyl Acetate and water molecule. **1**

(e) Oxidation: Carbon and its compounds get easily oxidized when subjected to combustion. The following equation shows the conversion of alcohols to carboxylic acid.

$$\underset{\text{Ethanol}}{CH_3—CH_2OH} \xrightarrow[\text{or Acidified } K_2Cr_2O_7 + \text{Heat}]{\text{Alkaline } KMnO_4 + \text{Heat}} \underset{\text{Acetic acid}}{CH_3COOH}$$

Alkaline potassium permanganate or acidified potassium dichromate are oxidising alcohols to acids, that is, adding oxygen to the starting material. Hence they are known as oxidising agents. **1**

26. (a) Diagram of human brain

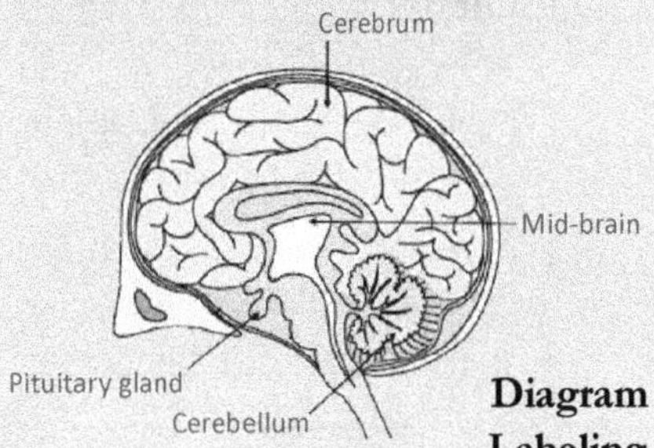

Diagram - 2
Labeling - 2

(b) The main thinking part of the brain is the Fore brain which control the voluntary actions, store information (memory), receives sensory impulses from various parts of the body and integrates it. **1**

27. (a) The role of seminal vesicles and the prostate glands: Seminal vesicles and prostate gland are part of male reproductive system. They add their secretions to the vas deferens which carries sperms from the testes so that sperms stay in a fluid medium. The secretions of seminal vesicles and prostate gland provide nutrition to the sperms and also make their further transport easier. **2**

(b) The contraceptive methods can be broadly divided into the following types:

- **Natural method:** In this method, the sexual act is avoided from day 10th to 17th of the menstrual cycle because during this period ovulation is expected and the chances of fertilization are very high. **1**
- **Barrier method:** Physical barrier method prevents the entry of sperm into the uterus. Barriers are available for both males and females. Condoms on the penis or similar coverings worn in the vagina can serve this purpose. **1**
- **Oral contraceptives:** In this method, the hormonal pills are

taken which prevent the entry of sperm into the uterus. However, since these pills change the hormonal balances, they can cause side effects too. 1

OR

Changes seen in girls at the time of puberty:

- Increase in breast size and darkening of skin of the nipples present at the tips of the breasts.
- Growth of hair in armpits and in the genital area.
- Appearance of thinner hair in other areas of skin like face, hands and legs.
- Beginning of menstrual cycle.
- More secretion of oil from the skin which results in the appearance of pimples.
- The hips broaden as extra fat is deposited in various parts of the body like hips and thighs. 3

Menstruation: Menstruation occurs in human females in each ovulation cycle when the egg released from the ovary is not fertilized and is transferred to the fallopian tube. At that time, the uterus prepares itself to receive embryo and the lining of uterus thickens and is supplied with blood to nourish the embryo. If the egg does not get fertilized, then the lining of the uterus is shed in fragments along with unfertilized egg and gets released in the form of blood and mucous from the vagina called menstruation. 2

28. **(a) Difference between Roasting and Calcination:** Roasting is the process of heating the ore strongly in the presence of excess of air whereas calcinations is the process of heating the ore strongly in the absence of air. In roasting, sulphur dioxide is released while in calcination carbon dioxide is released. 2

(b) Roasting is mostly done for sulphide ores because it is easier to obtain the metal from its oxide than from its sulphide. 1

(c) The reaction of iron (III) oxide (Fe_2O_3) with aluminium is used to join cracked railway tracks. The reaction is highly exothermic and is called thermite reaction. Iron is obtained in the molten state which fills the cracks.

$Fe_2O_3 + 2Al \rightarrow 2Fe + Al_2O_3 + \text{Heat}$ 2

OR

Given: a hammer, a battery, a bulb, wires and a switch.

(a) Using a hammer: If the sample breaks, this means it is brittle and hence it is a non metal. On the other hand if the sample flattens to form a sheet, this means that the sample is malleable and hence is a metal. 2

One can also use battery, wires, bulb and switch to make a circuit and use the given material to complete the circuit one by one, if the electric current flows and the bulb glows then it is metal and if not then it is non-metal. 2

(b) Though these tests give us rough idea in distinguishing between metals and non-metals but they are not reliable because there are exceptions both in metals as well as non-metals. For example Sodium (Na) metal is brittle and graphite can show conductivity. 1

29. **Tyndall effect:** The phenomena of scattering of light by dust, smoke and water droplets suspended in air is known as Tyndall effect. 1

Cause of Tyndall effect: The earth's atmosphere is a heterogeneous mixture of minute particles. These particles include smoke, tiny water droplets, suspended particles of dust and molecules of air. When a beam of light strikes such fine particles, the path of the beam becomes visible. The light reaches us, after getting diffused and reflected by these particles. The phenomenon of scattering of light by the colloidal particles gives rise to Tyndall effect. 2

Some applications of Tyndall effect are:

(a) When a fine beam of sunlight enters a smoke filled room through a small hole, the smoke particles become visible due to the scattering of light 1

(b) When sunlight passes through a canopy of a dense forest, the tiny water droplets in the mist scatter light and become visible. **1**

OR

Accomodation of eye: In order to focus far-off objects, the ciliary muscles relax, and in doing so, increase the curvature and focal length of the crystalline lens. Thus, the image of far-off object is clearly focussed on the retina, which is at the principal focus of crystalline lens.

Conversely, to focus near objects, the ciliary muscles contract and in doing so, decrease the curvature and hence, focal length of crystalline lens. Thus, the images of objects, nearer to the eye are clearly focussed on the retina, which is between F and 2F of crystalline lens. **2**

(i) QR is the refracted ray. ½

(ii) RS is the emergent ray. ½

(iii) Angle 1 is called angle of incidence. ½

(iv) Angle 3 is called angle of deviation. ½

(v) Angle 5 is the angle of refraction on face AB. ½

(vi) Angle 2 + Angle 3 = Angle 1+ Angle 4 . ½

30. **Ohm's law:** This law states that "the current flowing through a conductor is directly proportional to the potential difference across the ends of the conductor, provided the temperature and other physical conditions of the conductor remain the same". **1**

Experiment to verify Ohm's law

Procedure: **1**

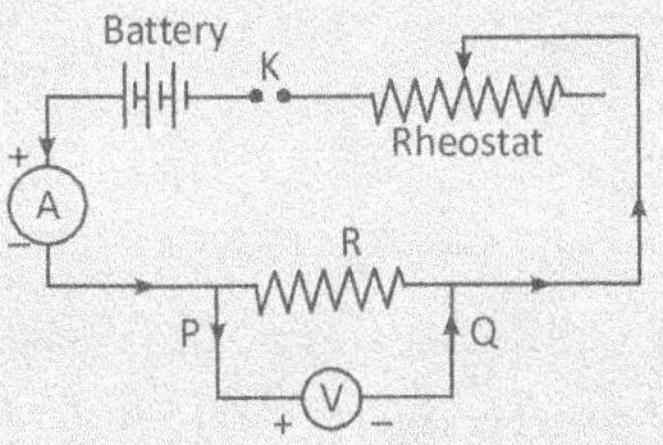

(a) Connect the various components as shown in the figure.

(b) Close the key, so that current begins to flow in the circuit.

(c) Note down the potential difference (V) across the conductor PQ of resistance R shown by the voltmeter and the corresponding current (I) shown by the ammeter.

(d) Now move the knob of rheostat so that the current in the circuit increases.

(e) Again note down the potential difference (V) across the conductor PQ of resistance R in the voltmeter and current in the circuit shown by ammeter.

(f) Repeat the experiment five times by increasing the current in the circuit by moving the knob of the rheostat in steps. **1**

Plot a graph between V and I by taking V along X-axis and I along Y-axis. We get a straight line passing through origin. **1**

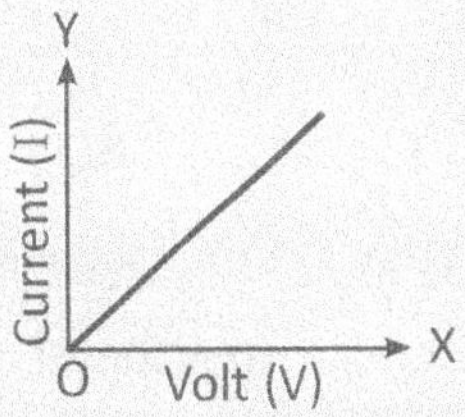

Conclusion: From the graph between V and I, we conclude that $I \propto V$, which is Ohm's law. Hence Ohm's law is verified experimentally.

Ohm's law does not hold under all conditions:

- Ohm's law does not hold for non-ohmic material such as electrolyte
- Ohm's law holds good only if the temperature and other physical conditions of the conductor remains the same **1**

SAMPLE PAPER 2

CBSE - Class 10

SCIENCE

Time Allowed: 3 Hours *Maximum Marks: 80*

General Instructions:

i. The question paper comprises three sections – A, B and C. Attempt all the sections.
ii. All questions are compulsory.
iii. Internal choice is given in each section.
iv. All questions in Section A are one-mark questions comprising MCQ, VSA type and assertion-reason type questions. They are to be answered in one word or in one sentence.
v. All questions in Section B are three-mark, short-answer type questions. These are to be answered in about 50 - 60 words each.
vi. All questions in Section C are five-mark, long-answer type questions. These are to be answered in about 80 - 90 words each.
vii. This question paper consists of a total of 30 questions.

SECTION - A

1. State the location and the function of gastric glands? **1**

2. What is the function of micropyle? **1**

3. **Answer question numbers 3(a)-3(d) on the basis of your understanding of the following paragraph and the related studied concepts.**

All acids have similar chemical properties. For example all acids generate hydrogen gas on reacting with metals, so hydrogen seems to be common to all acids. To investigate whether all compounds containing hydrogen are acidic following set up was taken.

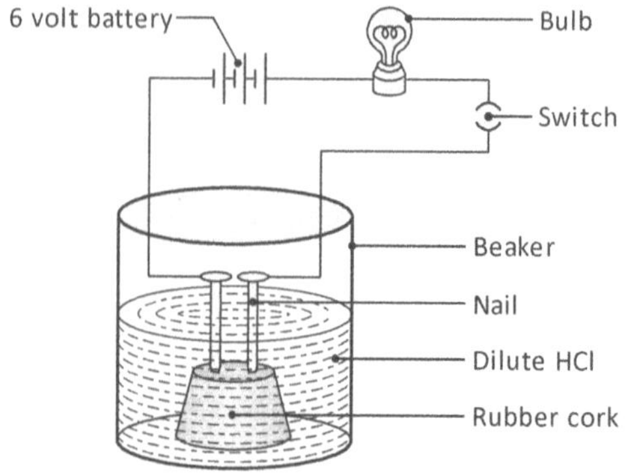

Based on the above set up answer the following questions:

3(a) What do you observe on passing electric current? **1**

3(b) If you will repeat the experiment separately with glucose and alcohol solutions,what will you observe? **1**

3(c) What does glowing of bulb indicates? **1**

3(d) Give reasons for the above observations. **1**

4. Question numbers 4(a) - 4(d) are based on the table given below. Study this table related to Absolute refractive index of some material media and answer the questions that follow:

Material medium	Refractive index	Material medium	Refrective index
Air	1.0003	Crown glass	1.52
Ice	1.31	Canada Balsam	1.53
Water	1.33	Rock salt	1.54
Alcohol	1.36	Carbon disulphide	1.63
Kerosene	1.44	Dense flint glass	1.65
Fused quartz	1.46	Ruby	1.71
Turpentine oil	1.47	Sapphire	1.77
Benzene	1.50	Diamond	2.42

4(a) Find out from the given table, the medium having highest optical density.

(i) Diamond **(ii)** Air

(iii) Ice **(iv)** Crown glass **1**

4(b) As light travels from a rarer medium to a denser medium it will have:

(i) Increased velocity **(ii)** Decreased velocity

(iii) Decreased wavelength **(iv)** Both (i) and (ii) **1**

4(c) You are given kerosene, turpentine and water. In which of these does the light travel fastest? **1**

4(d) The refractive index of diamond is 2.42. What is the meaning of this statement? Find out from the given table, the medium having lowest optical density. **1**

5. Which of the following statements is correct about receptors:

(i) Gustatory receptors detect taste while olfactory receptors detect smell

(ii) Both gustatory and olfactory receptors detect smell

(iii) Auditory receptors detect smell and olfactory receptors detect taste

(iv) Olfactory receptors detect taste and gustatory receptors smell **1**

6. Which of the following statements about the given reaction are correct:

$$3Fe(s) + 4H_2O(g) \longrightarrow Fe_3O_4\,(s) + 4H_2\,(g)$$

(a) Iron metal is getting oxidized

(b) Water is getting reduced

(c) Water is acting as reducing agent

(d) Water is acting as oxidizing agent

(i) (a), (b) and (c) **(ii)** (c) and (d)

(iii) (a), (b) and (d) **(iv)** (b) and (d) **1**

OR

The following reaction is an example of a:

$$4NH_3\ (g) + 5O_2\ (g) \longrightarrow 4NO\ (g) + 6\ H_2O\ (g)$$

(a) Displacement reaction

(b) Combination reaction

(c) Redox reaction

(d) Neutralisation reaction

(i) (a) and (d) **(ii)** (a) and (c)

(iii) (a) and (c) **(iv)** (c) and (d) **1**

7. The important message conveyed by the 'Chipko Movement' is:

(i) To involve the community in forest conservation efforts

(ii) To ignore the community in forest conservation efforts

(iii) To cut down forest trees for developmental activities

(iv) Government agencies have the unquestionable right to order destruction of trees in forests **1**

8. Factors responsible for the rapid spread of bread mould on slices of bread are:

(a) Large number of spores

(b) Availability of moisture and nutrients in bread

(c) Presence of tubular branched hyphae

(d) Formation of round shaped sporangia

(i) (a) and (c) **(ii)** (b) and (d)

(iii) (a) and (b) **(iv)** (c) and (d) **1**

OR

Length of pollen tube depends on the distance between:

(i) Pollen grain and upper surface of stigma

(ii) Pollen grain on upper surface of stigma and ovule

(iii) Pollen grain in anther and upper surface of stigma

(iv) Upper surface of stigma and lower part of style **1**

9. Which of the following oxide(s) of iron would be obtained on prolonged reaction of iron with steam?

(i) FeO **(ii)** Fe_2O_3

(iii) Fe_3O_4 **(iv)** Fe_2O_3 and Fe_3O_4 **1**

10. Which of the following statements are usually correct for carbon compounds? These:

(a) Are good conductors of electricity

(b) Are poor conductors of electricity

(c) Have strong forces of attraction between their molecules

(d) Do not have strong forces of attraction between their molecules

(i) (a) and (c) **(ii)** (b) and (c)

(iii) (a) and (d) **(iv)** (b) and (d) **1**

11. To convert an AC generator into DC generator:

(i) Split ring type commutator must be used

(ii) Slip rings and brushes must be used

(iii) A stronger magnetic field has to be used

(iv) A rectangular wire loop has to be used **1**

12. A student sitting on the last bench can read the letters written on the blackboard but is not able to read the letters written in his text book. Which of the following statements is correct:

(i) The near point of his eyes has receded away

(ii) The near point of his eyes has come closer to him

(iii) The far point of his eyes has come closer to him

(iv) The far point of his eyes has receded away **1**

OR

Which of the following statements is correct?

(i) A person with myopia can see distant objects clearly

(ii) A person with hypermetropia can see nearby objects clearly

(iii) A person with myopia can see nearby objects clearly

(iv) A person with hypermetropia cannot see distant objects clearly

For question numbers 13 and 14, two statements are given- one labeled Assertion (A) and the other labeled Reason (R). Select the correct answer to these questions from the codes (i), (ii), (iii) and (iv) as given below

(i) Both A and R are true and R is correct explanation of the assertion.

(ii) Both A and R are true but R is not the correct explanation of the assertion.

(iii) A is true but R is false.

(iv) A is false but R is true.

13. **Assertion A** : 1 kilowatt = 1000 J s^{-1}. **1**

Reason R : Watt and J s^{-1} are SI units of power.

14. **Assertion A** : Veins have thick walls to collect blood from different organs. **1**

Reason R : Blood in veins are not under pressure.

SECTION - B

15. Suman and her husband have decided not to have more than 2 children. Describe two types of birth control methods which can be used by them to avoid pregnancy. **3**

16. A compound which is prepared from gypsum has the property pH hardening when mixed with right quantity of water.

(a) Identify the compound and write its chemical formula.

(b) Write the chemical equation for its preparation.

(c) List any two uses of the above compound. **3**

17. List three main factors responsible for the speciation and briefly describe each of them. **3**

OR

What are Mendel's laws of inheritance? **3**

18. Draw a schematic diagram of a circuit consisting of a battery of five 2 V cells, a 5 ohm resistor, a 10 ohm resistor and a 15 ohm resistor, an ammeter and a plug key, all connected in series. Calculate the electric current passing through the above circuit when the key is closed. **3**

OR

Judge the equivalent resistance when the following are connected in parallel:

(a) 1 Ω and 10^6 Ω

(b) 1 Ω and 10^3 Ω and 10^6 Ω **3**

19. An element P with atomic number 20 reacts with an element Q with atomic number 17 to form a compound. Answer the following question giving reasons:
Write the position of P and Q in the Modern Periodic Table and the molecular formula of the compound formed when P reacts with Q. **3**

20. Explain giving reasons why the sky appears blue to an observer from the surface of earth? What will the colour of the sky be for an astronaut staying in the international space station orbiting the earth? Justify your answer. **3**

21. What is an alloy? Name the constituents of 22 carat gold. Why is 24-carat gold converted into 22- carat gold? **3**

OR

Answer the following:

(a) Write the electron-dot structures for sodium, oxygen and magnesium.

(b) Show the formation of Na_2O and MgO by the transfer of electrons.

(c) What are the ions present in these compounds? **3**

22. Answer the following:

(a) State three factors which can cause overloading of domestic electric circuits.

(b) State the function of a 'fuse' in an electric circuit. **3**

23. With the help of a flowchart, how will you show the breakdown of glucose in a cell to provide energy:

(a) In the absence of oxygen

(b) In the presence of oxygen

(c) When there is lack of oxygen **3**

24. In human beings, the statistical probability of getting either a male or a female child is 50%. Based upon the evidence, explain your answer with the help of a diagram. **3**

SECTION - C

25. Name any three of energy of the oceans which can be converted into usable energy forms . Describe how it is done in each case. What is the likelihood of their use on a large scale? **5**

OR

How has the traditional use of wind and water energy been modified for our convenience? Can any source of energy be pollution-free? Why or why not? **5**

26. Explain the following:

(a) Reactivity of Al decreases if it is dipped in HNO_3.

(b) Carbon cannot reduce the oxides of Na or Mg.

(c) NaCl is not a conductor of electricity in solid state whereas it does conduct electricity in aqueous solution as well in molten state.

(d) Iron articles are galvanized.

(e) Metals like Na, K are never found in their free state in nature. **5**

27. Answer the following:

(a) Draw the structure of neuron and label it.

(b) Name the part of neuron:

(i) Where the information is required

(ii) Through which information travels as an electrical impulse

(c) What are the short fibre and long fibre of a neuron known as?

OR

Name various plant hormones. Also give their physiological effects on plant growth and development. **5**

28. Answer the following:

(a) Define the principal focus of a concave mirror.

(b) Why are convex mirrors preferred over plane mirrors as rear view mirrors?

(c) An object is placed at a distance of 30 cm from a convex mirror, the magnification produced is 1/2. Where should the object be placed to get a magnification of 1/3? **5**

29. Answer the following:

(a) Define electric power.

(b) Two identical resistors each of resistance 12 ohm are connected, (i) in series (ii) in parallel, in turn to a battery of 6 V. Calculate the ratio of power consumed in the combination of resistors in the two cases. **5**

30. Both soap and detergent are some type of salts. What is the difference between them? Describe in brief the cleansing action of soap. **5**

OR

Discuss briefly any two physical and three chemical properties of ethanol. **5**

2

SOLUTION

CBSE - Class 10

SECTION - A

1. **Gastric glands** are located in the walls of the stomach. Their function is to secrete gastric juice which contains three substances: hydrochloric acid, the enzyme pepsin and mucus. 1

2. **Micropyle** is a small opening at the surface of an ovule through which the pollen tube enters the ovule. So we can say Micropyle allows pollen access to the egg inside the protected ovule. 1

3. **(a)** The bulb will start glowing in the case of acids i.e. HCl on passing electric current. 1

3. **(b)** The bulb will not glow with glucose and alcohol solutions. 1

3. **(c)** Glowing of the bulb indicates that there is a flow of electric current through the solution. 1

3. **(d)** The electric current is carried through the solution by ions. Since the cation present in acids is H^+, this suggests that acids produce hydrogen ions, $H^+(aq)$, in solution, which are responsible for their acidic properties. Substances like glucose and alcohol do not dissociate to give H^+ ions and hence are not acidic. 1

4. **(a) (i)** Diamond 1

4. **(b) (iv)** Both (i) and (ii) 1

Explanation: When light rays travel from rarer to denser medium, its velocity and wavelength both decreases as $v = \nu\lambda$.

4. **(c)** We know from the definition of refractive index, that the speed of light is higher in a medium with lower refractive index. So, the light travels fastest in water relative to kerosene and turpentine. 1

4. **(d)** The refractive index is defined as the ratio of speed of light in air to the speed of light in the substance. If we say that the refractive index of diamond is 2.42, it means that the ratio of the speed of light in air and the speed of light in diamond is 2.42. Since, the refractive index of diamond is quite high, it means that the speed of light in diamond is very low. 1

5. **(i)** Gustatory receptors detect taste while olfactory receptors detect smell. 1

Explanation: Gustatory receptors are the taste receptors which are present on the surface of tongue in the form of taste buds. Olfactory receptors help to sense the smell and are located over the roof of nasal cavity.

6. **(iii)** (a), (b) and (d) 1

Explanation: Addition of oxygen to Fe is an oxidation process whereas lose of oxygen from H_2O to H_2 is a reduction step. Since water is source of oxygen therefore it acts as oxidizing agent.

OR

(iii) (a) and (c) 1

Explanation: A Redox reaction is combination of oxidation (removal of hydrogen) and reduction (addition of hydrogen). Displacement reaction involves displacement of some part of a compound with other atom like H atoms of NH_3 are displaced by oxygen.

7. (i) To involve the community in forest conservation efforts **1**

Explanation: 'Chipko Movement' represents sacred feelings of community towards the local forest areas.

8. (iii) (a) and (b) *i.e.* Large number of spores and Availability of moisture and nutrients in bread. **1**

Explanation: Bread mold prefers damp and warm substratum with ample supply of nutrients on which its air-borne spores land and germinate to produce mycelium.

OR

(ii) Pollen grain on upper surface of stigma and ovule. **1**

Explanation: Pollen tube carries male gametes to ovule and hence, is long equal to the distance between stigma and ovary.

9. (iii) Fe_3O_4 **1**

Explanation: Prolong heating of red hot iron with steam form Fe_3O_4 with hydrogen gas.

$$3Fe + 4H_2O \longrightarrow Fe_3O_4 + 4H_2$$

10. (iv) (b) and (d) **1**

Explanation: Carbon having four valence electrons forms only covalent compounds which exhibit less intermolecular attractions and do not have any free electrons to carry electric current. Therefore, these are poor conductors of electricity.

11. (i) Split ring type commutator must be used **1**

Explanation: AC generator has slip rings while the DC generator has a split ring type commutator. To convert an AC generator into DC generator the split ring type commutator is used with which unidirectional current is obtained.

12. (i) The near point of his eyes has receded away **1**

Explanation: The student is suffering from hyper-metropia wherein distant images are clear but the nearby images are blurry.

OR

(iii) A person with myopia can see nearby objects clearly. **1**

Explanation: Nearsightedness, or myopia is inability to see the far located objects clearly.

13. (i) Both A and R are true and R is the correct explanation of A. **1**

Explanation: 1 kilowatt = 1000 watts and 1 kilowatt = 1000 J s^{-1}

Therefore 1 watt = 1 J s^{-1}

Thus we can say that watt and Js^{-1} both are SI units of power.

Hence, the correct option is (i).

14. (i) Both A and R are true and R is the correct explanation of A. **1**

SECTION - C

15. The **two common type of birth control methods** which can be used by Suman and her husband are:

(a) Barrier Method: Physical barrier method prevents the entry of sperm into the uterus. Barriers are available for both males and females. Condoms on the penis or similar coverings worn in the vagina can serve this purpose. **1½**

(b) Chemical Method: In this method, the hormonal pills are taken which prevent the entry of sperm into the uterus. However, since these pills change the hormonal balances, they can cause side effects too. **1½**

16. A compound which is prepared from gypsum has the property of pH hardening when mixed with right quantity of water.

(a) The compound is Plaster of Paris / calcium sulphate hemihydrate. **½**

Chemical formula: $CaSO_4 . \frac{1}{2} H_2O$ **½**

(b) Chemical equation for its preparation: **1**

$$\underset{\text{Gypsum / Calcium sulphate dehydrate}}{CaSO_4.2H_2O} \xrightarrow{100°C} \underset{\text{Plaster of Paris / Calcium sulphate hemihydrate}}{CaSO_4.\tfrac{1}{2}H_2O} + 1\tfrac{1}{2}H_2O$$

(c) Two uses of Plaster of Paris:

(i) In making chalks for writing on the blackboard. ½

(ii) In medical science, used for setting fractured bones in the right position. ½

17. Three main factors responsible for the speciation are:

(a) Natural selection: Those individuals whose genes are best suited to the environment are more likely to survive and pass on their genes to the next generation. This is natural selection. Gradually, favourable genes will start to predominate in the population and less favourable genes will decline. **1**

(b) Genetic drift: It is caused by drastic changes in the frequencies of particular genes by chance alone. Genetic drift, with changes in the gene flow imposed by isolation mechanism, acts as an agent of speciation which ultimately results in evolution. **1**

(c) Geographical isolation: Geographical isolation is caused by various types of barriers such as mountain ranges, rivers and seas. It leads to reproductive isolation due to which there is no flow of genes between separated groups of population which ultimately results in speciation. **1**

OR

Mendel's laws of inheritance:

(a) Law of dominance: When two homozygous individuals with one or more sets of contrasting characters are crossed the characters that appear in the F_1 hybrids are dominant characters. **1**

(b) Law of segregation: Contrasting characters brought together in a hybrid remain together without being contaminated and when gametes are formed from the hybrid the two separate from each other and only one enters each gamete. **1**

(c) Law of independent assortment: In inheritance of more than one pair of contrasting characters simultaneously, the factors for each pair of characters assort independently of other pairs. **1**

18. Circuit diagram will be:

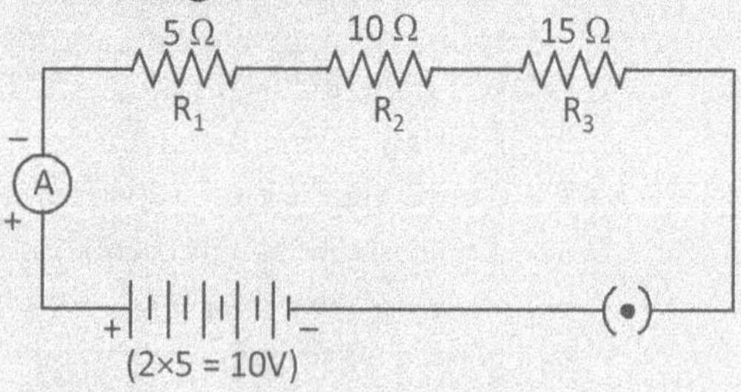

1

It is given that five cells of 2 V are connected in series, so total voltage of the battery

$$V = 2 \times 5 = 10 \text{ V}$$ ½

Three resistors of 5Ω, 10Ω and 15Ω are connected in series, so the net resistance

$$R = 5\Omega + 10\Omega + 15\Omega = 30\Omega.$$ ½

According to Ohm's law

$$V = IR \quad \text{and} \quad I = \frac{V}{R}$$

On substituting resultant voltage(V) as 10 V and resultant resistance as 30Ω, we get

$$I = \frac{10V}{30\Omega} = 0.33 \text{ A}$$ **1**

The electric current passing through the above circuit when the key is closed will be 0.33 A

OR

We know that when resistors are connected in parallel then equivalent resistance is given by the relation

$$\frac{1}{R} = \frac{1}{R_1} + \frac{1}{R_2} + \frac{1}{R_3}$$

Equivalent resistance when the following are connected in parallel –

(a) 1 Ω and 10^6 Ω are connected in parallel then

$$\frac{1}{R} = \frac{1}{1} + \frac{1}{10^6} = \frac{10^6 + 1}{10^6} \approx \frac{10^6}{10^6} \approx 1\Omega$$

Equivalent resistance will be approximately 1 ohm but less than 1 ohm. 1½

(b) 1 Ω, 10^3 Ω and 10^6 Ω are connected in parallel then,

$$\frac{1}{R} = \frac{1}{1} + \frac{1}{10^3} + \frac{1}{10^6}$$

$$= \frac{1 + 10^3 + 10^6}{10^6} = \frac{1001001}{10^6}$$

Therefore, equivalent resistance (R) = 0.999 ohm 1½

19. Atomic number of element P is 20

Electronic configuration of P will be 2, 8, 8, 2

Valence electron = 2

Position of P in the Modern Periodic table will be

Period = 4, Group = 2 1

Atomic number of element Q is 17

Electronic configuration of Q will be 2, 8, 7

Valence electron = 1

Position of Q in the modern Periodic table will be

Period =3, Group = 10 +7 = 17 1

When P reacts with Q, it loses the two valence electrons (valency 2). These two valence electrons are accepted by two Q atoms (valency 1).

Hence, the **formula of the compound formed between P and Q** is PQ_2. 1

20. The scattering of various components of sunlight is purely dependent on the wavelength of the light. Sunlight, reaching the surface of the earth is scattered in all directions by the gases and particles present in the atmosphere. Blue light having shortest wavelength is scattered most by the atmospheric particles. Thus, **sky appears blue to an observer from the surface of the Earth.** 2

For an astronaut staying in the international space station orbiting the Earth, the colour of the sky will be black because there is no atmosphere in the outer space that can scatter the sunlight. 1

21. An alloy is a homogeneous mixture of two or more metals, or a metal and a non metal. 1

The constituent of 22-carat gold is either silver or copper. 1

24-carat gold is converted into 22-carat gold as 24-carat gold is pure gold which is very soft. It is therefore not suitable for making jewellery or gold ornaments. For this purpose, 22 carat gold is preferred which is an alloy of 22 parts by mass of gold and 2 parts by mass of copper or silver. It is harder than pure gold. 1

OR

(a) Electron-dot structures for sodium, oxygen and magnesium:

Sodium: $\dot{\text{Na}}$ Oxygen: $:\ddot{\text{O}}:$

Magnesium: $\ddot{\text{Mg}}$

(b) Formation of Sodium oxide: 1

Two sodium atoms transfer their 2 outermost electrons to an oxygen atom. By losing two electrons, the two sodium atoms form two sodium ions ($2Na^+$). And by gaining two electrons, the oxygen atom forms an oxide ion (O^{2-}).

$$\begin{matrix}\dot{\text{Na}}\\ \dot{\text{Na}}\end{matrix} + :\ddot{\text{O}}: \longrightarrow Na_2O$$ ½

Formation of Magnesium Oxide:

When magnesium reacts with oxygen, the magnesium atom transfers its two outermost electrons to an oxygen atom. By losing two electrons, the magnesium atoms form a magnesium ion (Mg^{2+}) and by gaining two electrons, the oxygen atom forms an oxide ion (O^{2-}).

$$\ddot{\text{Mg}} + :\ddot{\text{O}}: \longrightarrow MgO$$ ½

(c) The ions present in sodium oxide compound (Na_2O) are sodium ions ($2Na^+$) and oxide ions (O^{2-}). ½

Ions present in Magnesium oxide compound (MgO) are magnesium ions Mg^{2+} and oxide ions (O^{2-}). ½

22. **(a) Three factors which can cause overloading are:**

(i) When the live wire and the neutral wire come into direct contact.

(ii) Accidental hike in the supply voltage.

(iii) By connecting too many appliances to a single socket. 1½

(b) Function of a 'fuse' in an electric circuit: : Electric fuse wire is a safety wire connected in series with the live wire. Fuse wire melts down in case of supply of large current supply or malfunctioning in the electric connections thereby stopping the flow of electric current and preventing damage to the appliance due to overloading or short circuiting. 1½

23. Flowchart to show the breakdown of glucose in a cell to provide energy:

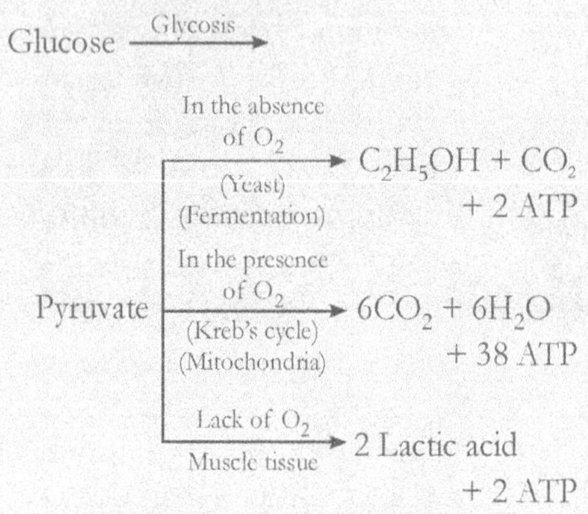

1
1
1

24. In human beings, the statistical probability of getting either a male or a female child is 50 %.

Females have a perfect pair of sex chromosome, XX

Males have mismatched pair of sex chromosomes, XY

There is an equal probability of fertilization of ovum with the sperm carrying either X or Y chromosomes. In case the ovum fertilizes with sperm carrying X- chromosomes, the zygote develop into a female (XX) child. Fertilization of ovum with Y-chromosomes carrying sperm result into male (XY) child. 1

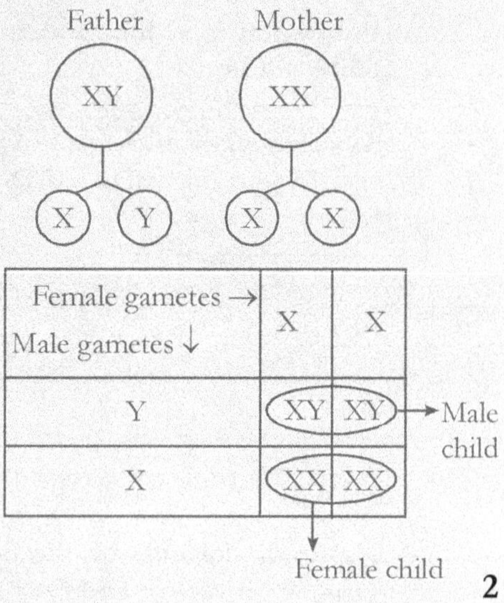

2

SECTION - C

25. The energy from sea or ocean water is available in the following forms:

(a) Energy of sea waves.

(b) Tidal energy.

(c) Ocean thermal energy. ½

Tidal Energy: Due to the gravitational pull of mainly the moon on the spinning earth, the level of water in the sea rises and falls. This phenomenon is called high and low tides and the difference in sea-levels gives us tidal energy. Tidal energy is harnessed by constructing a dam across a narrow opening to the sea. A turbine fixed at the opening of the dam converts tidal energy to electricity. 1½

Wave Energy: The waves are generated by strong winds blowing across the sea. The kinetic energy possessed by huge waves near the sea-shore rotates the turbine of a generator. Hence, electricity is produced. 1½

Ocean Thermal Energy: The water at the surface of the sea or ocean is heated by the Sun while the water in deeper sections is relatively cold. This difference in temperature is exploited to obtain energy in ocean-thermal-energy conversion plants.

Ocean Thermal Energy Conversion plants: The warm surface-water is used to boil a volatile liquid like ammonia. The vapours of the liquid are then used to run the turbine of generator. The cold water from the depth of the ocean is pumped up and condenses vapour again to liquid. This process is repeated time and again to convert ocean thermal energy into electric energy. 1½

OR

The traditional use of wind and water energy been modified for our convenience.

Earlier, the windmills were used to harness wind energy to do mechanical work such as lifting or drawing water from a well. But now a day's windmills are used to generate electricity. 1½

Traditionally, waterfalls were used as a source of energy. Nowadays to use energy of flowing water, large dams are built in hilly regions and hydro-electric power stations are used in order to harness potential energy of stored water. 1½

No source of energy can be called pollution-free because the use of any source of energy disturbs the environment in one way or the other. A source of energy like a solar cell is pollution free in actual operation but the assembly of the device might have caused some damage to the environment. 2

26. **(a) Reactivity of Al decreases if it is dipped in HNO_3**

When aluminium is dipped in nitric acid, a layer of aluminium oxide Al_2O_3 is formed on the metal. This happens because nitric acid is a strong oxidizing agent. This layer is hard and prevents further reaction of aluminium. Due to this, the reactivity of aluminium decreases. 1

(b) Carbon cannot reduce the oxides of Na or Mg

Sodium and magnesium have higher affinity towards oxygen than towards carbon because these are highly reactive metals. Hence, carbon cannot reduce the oxides of Na or Mg. 1

(c) NaCl is not a conductor of electricity in solid state whereas it does conduct electricity in aqueous solution as well in molten state.

Ionic compounds do not conduct electricity in solid state but they conduct electricity in aqueous solution and in molten state. Hence, this property is shown by sodium chloride. 1

(d) Iron articles are galvanized.

Iron articles are galvanized to prevent rusting of iron. After galvanization, zinc being more reactive than iron, works as a protective layer for iron articles. 1

(e) Metals like Na, K are never found in their free state in nature.

Metals like Na, K, Ca and Mg are highly reactive metals and react with the gases present in the air. Hence they are not found in their free state in nature. 1

27. (a) The structure of neuron:

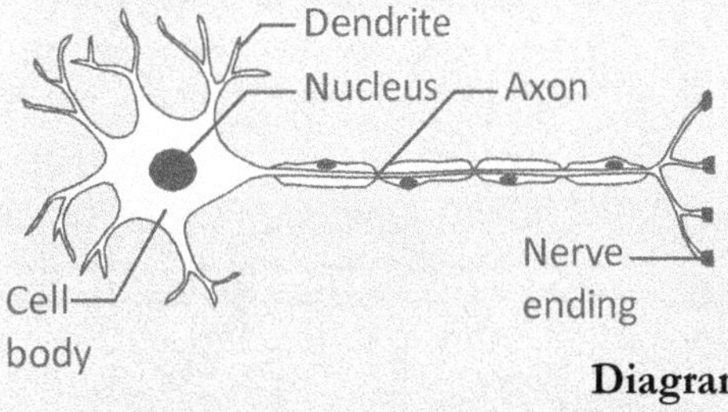

Diagram 1
Labeling 1

Fig. Neuron

(b) The part of neuron:

(i) **Where the information is required:** at the end of the dendrite tip of a nerve cell. 1

(ii) **Through which information travels as an electrical impulse:** from the dendrite to the cell body and then along the axon to its end. 1

(c) The short fibres of a neuron are dendrites and long fibres are axons. 1

OR

Plant Hormone	Physiological Effect
1. Auxin	• Promotes lengthening and apical dominance. • Promotes cell elongation and division • Stimulates root formation and development of seedless fruit
2. Gibberellin	• Promotes Stem elongation, breaking seed dormancy • Mobilization of endosperm reserves • Stimilates flower initiation and fruit set
3. Cytokinins	• Promotes cell division and delay leaf ageing • Stimulate leaf expansion
4. Abscisic Acid	• Growth retardation hormone • Reverses the effects of auxin and gibberellins on growth and development
5. Ethylene	• Growth and development of floral organs • Essential for fruit ripening, promotes senescence and abscission of leaves

1 × 5 = 5

28. (a) **Principal focus of a concave mirror:** The principal focus of the concave mirror is a point on the principal axis of the mirror, where incident rays of light parallel to the principal axis actually meet after reflection from the mirror surface. **1**

(b) **Convex mirrors are preferred over plane mirrors as rear view mirrors** because they give an erect, virtual, full size diminished image of distant objects with a wider view. Thus, convex mirrors enable the driver to view much larger area than would be possible with a plane mirror. **1**

(c) Given $u = 30$ cm, $m = \frac{1}{2}$

Using $m = -\frac{v}{u}$, we get

$$\frac{1}{2} = \frac{-v}{-30}$$

$$v = 15 \text{ cm}$$ **1**

Also we know that,

$$\frac{1}{f} = \frac{1}{v} + \frac{1}{u}$$

$$\frac{1}{f} = \frac{1}{15} + \frac{1}{-30} = \frac{2-1}{30} = \frac{1}{30}$$

$$f = +30 \text{ cm}$$ **1**

Now to get the magnification of 1/3 we have to find the value of u.

$$m = -\frac{v}{u}$$

$$\frac{1}{3} = -\frac{v}{u}$$

$$v = -\frac{u}{3}$$

Using $\frac{1}{f} = \frac{1}{v} + \frac{1}{u}$

$$\frac{1}{30} = \frac{-3}{u} + \frac{1}{u} = \frac{-2}{u}$$

$$u = -60 \text{ cm}$$ **1**

Hence object should be placed at a distance of 60 cm in front of convex mirror to get 1/3 magni-fication.

29. (a) **Electric power:** is defined as the amount of electric energy consumed in a circuit per unit time.

S.I. unit of Electric Power is watt (or W) **1**

(b) Two identical resistors each of resistance 12 ohm are connected, 1) in series 2) in parallel, in turn to a battery of 6 V.

Here, V = 6 V

(i) In series

Net resistance $R = R_1 + R_2$

Net resistance R = 12 + 12

$= 24\Omega$ ½

Power consumed,

$$P_1 = \frac{V^2}{R} = \frac{36}{24} = 1.5W$$ **1**

(ii) In parallel

$$\frac{1}{R} = \frac{1}{R_1} + \frac{1}{R_2}$$

$$= \frac{1}{12} + \frac{1}{12} = \frac{2}{12}$$

Net resistance $R = 6\Omega$ ½

Power consumed,

$$P_2 = \frac{V^2}{R} = \frac{36}{6} = 6W$$ **1**

Ratio $\frac{P_2}{P_1} = \frac{6}{1.5} = 4 : 1$ **1**

30. Difference between soaps and detergents:

Soaps	Detergents
Soaps are sodium or potassium salts of long chain carboxylic acids.	Detergents are generally ammonium or sulphonate salts of long chain carboxylic acids.
Soaps are not effective for cleaning in hard water.	Detergents are effective for cleaning in hard as well as soft water.
Soaps are biodegradable.	Detergents are non - biodegradable.

1½

Cleansing action of soap can be described as follows:

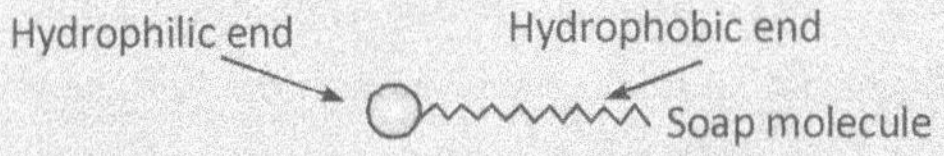

½

When a cloth with dirt attached to it is immersed in water containing soap, then the ionic end of soap orients itself towards water and the hydrocarbon chain orients itself along the dirt. Thus, clusters of molecules are formed in which the hydrophobic tails are in the interior of the cluster and the ionic ends are on the surface of the cluster. So, the dirt particles are surrounded by the soap molecules. This formation is called a micelle. Soap in the form of a micelle is able to clean, since the oily dirt will be collected in the centre of the micelle. The micelles stay in solution as a colloid and will not come together to precipitate because of ion-ion repulsion. Now, when water is agitated, the dirt suspended in the micelles is also easily rinsed away. **2**

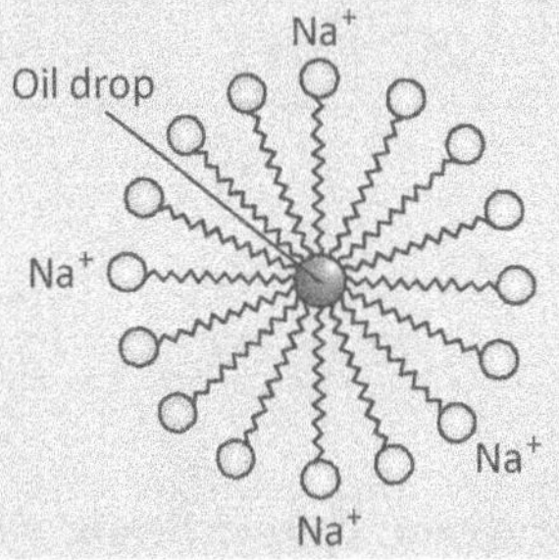

1

OR

Properties of Ethanol

Physical properties:

1. Ethanol exists in liquid state at room temperature. **1**
2. Ethanol is soluble in water in all proportions. **1**
3. Ethanol has a distinct smell and a burning taste. **1**

Chemical Properties:

1. **Reaction with Metals :**

   Sodium reacts with ethanol to form sodium ethoxide with the evolution of hydrogen gas.

   $$\underset{\text{(Ethanol)}}{C_2H_5OH} + Na \longrightarrow \underset{\text{(Sodium Ethoxide)}}{C_2H_5ONa} + H_2$$ **1**

2. **Reaction with conc. H_2SO_4 :**

   When ethanol is heated with concentrated sulphuric acid, ethene is collected over water. This is called dehydration of Alcohol.

   $$\underset{\text{(Ethanol)}}{2CH_3CH_2OH} \xrightarrow[H_2SO_4]{\text{Hot conc.}} \underset{\text{(Ethene)}}{2CH_2 = CH_2} + H_2O$$ **1**

SAMPLE PAPER 3

CBSE - Class 10

SCIENCE

Time Allowed: 3 Hours *Maximum Marks: 80*

General Instructions:

i. The question paper comprises three sections – A, B and C. Attempt all the sections.
ii. All questions are compulsory.
iii. Internal choice is given in each section.
iv. All questions in Section A are one-mark questions comprising MCQ, VSA type and assertion-reason type questions. They are to be answered in one word or in one sentence.
v. All questions in Section B are three-mark, short-answer type questions. These are to be answered in about 50 - 60 words each.
vi. All questions in Section C are five-mark, long-answer type questions. These are to be answered in about 80 - 90 words each.
vii. This question paper consists of a total of 30 questions.

SECTION - A

1. What is the name of the phenomenon in which the right side of an object appears to be the left side of the image in a plane mirror? 1

2. Name two simple organisms having the ability of regeneration. 1

3. **Answer question numbers 3(a)-3(d) on the basis of your understanding of the given diagram and the related studied concepts.**

The following diagram shows a part of the periodic table in which the elements are arranged according to their atomic numbers. (The letters given here are not the chemical symbols of the elements):

a 3	b 4		c 5	d 6	e 7	f 8	g 9	h 10
i 11	j 12		k 13	l 14	m 15	n 16	o 17	p 18

3(a) Which element has a bigger atom, a or f? 1

3(b) Which element has a higher valency, k or o? 1

3(c) Which element is more metallic, i or k? 1

3(d) Select a letter which represents a non-metal of valency 2. 1

4. **Question numbers 4(a) - 4(d) are based on the graph given below. Study this graph and answer the questions that follow:**

The values of potential difference V applied across a resistor and the corresponding values of current I flowing in the resistor are plotted in a graph given below:

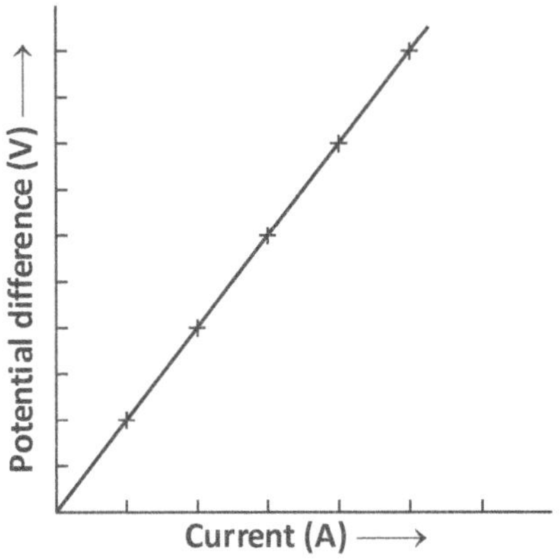

4(a) Name the law which is illustrated by the above V-I graph. **1**

4(b) Write down the formula which states the relation between potential difference, current and resistance. **1**

4(c) What is the maximum resistance which can be made using five resistors each of 1/5 Ω?

(i) 1/5 Ω **(ii)** 10 Ω

(iii) 5 Ω **(iv)** 1 Ω **1**

4(d) Which of the following represents voltage?

(i) $\frac{\text{Work done}}{\text{Current} \times \text{Time}}$ **(ii)** Work done × Charge

(iii) $\frac{\text{Work done} \times \text{Time}}{\text{Current}}$ **(iv)** Work done × Charge × Time **1**

5. Sodium carbonate is a basic salt because it is a salt of:

(i) Strong acid and strong base **(ii)** Weak acid and weak base

(iii) Strong acid and weak base **(iv)** Weak acid and strong base **1**

OR

Calcium phosphate is present in tooth enamel. Its nature is:

(i) Basic **(ii)** Acidic

(iii) Neutral **(iv)** Amphoteric **1**

6. During respiration exchange of gases take place in:

(i) Trachea and larynx **(ii)** Alveoli of lungs

(iii) Alveoli and throat **(iv)** Throat and larynx **1**

OR

What prevents backflow of blood inside the heart during contraction?

(i) Valves in heart **(ii)** Thick muscular walls of ventricles

(iii) Thin walls of atria **(iv)** All of these

7. In torches, search lights and headlights of vehicles, the bulb is placed:

(i) between the pole and the focus of the reflector

(ii) very near to the focus of the reflector

(iii) between the focus and centre of curvature of the reflector

(iv) at the centre of curvature of the reflector **1**

8. One of the following is not a direct stakeholder in the management (or conservation) of forests. This is:

(i) the people who have paper mills

(ii) the people who run the forest department

(iii) the people who campaign for the conservation of forests

(iv) the people who live in urban areas 1

9. Buckminsterfullerene is an allotropic form of:

(i) Phosphorus (ii) Sulphur

(iii) Carbon (iv) Tin 1

10. The correct sequence of organs in the male reproductive system for transport of sperms is:

(i) Testis → vas deferens → urethra

(ii) Testis → ureter → urethra

(iii) Testis → urethra → ureter

(iv) Testis → vas deferens → ureter 1

11. Which among the following diseases is not sexually transmitted:

(i) Syphillis (ii) Hepatitis

(iii) HIV-AIDS (iv) Gonorrhoea 1

12. There are four fuels which all contain only carbon and hydrogen. The fuel having highest calorific value will be one which has:

(i) more of carbon but less of hydrogen

(ii) less of carbon but more of hydrogen

(iii) equal proportions of carbon and hydrogen

(iv) less of carbon as well as less of hydrogen 1

OR

Fuel used in thermal power plants is:

(i) Water (ii) Uranium

(iii) Biomass (iv) Fossil fuels 1

For question numbers 13 and 14, two statements are given- one labeled Assertion (A) and the other labeled Reason (R). Select the correct answer to these questions from the codes (i), (ii), (iii) and (iv) as given below :

(i) Both A and R are true and R is correct explanation of the assertion.

(ii) Both A and R are true but R is not the correct explanation of the assertion.

(iii) A is true but R is false.

(iv) A is false but R is true.

13. **Assertion A** : Sky appears in blue colour.

Reason R : Blue colour in sunlight travelling through atmosphere undergoes maximum scattering. 1

14. **Assertion A** : Human being has a complex respiratory system.

Reason R : Human skin is impermeable to gases. 1

SECTION - B

15. What is nuclear fusion reaction? List any two advantages of nuclear fusion reactions. 3

16. State the laws of refraction of light. If the speed of light in vacuum is 3×10^8 m/s find the absolute refractive index of a medium in which light travels with a speed of 1.4×10^8 m/s. 3

OR

Which spherical mirror is used as the following and why?

(a) Shaving mirror

(b) Rear view mirror in vehicles

(c) Reflectors in search lights 3

17. Define the term decomposition reaction. Give one example each of thermal decomposition and electrolytic decomposition. **3**

OR

On adding a drop of barium chloride solution to an aqueous solution of sodium sulphite, white precipitate is obtained. **3**

(a) Write a balanced chemical equation of the reaction involved.

(b) What other name can be given to this precipitation reaction?

(c) On adding dilute hydrochloric acid to the reaction mixture, white precipitate disappears. Why?

18. Draw longitudinal section of a bisexual flower and label the following parts on it:

(a) Anther **(b)** Ovary **(c)** Stigma **(d)** Style **3**

19. Answer the following questions:

(a) List a distinguishing feature between the resistance and resistivity of a conductor.

(b) A wire is stretched so that its length becomes 6/5 times its original length. If its original resistance is 25 ohm, find its new resistance and resistivity. **3**

20. A student has been collecting silver coins and copper coins. One day, she observed a black coating on silver coins and a green coating on copper coins. Which chemical phenomenon is responsible for these coatings? Write the chemical name of black and green coatings. **3**

21. A person is taking the insulin injection every day.

(a) Name the disease he is suffering from.

(b) Mention the hormone whose imbalance has caused this disease.

(c) What changes can you make in the life style of the patient to help him/her control this disease? **3**

22. Can a freely suspended current carrying solenoid stay in any direction? Justify your answer. What will happen when the direction of current in the solenoid is reversed? Explain. **3**

23. Answer the following questions:

(a) In the following reactions, name the reactants which undergo oxidation and reduction:

(i) $CuO(s) + H_2(g) \longrightarrow Cu(s) + H_2O(g)$

(ii) $CuO(s) + Zn(s) \longrightarrow ZnO(s) + Cu(s)$

(b) Also state one industrial application of reduction. **3**

24. What is water harvesting? How can this technique be used in the conservation of water? **3**

OR

What is wildlife? How is wildlife important for us? **3**

SECTION - C

25. What are the differences between aerobic and anaerobic respiration? Name some organisms that use anaerobic mode of respiration. Name the final product obtained in anaerobic respiration if it takes place in a plant (like yeast). **5**

OR

What are the necessary conditions for autotrophic nutrition and what are its by-products? Where do plants get each of the raw materials required for photosynthesis? **5**

26. Answer the following questions:

(a) What is dispersion of white light? What is the cause of such dispersion? Draw a diagram, to show the dispersion of white light by a glass prism.

(b) A glass prism is able to produce a spectrum when white light passes through it but a glass slab does not produce any spectrum. Explain why it is so. **5**

27. Account for the following:

(a) State the relation between hydrogen ion concentration of an aqueous solution and its pH.

(b) An aqueous solution has a pH value of 7.0. Is this solution acidic, basic and neutral?

(c) Which has a higher pH value, 1 M HCl or 1 M NaOH solution?

(d) Tooth enamel is one of the hardest substances in our body. How does it undergo damage due to eating chocolates and sweets? What should we do to prevent it?

(e) How do $[H^+]$ ions exist in nature? **5**

OR

(a) A student prepared solutions of (i) an acid and (ii) a base in two separate beakers. She forgot to label the solutions and litmus paper is not available in the laboratory. Since, both the solutions are colourless, how will she distinguish between the two? **5**

(b) What is an olfactory indicator? Name two olfactory indicators. What is the effect of adding sodium hydroxide solution to these olfactory indicators?

28. Answer the following questions:

(a) Two carbon compounds X and Y have the molecular formula C_4H_8 and C_5H_{12} respectively. Which one of these is most likely to show addition reaction? Justify your answer. Also give the chemical equation to explain the process of addition reaction in this case.

(b) Give reasons why carbon compounds:

(i) Generally have low melting and boiling points

(ii) Do not conduct electricity in molten state **5**

29. A household uses the following electric appliances:

(a) Refrigerator of rating 400 W for 10 h each day

(b) Two electric fans of rating 80 W each for 6 h daily

(c) Six electric tubes of rating 18 W each for 6 h daily

Calculate electricity bill for the household for month of June if cost of electrical energy is 3 per unit. **5**

OR

(a) State the physical quantity which is equal to the ratio of potential difference and current. Define its SI unit

(b) Find the equivalent resistance across the two ends A and B of this circuit.

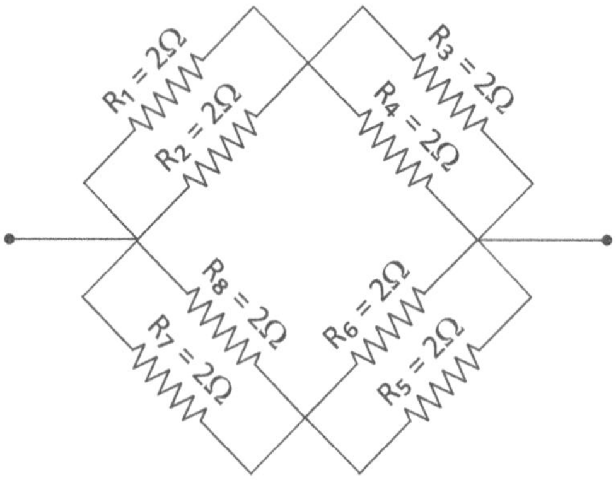

5

30. Answer the following questions:

(a) Why did Mendel choose garden pea plant for his experiments? Write two reasons.

(b) List two contrasting visible characters of garden pea Mendel used for his experiment.

(c) Explain how Mendel interpreted his results to show that the traits may be dominant or recessive. **5**

SOLUTION

3

CBSE - Class 10

SECTION - A

1. Lateral inversion is the phenomenon in which the right side of an object appears to be the left side in its image in a plane mirror. **1**

2. Hydra and Planaria are two simple **organism having the ability of regeneration**. **1**

3. **(a)** a (size decreases from left to right in a period). **1**

3. **(b)** k (valency of k = 3; valency of o = 1). **1**

3. **(c)** i (metallic character decreases from left to right in a period). **1**

3. **(d)** f (or n) **1**

4. **(a)** Ohm's law **1**

4. **(b)** Potential difference = Current × Resistance **1**

4. **(c)** **(iv)** 1Ω **1**

Explanation: The maximum resistance is obtained when resistors are connected in series combination.

Thus equivalent resistance obtained by connecting five resistors of resistance 1/5 Ω each, in series = (1/5 + 1/5 + 1/5 + 1/5) = 1Ω

(d) (i) $\frac{\text{Work done}}{\text{Current} \times \text{Time}}$ **1**

Explanation:

Work done = Charge × Potential difference

⇒ Work done = (Current × Time) × Potential difference

[∵ Charge = Current × Time]

⇒ Potential difference

$= \frac{\text{Work done}}{\text{Current} \times \text{Time}}$

5. **(iv)** Weak acid and strong base. **1**

Explanation: Sodium carbonate (Na_2CO_3) is the salt of carbonic acid (H_2CO_3) and sodium hydroxide (NaOH). Here NaOH is a strong base and carbonic acid is a weak acid.

OR

(i) Basic **1**

Explanation: Calcium phosphate $Ca_3(PO_4)_2$ is a salt of weak acid and strong base so it is a basic salt.

$$\underset{\text{Calcium hydroxide}}{3Ca(OH)_2} + \underset{\text{Phosphoric acid}}{2H_3PO_4} \longrightarrow \underset{\text{Calcium phosphate}}{Ca_3(PO_4)_2} + 6H_2O$$

6. **(ii)** Alveoli of lungs **1**

Explanation: An alveolar sac is made up of simple squamous epithelium and is surrounded by blood capillaries. Thin walls and increased surface area favor the gaseous exchange which takes place between the oxygen rich alveolar air and the carbon dioxide rich blood in the capillaries at alveolar surface. Oxygen diffuses across the alveolar and capillary walls to enter bloodstream, while carbon dioxide diffuses from the blood across these walls to enter the alveoli.

OR

(i) Valves in heart **1**

Explanation: Valves ensure that blood does not flow backwards when the atria or ventricles contract.

Semilunar valves, the valves present between ventricles and their attached vessels, serve to prevent the backflow of blood to ventricles from their respective attached vessels. Likewise, atrioventricular (AV) valve between atrium and ventricle directs the flow of blood and prevents any backflow into atria.

7. (ii) very near to the focus of the reflector **1**

Explanation: In torches, search lights and headlights of vehicles, the bulb is placed very near to the focus of the reflector (or concave mirror). It is due the reason that light rays after falling on reflecting surface become parallel to the principal axis of the mirror, and a concentrated beam of light is obtained.

8. (i) the people who live in urban areas **1**

Explanation: People living in urban areas do not directly contribute in the management of forests. Thus, they are not the direct stakeholders.

9. (iii) Carbon **1**

Explanation: Buckminsterfullerene is an allotrope of carbon with 60 carbon atoms which are joined together in a spherical shape.

10. (i) Testis → vas deferens → urethra **1**

Explanation: Vas deferens delivers sperms from testes to urethra coming from the urinary bladder.

11. (ii) Hepatitis **1**

Explanation: Hepatitis is water borne viral disease.

12. (ii) less of carbon but more of hydrogen **1**

Explanation: The fuel with the highest calorific value would have less carbon and more hydrogen, because hydrogen has a higher calorific value than carbon.

OR

(iv) Fossil Fuels **1**

Explanation: Large amount of fossil fuels are burnt every day in power stations to heat up water to produce steam which further runs the turbine to generate electricity.

13. (i) Both A and R are true and R is correct explanation of the assertion. **1**

Explanation: Blue colour of the sky is due to scattering of blue colour to the maximum extent by dust particles. Blue colour appears to be coming from the sky. Blue colour has the least wavelength. Hence, the correct option is (a).

14. (ii) Both Assertion and Reason are correct but the Reason is not the correct explanation of the Assertion. **1**

SECTION - B

15. Nuclear fusion reaction: The process in which nuclei of two or more light nuclei atoms fuse together to form a heavier nucleus along with the release of large energy is called nuclear fusion. **1**

Two advantages of nuclear fusion reactions are:

(a) There is barely any waste in this reaction *i.e.* the only byproduct of nuclear fusion is helium, which is safe and non toxic. **1**

(b) This reaction is highly energy efficient system *i.e.* energy released in nuclear fusion is much more than the energy released in nuclear fission reaction. **1**

16. The laws of refraction states that:

First law: The incident ray, the refracted ray and the normal to the surface separating the two media, all three lie in the same plane. **1**

Second law: The ratio of the sine of the angle of incidence to the sine of the angle of refraction is constant.

i.e. $\frac{\sin i}{\sin r} = \text{constant } (n)$ **1**

This constant is known as the relative refractive index of medium in which refracted ray travels with respect to the medium in which incident ray travels. It is denoted by '*n*'.

Refractive index of a medium

$$= \frac{\text{speed of light in vacuum}}{\text{speed of light in the medium}}$$

$$= \frac{3 \times 10^8}{1.4 \times 10^8}$$

$= 2.14$ 1

OR

The spherical mirror used in:

(a) Shaving mirror: Concave mirror. This is because when an object is placed close to a concave mirror, an erect and enlarged image of the object is formed. 1

(b) Rear view mirror in vehicles: Convex mirror. This is because this mirror forms an erect and diminished image of the object behind the vehicle giving a wide field of view. It means the driver of a vehicle can see the traffic over large area behind his vehicle. 1

(c) Reflectors in search lights: Concave mirror. This is because the beam of light after reflecting from the concave mirror emerges as a parallel beam of light which illuminates the road ahead of the vehicle. 1

17. **Decomposition Reaction:** It is a very simple type of chemical reaction in which a single compound breaks down into two or more simpler substances under suitable condition. 1

Thermal Decomposition (Thermolysis) reaction: Decomposition reactions which take place by absorption of heat.

Thermal decomposition of lead nitrate.

$$\underset{\text{Lead nitrate (white)}}{2Pb(NO_3)_2} \xrightarrow{\Delta} \underset{\text{Lead oxide (Yellow)}}{2PbO} + \underset{\text{Nitrogen dioxide (Brown fumes)}}{4NO_2} + \underset{\text{Oxygen}}{O_2}$$ 1

Electrolytic Decomposition (Electrolysis) reaction: Decomposition reactions where energy is supplied in the form of electricity.

Electrolytic decomposition of molten sodium chloride.

$$\underset{\text{Sodium chloride}}{2NaCl} \xrightarrow{\text{electricity}} \underset{\text{Sodium metal}}{2Na} + Cl_2$$ 1

OR

(a) $Na_2SO_3\,(aq) + BaCl_2\,(aq) \longrightarrow BaSO_3(s) + 2NaCl\,(aq)$ 1

(b) Double displacement reaction 1

(c) On adding dilute hydrochloric acid to the reaction mixture, white precipitate disappears. This is because addition of HCl dissolves the white precipitate of $BaSO_3$ and form soluble $BaCl_2$.

$BaSO_3(s) + 2HCl\,(aq) \longrightarrow BaCl_2\,(aq) + H_2O\,(l) + SO_2\,(g)$ 1

18. **Longitudinal section of a bisexual flower**

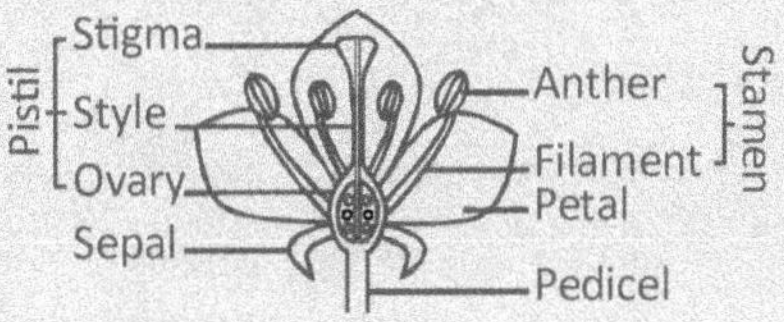

Diagram (1)
Labeling (2)

19. **(a) A distinguishing feature between the resistance and resistivity of a conductor:**

Resistance of a conductor depends on the length and area of cross-section of the conductor. On the other hand, resistivity depends upon the properties of the metal used in conductor. Unit of resistance is ohm and unit of resistivity is ohm-meter. 1

(b) We know that

$$R = \rho \frac{l}{A}.$$

So when length of wire increases, its area of cross-section decreases but its volume remains the same.

Volume $\quad V = Al$ or $A = \frac{V}{l}$

$$R = \rho \frac{l}{A} = \rho \frac{l^2}{V}$$

Increasing l by 6/5, we get

$$l' = \frac{6}{5}l$$

This gives $R' = \rho\frac{l'^2}{V} = \frac{36}{25}R$

Now, $R = 25$ Ohm

Therefore,

New resistance $R' = \frac{36}{25} \times 25$

$= 36$ Ohm. 1

Resistivity is independent of its length and area of cross-section, therefore new resistivity will be same. 1

20. The phenomenon is called corrosion. 1

Black coating on silver coins is silver sulphide formed due to attack of H_2S gas present in the atmosphere on the silver.

$$\underset{\text{Silver}}{2Ag(s)} + \underset{\text{Hydrogen sulphide}}{H_2S(g)} \longrightarrow \underset{\text{Silver sulphide}}{Ag_2S(s)} + \underset{\text{Hydrogen}}{H_2(g)}$$ 1

Green coating on copper coins is basic copper carbonate formed due to attack of moist air (CO_2, O_2 and H_2O vapours) on copper.

$$\underset{\text{Copper}}{2Cu} + \underbrace{CO_2 + O_2 + H_2O}_{\text{Moist air}} \longrightarrow \underset{\text{Basic copper carbonate}}{CuCO_3.Cu(OH)_2}$$ 1

21. A person is taking the insulin injection every day.

(a) The disease he is suffering from is Diabetes (Type – II) 1

(b) The hormone whose imbalance has caused this disease is Insulin as it controls the metabolism of sugar. 1

(c) Diabetes is a metabolic disease and can be controlled with balanced diet and regular exercise. 1

22. Solenoid is a closely bound cylindrical coil of insulated metallic wire. A current carrying freely suspended solenoid behaves like a magnet and when suspended freely, it rests in north-south direction. 1

A current carrying solenoid behaves like a bar magnet with fixed polarities at its ends. The end of the current carrying solenoid at which the current flows anticlockwise behaves as a north pole while that end at which the direction of current is clockwise behaves as a south pole. The direction of magnetic field is always perpendicular to the direction of current flow and the magnitude of the magnetic field inside a solenoid is directly proportional to the current flowing through the solenoid. 1½

Thus, when the current through the solenoid is reversed, the direction of magnetic field is reversed. ½

23. (a) Oxidation is loss of electrons and reduction is gain of electrons.

(i) The reactants are copper oxide_ and hydrogen. Copper has gained 2 electrons and each hydrogen atom has lost 1 electron. So copper has been reduced and hydrogen has been oxidized. 1

(ii) The reactants are copper oxide and zinc. Copper has gained 2 electrons and zinc atom has lost 2 electrons. So, copper has been reduced and zinc has been oxidized. 1

(b) One industrial application of reduction: In industries, metallic ores are reduced to obtain the metal from them. For example Calcium carbonate is reduced in industries to get CaO and CO_2. 1

24. Water harvesting: Water harvesting refers to all the processes and steps that are taken for scientific conservation of fresh water. 1

Water harvesting helps in the conservation of water as:

(a) It increases the ground water resources as its purpose is not to hold rainwater on the surface of the earth but to make rainwater percolate under the ground so as to recharge groundwater. 1

(b) It reduces storm water discharge and overloading of sewage treatment plants. 1

OR

Wildlife: It means all those naturally occurring animals, plants and their species, which are not cultivated, domesticated and tamed. **1**

Wildlife is important to us because:

(a) It maintains ecological balance in nature.

(b) It also maintains the forests by facilitating growth of plants in different places by dispersing of seeds.

(c) They provide great aesthetic value for human beings as they are a symbol of national pride and represent the cultural heritage.

(d) Wildlife enhance the natural beauty of the earth.

(e) Scientists have gained knowledge by studying wildlife and also discovered various medicinal products. **2**

SECTION - C

25. Differences between aerobic and anaerobic respiration.

Aerobic Respirations	Anaerobic Respirations
1. Aerobic respiration takes place in the presence of oxygen.	1. Anaerobic respiration takes place in the absence of oxygen.
2. In Aerobic respiration complete break-down (oxidation) of food takes place.	2. In Anaerobic respiration partial breakdown (oxidation) of food occurs.
3. End products of Aerobic respiration are carbon dioxide and water.	3. End products of Anaerobic respiration are ethyl alcohol (or lactic acid) and carbon dioxide
4. Large amount of energy is released.	4. Small amount of energy is released.

3

Some **organisms that use anaerobic mode of respiration** are yeast and human beings (muscles). **1**

The **final product obtained in anaerobic respiration,** if it takes place in a plant (like yeast), are ethanol and carbon dioxide accompanied by small amount of energy. **1**

OR

For autotrophic nutrition to take place, **the conditions necessary** are light, chlorophyll, carbon dioxide and water. **1**

The major by-product of the autotrophic nutrition is oxygen which is released through stomata into the air and carbohydrate (food) which is stored in the plant as starch. **1**

Autotrophic nutrition involves making of food by green plants by the process of photosynthesis using the following necessary conditions:

(a) Chlorophyll is present in the living cells of the leaves.

(b) Supply of water to green parts or cells of the plant either through roots or by surrounding environment.

(c) Availability of sufficient amount of sunlight to provide light energy required to carry out photosynthesis.

(d) Sufficient supply of carbon dioxide which is one of the important components for the formation of carbohydrates during photosynthesis. Stomata in leafs allow the carbon dioxide gas to enter into the plant. **3**

26. **(a) Dispersion of white light:** The phenomena of splitting up of white light into seven colours on passing through a transparent medium like a glass prism is called dispersion of light. 1

Causes of such dispersion: When a white light passes through a glass prism, different constituent colours come out of the prism at different angles.This gives rise to the dispersion of white light. 1

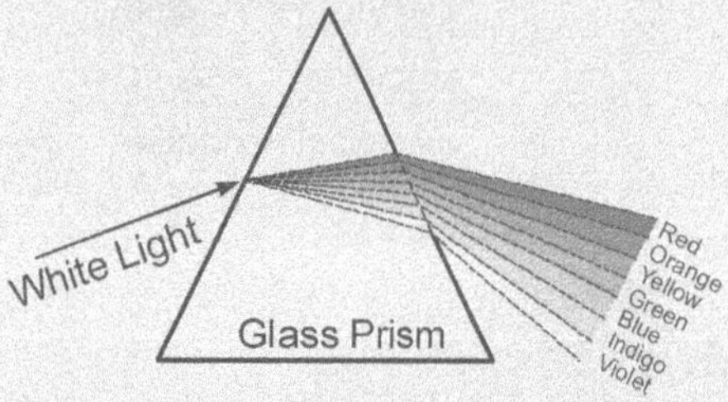

1

(b) A glass prism is able to produce a spectrum when white light passes through it but a glass slab does not produce any spectrum. This is because when white light enters the glass slab, dispersion of light takes place. The angle of refraction for violet colour is more than the red colour on entering the glass slab. But all colours of light return to the original direction of propagation while refracting from other side of the glass slab and thus white light emerges out of the glass slab without producing any spectrum. 2

27. **(a) Relation between hydrogen ion concentration of an aqueous solution and its pH:** If H^+ ion concentration is more, pH will be less because pH of a solution is inversely proportional to H^+ ions concentration.

If $[H^+] = 10^{-x}$ M,

then pH $= x$ 1

(b) An aqueous solution has a pH value of 7.0. The solution is neutral. 1

(c) 1 M HCl means

$$[H^+] = 10^0 \text{ M}$$

Therefore

$$\text{pH} = 0$$

1 M NaOH means

$$[OH^-] = 1 \text{ M}$$

Therefore

$$[H^+] = \frac{10^{-14}}{[OH^-]} = 10^{-14} \text{ M}$$

$$\text{pH} = 14$$

Hence, 1 M NaOH solution has more pH value. 1

(d) Tooth enamel is made up of calcium phosphate which gets corroded when the pH in the mouth is below 5.5. Bacteria present in the mouth produce acids by degradation of sugar and food particles in the mouth after eating. It can be prevented by using Tooth pastes, which are basic. 1

(e) H^+ ions do not exist independently as it gains the unshared electron pairs on the oxygen in the water molecule to form a hydronium ion.

$$H^+ + H_2O \longrightarrow H_3O^+$$ 1

OR

(a) Other then litmus paper, pH indicators can also be used to distinguish between an acidic and an alkaline solution. Some common pH indicators are methyl orange, phenolphthalein. They show characteristic colour change in acidic and alkaline medium.

Some natural indicators such as turmeric, red cabbage juice can also used to identify acidic and alkaline behavior of solutions.

pH Indicator	Colour in acidic medium	Colour in basic medium
Phenolphthalein	Colourless	Pink
Methyl Orange	Red/Pink	Yellow
Turmeric	Yellow	Reddish Brown

2

(b) **Olfactory Indicators:** Substances which change their smell when mixed with acid or base are known as olfactory indicators. **1**

Two olfactory indicators are onion and vanilla. **1**

When sodium hydroxide solution is added to an olfactory indicator it loses its characteristic smell. **1**

28. **(a)** Compound X has the molecular formula = C_4H_8 (C_nH_{2n}, alkene)

Compound Y has the molecular formula = C_5H_{12} (C_nH_{2n+2} , alkane)

C_4H_8 is unsaturated hydrocarbon, *i.e.* alkene (butene) and C_5H_{12} is a saturated hydrocarbon *i.e.* alkane (pentane). **1**

Saturated compounds undergo substitution reaction. Unsaturated compounds undergo addition reaction at the multiple bonds. **1**

For example:

1- butene and 2-butene will add a chlorine molecule (Cl_2) to form 1,2-dichlorobutane and 2,3-dichlorobutane, respectively. The reaction will be:

$$CH_3—CH_2—CH{=}CH_2 + Cl_2 \rightarrow CH_3—CH_2—CH(Cl)—CH_2Cl$$

Or

$$CH_3—CH{=}CH—CH_3 + Cl_2 \rightarrow CH_3—CH(Cl)—CH(Cl)—CH_3$$ **1**

(b) **(i)** **Carbon compounds generally have low melting and boiling points** because the force of attraction between the molecules of carbon compounds is not very strong. These weak intermolecular forces make them very easy to pull apart from each other. Since they are easy to separate, carbon compounds have low melting and boiling points. **1**

(ii) **Carbon compounds do not conduct electricity in the molten state** because bonding in carbon compounds does not involve any formation of ions and thus there are no free electrons that can conduct electricity. **1**

29. **(a)** Energy consumed by refrigerator of rating 400 W for ten hours each day

$$= \text{Power} \times \text{time}$$

$$E = P \times t$$

$$= 400\ \text{W} \times 10\ \text{h}$$

$$= 4000\ \text{Wh} = 4\ \text{kWh}$$ **1**

(b) Energy consumed by two electric fans of rating 80 W each for twelve hours each day is

$$E = 2 \times P \times t$$

$$= 2 \times 80\ \text{W} \times 12\ \text{h}$$

$$= 1920\ \text{Wh} = 1.92\ \text{kWh}$$ **1**

(c) Energy consumed by six electric tubes of rating 18 W each for 6 hours each day is

$$E = 6 \times P \times t$$

$$= 6 \times 18\ \text{W} \times 6\ \text{h}$$

$$= 648\ \text{Wh} = 0.648\ \text{kWh}$$ **1**

Therefore **Total energy consumed by appliances in one day**

$$= 4\ \text{kWh} + 1.92\text{kWh} + 0.648\ \text{kWh}$$

$$= 6.568\ \text{kWh}$$

Total energy consumed in the month of June (30 days)

$$= 6.568 \times 30\ \text{kWh} = 197.04\ \text{unit}$$ **1**

Cost of 1 unit

= ₹ 3.00

Cost of 197.04 units

= ₹ 3.00 × 197.04 = ₹ 591.12

Thus, the electricity bill of month of June = ₹ 591.12 **1**

OR

(a) The physical quantity which is equal to the ratio of potential difference and current is Electrical Resistance R. Its SI unit is ohm (Ω).

$$1\ \text{ohm} = \frac{1\ \text{volt}}{1\ \text{ampere}}$$

The resistance of a conductor is said to be one ohm, if the potential difference applied across its ends is 1 volt and a current of 1 A flow through it. **2**

(b) $$\frac{1}{R_{1,2}} = \frac{1}{R_1} + \frac{1}{R_2}$$

$$= \frac{1}{2} + \frac{1}{2} = \frac{2}{2} = 1\Omega$$

$$R_{1,2} = 1\Omega$$

Similarly,

$$R_{3,4} = 1\Omega$$

$$R_{5,6} = 1\Omega$$

$$R_{7,8} = 1\Omega$$

Now $R_{1,2}$ and $R_{3,4}$ are connected in series

$$R_{1,2,3,4} = R_{1,2} + R_{3,4}$$

$$= 1 + 1 = 2\Omega$$ **1**

Also, $R_{5,6}$ and $R_{7,8}$ are connected in series

$$R_{5,6,7,8} = R_{5,6} + R_{7,8}$$

$$= 1 + 1 = 2\Omega$$ **1**

Now, equivalent resistance

$$\frac{1}{R} = \frac{1}{R_{1,2,3,4}} + \frac{1}{R_{5,6,7,8}}$$

$$= \frac{1}{2} + \frac{1}{2} = \frac{2}{2} = 1\Omega$$

Thus, we can say that the equivalent resistance between A and B is 1Ω. **1**

30. (a) Mendel choose garden pea plant for his experiments because

- Pea plant has several contrasting characters like height, flower colour, seed colour and shape.
- Normally allows self pollination but cross pollination can also be done.
- It has short life span and also is easy to cultivate. **1½**

(b) Contrasting characters of garden pea plants:

Colour of seeds:

Dominant – Yellow

Recessive – Green

Shape of seeds:

Dominant – Round

Recessive – Wrinkled. **1**

(c) Mendel took pea plants with different characteristics – a pure breed tall plant and a pure breed dwarf plant. Pure breed plant means, both versions of a trait are identical.

(i) Pure tall pea plant (TT) - Both trait T are identical, which represents tallness in the plant.

(ii) Pure dwarf pea plant (tt) - Both trait t are identical, which represents dwarfness in the plant.

He produced progeny from them by cross pollination of TT and tt plants and calculated the percentages of tall or short progeny. He observed that all F1 generations of plants were tall. Mendel allowed only self-pollination in F1 progeny. He found that in F2 progeny 75% plants were tall and only 25% plants were dwarf.

The result of his experiment shows that trait may be dominant or recessive.

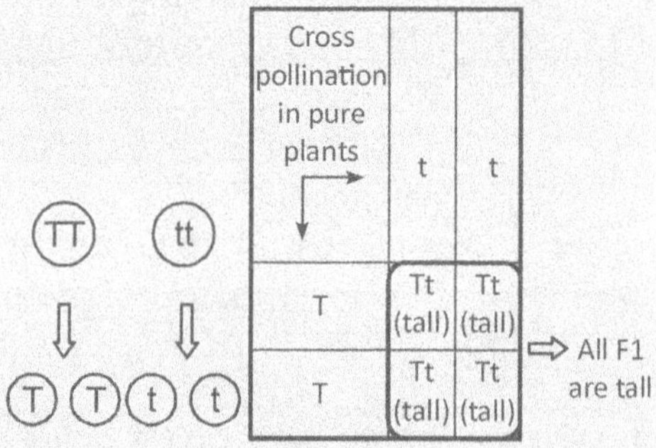

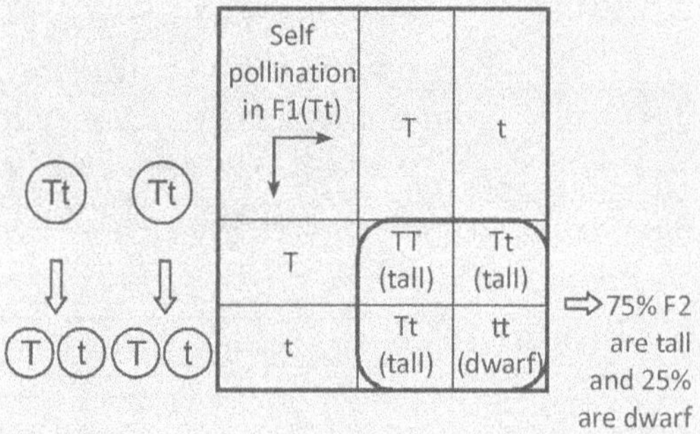

2½

4

SAMPLE PAPER

CBSE - Class 10

SCIENCE

Time Allowed: 3 Hours *Maximum Marks: 80*

General Instructions:

i. The question paper comprises three sections – A, B and C. Attempt all the sections.
ii. All questions are compulsory.
iii. Internal choice is given in each section.
iv. All questions in Section A are one-mark questions comprising MCQ, VSA type and assertion-reason type questions. They are to be answered in one word or in one sentence.
v. All questions in Section B are three-mark, short-answer type questions. These are to be answered in about 50 - 60 words each.
vi. All questions in Section C are five-mark, long-answer type questions. These are to be answered in about 80 - 90 words each.
vii. This question paper consists of a total of 30 questions.

SECTION - A

1. The atomic radii of three elements A, B and C of a periodic table are 186 pm, 104 pm and 143 pm respectively. Giving a reason, arrange these elements in the increasing order of atomic numbers in the period. **1**

2. Name one substance which is produced in anaerobic respiration by an organism but not in aerobic respiration. **1**

3. **Answer question numbers 3(a)-3(d) on the basis of your understanding of the following paragraph and the related studied concepts.**

A chemical bond is an attractive force that holds the atoms together in a molecule or a compound. The element carbon is known to have the unique ability to form bonds with other similar atoms or atoms of other elements. This property of carbon has resulted in its having very large number of compounds. The carbon-carbon band is also known to be very strong and hence stable. Answer the following questions based on the given information:

3(a) Name the chemical bond formed between carbon-carbon atoms. **1**

3(b) How is this bond formed? **1**

3(c) Why are carbon and its compounds used as fuels for most applications? **1**

3(d) Name two allotropes of carbon. **1**

4. **Question numbers 4(a)-4(d) are based on the table given below. Study this table and answer the questions that follow about metals A, B, C and D.**

Samples of four metals A, B, C and D were taken and added to the following solution one by one. The results obtained have been tabulated as follows:

Metal	Iron sulphate	Copper sulphate	Zinc sulphate	Silver nitrate
A.	No reaction	Displacement		
B.	Displacement		No reaction	
C.	No reaction	No reaction	No reaction	Displacement
D.	No reaction	No reaction	No reaction	No reaction

4(a) Which is the most reactive metal?

(i) A | **(ii)** B

(iii) C | **(iv)** D — 1

4(b) The metal which is stored in kerosene:

(i) Phosphorus | **(ii)** Magnesium

(iii) Sodium | **(iv)** Magnesium — 1

4(c) What would you observe if B is added to a solution of copper (II) sulphate? 1

4(d) Arrange the metals A, B, C and D in the order of decreasing reactivity. 1

5. The filtration units of kidneys are called:

(i) Ureter | **(ii)** Urethra

(iii) Neurons | **(iv)** Nephrons — 1

6. You are given water, mustard oil, glycerine and kerosene. In which of these media, a ray of light incident obliquely at some angle would bend the most?

(i) Kerosene | **(ii)** Water

(iii) Mustard oil | **(iv)** Glycerine — 1

7. Which of the following statement is incorrect:

(i) economic development is linked to environmental conservation

(ii) sustainable development meets the current basic human needs and also preserves resources for future generations

(iii) sustainable development does not take into consideration the viewpoints of all stakeholders

(iv) sustainable development is a long planned and persistent development — 1

8. According to Mendeleev's periodic law, the elements were arranged in the periodic table in the order of:

(i) Increasing atomic number | **(ii)** Decreasing atomic number

(iii) Increasing atomic masses | **(iv)** Decreasing atomic masses — 1

OR

In Mendeleev's periodic table, gaps were left for the elements to be discovered later. Which of the following elements found a place in the periodic table later?

(i) Germanium | **(ii)** Chlorine

(iii) Oxygen | **(iv)** Silicon — 1

9. A cross between a tall plant (TT) and short pea plant (tt) resulted in progeny that were all tall plants because:

(i) Tallness is the dominant trait

(ii) Shortness is the dominant trait

(iii) Tallness is the recessive trait

(iv) Height of pea plant is not governed by gene 'T' or 't' — 1

10. Offspring formed as a result of sexual reproduction exhibit more variations because:

(i) Sexual reproduction is a lengthy process

(ii) Genetic material comes from two parents of the same species

(iii) Genetic material comes from two parents of different species

(iv) Genetic material comes from many parents **1**

OR

Reproduction is essential for living organisms to order to:

(i) Keep the individual organism alive

(ii) Fulfill their energy requirement

(iii) Maintain growth

(iv) Continue the species generation after generation **1**

11. Electrical resistivity of a given metallic wire depends upon:

(i) Its length **(ii)** Its thickness

(iii) Its shape **(iv)** Nature of the material **1**

OR

The instrument used for measuring electric current is :

(i) galvanometer **(ii)** ammeter

(iii) voltmeter **(iv)** potentiometer **1**

12. The size of the pupil of the eye is adjusted by:

(i) cornea **(ii)** ciliary muscles

(iii) optic nerve **(iv)** iris **1**

For question numbers 13 and 14, two statements are given-one labeled Assertion (A) and the other labeled Reason (R). Select the correct answer to these questions from the codes (i), (ii), (iii) and (iv) as given below:

(i) Both A and R are true and R is correct explanation of the assertion.

(ii) Both A and R are true but R is not the correct explanation of the assertion.

(iii) A is true but R is false.

(iv) A is false but R is true.

13. **Assertion A :** Pupil is black in colour. **1**

Reason R : Pupil is black in colour as no light is reflected in it.

14. **Assertion A :** Concave mirrors are used as reflectors in torches, vehicle headlights and in search lights. **1**

Reason R : When an object is placed beyond the centre of curvature of a concave mirror, the image formed is real and inverted.

SECTION - B

15. Answer the following questions:

(a) What is meant by vegetative propagation?

(b) List four advantages of vegetative propagation. **3**

16. A student wants to project the image of a candle flame on a screen 60cm in front of a mirror by keeping the flame at a distance of 15cm from its pole.

(a) State the type of the mirror.

(b) Find the linear magnification of the image produced.

(c) Find the distance between the object and its image. **3**

OR

A divergent lens has a focal length of 20cm. At what distance should an object be placed so that the image is formed 10 cm away from the lens. What is the magnification produced by the lens? **3**

17. The farmers have been cultivating a food plant X for over two thousand years and have produced as many as five entirely different looking vegetables A, B, C, D and E from it.

(a) What could be the plant X? Based upon the evidence, explain your choice.

(b) What are A, B, C, D and E? Based upon the evidence, explain your choice.

(c) What is the process of evolution involved in this example known as? **3**

18. Study the following circuit and answer the questions that follows:

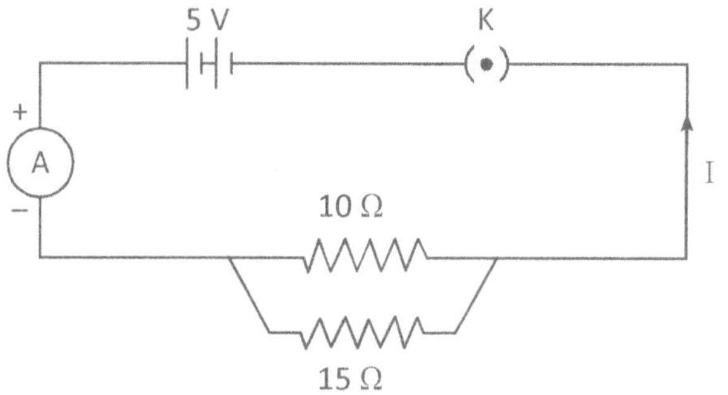

(a) State the type of combination of two resistors in the circuit.

(b) How much current is flowing through **(i)** 10 ohms and **(ii)** 15 ohms resistor?

(c) What is the ammeter reading? **3**

19. Identify the type of chemical reaction in the following statements and define each of them:

(a) Digestion of food in our body

(b) Rusting of iron

(c) Heating of manganese dioxide with aluminium powder **3**

OR

What do you mean by endothermic and exothermic reactions? Which among the following changes are exothermic or endothermic in nature?

(a) Decomposition of ferrous sulphate.

(b) Dilution of an acid.

(c) Dissolution of ammonium chloride in water.

(d) Sublimation of camphor (crystals). **3**

20. Answer the following questions:

(a) What is the principle of electric motor?

(b) What is the role of split ring in an electric motor? **3**

21. "It is possible that a trait is inherited but may not be expresse(iv)" Give a suitable example to justify this statement. **3**

OR

Cite the evidence on the basis of which it is concluded that birds have evolved from reptiles. **3**

22. Answer the following questions:

(a) Predict which of the following elements will form cation and which will form anions?

(i) Na **(ii)** Al **(iii)** Cl **(iv)** O **3**

(b) Also name two elements that are inert in nature. **3**

23. Rahul wants to build up his body very quickly without following right exercise regime and balanced diet. Instead he started eating readymade food supplement.

(a) In your opinion was the step taken by Rahul is right? Justify your answer.

(b) What are the harmful effects of taking artificial health supplement without consulting a physician? **3**

24. Answer the following questions:

(a) A knife, which is used to cut a fruit, was immediately dipped into water containing drops of blue litmus solution. If the colour of the solution is changed to red, what inference can be drawn about the nature of the fruit and why?

(b) How is the strength of an acid affected when some water is added to it? **3**

SECTION - C

25. Name the hormone which regulates carbohydrate, protein and fat metabolism in our body. Which gland secrets this hormone? Why is it important for us to have iodized salt in our diet? Name the disease caused due to deficiency of iodine and mention its main symptom. **5**

26. Answer the following questions:

(a) Write the chief ore of iron. Write its formula.

(b) What do you mean by concentration of ore? What is gangue?

(c) Draw labeled diagram for electrolytic refining of copper metal. **5**

27. A beam of white light falling on a glass prism gets split up into seven colours marked 1 to 7 as shown in the diagram:

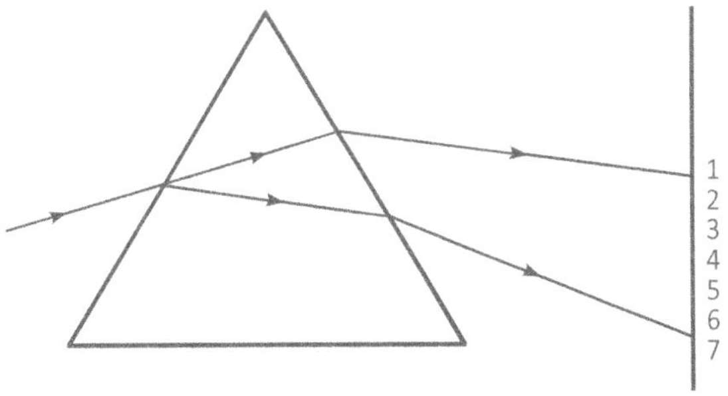

(a) The colour at position marked 3-and 5 are similar to the colour of the sky and the colour of gold metal respectively. Is the above statement made by the student correct or incorrect? Justify.

(b) Which of the above shown positions corresponds approximately to the colour of:

(i) a solution of potassium permanganate?

(ii) danger or stop signal lights? **5**

28. Answer the following questions:

(a) What is solenoid? Draw field lines of the magnetic field through and around a current-carrying solenoid.

(b) If field lines of a magnetic field are crossed at a point, what does it indicate? **5**

OR

How does a solenoid behave like a magnet? Can you determine the north and south poles of a current–carrying solenoid with the help of a bar magnet? Explain. **5**

29. Why certain compounds are called hydrocarbons? Write the general formula for homologous series of alkanes, alkenes and alkynes and also draw the structure of the member of each series. Write the name of the reaction that converts alkenes into alkanes and also write a chemical equation to show the necessary conditions for the reaction to occur. **5**

OR

Distinguish between esterification and saponification reactions with the help of the chemical equations for each. State one use of each:

(i) Esters **(ii)** Saponification process **5**

30. Answer the following questions:

(a) What is Chipko movement?

(b) Why should we conserve forests?

(c) List four stakeholders which may be useful in the conservation of forests. **5**

OR

Answer the following:

(a) What is meant by rainwater harvesting?

(b) What are the various advantages of water stored in ground? **5**

4

SOLUTION

CBSE - Class 10

SECTION - A

1. Since atomic size decreases along a period and the atomic number increases. So, the element with smaller radii, has the highest atomic number. **1**

   Hence, B has the highest atomic number followed by C and A

   i.e. A < C < B **1**

2. Substance which is produced in anaerobic respiration but not in aerobic respiration is Ethanol. **1**

3. **(a)** Covalent bond is formed between carbon-carbon atoms. **1**

3. **(b)** They are formed by the sharing of electrons. **1**

3. **(c)** Most of the carbon compounds give a lot of heat and light when burnt in air. Saturated hydrocarbons burn with a clean flame and no smoke is produced. The carbon compounds, used as a fuel, have high caloric values. Therefore, carbon and its compounds are used as fuels for most applications. **1**

3. **(d)** (i) Diamond, (ii) Graphite **1**

4. **(a)** **(ii)** B **1**

   Explanation: Among A, B, C and D we can say that B is the most reactive metal.

3. **(b)** **(iii)** Sodium **1**

   Explanation: **Sodium** is a very reactive metal. It is **kept in kerosene** to prevent it from coming in contact with oxygen and moisture. If this happens, it will react with the moisture present in air and form **sodium** hydroxide. This is a strongly exothermic reaction, and lot of heat is generated.

   (c) If B is added to a solution of copper (II) sulphate, then it would displace copper as it is more reactive than copper.

   $B + CuSO_4$

   $\longrightarrow$ Displacement Reaction **1**

   (d) The arrangement of the metals in the order of decreasing reactivity is: B > A > C > D **1**

5. **(iv)** Nephrons **1**

   Explanation: Nephrons are the structural and functional filtration unit of a kidney that serves in filtration, reabsorption and secretion. Ureters are small muscular tubes that extend from the kidney and carry urine into the urinary bladder. The urethra is a canal that carries urine from bladder and expels it out of body. Neurons are structural and functional unit of nervous system.

6. **(iv)** Glycerine **1**

   Explanation: Out of the given four materials, the refractive index of glycerine is highest. So, greatest deviation of incident light ray is observed in case of glycerine.

7. **(iii)** Sustainable development does not take into consideration the viewpoints of all stakeholders. **1**

8. **(iii)** Increasing atomic masses **1**

Explanation: The Mendeleev's periodic law is an arrangement of elements in increasing order of their atomic masses as Mendeleev's periodic law states that, the physical and chemical properties of elements are a periodic function of their atomic masses.

OR

(i) Germanium **1**

Explanation: Germanium element found a place in the periodic table later in the place of Eka–silicon in Mendeleev's periodic table.

9. (i) Tallness is the dominant trait **1**

Explanation: According to law of dominance, a trait is represented by two contrasting factors of a gene in a heterozygous individual; the allele/ factor that can express itself in heterozygous individual is called as dominant trait. The other factor, whose effect is masked by presence of dominant factor, is called recessive factor.

10. (ii) Genetic material comes from two parents of the same species **1**

Explanation: Sexual reproduction produces genetic variations by meiosis during gamete formation and fertilization of male and female gametes.

OR

(iv) Continue the species generation after generation. **1**

Explanation: Reproduction serves to continue the species which would other-wise extinct due to struggle for survival and natural/accidental death of individuals.

11. (iv) Nature of the material **1**

Explanation: The resistivity of a material is constant for a particular temperature at a constant temperature. Resistivity of material does not depend on length, thickness and shape of the material. It only depends on the temperature.

OR

(ii) ammeter **1**

Explanation: The instrument used for measuring electric current is ammeter.

12. (iv) iris **1**

Explanation: The iris controls the size of the pupil.

13. (i) Both Assertion and Reason are correct and the Reason is the correct explanation of the Assertion. **1**

14. (ii) Both Assertion and Reason are correct but the Reason is not the correct explanation of the Assertion. **1**

SECTION - B

15. (a) Vegetative propagation: When a part of the plant – stem, root or leaf gets detached and develops into an independent individual, the process is referred to as vegetative propagation. Thus we see that in vegetative propagation, new plants are obtained from the parts of old plants without the help of any reproductive organs. **1**

(b) Advantages of vegetative propagation:

- The new plants produced will be exactly same like the parent plants. ½
- The trees grown from cutting or grafting start to bear fruits much earlier as compared to the trees that grow from seeds. ½
- Many plants can be grown from just one parent plant by this method. ½
- We can also get seedless plants by this method. ½

16. (a) Type of mirror: He should use concave mirror as it forms a real image on the same side of the mirror. **1**

(b) Flame is placed at 15cm distance from pole, so

Object distance,

$u = -15\text{cm}$

Screen is placed 60cm distance from its pole, so

Image distance,

$v = -60\text{cm}$

Now, magnification

$$= -\frac{\text{image distance}}{\text{object distance}}$$

$$= -\frac{v}{u} = -\frac{(-60\text{cm})}{(-15\text{cm})}$$

$$= -4$$

Hence, linear magnification of the image is −4 **1**

(c) Distance between the object and its image = distance of screen from pole − distance of object from pole = 60cm − 15cm = 45cm **1**

OR

Divergent lens is concave lens–

$f = -20$ cm

and $v = -10$ cm

because a concave lens always forms a virtual image on the same side as the object.

$$\frac{1}{f} = \frac{1}{v} - \frac{1}{u}$$

[Lens Formula]

$$-\frac{1}{20} = -\frac{1}{u} - \frac{1}{10}$$

$$-\frac{1}{u} = \frac{1}{10} - \frac{1}{20}$$

$$-\frac{1}{u} = \frac{2-1}{20}$$

$$-\frac{1}{u} = \frac{1}{20}$$

$u = -20$ cm **2**

$$m = \frac{v}{u} = -\frac{10}{-20} = \frac{1}{2}$$

$= 0.5$ **1**

Thus, object should be placed at a distance of 20 cm from the lens and magnification produced by the lens is 0.5

17. The farmers have been cultivating a food plant X for over two thousand years and have produced as many as five entirely different looking vegetables A, B, C, D and E from it.

(a) The plant X would be Wild cabbage. **1**

(b) A, B, C, D and E could be Cabbage, Broccoli, Cauliflower, Kohlrabi and Kale. **1**

(c) The process of evolution involved in this example is known as Artificial selection. **1**

18.

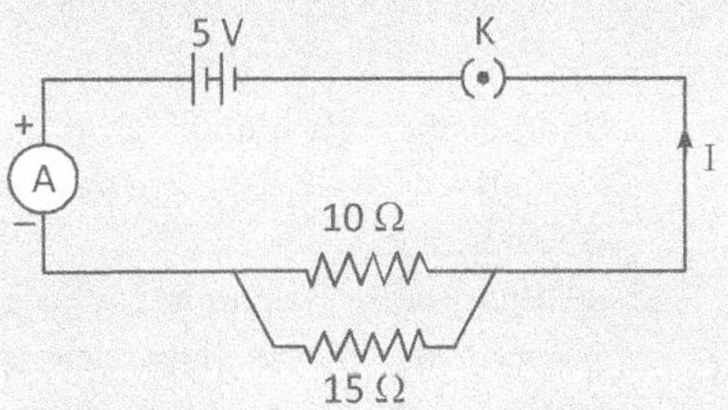

(a) Resistors in the circuit are connected in parallel combination. **½**

(b) (i) Let I_1 be the current flowing through R_1 = 10 ohm

Now $I_1R_1 = V$

$$I_1 = \frac{V}{R_1} = \frac{5}{10} = 0.5\text{A}$$ **1**

(ii) Let I_2 be the current flowing through R_2 = 15 ohm

Now $I_2R_2 = V$

$$I_2 = \frac{V}{R_2} = \frac{5}{15} = 0.33\text{A}$$ **1**

(c) Ammeter reading

$= I_1 + I_2$

$= 0.5\text{ A} + 0.33\text{ A}$

$= 0.83\text{ A}$ **½**

19. Type of chemical reaction in the following statements and define each of them:

(a) Digestion of food in our body is Decomposition reaction.

A decomposition reaction is a type of reaction in which a single compound breaks down into two or more elements or a new compound. **1**

(b) Rusting of iron is Oxidation Reaction.

Oxidation Reaction – Oxidation is the process which involves gain of oxygen or loss of hydrogen or which involves loss of electrons during a reaction. 1

(c) Heating of manganese dioxide with aluminium powder is Displacement Reaction.

A reaction in which the most reactive element displaces the less reactive element from its compound is known as Displacement Reaction. 1

OR

Exothermic Reaction: A chemical reaction in which heat is given out is known as exothermic reaction.

Endothermic Reaction: A chemical reaction in which heat energy is absorbed is known as endothermic reaction. 1

(a) Decomposition of ferrous sulphate is Endothermic reaction. ½

(b) Dilution of an acid is Exothermic Reaction. ½

(c) Dissolution of ammonium chloride in water is Endothermic reaction. ½

(d) Sublimation of camphor (crystals) is Endothermic reaction. ½

20. (a) Electric motor works on the principle that a current carrying conductor placed perpendicular to a magnetic field experiences a force. 1

(b) The split ring in an electric motor reverses the direction of current in the armature coil of the motor. Therefore, the direction of the force acting on the two arms of the coil is also reversed. As a result of this, the coil of motor continues to rotate in same direction. 2

21. It is possible that a trait is inherited but may not be expressed. This can be seen in the Mendel experiment. When pure tall pea plants are crossed with pure dwarf pea plants, only tall pea plants are obtained in F_1 generation. On crossing tall plants of F_1, both tall and dwarf plants are obtained in F_2 generation in the ratio 3:1. Reappearance of the dwarf character, a recessive trait in F_2 generation shows that the dwarf trait was present in individuals of F_1 but it did not got expressed, *i.e.* it was merely concealed or suppressed in the first generation to re–emerge in the second generation. 3

OR

Evidence on the basis of which it is concluded that birds have evolved from reptiles are:

(i) Fossils showing imprints of feathers along with the bones found in dinosaurs and reptiles are found.

(ii) The function of feathers initially was to provide insulation but later on they became useful for flight in birds only. Similarly, some dinosaurs had feathers, although they could not fly using the feathers.

(iii) Birds seem to have later adapted the feathers to flight. This, of course, means that birds are very closely related to reptiles, since dinosaurs were reptiles. 3

22. (a) Elements which will form cations: Na and Al (Sodium and Aluminium) 1

Elements which will form anions: Cl and O (Chlorine and Oxygen) 1

(b) He and Ne (Helium and Neon) are two inert elements 1

23. (a) In my opinion, Rahul is not doing right. If you don't eat a nutritious variety of food, some supplements might help us to get adequate amounts of only some of the essential nutrients. Supplements can't be substitute for the variety of foods that are present in a healthy diet for overall development of the body. 1

(b) There are many harmful effects of taking artificial health supplement without consulting a physician as this can lead to addiction and can lead to severe deficiency of some minerals and a spike in presence of some minerals in the body thereby leading to adverse affect on the health along with other side effects. Also supplements don't contain essential dietary fibers necessary for proper digestion which is provided by fresh food. 2

24. (a) The fruit may be a citrus fruit or its juice may contain an acid, which is why the traces of acid remained on the knife that turned the blue litmus red. 1½

(b) The strength of an acid decreases when some water is added to it as when we add water to an acid, the H^+ ion combines with water molecule thus producing hydronium ion (H_3O^+). As the proton (H^+) combines with water molecules, the concentration of free hydrogen ions gets reduced thereby reducing the strength of the acid. 1½

SECTION -C

25. The hormone which regulates carbohydrate, protein and fat metabolism in our body is thyroxine. 1

Thyroxine hormone is secreted by thyroid gland. 1

It is important for us to have iodized salt in our diet. This is because iodine is needed by the thyroid gland for the production thyroxin hormone. This hormone regulates fat, protein and carbohydrate metabolism in our body so as to produce the best balance for growth. So, if we take iodised salt, there can be no deficiency of iodine in the body. 1

The disease caused due to deficiency of iodine is goitre as there would be reduction in the formation of thyroxine hormone. 1

One of the main symptoms of this disease is that the neck of the person appears to be swollen. 1

26. (a) Chief ore of iron is haematite. Its formula is Fe_2O_3. 1

(b) Concentration of ore means removal of unwanted impurities from the ore. The earthy, sandy and rocky impurities associated with mineral are called gangue. 2

(c) Diagram for electrolytic refining of copper metal:

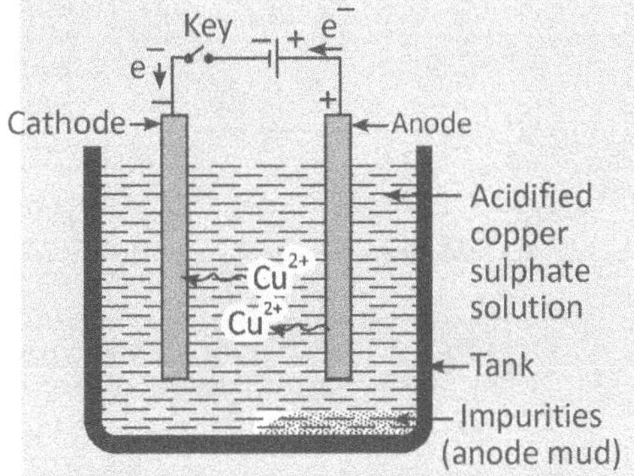

2

Electrolytic Refining of Copper Metal

27. A beam of white light falling on a glass prism gets split up into seven colours as shown in the diagram:

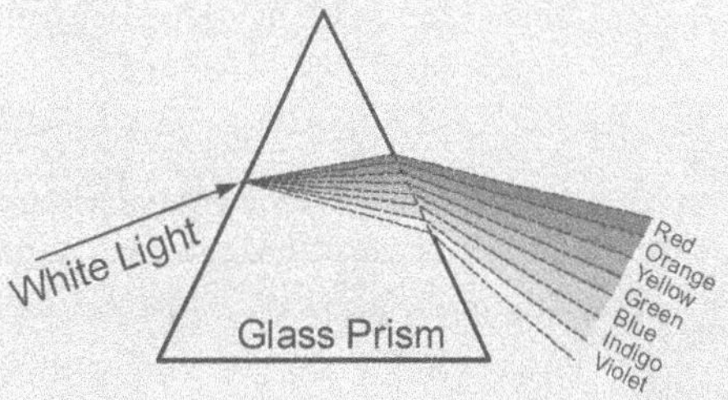

1

(a) The colours at position marked 3 and 5 are yellow and blue respectively. On, the other hand, student has identified them as blue and yellow. Hence the statement made by the student is incorrect. 2

(b) (i) Position 7 is the position of violet colour, which corresponds to the colour of a solution of potassium permanganate. 1

(ii) Position 1 is the position of red colour, which corresponds to the colour of 'danger' or stop signal lights. **1**

28. **(a)** **Solenoid**: A coil of many circular turns of insulated copper wire wrapped closely in the shape of a cylinder is called a solenoid. **1**

Magnetic field around a current carrying solenoid is shown in the figure.

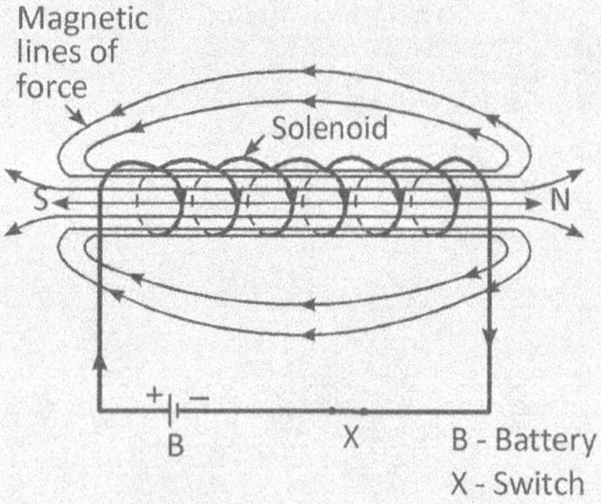

Field lines of the magnetic field through and around a current carrying solenoid **2**

These appear to be similar to that of a bar magnet. One end of the solenoid behaves like North Pole and the other end behaves like the South Pole. Magnetic field lines inside the solenoid are in the form of parallel straight lines. This means that the field is same at all the points inside the solenoid.

(b) No two field–lines are found to cross each other. If they did, it would mean that at the point of intersection, the compass needle would point towards two directions, which is not possible. **2**

OR

A solenoid is a current carrying coil. When current passes through the solenoid it creates a magnetic field around it. The magnetic field is uniform inside the solenoid. Thus, the solenoid behaves like a magnet. One end of the solenoid behaves as a magnetic north pole, while the other behaves as the South Pole. The field lines inside the solenoid are in the form of parallel straight lines. This indicates that the magnetic field is the same at all points inside the solenoid. That is, the field is uniform inside the solenoid. **2**

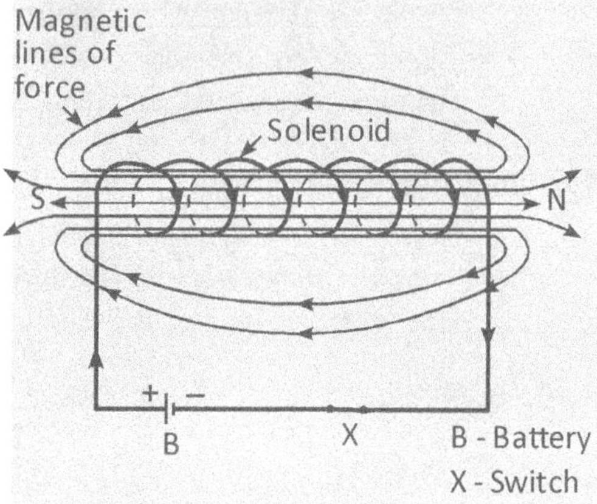

1

The north and south poles of the solenoid can be determined by bringing one pole of a bar magnet next to the solenoid and checking whether it is attracted to or repelled by the solenoid. If it is repelled, they are like poles and unlike poles in the vice versa case. **2**

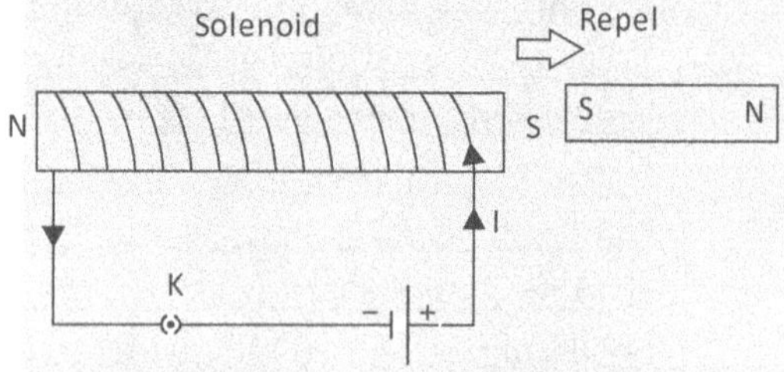

29. Certain compounds are called hydrocarbons because they are formed mainly from carbon and hydrogen. **1**

The general formula for homologous series of alkanes, alkenes and alkynes:

General formula of Alkanes = C_nH_{2n+2}
where n = number of carbon atoms

General formula of Alkenes = C_nH_{2n}
where n = number of carbon atoms

General formula of Alkynes = C_nH_{2n-2}
where n = number of carbon atoms **1**

Structure of the first member of each series:

Structure of Alkane (Methane):

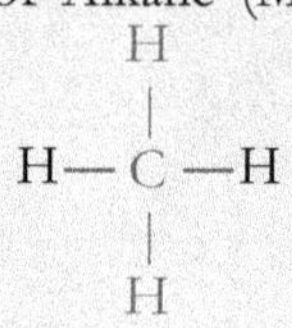

Structure of Alkene (Ethene):

```
      H   H
      |   |
H — C = C — H
```

Structure of Alkyne (Ethyne):

$H—C \equiv C—H$ **1**

The name of the reaction that converts alkenes into alkanes is Catalytic Hydrogenation reaction. It involves the adding of the H atoms. The reaction is favoured at 300 degree celsius in the presence of Nickel/Platinum/Palladium catalyst. **1**

Hydrogenation of Ethene

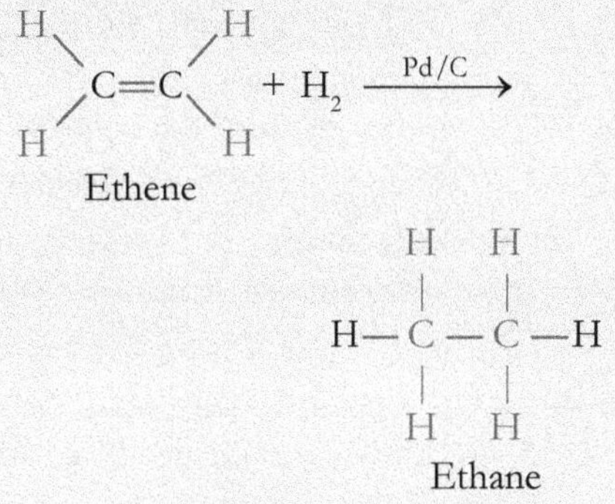

1

OR

Esterification	Saponification
A process in which an alcohol and a carboxylic acid reacts in the presence of conc. H_2SO_4 to form an ester.	A process in which an ester reacts with sodium hydroxide to form sodium salt of an acid and a alcohol.
$\underset{\text{Ethanoic acid}}{CH_3COOH} + \underset{\text{Ethanol}}{C_2H_5OH} \longrightarrow \underset{\text{Ethyl ethanoate (ester)}}{CH_3COOC_2H_5 + H_2O}$	$\underset{\text{Ethyl ethanoate}}{CH_3COOC_2H_5} + NaOH \longrightarrow \underset{\text{Ethanol}}{C_2H_5OH} + \underset{\text{Sod. ethanoate}}{CH_3COONa}$
Esters are formed	Soaps are formed
Esterification reaction needs a catalyst like sulphuric acid	Saponification reaction does not need a catalyst.

3

Uses of Esters and Saponification process:

Esters are used in making perfumes and flavouring agents.

Saponification process is used in preparation of soap. **2**

30. **(a)** Chipko Movement: The movement started in Reni village in Garhwal to protect the trees by hugging them and not allowing cutting of these trees is called Chipko Movement. **1**

(b) We should conserve forests:

(i) to maintain ecological balance of ecosystem.

(ii) to conserve and maintain biological diversity.

(iii) to produce a large quantity of raw materials for industry.

(iv) to prevent global warming, soil erosion and floods. **2**

(c) Four stakeholders that may be useful in the conservation of forests are:

(i) **The people** who live in and around forests and are dependent to some extent on forest produce to lead their life.

(ii) **The forest department** of the Government which owns the forest land and controls the resources from the forest.

(iii) **The industrialists** who use forest products for their factories.

(iv) **The forest and wildlife activists** who want to see the forests in their pristine form. **2**

OR

(a) **Rainwater harvesting:** The harvesting of rainwater simply involves the collection of water from surfaces on which rain falls, and subsequently storing this water for later use. Normally water is collected from the roofs of buildings and stored in rainwater tanks. **2**

(b) Advantages of water stored in ground:

- The water stored in ground does not evaporate and is protected from contamination by human and animal wastes.
- The water stored in ground spreads out to recharge wells and provide moisture for crops over a wide area.
- The water stored in ground does not promote breeding of mosquitoes (unlike stagnant water collected in ponds or artificial lakes.)
- The water stored in ground is utilized for the benefit of local population. **3**

SAMPLE PAPER 5

CBSE - Class 10

SCIENCE

Time Allowed: 3 Hours *Maximum Marks: 80*

General Instructions:

i. The question paper comprises three sections – A, B and C. Attempt all the sections.
ii. All questions are compulsory.
iii. Internal choice is given in each section.
iv. All questions in Section A are one-mark questions comprising MCQ, VSA type and assertion-reason type questions. They are to be answered in one word or in one sentence.
v. All questions in Section B are three-mark, short-answer type questions. These are to be answered in about 50 - 60 words each.
vi. All questions in Section C are five-mark, long-answer type questions. These are to be answered in about 80 - 90 words each.
vii. This question paper consists of a total of 30 questions.

SECTION - A

1. Name the acid along with its chemical formula present in ant sting. 1

2. What is the difference in the molecular mass of any two adjacent homologues? 1

3. **Answer question numbers 3(a)-3(d) on the basis of your understanding of the following paragraph and the related studied concepts.**

The reproductive parts of angiosperms are located in the flower. The different parts of a flower are sepals, petals, stamens and carpels. Stamens and carpels are the reproductive parts of a flower which contain the germ-cells. The flower may be unisexual (papaya, watermelon) when it contains either stamens or carpels or bisexual (Hibiscus, mustard) when it contains both stamens and carpels. Stamen is the male reproductive part and it produces pollen grains that are yellowish in colour. Carpel is present in the centre of a flower and is the female reproductive part.

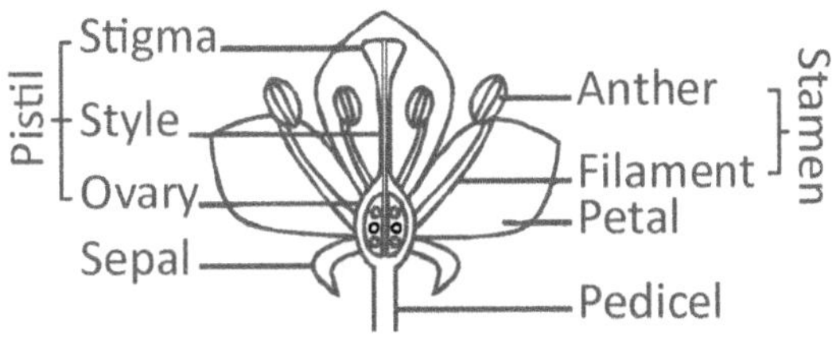

3(a) Where are the plant's sex organs located? 1

3(b) What is the function of a flower? **1**

3(c) Where is the male and female gamete formed in flowering plants? **1**

3(d) What changes take place in the flower after fertilisation which lead to the formation of seeds and fruit? **1**

4. Analyse the following observation table showing variation of image-distance (v) with object-distance (u) in case of a convex lens and answer the questions that follow without doing any calculations:

S.No.	Object-Distance u (cm)	Image-Distance v (cm)
1.	–60	+12
2.	–30	+15
3.	–20	+20
4.	–15	+30
5.	–12	+60
6.	–9	+90

4(a) What is the focal length of the convex lens? State reason for your answer. **1**

4(b) For what object-distance (u) is the corresponding image-distance (v) not correct? How did you arrive at this conclusion? **1**

4(c) A concave mirror gives real, inverted and same size image if the object is placed

(i) At focus **(ii)** At infinity

(iii) At C *i.e.* centre of curvature **(iv)** Beyond centre of curvature **1**

4(d) Focal length of plane mirror is:

(i) At infinity **(ii)** Zero

(iii) Negative **(iv)** None of these **1**

OR

In which of the following, the image of an object placed at infinity will be highly diminished and point sized?

(i) Concave mirror only

(ii) Convex mirror only

(iii) Convex lens only

(iv) Concave mirror, convex mirror, concave lens and convex lens **1**

5. Silver articles become black on prolonged exposure to air. This is due to the formation of:

(i) Ag_3N **(ii)** Ag_3O

(iii) Ag_2S **(iv)** Ag_2S and Ag_3N **1**

OR

Galvanisation is a method of protecting iron from rusting by coating it with a thin layer of:

(i) Gallium **(ii)** Aluminium

(iii) Zinc **(iv)** Silver **1**

6. Posture and balance of the body is controlled by:

(i) Cerebrum **(ii)** Cerebellum

(iii) Medulla **(iv)** Pons **1**

OR

Spinal cord originates from:

(i) Cerebrum **(ii)** Medulla

(iii) Pons **(iv)** Cerebellum 1

7. Expand the abbreviation GAP:

(i) Governmental Agency for Pollution Control

(ii) Gross Assimilation by Photosynthesis

(iii) Ganga Action Plan

(iv) Governmental Agency for Animal Protection 1

8. Arrange the following elements in the order of their decreasing metallic character Na, Si, Cl, Mg, Al:

(i) Cl > Si > Al > Mg > Na **(ii)** Na > Mg > Al > Si > Cl

(iii) Na > Al > Mg > Cl > Si **(iv)** Al > Na > Si > Ca > Mg 1

9. Match the chemical substances given in Column I with their appropriate application given in Column II:

	Column I		**Column II**
A.	Bleaching Powder	1.	Preparation of glass
B.	Baking Soda	2.	Production of H_2 and Cl_2
C.	Washing Soda	3.	Decolourisation
D.	Sodium Chloride	4.	Antacid

Codes:	**A**	**B**	**C**	**D**
(i)	2	1	4	3
(ii)	3	2	4	1
(iii)	3	4	1	2
(iv)	2	4	1	3

1

10. One coulomb charge is equivalent to the charge contained in:

(i) 2.6×10^{19} electrons **(ii)** 6.2×10^{19} electrons

(iii) 2.65×10^{18} electrons **(iv)** 6.25×10^{18} electrons 1

11. A current-carrying conductor is held in exactly vertical direction. In order to produce a clockwise magnetic field around the conductor, the current should passed in the conductor:

(i) from top towards bottom **(ii)** from left towards right

(iii) from bottom towards top **(iv)** from right towards left 1

12. Which of the following represents a possible food chain found in a pond :

	Primary producers	**Primary consumers**	**Secondary consumers**
(i)	green algae	fish	mosquito larvae
(ii)	fish	green algae	mosquito larvae
(iii)	mosquito larvae	fish	green algae
(iv)	green algae	mosquito larvae	fish

1

For question numbers 13 and 14, two statements are given- one labeled Assertion (A) and the other labeled Reason (R). Select the correct answer to these questions from the codes (i), (ii), (iii) and (iv) as given below:

(i) Both A and R are true and R is correct explanation of the assertion.

(ii) Both A and R are true but R is not the correct explanation of the assertion.

(iii) A is true but R is false.

(iv) A is false but R is true.

13. **Assertion A :** Bending a wire does not effect electrical resistance.

Reason R : Resistance of wire is proportional to resistivity of material. **1**

14. **Assertion A :** Autotrophs can produce food on its own.

Reason R : Green plants can absorb energy of sunlight that fall on the leaves. **1**

SECTION - B

15. **(a)** Mention any four information given by a chemical equation.

(b) State the law of conservation of mass as applicable in a chemical reaction. **3**

16. The inner lining of the small intestine has numerous finger like projections. What are they called? List their functions. **3**

17. What is the significance of fossils in deciding evolutionary relationships. **3**

OR

How can you interpret that Variation is beneficial to the species but not necessarily for the individual? Give reasons to support your answer. **3**

18. **(a)** Define a magnetic field line.

(b) Imagine that you are sitting in a chamber with your back to one wall. An electron beam, moving horizontally from back wall towards the front wall, is deflected by a strong magnetic field to your right side. What is the direction of magnetic field? **3**

OR

What is the function of an earth wire? Why is it necessary to earth metallic appliances? **3**

19. Give reasons for the following:

(a) Ionic compounds have high melting and boiling point

(b) Ionic compounds conduct electricity in molten state

(c) Ionic compounds are solid at room temperature and are somewhat hard **3**

20. Charcoal is better fuel than wood. Explain why? **3**

21. State and explain at least six phenomena observed in nature subsequent to scattering of light. **3**

22. State the rule to determine the direction of a **(i)** magnetic field produced around a straight conductor-carrying current, **(ii)** force experienced by a current-carrying straight conductor placed in a magnetic field which is perpendicular to it, and **(iii)** current induced in a coil due to its rotation in a magnetic field. **3**

23. What 3 criteria's provide evidences in favour of evolution in organisms? State the role of each in brief. **3**

24. A sweet smelling compound A with molecular formula $C_4H_8O_2$ on hydrolysis with dil. H_2SO_4 gives two compounds B and C. Compound B on oxidation with $K_2Cr_2O_7/H_2SO_4$ gives C. Identify A, B and C. **3**

OR

A mixture of oxygen and ethyne is burnt for welding. Can you tell why a mixture of ethyne and air is not used? **3**

SECTION - C

25. Five solutions A, B, C, D and E when tested with universal indicator showed pH as 4, 1, 11, 7 and 9 respectively. Which solution is:

(a) Neutral **(b)** Strongly alkaline **(c)** Strongly acidic

(d) Weakly acidic **(e)** Weakly alkaline **5**

Arrange the pH in increasing order of hydrogen ion concentration.

OR

Write word equations and them balanced equations for the reaction taking place when:

(a) dilute sulphuric acid reacts with zinc granules

(b) dilute hydrochloric acid reacts with magnesium ribbon

(c) dilute sulphuric acid reacts with aluminium powder

(d) dilute hydrochloric acid reacts with iron fillings

(e) sodium hydroxide reacts with hydrochloric acid **5**

26. Compare and contrast the arrangement of elements in Mendeleev's Periodic Table and Modern Periodic Table. **5**

27. What is pollination? How does it occur in plants? How does it occur in plants? How does pollination lead to fertilization? Explain. **5**

OR

Answer the following:

(a) What could be the reasons for adopting contraceptive methods?

(b) Describe in brief any three methods of contraception. **5**

28. A student wants to project the image of a candle flame on a screen 60 cm in front of a mirror by keeping the candle flame at a distance of 15 cm from its pole.

(a) Which type of mirror should the student use?

(b) Find the magnification of the image produced.

(c) Find the distance between the object and its image.

(d) Draw a ray diagram to show the image formation in this case and mark the distance between the object and its image. **5**

29. **(a)** Name an instrument that measures electric current in a circuit. Define unit of electric current.

(b) How is static electricity different from current electricity?

(c) Mention some important uses of electricity in our daily life. **5**

OR

(a) On what factors does the resistance of a conductor depend?

(b) Give one example to show how the resistance depends on the nature of material of the conductor.

(c) Calculate the resistance of an aluminium cable of length 10 km and diameter 2.0 mm if the resistivity of aluminium is 2.7×10^{-8} Ωm. **5**

30. The liquid connective tissue A circulates in our body continuously without stopping. This tissue contains a pigment B which imparts it a colour C. The tissue A consists of four components D, E, F and G. The component D fights infection and protects us from diseases. The component E helps in the clotting of tissue A if a person gets a cut. The component F is a liquid which consists mainly of water with many substances dissolved in it and component G carries oxygen from the lungs to all parts of the body.

(a) What is : **(i)** tissue A **(ii)** pigment B and **(iii)** colour C?

(b) Name : **(i)** D **(ii)** E **(iii)** F and **(iv)** G.

(c) Name one substance which is transported by tissue A in the human body.

(d) Which two components of tissue A are the cells without nucleus?

(e) Name any two organisms which do not have liquid like A in their body. **5**

SOLUTION

5

CBSE - Class 10

SECTION - A

1. The acid present in ant sting is methanoic acid (formic acid). The chemical formula is HCOOH. **1**

2. Two successive homologous would differ by one carbon atom and two hydrogen atoms in terms of atoms in their molecules and thus differ by 14 amu in terms of molecular mass. **1**

3. **(a)** Plant's sex organs are located in the flower. **1**

3. **(b)** The function of a flower is to make male and female gametes and to ensure that fertilisation will take place to make new seeds for the reproduction of plant. **1**

3. **(c)** The male gemate is formed in the anther of a flower and female gamete is formed in ovary of a flower. **1**

3. **(d)** The fertilised egg divides several times to form an embryo within the ovule which develops a tough coat around it and is gradually converted into a seed. The ovary of the flower develops and becomes a fruit with seeds inside it. **1**

4. **(a)** From S.No. 3, we can say that the radius of curvature of the lens is 20 cm because when an object is placed at the centre of curvature of a convex lens its image is formed on the other side of the lens at the same distance from the lens. And, we also know that focal length is half of the radius of curvature.

   Thus, focal length of the lens is + 10 cm. **1**

4. **(b)** S.No. 6 is not correct as for this observation the object distance is between focus and pole, and for such cases the image formed is always virtual but in this case a real image is forming as the image distance is positive. **1**

4. **(c)** **(iii)** At Centre of curvature. **1**

   Explanation: The image formed by the concave mirror is inverted and of the same size as the object only if the object is placed at the centre of curvature.

4. **(d)** **(i)** at infinity **1**

   OR

   (iv) Convex mirror, convex mirror, concave lens and convex lens **1**

   Explanation: The incident rays coming from an object placed at infinity will be parallel to the principal axis and the rays parallel to the principal axis, after reflection/refraction by concave mirror, convex mirror, concave lens and convex lens, will pass or appear to pass through the principal focus. Hence, image will be highly diminished and point sized. **1**

5. **(iii)** Ag_2S **1**

   Explanation: Silver metal reacts with atmospheric sulphur compounds like H_2S gas and form black coating of Ag_2S over surface.

OR

(iii) Zinc 1

Explanation: Zinc (Zn) metal is used to protect iron surface from rusting.

6. (ii) Cerebellum 1

Explanation: Cerebellum coordinates the voluntary movements of skeletal muscles as well as posture, balance and equilibrium.

OR

(ii) Medulla 1

Explanation: Spinal cord begins in continuation with medulla and extends downwards.

7. (iii) Ganga Action Plan 1

Explanation: GAP, 1985 came in existence to check water pollution in river Ganga.

8. (ii) Na > Mg > Al > Si > Cl 1

Explanation: As we move from left to right in periodic table, metallic characters decreases and non-metalliccharacters increases. Here Na, Si, Cl, Mg, Al belong to same period so we have to check their position in period. 1

9. (iii) Codes :

A	B	C	D
3	4	1	2

1

Explanation:

- Bleaching powder ($CaOCl_2$)–Used for bleaching or decolourisation of clothes.
- Baking soda ($NaHCO_3$)- Used as an antacid for relieving stomach acidity.
- Washing soda (Na_2CO_3)- Used in preparation of glass.
- Sodium chloride (NaCl)- Used for production of H_2 and Cl_2 gases.

10. (iv) 6.25×10^{18} electrons 1

Explanation: Since the charge of an electron is 1.6×10^{-19}C

6.25×10^{18} electrons taken together constitute ($6.25 \times 10^{18} \times 1.6 \times 10^{-19}$ C) or 1 coulomb of charge.

11. (i) from top towards bottom 1

Explanation : It is given that the current-carrying conductor is held in exactly vertical direction. In order to produce a clockwise magnetic field around the conductor, the current should be passed in the conductor from top towards bottom. It is concluded by applying right-hand thumb rule. 1

12. (iv) green algae—mosquito larvae—fish 1

Explanation: In a pond, green algae are the primary producers. Green algae are consumed by mosquito larvae, which therefore become the primary consumers. Mosquito larvae are consumed by fish, which then become the secondary consumers.

13. (i) Both assertion and reason are true and the reason is the correct explanation of the assertion. 1

Explanation: Resistance wire = R

$= \frac{\rho l}{A}$, where ρ is resistivity of material which does not depend on the geometry of wire. Since when wire is bended, resistivity, length and area of cross-section does not change, therefore resistance of wire also remain same.

14. (ii) Both A and R are true but R is not the correct explanation of the assertion. 1

Explanation: All the green plants are called autotrophs. This is due to the fact that the green plants make their own food from very simple substances like carbon dioxide and water that is present in the surroundings.

SECTION - B

15. (a) A balanced chemical equation tells:

(i) number of molecules of reactants and products involved.

(ii) chemical formula of reactants and products involved.

(iii) catalyst involved in the reaction if any.

(iv) physical state of reactants and products involved. **2**

(b) The Law of Conservation of Mass states that matter can neither be created nor destroyed in a chemical reaction. The mass of the products in a chemical reaction is equal to the mass of the reactants. **1**

16. The inner lining of the small intestine contains numerous finger like projections called villi. **1**

Functions of villi:

(a) The villi increase the surface area for absorption of food.

(b) Villi are richly supplied with blood vessels which transport the absorbed food into the blood to each and every cell of the body. There it is utilized to obtain energy and for repair of old tissues. **2**

17. Importance of fossils in deciding evolutionary relationships:

Fossils are the remains of organisms that once existed on the earth. They represent the ancestors of plants and animals that are alive today. They provide evidences of evolution by showing characteristics of past organisms and link between progressive changes that have occurred in present living organism to give new species. The fossils found in upper strata of rocks are considered to be newer than those found in the lower strata. It is also seen from the fossils that the organisms become more complex in the upper strata when compared to the lower strata which indicates towards the evolutionary process. Also transitional fossils like Archeopteryx are known which were intermediaries between reptiles and birds. **3**

OR

Variation is beneficial for the survival of species but not necessarily for the individual as variation makes species more adapted to survive with the changing conditions. At the species level, these variations can make difference at each generation but at individual level an organism is not evolving but aging. Variation is not necessary in case of an individual because it does not result into evolutionary change. If an individual naturally accumulates variation in his gene composition through mutation or any other source, it could be harmful. Thus variation at individual level is not useful as a person does not evolve by these variations. **3**

18. (a) The space or region around a magnet within which its influence can be felt by another magnet is called magnetic field. It is a vector quantity which has both magnitude and direction. **1**

(b) Movement of electron beam from back wall to front wall is equivalent to the flow of electric current from front wall to the back wall. Now the deflection of the beam towards right means direction of force is towards the right side. According to Fleming's left hand rule, the magnetic field inside the chamber is in downward direction *i.e.* perpendicular to the plane of the paper and directed inwards. **2**

OR

Earth wire acts as a safety measure. The main function of the earth wire is to ensure that any excess current passing through an appliance gets diverted to earth, ensuring humans using appliance don't get electric shock. It also prevents live wire from getting overloaded. **1**

The earth wire is attached to the metallic body of an electrical appliance. This helps in preventing accidental electric shock while using electrical appliances having metallic bodies, such as refrigerator, electric iron, etc. When the live wire touches the metal casing of the appliance, 'earthing' ensures that the electric current flows from the casing of the appliance to the earth through the earth wire. 2

19. (a) **Ionic compounds have high boiling and melting point** due to the presence of strong bond between cations and anions. To break or overcome these strong forces of attraction, a large amount of energy is required. 1

(b) **Ionic compounds conduct electricity in molten state.** Conductivity depends on the presence of number of mobile ions. Solid ionic compounds cannot conduct electricity because of the absence of ions (electrons) in the crystal structure. When the ionic compounds is present in molten state, crystal structure deforms and they can easily conduct electricity with the mobile ions. 1

(c) **Ionic compounds are solid at room temperature and are somewhat hard.** Due to the presence of strong force of attraction between the positive and negative ions a solid ionic compound formed becomes hard and solid at room temperature. 1

20. **Charcoal is better fuel than wood.** It is because:

(a) It has a higher calorific value than wood *i.e.* the amount of heat produced by burning charcoal is much more than heat produced by burning wood.

(b) It does not produce that much smoke on combustion and hence it causes less air pollution.

(c) It is easier to handle as it burns easily as compared to wood. 3

21. **Phenomena observed in nature subsequent to scattering of light:**

(a) The sun is red in colour during sunrise and sunset but it is white when seen overhead.

(b) Formation of rainbow. After it rains, small particles of water vapor still persist in the atmosphere. When sunlight passes through these particles (the raindrops), they refract the light, disperse it, then internally reflect it and finally refract it

(c) Bluish colour of sky and oceans.

(d) Sunlight flittering through clouds.

(e) Danger signals are usually red as red, having the longest wavelength, is scattered the least.

(f) Visible path of light as it enters a dark room. 3

22. **Rule to determine the direction:**

(a) Right hand thumb rule which states that that if one holds a straight current carrying conductor with right hand such that the thumb points towards the direction of current, then fingers will wrap around the conductor in the direction of field lines of the magnetic field.

This rule determines the magnetic field produced around a straight conductor carrying current. 1

(b) Fleming's Left Hand Rule, which states that if the first finger points in the direction of magnetic field and second finger in the direction of current, then the thumb will point in the direction of motion or the force acting on the conductor.

This determines force experienced by a current-carrying straight conductor placed in a magnetic field which is perpendicular to it. 1

(c) Fleming's Right Hand Rule, which states that if the forefinger indicates the direction of the magnetic field and thumb shows the direction of motion of conductor, then the middle finger will show the direction of induced current. 1

This rule determines the current induced in a coil due to its rotation in a magnetic field.

23. Three factors that provide evidences are:

(a) Homologous organs suggest that the organisms with same basic structure perform different functions and may have similar origin.
Example: forelimbs of cat used for running and bats and birds use them for flying. Hence they indicate origin from a common ancestor. **1**

(b) Analogous organs are organs which look alike and perform same functions but may have different origin in different species.
Example: the wings of a bat and the wings of a bird are analogous. It indicates that birds and bats may be developed from the flying mammals. **1**

(c) Fossils allow us to make estimates and helps in tracing the evolutionary history of an organism. They are the preserved traces or impressions of the body parts of living organisms.

Example: archaeopteryx serves as a connecting link between birds and reptiles. It is the fossil evidence to show that birds evolved from reptiles. **1**

24. Since A is a sweet smelling compound, it must be an ester.

Since A an ester with molecular formula $C_4H_8O_2$ on hydrolysis with dil. H_2SO_4 gives two compounds B and C, therefore B must be an alcohol and C must be an acid.

Compound B on oxidation with $K_2Cr_2O_7/H_2SO_4$ gives C, both B and C must contain same number of carbon atoms. This is possible only if B is an alcohol with 2 carbon atoms and C is an acid with 2 carbon atoms. Therefore, B must be ethanol and C must be ethanoic acid. Thus A will be ethyl ethanoate. **1**

Compound A	Ethyl ethanoate *i.e.* $CH_3COOCH_2CH_3$
Compound B	Ethanol *i.e.* C_2H_5OH
Compound C	Ethanoic acid *i.e.* CH_3COOH **1**

$$CH_3COOC_2H_5 + H_2O \xrightarrow[+\text{Heat}]{\text{dil. } H_2SO_4} C_2H_5OH + CH_3COOH$$

where H_2SO_4 acts as a catalyst.

$$C_2H_5OH \xrightarrow{K_2Cr_2O_7/H_2SO_4 + \text{Heat}} CH_3COOH + H_2O$$

where $K_2Cr_2O_7$ acts as a catalyst. (This is an oxidation reaction) **1**

OR

Air is a mixture of many gases and carbon dioxide is one of them. When ethyne is allowed to burn with air, gases other than oxygen present in air prevent ethyne from complete combustion thereby producing a yellow flame with lot of black smoke and high temperature required for welding is not achieved. But if ethyne is burnt with only oxygen, ethyne is burnt with clean flame and complete combustion takes place and thus it gives a high temperature of 3000°C which gives proper welding. **2**

This is the reason why ethyne is burnt with only oxygen and not with the air for welding.

$$2\,HC{\equiv}CH + 5O_2 \longrightarrow 4CO_2 + 2H_2O + \text{heat and light}$$ **1**

SECTION - C

25. Given pH for the solutions are
A = 4, B = 1, C = 11, D = 7, E = 9.

Hydrogen ions concentration increases with decrease in pH value and thus strength of acid increases with decrease in pH value from 7 to 0.

On the other hand hydroxide ions concentration decreases with increase in pH value and thus strength of acid increases with increase in pH value from 7 to 14.

While neutral solution has pH value = 7.

Therefore,

(a) Solution D is neutral having pH value equal to 7.

(b) Solution C is strongly alkaline as its pH value is equal to 11

(c) Solution B is strongly acidic as its pH value is equal to 1

(d) Solution A is weakly acidic as its pH value is equal to 4

(e) Solution E is weakly alkaline as its pH value is equal to 9 **(½ × 5 = 2.5)**

Hydrogen ion concentration of the given solutions will be

A = 10^{-4} M, B = 10^{-1}M, C = 10^{-11}M, D = 10^{-7}M, E = 10^{-9}M.

Hence arrangement of given pH value in increasing order of hydrogen ion concentration:

C (11) < E (9)< D (7) < A (4) < B(1)

(½ × 5 = 2.5)

OR

Word equations and balanced equations for the reaction taking place when

(a) dilute sulphuric acid reacts with zinc granules.

Sulphuric acid + Zinc ⟶ Zinc sulphate + Hydrogen

$H_2SO_4 + Zn \longrightarrow ZnSO_4\,(aq) + H_2\,(g)$ **1**

(b) dilute hydrochloric acid reacts with magnesium ribbon.

Hydrochloric acid + Magnesium ⟶ Magnesium chloride + Hydrogen

$2HCl + Mg \longrightarrow MgCl_2 + H_2\,(g)$ **1**

(c) dilute sulphuric acid reacts with aluminium powder.

Sulphuric acid + Aluminium ⟶ Aluminium sulphate + Hydrogen

$3H_2SO_4 + 2\,Al \longrightarrow Al_2(SO_4)_3 + 3H_2\,(g)$ **1**

(d) dilute hydrochloric acid reacts with iron fillings.

Hydrochloric acid + Iron Fillings ⟶ Iron chloride + Hydrogen

$2HCl + Fe \longrightarrow FeCl_2 + H_2\,(g)$ **1**

(e) sodium hydroxide reacts with hydrochloric acid.

Hydrochloric acid + Sodium hydroxide ⟶ Sodium chloride + water

$HCl + NaOH \longrightarrow NaCl + H_2O$ **1**

26.

Mendeleev's Periodic Table	**Modern Periodic Table**
Elements are arranged in increasing order of their atomic masses.	Elements are arranged in increasing order of their atomic numbers.
In Mendeleev periodic table, the position of isotopes was not justified.	In Modem periodic table, the classification is based on the atomic number and not atomic mass and hence the position of isotopes is fully justified.
Electronic configuration of an element cannot be predicted from its position in the periodic table.	Electronic configuration of an element can be easily predicted from its position in the periodic table.
Many metals and nonmetals are grouped together.	Metals and nonmetals are widely separated from one another.
Some elements with higher atomic masses have been placed before elements of lower atomic masses.	No. such discrepancy arises because elements are placed in increasing order of their atomic masses.
Groups for Noble gas was not discovered by Mendeleev's periodic Table	A Noble gas was placed separately in modern periodic table.

5

27. **Pollination:** The transfer of pollen from anther of a stamen to the stigma of a carpel is called pollination. **1**

If this transfer of pollen occurs in the same flower, it is referred to as self-pollination, whereas if the pollen is transferred from one flower to another, it is known as cross-pollination. This transfer is carried out by different agencies like wind, water, insects (like bees and butterflies), or animals. **2**

Fertilization: After a pollen grain falls on the stigma, the next step is fertilization. A tube grows out of pollen grain and travels through the style to reach the female germ cells present in ovule in the ovary. Out of the two male gametes present in pollen tube one fuses with egg to form zygote. This fusion is called fertilization. After fertilization, the zygote divides several times to form an embryo within the ovule. The ovule develops a tough coat and gradually turns into a seed. The ovary grows rapidly and ripens to form a fruit. Meanwhile the petals, sepals, stamens, style and stigma may shrivel and fall off. **2**

OR

(a) **Contraceptive methods are mainly adopted because of the following reasons:**
- To avoid unwanted pregnancies.
- To keep the population of a country under control.
- To limit the number of children a couple wants to have.
- To maintain adequate gap between two consecutive children.
- To prevent the transfer of sexually transmitted diseases. **2**

(b) Different contraceptive methods that can be used are:
- **Natural method:** In this method, the sexual act is avoided from day 10th to 17th of the menstrual cycle because during this period ovulation is expected and the chances of fertilization are very high. **1**
- **Barrier method:** Physical barrier method prevents the entry of sperm into the uterus. Barriers are available for both males and females. Condoms on the penis or similar coverings worn in the vagina can serve this purpose. **1**
- **Oral contraceptives:** In this method, the hormonal pills are taken which prevent the entry of sperm into the uterus. However, since these pills change the hormonal balances, they can cause side effects too. **1**

28. (a) The student should use a Concave Mirror, as it forms a real image on the same side of the mirror. **1**

(b) Object distance, $u = -15$ cm

Image distance, $v = -60$ cm

Magnification, $m = -\frac{v}{u} = -\left(\frac{-60}{-15}\right)$

$= -4$ **1**

(c) Distance of image from the object

$= v - u$ **1**

$= -60 - (-15)$

$= -16 + 15 = -45$

∴ The image is formed at a distance of 45 cm from the object.

(d)

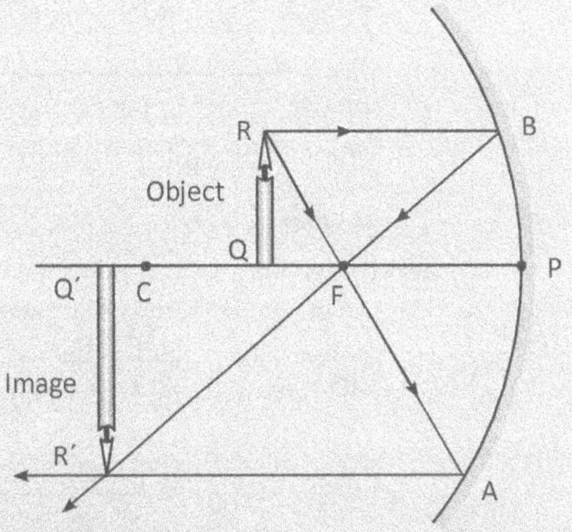

29. (a) Ammeter is used to measure electric current in a circuit.

The SI unit of current is Ampere. Current through a conductor is said to be one ampere, when one coulomb of charge flows through any section of a conductor in one second. **1**

(b) Electricity is basically categorised into static and current electricity. The difference between the two is as follows:

Static electricity	Current electricity
1. Static electricity is caused by the building up of electrical charges on surfaces of objects	1. Current electricity is caused by the flow of the electrons along a conductor.
2. Static current happens sporadically and is usually uncontrolled.	2. Current electricity is normally controlled and is used in a wide range of applications.
3. Static electricity is generated by friction or sudden contact – for instance, rubbing two materials against each other.	3. Current electricity is generated by batteries and power plants.

(c) Electricity has a wide range of applications:

- Electricity is used in heating, lighting, cooking, operating fans, geysers etc. in our houses, hospitals, hotels, office buildings, food storage plants.
- Electricity is used in industries to run various types of machines.
- In transportation, to pull electric trains, trams etc.
- Electricity is used for irrigation purposes in agriculture. **2**

OR

(a) Resistance of a conductor depends on the following factors:

Length of the conductor, area of cross section of the conductor, nature of material of the conductor and temperature of the conductor **1**

(b) If we take two similar wires of same length and same diameter, one of copper metal and other of nichrome alloy, we will find that the resistance of nichrome wire is about 60 times more than that of the copper wire.

This shows that the resistance depends on the nature of material of the conductor. **2**

(c) l = 10 km = 10000 m; d = 2 mm; r = 1 mm = 10^{-3} m; $\rho = 2.7 \times 10^{-8}$ Ωm

$$R = \rho\frac{l}{A}$$

$$= 2.7 \times 10^{-8} \times \frac{10000}{3.14 \times (10^{-3})^2}$$

$$= 0.859 \times 10^2\ \Omega$$

$$\approx 86\ \Omega$$ **2**

30. **(a)** **(i)** Tissue A is blood

(ii) pigment B is Haemoglobin and

(iii) colour C is Red. **1**

(b) **(i)** D is white blood cells

(ii) E is Platelets

(iii) F is Plasma and

(iv) G is Red blood cells. **1**

(c) Digested food is transported by tissue A (blood) in the human body. **1**

(d) E (Platelets) and G (Red blood cells) are two components of tissue A (blood) are the cells without nucleus. **1**

(e) Two organisms which do not have blood in their body are Amoeba and grasshopper. **1**

SAMPLE PAPER 6

CBSE - Class 10

SCIENCE

Time Allowed: 3 Hours *Maximum Marks: 80*

General Instructions:

i. The question paper comprises three sections – A, B and C. Attempt all the sections.

ii. All questions are compulsory.

iii. Internal choice is given in each section.

iv. All questions in Section A are one-mark questions comprising MCQ, VSA type and assertion-reason type questions. They are to be answered in one word or in one sentence.

v. All questions in Section B are three-mark, short-answer type questions. These are to be answered in about 50 - 60 words each.

vi. All questions in Section C are five-mark, long-answer type questions. These are to be answered in about 80 - 90 words each.

vii. This question paper consists of a total of 30 questions.

SECTION - A

1. What is gestation period? **1**

2. What happens when egg is not fertilized? **1**

3. **Answer question numbers 3(a)-3(d) on the basis of your understanding of the following paragraph and the related studied concepts.**

Atoms of eight elements A, B, C, D, E, F, G and H have the same number of electron shells but different number of electrons in their outermost shells. It was found that elements A and G combine to form an ionic compound. This ionic compound is added in a small amount to almost all vegetables and dishes during cooking. Oxides of elements A and B are basic in nature while those of elements E and F are acidic. The oxide of element D is, however, almost neutral. Based on the above information, answer the following questions:

3(a) To which group or period of the periodic table do these elements belong? **1**

3(b) What would be the nature of compound formed by a combination of elements B and F? **1**

3(c) Which two of these elements could definitely be metals and which would be non metals? **1**

3(d) Which one of the eight elements is most likely to be found in gaseous state at room temperature? **1**

4. Analyse the following table showing refractive indices of four media A, B, C and D and answer the questions that follow:

The refractive indices of four media A, B, C and D are given in the following table:

Medium	A	B	C	D
Refractive Index	1.33	1.50	1.52	2.40

4(a) If light, travels from one medium to another, in which case the change in speed will be minimum. **1**

4(b) If light, travels from one medium to another, in which case the change in speed will be maximum. **1**

4(c) A light ray enters from medium A to medium B as shown in the figure. The refractive index of medium B relative to A will be:

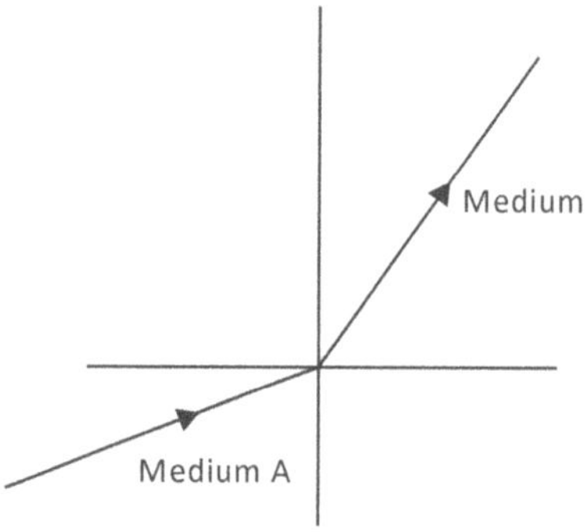

(i) Greater than unity **(ii)** Less than unity
(iii) Equal to unity **(iv)** Zero **1**

4(d) The laws of reflection hold good for

(i) plane mirror only **(ii)** concave mirror only
(iii) convex mirror only **(iv)** all mirrors irrespective of their shape **1**

5. Which of the following statements about the autotrophs is incorrect:

(i) They synthesize carbohydrates from carbon dioxide and water in the presence of sunlight and chlorophyll
(ii) They store carbohydrates in the form of starch
(iii) They convert carbon dioxide and water into carbohydrates in the absence of sunlight
(iv) They constitute the first trophic level in food chains **1**

6. The solution of one of the following compounds will not conduct electricity. This compounds is:

(i) NaCl **(ii)** CCl_4
(iii) $MgCl_2$ **(iv)** $CaCl_2$ **1**

7. In a flower, the parts that produce male and female gametes (germ cells) are:

(i) Stamen and anther **(ii)** Filament and stigma
(iii) Anther and ovary **(iv)** Stamen and style **1**

8. A cell, a resistor, a key and an ammeter are arranged as shown in the circuit diagrams of figure. The current recorded in the ammeter will be:

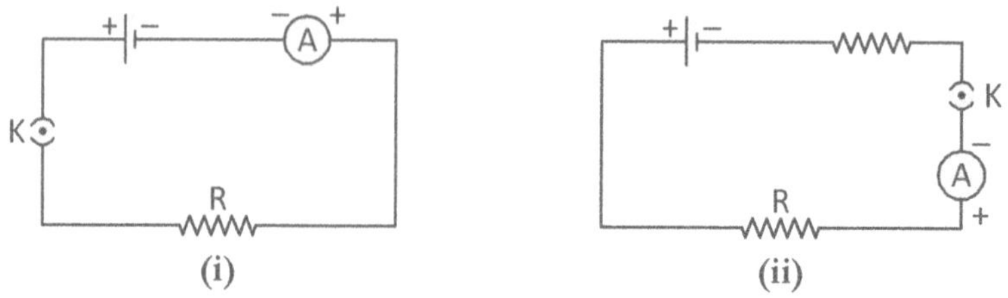

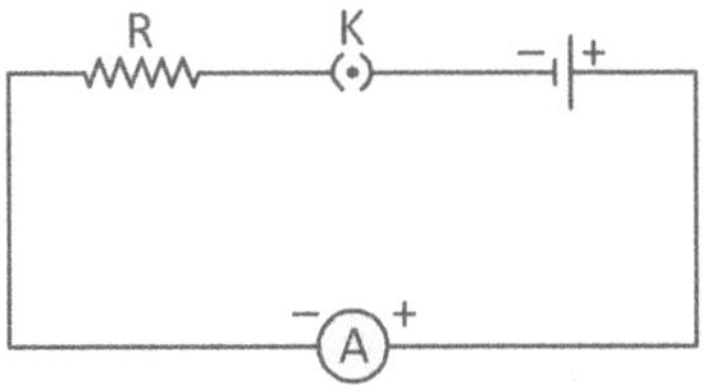

(iii)

(i) Maximum in (i) **(ii)** Maximum in (ii)

(iii) Maximum in (iii) **(iv)** The same in all the cases **1**

9. Which one of the following is an artificial ecosystem:

(i) Pond **(ii)** Crop field

(iii) Lake **(iv)** Forest **1**

10. Which of the following are present in a dilute aqueous solution of hydrochloric acid:

(i) $H_3O^+ + Cl^-$ **(ii)** $H_3O^+ + OH^-$

(iii) $Cl^- + OH^-$ **(iv)** Unionised HCl **1**

OR

Identify the correct representation of reaction occurring during chloralkali process:

(i) $2NaCl\ (l) + 2H_2O\ (l) \longrightarrow 2NaOH\ (l) + Cl_2\ (g) + H_2\ (g)$

(ii) $2NaCl\ (l) + 2H_2O\ (aq) \longrightarrow 2NaOH\ (aq) + Cl_2\ (g) + H_2\ (aq)$

(iii) $2NaCl\ (aq) + 2H_2O\ (l) \longrightarrow 2NaOH\ (aq) + Cl_2\ (aq) + H_2\ (aq)$

(iv) $2NaCl\ (aq) + 2H_2O\ (l) \longrightarrow 2NaOH\ (aq) + Cl_2\ (g) + H_2\ (g)$ **1**

11. Some dinosaurs had feathers although they could not fly but birds have feathers that help them to fly. In the context of evolution this means that:

(i) Reptiles have evolved from birds

(ii) There is no evolutionary connection between reptiles and birds

(iii) Feathers are homologous structures in both the organisms

(iv) Birds have evolved from reptiles **1**

OR

Two pink coloured flowers on crossing resulted in 1 red, 2 pink and 1 white flower progeny. The nature of the cross will be

(i) Double fertilization **(ii)** Self pollination

(iii) Cross fertilization **(iv)** No fertilization **1**

12. For a current in a long straight solenoid N and S-poles are created at the two ends. Among the following statements, the incorrect statement is:

(i) The field lines inside the solenoid are in the form of straight lines, which indicates that the magnetic field is the same at all points inside the solenoid

(ii) The strong magnetic field produced inside the solenoid can be used to magnetise a piece of magnetic material like soft iron, when placed inside the coil

(iii) The pattern of the magnetic field associated with the solenoid is different from the pattern of the magnetic field around a bar magnet

(iv) The N and S-poles exchange position when the direction of current through the solenoid is reversed **1**

OR

Commercial electric motors do not use

(i) An electromagnet to rotate the armature

(ii) Effectively large number of turns of conducting wire in the current carrying coil

(iii) A permanent magnet to rotate the armature

(iv) A soft iron core on which the coil is wound

For question numbers 13 and 14, two statements are given- one labeled Assertion (A) and the other labeled Reason (R). Select the correct answer to these questions from the codes (i), (ii), (iii) and (iv) as given below:

(i) Both A and R are true and R is correct explanation of the assertion.

(ii) Both A and R are true but R is not the correct explanation of the assertion.

(iii) A is true but R is false.

(iv) A is false but R is true.

13. **Assertion A :** The stars twinkle while the planets do not.

Reason R : The stars are much bigger in size than the planets. **1**

14. **Assertion A :** Human beings have a complex respiratory system.

Reason R : Human skin is impermeable to gases. **1**

SECTION - B

15. Name two elements you would expect to show chemical reactions similar to magnesium. What is the basis for your choice? **3**

OR

Nitrogen (atomic number 7) and phosphorus (atomic number 15) belong to group 15 of the Periodic Table. Write the electronic configuration of these two elements. Which of these will be more electronegative? Why? **3**

16. Design an experiment to demonstrate hydrotropism. **3**

OR

(a) What is the gap between two neurons known as?

(b) What is the difference between a reflex action and walking? **3**

17. Differentiate between strong and weak acids. Identify the strong and weak acids from the following list of acids:

Hydrochloric acid, acetic acid, formic acid, nitric acid. **3**

18. Answer the following:

(a) Which hormone is responsible for the changes noticed in females at puberty?

(b) Dwarfism results due to deficiency of which hormone?

(c) Blood sugar level rises due to deficiency of which hormone?

(d) Iodine is necessary for the synthesis of which hormone?

(e) Name the gland which controls the secretion of hormones from the pituitary.

(f) Name the hormone that prepares our body in emergency situation. **3**

19. (a) What is the nature of the image formed at the retina of human eye?

(b) What happens to the image distance in the eye when we increase the distance of an object from the eye? **3**

20. (a) What is the resistance of a conductor?

(b) What happens to the electrical resistance when mercury is cooled to 4.12 K?

(c) What name is given to this phenomenon? **3**

21. A metal M forms an oxide having the formula M_2O_3. It is dissolved both in dilute sulphuric and dilute sodium hydroxide solution. Identify the metal and write equations for the reaction involved. What criteria would you use to assess it? **3**

22. Define Ecosystem. Briefly describe the two types of ecosystem. **3**

23. An electric iron is used on a 240V supply and draws a current of 4 Ampere.

(a) What is its power?

(b) What is its resistance?

(c) What is the cost of using the iron for the month of January 10 hours a day if 1 KWH costs rupees 3.40? **3**

OR

(a) Draw a diagram to show how two resistors R_1 and R_2 should be connected so that the total resistance of the circuit is minimum.

(b) In a circuit, if two resistors of 4 Ω and 8 Ω are connected in parallel, find ratio of current passing through the two resistors. **3**

24. Explain how forests and wild life play a key role in the ecological system. **3**

SECTION - C

25. Describe the structure and functioning of nephrons. **5**

OR

What are the methods used by plants to get rid of excretory products? **5**

26. **(a)** Name an allotrope of carbon which consists of fused benzene rings.

(b) Why is carbon tetravalent?

(c) What would be the electron dot structure of a molecule of sulphur which is made up of eight atoms of sulphur?

(d) What are the two properties of carbon which lead to the huge number of carbon compounds we see around us? **5**

OR

(a) Why are carbon and its compounds used as fuels for most applications?

(b) In the electrolytic refining of a metal M, what would you take as the anode, the cathode and the electrolyte? **5**

27. A cross was made between pure breeding pea plants one with round and green seeds and the other with wrinkled and yellow seeds.

(a) Write the phenotype of F1 progeny. Give reason for your answer.

(b) Write the different types of F2 progeny obtained along with their ration when F1 progeny was selfed. **5**

28. **(a)** Define focal length of a spherical lens.

(b) An object of size 7.0 cm is placed at 27cm in front of a concave mirror of focal length 18cm. At what distance from the mirror should a screen be placed, so that a sharp focused image can be obtained? Find the size and the nature of the image.

(c) Draw a ray diagram to show the formation of image in the above situation. **5**

29. **(a)** Write the balanced chemical equations for the following reactions.

(i) Calcium hydroxide + Carbon dioxide $\longrightarrow$ Calcium carbonate + Water

(ii) Zinc + Silver nitrate $\longrightarrow$ Zinc nitrate + Silver

(iii) Aluminium + Copper chloride $\longrightarrow$ Aluminium chloride + Copper

(b) Why is respiration considered an exothermic reaction? Explain. **5**

30. Explain the underlying principle and working of an electric generator by drawing a labeled diagram. **5**

OR

Explain the phenomenon of electromagnetic induction. Describe an experiment to show that a current is set up in a closed loop when an external magnetic field passing through the loop increases or decreases. **5**

SOLUTION

6

CBSE - Class 10

SECTION - A

1. The time period from the fertilization of foetus inside the uterus up to the birth of the baby is called gestation period. **1**

2. The ovary releases one egg every month and the uterus prepares for the launching of the zygote by thickening its walls. If the egg is not fertilized, the uterus lining slowly breaks down and sheds through the vagina as blood and mucus. This cycle takes place roughly every month and is known as menstruation and lasts for about two to eight days. **1**

3. **(a)** They all belong to the 3rd period. **1**

3. **(b)** The compound between B and F will be ionic in nature. **1**

3. **(c)** A and B are metals as they form basic oxides, E and F are non metals as they form acidic oxides. **1**

3. **(d)** Element H will be found in gaseous state at room temperature as it is the 8th element of the group so it would have 8 electrons in its outermost shell which is the electronic configuration of a Nobel gas. **1**

4. **(a)** Minimum change is seen as light moves between 1.50 and 1.52, *i.e.* B and C. **1**

4. **(b)** Maximum change when light moves between 1.33 and 2.40, *i.e.* A and D. **1**

4. **(c) (i)** Greater than unity **1**

Explanation: Since light rays in medium B goes towards normal. So it has greater restrictive index and lesser velocity of light with respect to medium A. So refractive index of medium B with respect to medium A is greater than unity.

4. **(d) (iv)** all mirrors irrespective of their shape. **1**

Explanation: The laws of reflection hold good for light reflected form any smooth surface *i.e.*, all mirrors regardless of its shape.

5. **(iii)** They convert carbon dioxide and water into carbohydrates in the absence of sunlight option is incorrect. **1**

Explanation: Autotrophs obtain the required carbon and energy requirements from carbon dioxide and Sunlight. They combine carbon dioxide and water to form carbohydrates. The main photosynthetic pigment is chlorophyll, which helps to trap the Sunlight to carry out the light reaction of photosynthesis to synthesise carbohydrates.
Since autotrophs are the only organisms that can fix the atmospheric carbon dioxide into organic compounds, these organisms occupy first trophic level in food chain and serve as a source of food and energy for organisms of higher trophic levels.

6. **(ii)** CCl_4 **1**

Explanation: Because it is a covalent compound formed by sharing of electrons.

7. **(iii)** Anther and ovary **1**

Explanation: Anther produces pollen and ovary produces egg cell.

8. **(iv)** The same in all the cases **1**

Explanation: In series connections the order of elements in the circuit will not affect the amount of current flowing in the circuit.

9. **(ii)** Crop field **1**

Explanation: Crop field is an agricultural land created by human.

10. **(i)** $H_3O^+ + Cl^-$ **1**

Explanation: A strong acid like HCl dissociates completely in its aqueous solution and form hydronium ions with its respective anion.

$HCl + H_2O \longrightarrow H^+ + Cl^- + H_2O$

$H_2O + H^+ \longrightarrow H_3O^+$

(Hydronium ion)

OR

(iv) $2NaCl\ (aq) + 2H_2O\ (l) \longrightarrow 2NaOH\ (aq) + Cl_2\ (g) + H_2\ (g)$ **1**

Explanation: Chloro-alkali process is an industrial process that is used to form sodium hydroxide by electrolysis of aqueous solution of sodium chloride. It forms sodium hydroxide with hydrogen and chlorine gas as by-products.

11. **(iv)** Birds have evolved from reptiles **1**

Explanation: Development of flight feathers in reptilian ancestors of birds lead to evolution of birds (Aves).

OR

(iii) Cross fertilization **1**

Explanation: Cross fertilization is transfer of pollen from one plant to the stigma of flower borne on different plant of same species.

12. **(iii)** The pattern of the magnetic field associated with the solenoid is different from the pattern of the magnetic field around a bar magnet **1**

Explanation: Only option (c) is incorrect because the pattern of magnetic fields due to solenoid and bar magnet is almost same.

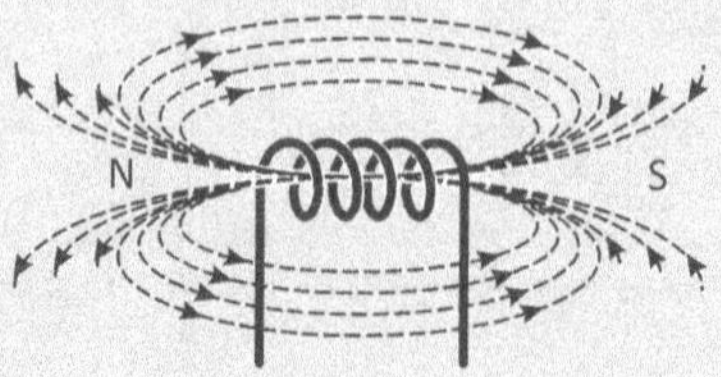

Solenoid

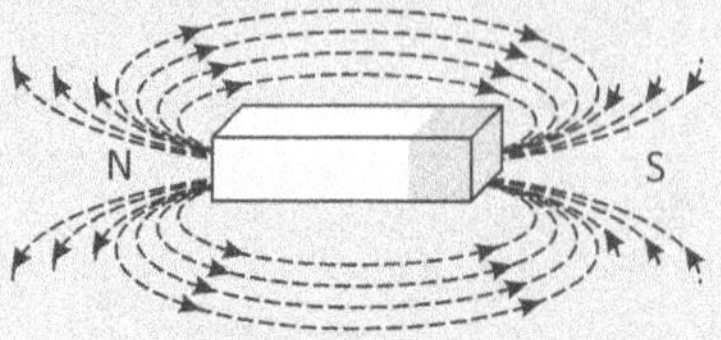

Bar Magnet

OR

(iii) A permanent magnet to rotate the armature **1**

Explanation: An electric motor is a device that converts electric energy into mechanical energy.

An electric motor has an **electromagnet instead of permanent magnet** (as permanent magnet does not produce strong magnetic field).

Large number of turns of the conducting wire in the current-carrying coil to produce stronger magnetic field. It also has a soft iron core on which the coil is wound also known as armature.

13. **(ii)** Both Assertion and Reason are true but reason is not the correct explanation of the assertion. **1**

Explanation: The stars twinkle while the planets do not. It is due to variation in density of atmospheric layer. As the stars are very far and giving light continuously to us. So, the light coming from stars is found to change their intensity continuously. Hence they are seen twinkling. Also stars are much bigger in size than planets but it has nothing to deal with twinkling phenomenon.

14. **(ii)** Both A and R are true but R is not the correct explanation of the assertion. **1**

Explanation: Both assertion and reasoning are true and Reason is not the correct explanation of the assertion.

SECTION - B

15. Magnesium (Mg) belongs to group 2 known as alkaline earth family. The two other elements belonging to the same group are Calcium (Ca) and Strontium (Sr) which are expected to show chemical reactions similar to Magnesium (Mg). The basis of choice is the electronic distribution in the valence shell of these elements. All of them have two valence electrons each. And since chemical properties are due to valence electrons, they show same chemical reactions. 2

	K	L	M	N	O
Mg(Z = 12)	2	8	2	-	-
Ca(Z = 20)	2	8	8	2	-
Sr(Z = 38)	2	8	18	8	2

1

OR

Electronic configurations of the two elements are:

Element	K	L	M
Nitrogen (7)	2	5	
Phosphorous (15)	2	8	5

1

Nitrogen is more electronegative than phosphorus. On moving down a group, the number of shells increases. Therefore, the valence electrons move away from the nucleus and the effective nuclear charge decreases. This causes the decrease in the tendency to attract electrons and hence electro-negativity decreases. 2

16. Experiment to demonstrate hydrotropism :

Aim: To demonstrate hydrotropism

Materials Required: Bean seeds, a deep container, sand and a porous flower pot.

Experiment:

Fill the container with sand. Make a pit on one side of the container and insert seeds on this side. Make a pit on other side of the container and insert the porous pot on the other side. Fill the porous pot with water. Now, keep aside the entire set-up for a week.

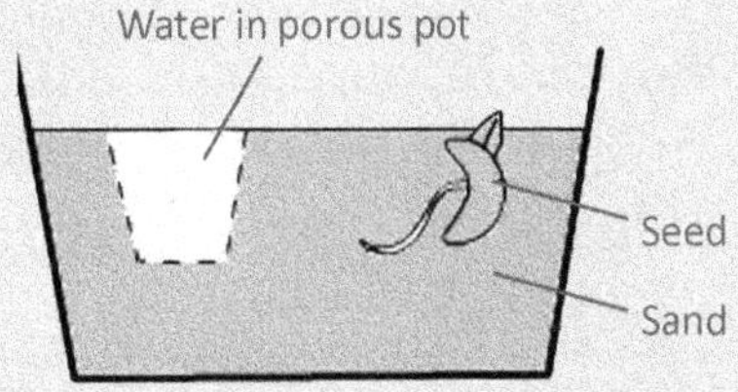

Setup Showing Hydrotropism

Observation:

After a week, when seeds are taken out, it is observed that the roots of the germinating seeds will grow in the direction of porous pot. This experiment demonstrates the phenomenon of hydrotropism in roots. 3

OR

(a) The gap between two neuron is called a synapse. 1

(b) Difference between reflex action and walking:

A reflex action is a rapid, automatic response to a stimulus which is not under the voluntary control of the brain. It does not involve any thinking. It involves only our spinal cord. For example, we close our eyes immediately when the bright light is focused on our eyes.

Walking is a voluntary action which requires our thinking. It is under our conscious control and involves thinking by the brain. The central nervous system (brain and spinal cord) takes part in the action of walking. 2

17. Difference between strong and weak acids.

Strong acid	Weak acid
Acids which dissociate completely in the aqueous solution to produce a large amount of H^+ ions are called strong acids. They conduct electricity to a large extent. They have pH between 0 to 3.	Acids which dissociate only partially in the aqueous solution to produce a small amount of H^+ ions are called week acids. They conduct electricity to a small extent. They have pH between 5 and 7.

2

Strong acid: Hydrochloric acid, nitric acid.

Week acid: Acetic acid, formic acid. **1**

18. **(a)** The female sex hormones 'oestrogen' and 'progesterone' made in ovaries are responsible for the changes noticed in females at puberty.

(b) Dwarfism results due to the deficiency of growth hormone.

(c) Blood sugar level rises due to deficiency of Insulin hormone.

(d) Iodine is necessary for the synthesis of thyroxine hormone.

(e) Hyprothalamus glands control the secretion of hormones from the pituitary.

(f) Hormone that prepares our body in emergency situation is adrenaline hormone. **½ × 6 = 3**

19. **(a)** The eye lens forms a real and inverted image on the retina of the eye. **1**

(b) There is no change to the image distance in the eye when we increase the distance of an object from the eye. To see closer or distant object clearly, the eyes, due to its ability of accommodation, can increase or decrease focal length of its lens, so that the image is always formed at retina. To see closer or distant objects, focal length of its lenses can be increased or decreased to some extent by the contraction and relaxation of the ciliary muscles. **2**

20. **(a)** The property of a conductor due to which it opposes the flow of current through it is called resistance. The resistance of a conductor is numerically equal to the ratio of potential difference across its ends to the current flowing through it. **1**

(b) When mercury is cooled to 4.12 K, the electrical resistance of mercury disappears completely and becomes zero. **1**

(c) This phenomenon of loss of electrical resistance of a substance on cooling it to an extremely low temperature is known as superconductivity. **1**

21. A metal M forms an oxide having the formula M_2O_3. It is dissolved both in dilute sulphuric and dilute sodium hydroxide solution. Identify the metal and write equations for the reaction involved.

Here the metal oxide dissolves in sulphuric as well as sodium hydroxide solution. That means metal oxide is showing acidic as well as basic character. So metal oxide is amphoteric oxide.

The metal is Aluminium (Al) and it forms aluminium oxide ($Al_2O\text{-}_3$) which is amphoteric that is it shows the nature of both acidic and basic. **1**

$Al_2O_3 + 3H_2SO_4 \longrightarrow Al_2(SO_4)_3 + 3H_2O$ **1**

$Al_2O_3 + 6NaOH \longrightarrow 2NaAlO_2 + H_2O$ **1**

22. **Ecosystem:** An Ecosystem is a self contained unit of living things (plants, animals and decomposers) and their non-living environment (soil, air and water). It needs only the input of sunlight energy for its functioning. **1**

Types of Ecosystem: There are two types of ecosystem:

Natural ecosystem: These ecosystems operate in the nature by themselves without any human interference. They can be terrestrial or aquatic. The common examples of terrestrial ecosystem are forest, grassland and desert. The common examples of aquatic ecosystem are ponds, lakes, rivers, sea.

Man-made or artificial ecosystem: These are maintained by man and hence are called Man-made ecosystems or artificial ecosystem. Man maintains the natural balance by the addition of energy and planned manipulations. Example: crop field, aquarium, garden. **2**

23. An electric iron is used on a 240V supply and draws a current of 4

Ampere. Therefore,

Voltage, $V = 240V$

Current, $I = 4A$

Time, $t = 31 \times 10$ hours

$= 310$ hours.

(a) Power, $P = V \times I$

$= 240 \times 4 = 960$ W **1**

(b) Resistance, $R = \frac{V}{I} = \frac{240}{4}$

$= 60$ ohms **1**

(c) Electric energy consumed

= Power × Time

$= 960 \times 310$

$= 297600$ watt hours

$= 297.6$ KWH

Cost of using the heater for 310 hours $= 297.6 \times$ ₹ 3.40

= ₹ 1011.84 **1**

OR

(a) Two resistors R_1 and R_2 should be connected in parallel so that the effective resistance of the circuit is minimum.

Here effective resistance, R_1

$$\frac{1}{R} = \frac{1}{R_1} + \frac{1}{R_2} \quad ...(1)$$

(b) $R_1 = 4\Omega$

$R_2 = 8\Omega$

Let, Potential difference = V

Then $I_1 = \frac{V_1}{R_1} = \frac{V}{4\Omega}$

$$I_2 = \frac{V_2}{R_2} = \frac{V}{8\Omega}$$

$$\frac{I_1}{I_2} = \frac{V/4\Omega}{V/8\Omega}$$

$$= \frac{8\Omega}{4\Omega} = \frac{2}{1}$$

$\Rightarrow$ $I_1 : I_2 = 2 : 1$ ...(2)

24. Role of forests in ecological system: We should conserve forests because they provide raw material for a number of industries. They maintain water cycle in nature by bringing in sufficient rainfall. They provide natural habitat to wild animals and birds. They are essential for maintaining ecological balance in nature. They also prevent soil erosion and floods.

Role of wildlife in ecological system: We should conserve wildlife to maintain ecological balance in nature. Wild animals like lions and tiger maintain the forest ecosystem because they keep the population of herbivorous animals under control and save the vegetation from overgrazing and its ill effects on environment. Wildlife should also be conserved to prevent the extinction of rare varieties of birds and animals found on earth. **3**

SECTION - C

25. Structure of nephrons: Nephron is the filtration unit of kidney. It consists of a tubule which is connected with urine collecting duct of the kidney at one end and a cup – shaped structure at the other end. This cup-shaped structure is called 'Bowman's capsule'. Every Bowman's capsule contains a cluster of capillaries called Glomerulus. The blood enters into Glomerulus through afferent arteriole of renal artery and leaves it through efferent arteriole. **2**

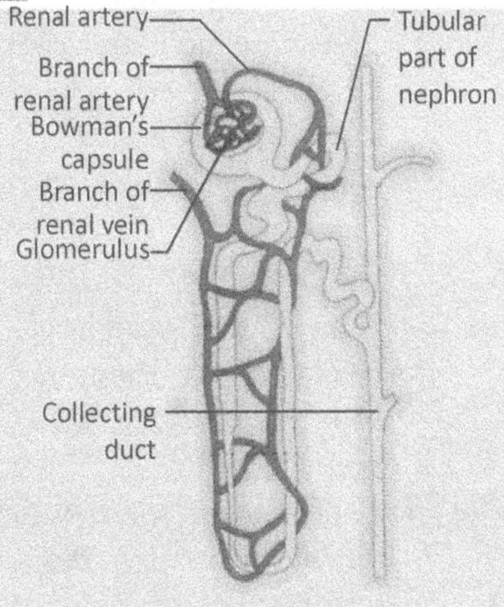

Structure of Nephron

Functioning of Nephron

- Filtration: Filtration of blood takes place in Bowman's capsule from the capillaries of glomerulus. The filtrate passes into the tubular part of the nephron. This filtrate contains glucose, amino acids, urea, uric acid, salts and a major amount of water.
- Re-absorption: As the filtrate flows along the tubule, useful substances such as glucose, amino acids, salts and water are re-absorbed into the blood by capillaries surrounding the nephron tubule.
- Urine: The filtrate which remains after re-absorption is called urine. Urine contains dissolved nitrogenous waste, *i.e.* urea and uric acid, excess salts and water. Urine is collected from nephrons by the collecting duct to carry it to the ureter and ultimately passed out of the body through urethra. 3

OR

To get rid of excretory products, plants use the following ways:

- The plants produce carbon dioxide as a waste product during respiration and oxygen as a waste product during photosynthesis. The plants get rid of gaseous waste products through stomata in their leaves and lenticels in stems.
- Many waste products are stored in vacuoles of the cells. Plant cells have comparatively large vacuoles. Some waste products are stored in the leaves. They are removed as the leaves fall off.
- Some waste products such as resins and gums are stored, especially in non-functional old xylem.
- Some waste products such as tannins, resins, gums are stored in bark, thereby removed as barks are peeled off.
- Plants excrete some waste products through roots into the soil around them.
- Plants also get rid of excess water through transpiration. 5

26. **(a)** Graphite is an allotrope of carbon which consists of fused benzene rings. 1

(b) Carbon atom has 4 electrons in its outermost shell. It needs 4 more electrons to complete its octet. Therefore it is tetravalent. 1

(c) Electron dot structure of a sulphur molecule:

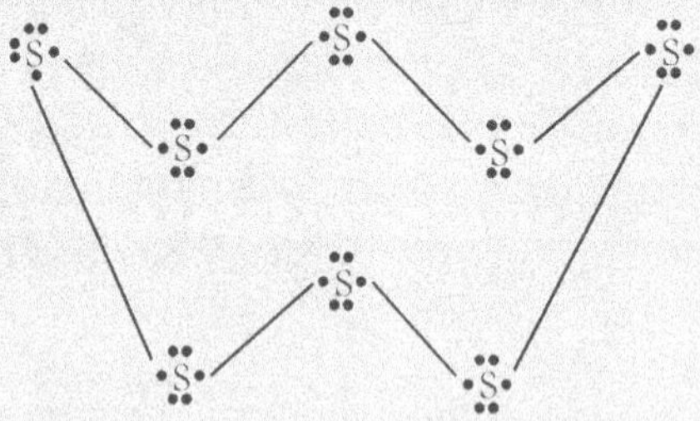

1

(d) The two features of carbon that give rise to a large number of carbon compounds or organic compounds are as follows :

Catenation: Carbon has the unique ability to form bonds with other atoms of carbon, giving rise to large molecules. This property is called catenation. These compounds may have long chains of carbon, branched chains of carbon or even carbon atoms arranged in rings.

Tetravalency: Since, carbon has a valency of four, it is capable of bonding with four other atoms of carbon or atoms of some other mono-valent element. Compounds of carbon are formed with oxygen, hydrogen, nitrogen, sulphur, chlorine and many other elements. 2

OR

(a) Most of the carbon compounds give large amount of heat and light on combustion due to high percentage of carbon and hydrogen present in them. Carbon compounds are used as fuel as they have optimum ignition temperature with high calorific value and are also easy to handle. Their combustion can also be controlled. Therefore, carbon and its compounds are used as fuels for most applications. **2**

(b) During electrolytic refining, impure metal is made anode and a thin strip of pure metal M is made cathode and the electrolyte used is the soluble salt of Metal M which is to be refined.

Anode → Impure metal M

Cathode → Thin strip of pure metal M

Electrolyte → Solution of salt of the metal M. **3**

27. **(a)** In the given cross, two traits were taken into account, which is a dihybrid cross. The round shape and yellow colour of seed is dominant over the wrinkled shape and green colour of seed in pea plant as observed by Mendel. Suppose R and Y denote dominant trait and r and y denote recessive trait. Genotype of the parent plant with round and green seeds – RRyy

Genotype of the parent plant with wrinkled and yellow seeds – rrYY

Therefore, the cross involved in the given question is

Parents: RRyy (Round green) × rrYY (Wrinkled yellow)

Gametes: Ry, rY

F_1 generation: RrYy (Round and Yellow)

The above cross shows round and yellow seeds in the F1 generation. It occurs because dominant traits (round and yellow) express itself, whereas recessive traits (wrinkled and green) get suppressed. **2**

(b) On selfing of F1 generation:

Phenotypic ratio 9:3:3:1

Round yellow: 9 Round green: 3 Wrinkled yellow: 3 Wrinkled green: 1

RrYy × RrYy

Gametes RY, rY, Ry, ry RY, rY, Ry, ry

F2	RY	rY	Ry	ry
RY	RRYY Round yellow	RrYY Round yellow	RRYy Round yellow	RrYy Round yellow
rY	RrYY Round yellow	rrYY Wrinkled yellow	RrYy Round yellow	rrYy Wrinkled yellow
Ry	RRYy Round yellow	RrYy Round yellow	RRyy Round green	Rryy Round green
ry	RrYy Round yellow	rrYy Wrinkled yellow	Rryy Round green	rryy Wrinkled green

3

28. **(a)** The distance between the principal focus and optical centre of a lens is known as focal length of the lens. It is denoted by f. **1**

(b) Size of object, h = 7.0 cm

Distance of object, u = – 27cm

Focal length, f = – 18cm

Distance of image, v =?

Height of image, h'=?

We know that,

$$\frac{1}{u}+\frac{1}{v}=\frac{1}{f},$$

$$\frac{1}{v}=\frac{1}{f}-\frac{1}{u}$$

$$= -\frac{1}{18} + \frac{1}{27}$$

$$= -\frac{1}{54}$$

$$v = -54 \text{ cm}$$

Thus, to obtain a sharp and focused image, screen will be placed at a distance of 54 cm in front of the concave mirror. 2

Magnification

$$m = \frac{h'}{h} = -\frac{v}{u}$$

$$= -\frac{-54}{-27}$$

$$= -2$$

Or $$h' = -\frac{v}{u} \times h$$

$$= \frac{54}{-27} \times 7$$

$$= -14$$

h' is negative, so image will be inverted.

Position of image = 54 cm in front of mirror.

Size of image = 14 cm, *i.e.* double size of object, *i.e.* enlarged.

Nature of image = Inverted and real

(Because magnification and distance of image are in negative) 2

29. **(a) Balanced chemical equations for the following reactions:**

(i) Calcium hydroxide + Carbon dioxide ⟶ Calcium carbonate + Water

$$Ca(OH)_2 + CO_2 \longrightarrow Ca(CO)_3 + H_2O$$

(ii) Zinc + Silver nitrate ⟶ Zinc nitrate + Silver

$$Zn + 2AgNO_3 \longrightarrow Zn(NO_3)_2 + 2Ag$$

(iii) Aluminium + Copper chloride ⟶ Aluminium chloride + Copper

$$2Al + 3CuCl_2 \longrightarrow 2AlCl_3 + 3Cu$$ 3

(b) Respiration is considered as an exothermic reaction because in respiration oxidation of glucose takes place which produces large amount of energy.

This is shown in following chemical equation:

$$C_6H_{12}O_6 + 6O_2 \longrightarrow 6CO_2 + 6H_2O + \text{Energy}$$ 2

30. **Underlying principle of an electric generator** : Electric generator is a device which converts mechanical energy into electrical energy. An electric generator is based on the principle of electromagnetic induction. When the coil of generator rotates in a magnetic field, induced current flows in a circuit connected with the coil. 1

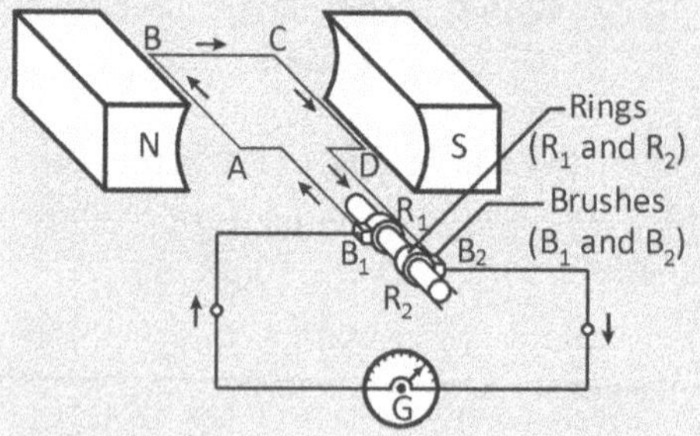

2

Working of Electric Generator:

When the axle is rotated in order to move the coil; the arm AB of the coil moves up and the arm CD moves down.

Due to Fleming's Right Hand rule, electric current is induced which flows from AB to CD and thus the current moves from the brush B_2 to B_1. Thus, the induced current moves in the direction ABCD.

Large number of turns; in the coil; results in add-on effect to produce a large amount of current.

The brushes in an electric generator pass on the induced current to the output wire. 2

OR

The process, by which a changing magnetic field in a conductor induces a current in another conductor, is called electromagnetic induction. In practice, we can induce the current in a coil either by moving it in a magnetic field or by changing the magnetic field around it. 1

Experiment: Take two different coils of copper wire having large number of turns (say 40 and 90 turns respectively). Insert them over a non-conducting cylindrical roll, as shown in the figure given below. Connect the coil-1, having a larger number of turns, in series with a battery and a plug key. 2

Also, connect the other coil-2 with a galvanometer as shown in the figure. Plug in the key. Observe the galvanometer. We will observe that the needle of the galvanometer instantly jumps to one side and just as quickly returns to zero, indicating a momentary current in coil-2.

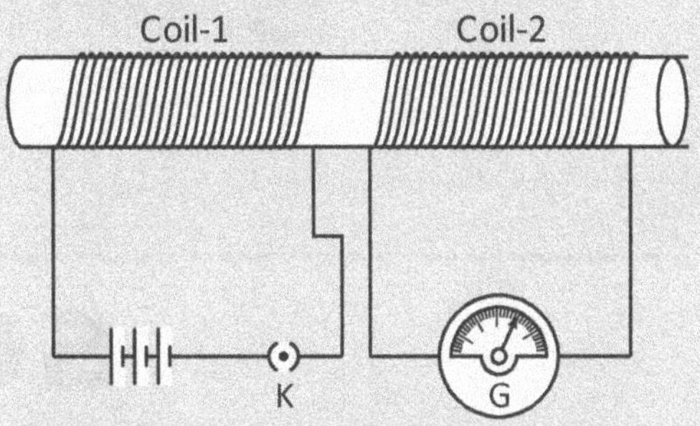

Disconnect coil-1 from the battery. You will observe that the needle momentarily moves but to the opposite side. It means that now the current flows in the opposite direction in coil-2. 2

7

SAMPLE PAPER

CBSE - Class 10

SCIENCE

Time Allowed: 3 Hours *Maximum Marks: 80*

General Instructions:

i. The question paper comprises three sections – A, B and C. Attempt all the sections.
ii. All questions are compulsory.
iii. Internal choice is given in each section.
iv. All questions in Section A are one-mark questions comprising MCQ, VSA type and assertion-reason type questions. They are to be answered in one word or in one sentence.
v. All questions in Section B are three-mark, short-answer type questions. These are to be answered in about 50 - 60 words each.
vi. All questions in Section C are five-mark, long-answer type questions. These are to be answered in about 80 - 90 words each.
vii. This question paper consists of a total of 30 questions.

SECTION - A

1. AB and CD, two spherical mirrors, form parts of a hollow spherical ball with its centre at O as shown in the diagram. If arc AB = $\frac{1}{2}$ arc CD, what is the ratio of their focal lengths? 1

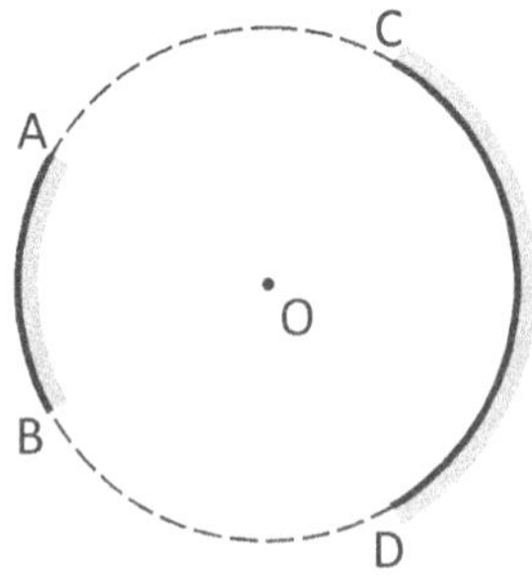

2. Give 2 examples of each:

(a) Organisms occupying the first trophic level

(b) Abiotic factors of an ecosystem 1

3. **Answer question numbers 3(a)-3(d) on the basis of your understanding of the following paragraph and the related studied concepts.**

Oxygen-rich blood from the lungs comes to the thin-walled upper chamber of the heart on the left, the left atrium. The left atrium relaxes when it is collecting this blood. It then contracts, while the next chamber, the left ventricle, expands, so that the blood is transferred to it. When the muscular left ventricle contracts in its turn, the blood is pumped out to the body. De-oxygenated blood comes from the body to the upper chamber on the right, the right atrium, as it expands. As the right atrium contracts, the corresponding lower chamber, the right ventricle, dilates. This transfers blood to the right ventricle, which in turn pumps it to the lungs for oxygenation. Since ventricles have to pump blood into various organs, they have thicker muscular walls than the atria do. Valves ensure that blood does not flow backwards when the atria or ventricles contract.

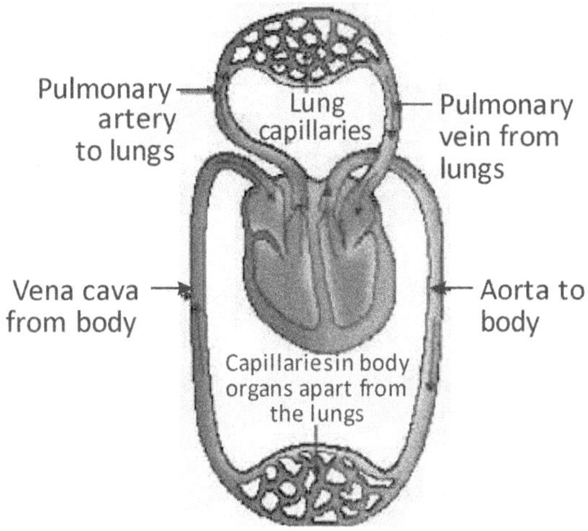

3(a) Name the organs of the circulatory system in humans. **1**

3(b) Name the red pigment which carries oxygen in the blood. **1**

3(c) How many chambers are there in the heart of an amphibian? **1**

3(d) Why is it necessary to separate oxygenated and deoxygenated blood in mammals and birds? **1**

4. Analyse the following table given below and answer the questions that follow:

Given alongside is a part of the periodic table. As we move vertically downward from Li to Fr:

Li	Be
Na	
K	
Rb	
Cs	
Fr	Ra

4(a) Which among the following has larger size of atoms?

(i) Li **(ii)** Na

(iii) Cs **(iv)** Fr **1**

4(b) Which one of the following does not increase while moving down to group of the periodic table?

(i) Atomic radius **(ii)** Metallic character

(iii) Valence **(iv)** Number of shells in an element **1**

4(c) Name two properties of elements whose magnitude change while going from top to bottom in a group of the periodic table. In what manner do they change? **1**

4(d) Rewrite the following statement after correction, if necessary:

"Groups have elements with consecutive atomic numbers" **1**

5. A constant current flows in a horizontal wire in the plane of the paper from east to west as shown in figure. The direction of magnetic field at a point will be north to south:

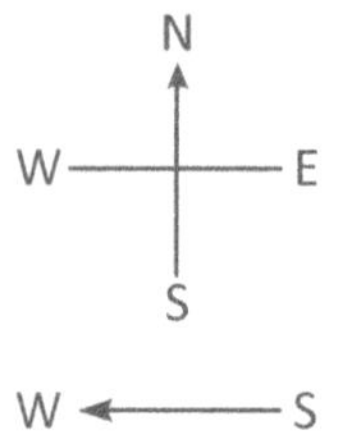

(i) Directly above the wire
(ii) Directly below the wire
(iii) At a point located in the plane of the paper on the north side of the wire
(iv) At a point located in the plane of the paper on the south side of the wire **1**

6. The theory of evolution of species by natural selection was given by:
(i) Mendel **(ii)** Darwin
(iii) Morgan **(iv)** Lamarck **1**

7. A current of 1 A is drawn by a filament of an electric bulb. Number of electron passing through a cross-section of the filament in 16 seconds would be roughly:
(i) 10^{20} **(ii)** 10^{16}
(iii) 10^{18} **(iv)** 10^{23} **1**

OR

What is the maximum resistance which can be made using five resistors each of 1/5 Ω?
(i) 1/5 Ω **(ii)** 10 Ω
(iii) 5 Ω **(iv)** 1 Ω **1**

8. Acid rain happens because:
(i) sun leads to heating of upper layer of atmosphere
(ii) burning of fossil fuels release oxides of carbon, nitrogen and sulphur in the atmosphere
(iii) electrical charges are produced due to friction amongst clouds
(iv) the earth atmosphere contains acids **1**

9. Offspring formed by asexual method of reproduction have greater similarity among themselves because:
(a) Asexual reproduction involves only one parent
(b) Asexual reproduction does not involve gametes
(c) Asexual reproduction occurs before sexual reproduction
(d) Asexual reproduction occurs after sexual reproduction
(i) (a) and (b) **(ii)** (a) and (c)
(iii) (b) and (d) **(iv)** (c) and (d) **1**

OR

Which of the following is not associated with growth of plant?
(i) Auxin **(ii)** Gibberellins
(iii) Cytokinins **(iv)** Abscisic acid **1**

10. The electronic configurations of three elements X, Y and Z are:
X : 2 Y : 2, 8, 7 Z : 2, 8, 2
Which of the following is correct regarding these elements?
(i) X is a metal **(ii)** Y is a metal
(iii) Z is a non-metal **(iv)** Y is a non-metal and Z is a metal **1**

11. Equal volumes of hydrochloric acid and sodium hydroxide solutions of same concentration are mixed and the pH of the resulting solution is checked with a pH paper. What would be the colour obtained? (You may use colour guide in the figure given below).

(i) Red **(ii)** Yellow

(iii) Yellowish green **(iv)** Blue **1**

Colour	Dark Red	Red	Red	Orange Red	Orange	Orange Yellow	Greenish Yellow	Green	Greenish Blue	Blue	Navy Blue	Purple	Dark Purple	Violet	Violet
pH	0	1	2	3	4	5	6	7	8	9	10	11	12	13	14

OR

Which of the following is/are true when $HCl_{(g)}$ is passed through water:

(a) It does not ionise in the solution as it is a covalent compound

(b) It ionises in the solution

(c) It gives both hydrogen and hydroxyl ion in the solution

(d) It forms hydronium ion in the solution due to the combination of hydrogen ion with water molecule

(i) Only (a) **(ii)** Only (c)

(iii) (b) and (d) **(iv)** (c) and (d) **1**

12. The least distance of distinct vision for a young adult with normal vision is about:

(i) 25 m **(ii)** 2.5 cm

(iii) 25 cm **(iv)** 2.5 m **1**

For question numbers 13 and 14, two statements are given- one labeled Assertion (A) and the other labeled Reason (R). Select the correct answer to these questions from the codes (i), (ii), (iii) and (iv) as given below:

(i) Both A and R are true and R is correct explanation of the assertion.

(ii) Both A and R are true but R is not the correct explanation of the assertion.

(iii) A is true but R is false. **(iv)** A is false but R is true.

13. **Assertion A :** Bile is essential for fat digestion.

Reason R : Fats cannot be digested without emulsification. **1**

14. **Assertion A :** The word AMBULANCE on the hospital vans is written in the form of its mirror image as ƎƆИA⅃UᙠMA.

Reason R : The image formed in a plane mirror is same size as that of the object. **1**

SECTION - B

15. Three elements A, B and C have 3, 4 and 2 electrons respectively in their outermost shell. Give the group number to which they belong in the Modern Periodic table. Also give their valencies. **3**

16. **(a)** Why do we apply paint on iron articles?

(b) Oil and fat containing food items are flushed with nitrogen. Why? **3**

17. A doctor has prescribed the corrective lens of power + 1.5 D. Find the focal length of the lens. What would you conclude about the prescribed lens- diverging or converging? **3**

18. What is the difference between permanent magnet and electromagnet? **3**

19. Metal M occurs in earth's crust as its oxide M_2O_3. An alloy of this metal is used in making aircrafts.

(a) What is the name of the metal M?

(b) Name the ore from of this metal containing M_2O_3.

(c) Write other two important uses of M. **3**

OR

Give an example of a metal which:

(a) is a liquid at room temperature

(b) can be easily cut with a knife

(c) is the best conductor of heat

(d) is a poor conductor of heat

(e) has low melting point

(f) does not react with water **3**

20. The diagram below is that of a typical biogas plant:

(a) Identify the parts indicated by 1, 2, 3 and 4

(b) Name the microorganism responsible for the fermentation of the slurry in the digester

(c) Name two chemicals present in the manure or spent slurry

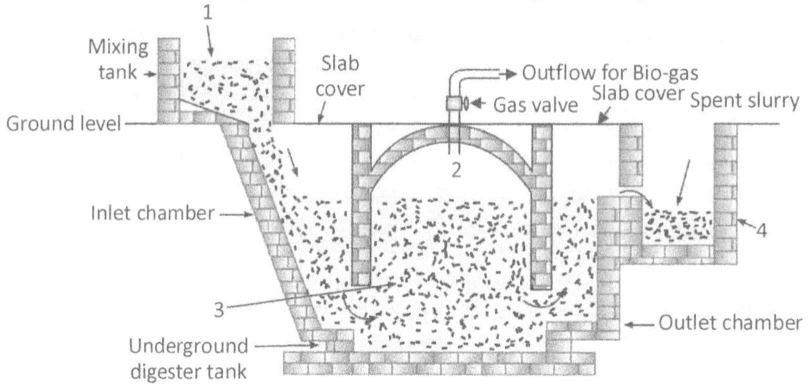

3

OR

What data would you use to assess the environmental consequences of the increasing demand for energy? **3**

21. How do Mendel's experiments show that traits are inherited independently? **3**

22. Study the circuit shown in which three identical bulbs B_1, B_2 and B_3 are connected in parallel with a battery of 4.5V.

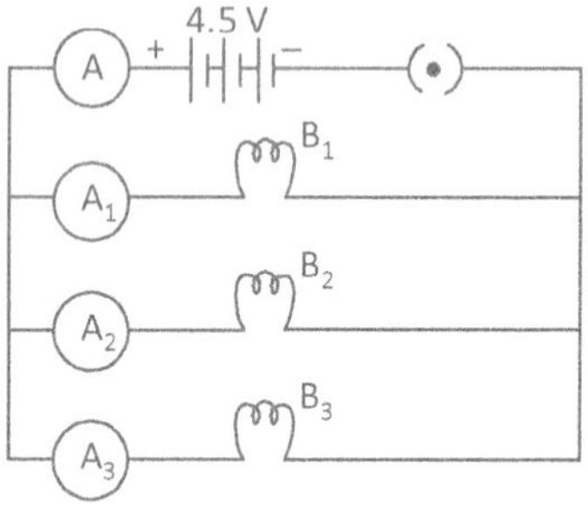

(a) What will happen to the glow of other two bulbs if the bulb B_3 gets fused?

(b) If the wattage of each bulb is 1.5 W, how much reading will the ammeter A show when all the three bulbs glow simultaneously?

(c) Find the total resistance of the circuit. **3**

23. How did 'Chipko Andolan' ultimately benefit the local people? Explain briefly. **3**

24. What happens when the following situations are initiated:

(a) A Planaria is cut into three different pieces

(b) Leaf of the Bryophyllum with notches falls on the soil

(c) Testosterone is released into the male reproductive system **3**

OR

(a) Name the hormone which is involved in phototropism.

(b) How is the movement of leaves of the sensitive plant different from the movement of a shoot towards light? **3**

SECTION - C

25. Draw the structures of the following compounds:

(a) Ethanoic acid **(b)** Bromopentane **(c)** Hexanal

(d) Butanone **(e)** Sodium ethanoate **5**

OR

(a) Give a chemical test to distinguish between saturated and unsaturated hydrocarbons.

(b) Name the products formed when ethane burns in air.

(c) Why is the reaction between methane and chlorine considered a substitution reaction? **5**

26. **(a)** Label the marked parts in the following diagram:

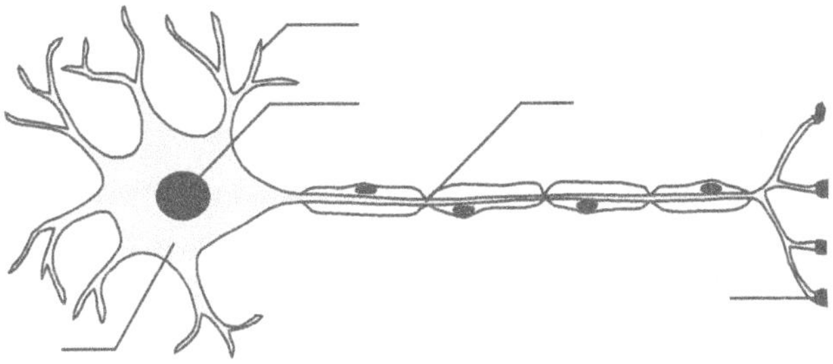

(b) Compare and contrast nervous and hormonal mechanisms for control and coordination in animals. **5**

27. **(a)** Draw a neat and labeled diagram to show the action of dilute sulphuric acid on zinc granules.

(b) Name the gas evolved.

(c) How will you test for the gas? **5**

28. Explain:

(a) Why a myopic person prefers to remove his spectacles, while reading a book?

(b) Why a hypermetropic person prefers to remove the spectacles while looking at the sky? **5**

OR

A person needs a lens of power –5.5 dioptres for correcting his distant vision. For correcting his near vision he needs a lens of power +1.5 dioptre. What is the focal length of the lens required for correcting?

(a) distant vision and **(b)** near vision **5**

29. Define the following processes:

(a) Fertilization **(b)** Menstruation **(c)** Binary Fission

(d) Vegetative propagation **(e)** Regeneration **5**

OR

(a) Distinguish between a gamete and zygote.

(b) Explain their roles in sexual reproduction. **5**

30. **(a)** Establish a relationship to determine the equivalent resistance R of a combination of three resistors having resistances R_1, R_2 and R_3 connected in series.

(b) Calculate the equivalent resistance of the combination of three resistors of 2W, 3W and 6W joined in parallel. **5**

SOLUTION

CBSE - Class 10

7

SECTION - A

1. The focal length will depend upon the radius of the sphere which forms the spherical mirror. In the above case since both the mirrors are made from the same sphere thus the radius of curvature for both of them will be same and hence the focal length will also be same. Thus the ratio for the two mirrors will be 1:1. **1**

2. **(a)** Organisms occupying the first trophic level: trees, shrubs, grass.
   (b) Abiotic factors of an ecosystem: soil, water, light. **1**

3. **(a)** The various organs of the circulatory system in humans are: heart, arteries, veins and capillaries. **1**

3. **(b)** The red pigment which carries oxygen in the blood is Haemoglobin. **1**

3. **(c)** Three chambered heart. **1**

3. **(d)** It is necessary to separate the oxygenated blood from mixing with deoxygenated blood as mammals and birds have high energy needs because they constantly require energy to maintain their body temperature. **1**

4. **(a)** **(iv)** Fr **1**

   Explanation: Fr has greater atomic size as the atomic size increases gradually from lithium to francium.

4. **(b)** **(iii)** Valence **1**

   Explanation: Elements of the same group have same number of valence electrons hence valency will remain same.

4. **(c)** On going down in a group of the periodic table, the atomic size and metallic character increases. When we move down from top to bottom in group 1 of alkali metals, the size of atom increases gradually from lithium to francium.

   In group 1 of alkali metals, lithium is the least metallic element whereas francium is the most metallic element. **1**

4. **(d)** Periods have elements with consecutive atomic numbers. **1**

5. **(ii)** Directly below the wire **1**

   Explanation: If we observe the direction of magnetic field by applying right hand thumb rule then, we will find that the direction of magnetic field is from North to South below the wire.

6. **(ii)** Darwin **1**

   Explanation: Darwin proposed the theory of natural selection to explain the process of evolution.

7. **(i)** 10^{20} **1**

   Explanation:

   Here current = 1 A

   Time t = 16 s

   Number of electrons n = ?

We know that

$$\text{current } i = \frac{Q}{t} = \frac{ne}{t}$$

$$e = 1.6 \times 10^{-19} C$$

$$n = \frac{it}{e} = \frac{16}{(1.6 \times 10^{-19} C)} = 10^{20}$$

OR

(iv) 1 Ω **1**

Explanation: The maximum resistance is obtained when resistors are connected in series combination.

Thus equivalent resistance obtained by connecting five resistors of resistance 1/5 Ω each, in series = (1/5 + 1/5 + 1/5 + 1/5 + 1/5) = 1 Ω

8. **(ii)** burning of fossil fuels release oxides of carbon, nitrogen and sulphur in the atmosphere. **1**

Explanation: The oxides of carbon, nitrogen and sulphur that are released by burning fossil fuels form acidic oxides. These lead to acid rain which affects our water and soil resources.

9. (a) and (b). **1**

Explanation: Asexual reproduction does not involve gamete formation and fertilization.

OR

(iv) Abscisic acid **1**

Explanation: Abscisic acid (ABA) is a growth retardation hormone.

10. **(iv)** Y is a non-metal and Z is a metal. **1**

Explanation: Element Y has 1 less electron to complete its octet which is a property of non-metals. On the other hand, element Z has 2 extra electrons to become stable which is a property of metals.

11. **(iii)** Yellowish green **1**

Explanation: Hydrochloric acid and sodium hydroxide are strong acid and base respectively. So mixing of strong acid and strong base will form neutral salt and water giving the pH value as 7.

OR

(iii) (b) and (d) **1**

Explanation: HCI being a polar covalent compound which can easily ionize in water to form hydronium ions (H_3O^+) and chloride ions (Cl^-).

12. **(iii)** 25 cm **1**

Explanation: The least distance for distant vision for a young adult with normal vision is 25 cm.

13. **(i)** Both A and R are true and R is the correct explanation of assertion. **1**

Explanation: Bile contains bile acids, which are critical for digestion and absorption of fats and fat-soluble vitamins in the small intestine.

14. **(ii)** Both A and R are true and R is not the correct explanation of the assertion. **1**

Explanation: The word AMBULANCE on the hospital vans is written in the form of its mirror image because any vehicle, which is ahead of the ambulance van, can see the laterally inverted alphabets correctly from his rear view mirror and make way for it to pass through.

SECTION - B

15. **(a)** Element A has 3 valence electrons, therefore its valency is 3 and thus belongs to group 13 (3+10). As such it could be any one of the following: B, Al, Ga, In or Tl. **1**

(b) Element B has 4 valence electrons, therefore its valency is 4 and thus belongs to group 14 (4+10). The element B could be any one of the following: C, Si, Ge, Sn or Pb. **1**

(c) Element C has 2 valence electrons; therefore its valency is 2 and thus belongs to group 2. The element C could be any one of the following: Be, Mg, Ca, Sr, Ba or Ra. **1**

16. **(a)** Paint covers the surface of the iron articles. Hence moist air cannot come in contact with iron. As a result it cannot attack iron and this prevents rusting. **1**

(b) Nitrogen being an inert gas does not react easily with the oil and fat present in the food substances. But oxygen reacts easily with fats present in the fatty food substances and is oxidized to form compounds which have a bad smell *i.e.* food becomes rancid. It is because of this reason that food items containing oil and fat are flushed with nitrogen gas before their packing to remove oxygen present in the pack and thereby protecting the food from rancidity. **2**

17. It is given that Power = +1.5 D

We know that Power

$$= \frac{1}{f(\text{m})} = \frac{100}{f(\text{cm})}$$ **1**

$$1.5 = \frac{100}{f}$$

$$f = \frac{100}{1.5} = \frac{10}{15}$$

$$= 66.67 \text{ cm.}$$

The focal length of the lens = 66.67 cm **1**

As the focal length is positive, the prescribed lens will be converging lens (convex lens). **1**

18. Difference between permanent magnet and electromagnet:

Permanent Magnet	**Electromagnet**
They are permanently magnetized.	They are temporarily magnetized.
They are usually made of hard materials.	They are usually made of soft materials.
Magnetic field of a permanent magnet is weak.	Electromagnet gives a strong magnetic field.
The strength of the magnetic field line are constant *i.e.* it cannot be varied.	The strength of the magnetic field lines can be varied according to our need by increasing or decreasing electric current through the solenoid.
The poles of a permanent magnet cannot be changed.	The poles of electro-magnet can be altered by reversing the direction of electric current through the solenoid.
Example of permanent magnet is a Bar Magnet.	Example of a temporary magnet is solenoid wounded across a nail and connected to a battery.

3

19. **(a)** Since the metal is used in making aircrafts, therefore, the metal must be light and resistant to corrosion. This metal M must be aluminium. **1**

(b) Its oxide has the formula Al_2O_3 and the ore is bauxite, $Al_2O_3 . 2H_2O$. **1**

(c) Aluminium is used in making utensils, electric wires etc. **1**

OR

Example of metals which:

(a) Metal which is a liquid at room temperature is Mercury.

(b) Metal which can be easily cut with a knife are Lithium, Sodium, Potassium.

(c) Metal which is the best conductor of heat is Silver.

(d) Metal which is a poor conductor of heat is Lead.

(e) Metal which has low melting point is Mercury.

(f) Metals such as Lead, Copper, Silver and Gold do not react with water at all. **½ × 6 = 3**

20. **(a)** 1 is Slurry of cattle dung and water

2 is Gas tank containing bio-gas

3 is Digester containing dung and water mixture

4 is Overflow tank **1**

(b) Anaerobic microorganisms are responsible for the fermentation of the slurry in the digester. **1**

(c) Nitrogen and Phosphorous are the two chemicals present in the manure. **1**

OR

Environmental consequences of the increasing demand for energy:

Industrialization and increase in population has increased the demand for energy. Fossil fuels are easily accessible sources of energy that fulfill this demand. The increased use of fossil fuels has a harsh effect on the environment such as:

(a) Burning of fossil fuels to meet increasing demand for energy causes air-pollution.

(b) Construction of dams on rivers to generate hydroelectricity destroys large ecosystem which get submerged under water in the dams.

(c) Large amount of methane (which is a greenhouse gas) is produced when submerged vegetation rots under anaerobic conditions. This results in global warming and a rise in the sea level. **1 × 3 = 3**

21. Mendel took two pairs of alternative expression of two traits of a pea plant and crossed them. When he crossed pure-bred tall pea plants with pure-bred dwarf pea plants, he found that only tall pea plants were produced in F1 generation. The F1 progeny showed only the dominant characteristics among each pair. Now, when he crossed tall pea plants of the F1 generation, he found that the F2 progeny were either tall or dwarf. There were no plants with intermediate height. This indicates that pairs with alternate characteristics behave independently of the other pair and are thus inherited independent of each other. **3**

22. **(a)** As the bulbs are in parallel connection, even if bulb B3 gets fused the remaining two bulbs will glow with the same brightness. **1**

(b) Same current flows through all the bulbs as they are connected in parallel.

Total wattage will be added

$$V = 4.5 \text{ V}$$

$$P = 1.5 \text{ W} + 1.5 \text{ W} + 1.5$$

$$\text{W} = 4.5 \text{ W}$$

So $$I = \frac{P}{V} = \frac{4.5\text{W}}{4.5\text{V}}$$

$$= 1\text{A}$$

The ammeter reading would be 1 Ampere **1**

(c) Also we know that

$$V = IR$$

Therefore

$$R = \frac{V}{I} = \frac{4.5V}{1A}$$

$$= 4.5 \text{ ohms}$$ **1**

23. Chipko Andolan or Hug the Trees Movement was a protest against the cutting down of trees of the forest. In this Andolan, the women of Reni village in Garhwal hugged the tree trunks and did not allow the contractors to cut the trees. This Andolan quickly spread to other parts of the country and forced the government to stop cutting of the trees and conserve them.

It therefore led to the efficient management of the forest and also resulted in conservation of soil and water which benefitted the local people as they continued to get food and other benefits from the forest. **3**

24. **(a)** When planaria is cut into three pieces, each piece will regenerate into a new planaria. **1**

(b) Buds that are produced in the notches along the leaf of bryophyllum fall on the soil and develop into new plants. **1**

(c) In men, testosterone plays a key role in the development of male sex organs and male features such as deeper voice, moustache, beard etc. All these changes are associated with male puberty which the boys attain at an age of 13 to 14 years. **1**

OR

(a) The hormone which is involved in phototropism is auxin **1**

(b) Difference between the movement of leaves of the sensitive plant different from the movement of a shoot towards light:

Movement of Leaves of the Sensitive Plant	Movement of a Shoot towards Light
1. It does not depend on the direction of stimulus applied.	1. It depends on the direction of stimulus applied.
2. Here the stimulus is touch.	2. Here the stimulus is light.
3. It is caused by the sudden loss of water from the swellings at the base of leaves.	3. It is caused by the unequal growth on the two sides of the shoot.
4. This movement is independent of the growth.	4. This movement is growth dependent.

2

SECTION - C

25. **(a)** Ethanoic Acid: CH_3COOH

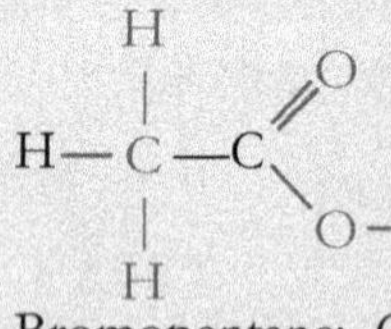

(b) Bromopentane: $C_5H_{11}Br$

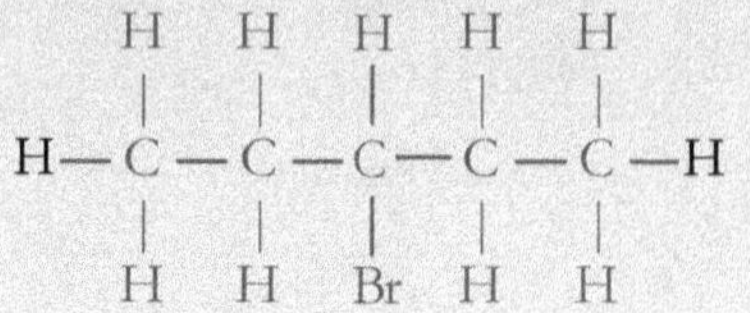

OR

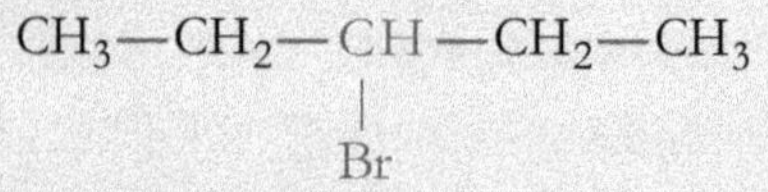

1

(c) Hexanal: $C_6H_{12}O$

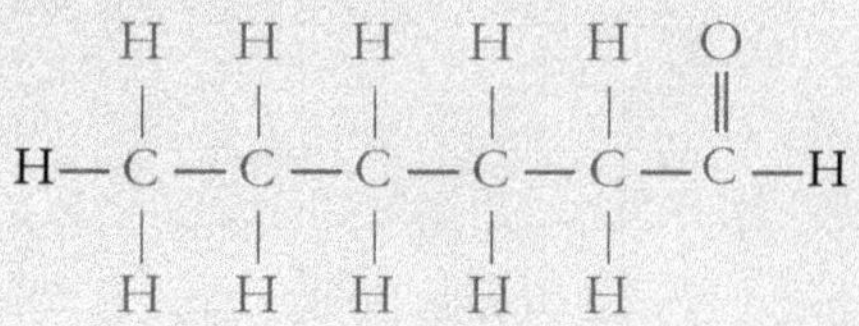

1

(d) Butanone: C_4H_8O

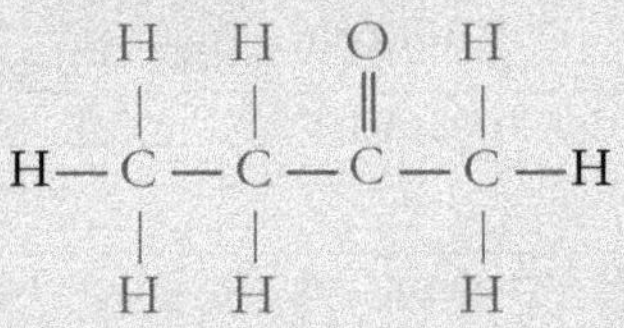

1

(e) Sodium Ethanoate: $C_2H_3NaO_2$

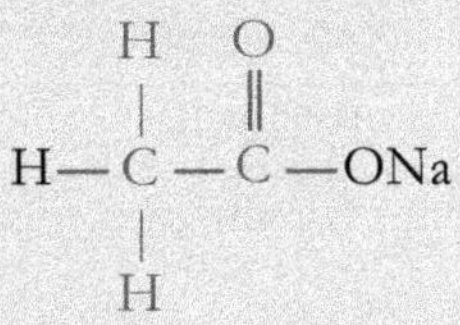

1

OR

(a) A chemical test to distinguish between saturated and unsaturated hydrocarbon is

Bromine water test:

Unsaturated hydrocarbon gives addition reaction with Bromine. So the colour of Bromine water gets decolourised.

$$CH_2{=}CH_2 + Br_2 \xrightarrow{CCl_4} Br{-}CH_2{-}CH_2{-}Br$$

$$CH{\equiv}CH + Br_2 \xrightarrow{CCl_4}$$

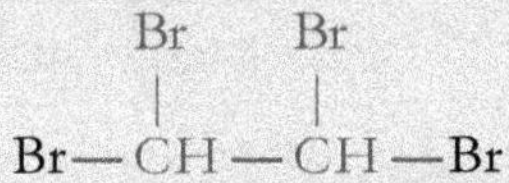

Whereas, saturated hydrocarbons do not react with Bromine water and so the colour of Bromine water does not get decolourised. 2

(b) When ethane ($CH_3{-}CH_3$) is burnt in air (oxygen), it forms carbon dioxide and water.

$$C_2H_6 + \frac{7}{2}O_2 \longrightarrow 2CO_2 + 3H_2O + \text{heat + light}$$

This reaction is called an exothermic reaction due to the evolution of heat. 1

(c) When ethane ($CH_3{-}CH_3$) is burnt in

(c) When methane reacts with chlorine in the presence of light, the following reaction takes place:

$$CH_4 + Cl_2 \xrightarrow{\text{Sunlight}} \underset{\text{(Chloromethane)}}{CH_3Cl} + HCl$$

Here hydrogen is getting substituted by chlorine:

$$\underset{\text{(Chloromethane)}}{CH_3Cl} + Cl_2 \xrightarrow{\text{Sunlight}} CH_2Cl_2 + HCl$$

$$CH_2Cl_2 + Cl_2 \xrightarrow{\text{Sunlight}} \underset{\text{(Chloroform)}}{CHCl_3} + HCl$$

$$CHCl_3 + Cl_2 \xrightarrow{\text{Sunlight}} \underset{\text{(Carbon tetrachloride)}}{CCl_4} + HCl$$

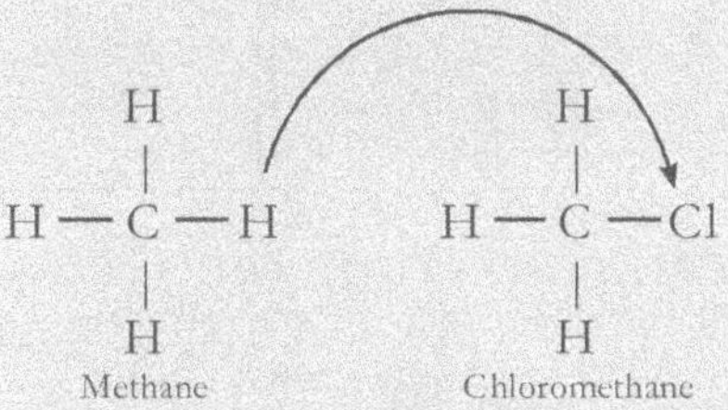

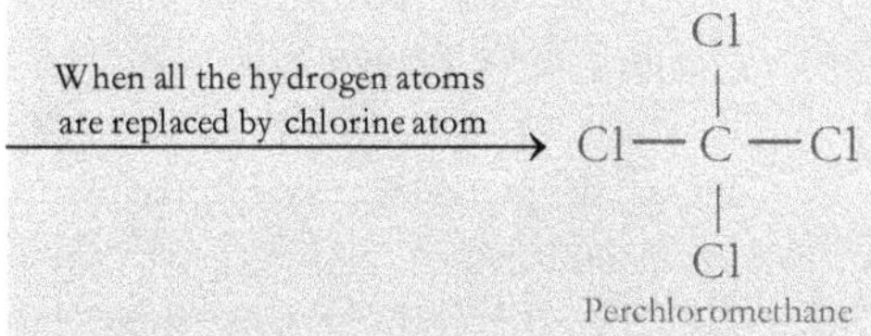

It is considered a substitution reaction because in this reaction hydrogen is substituted with chlorine. 2

26. (a) Labeled diagram of a Neuron:

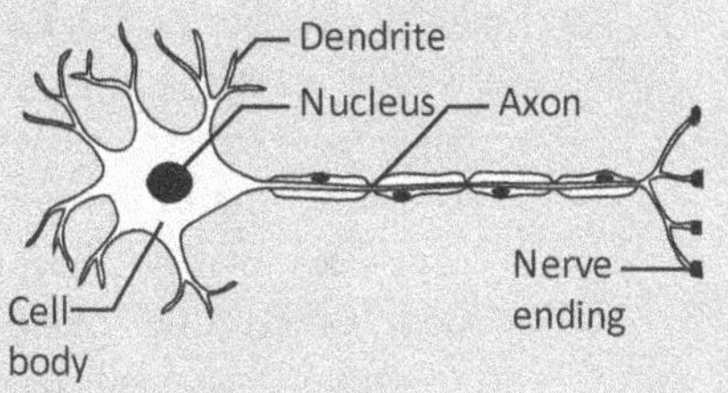

2

(b) Comparison of the nervous system and endocrine system:

Nervous system	Endocrine system
Nervous system is made of neurons.	Endocrine system is made of secretory cells.
Messages transmitted in the form of electrical impulses.	Messages transmitted in the form of chemicals called hormones.
Messages transmitted along nerve fibres.	Messages transmitted through blood stream.
Messages travel very quickly.	Messages travel more slowly.
Effect of message lasts for a very short while.	Effect of messages usually lasts longer.

3

27. (a) Action of dilute sulphuric acid on zinc granules.

2

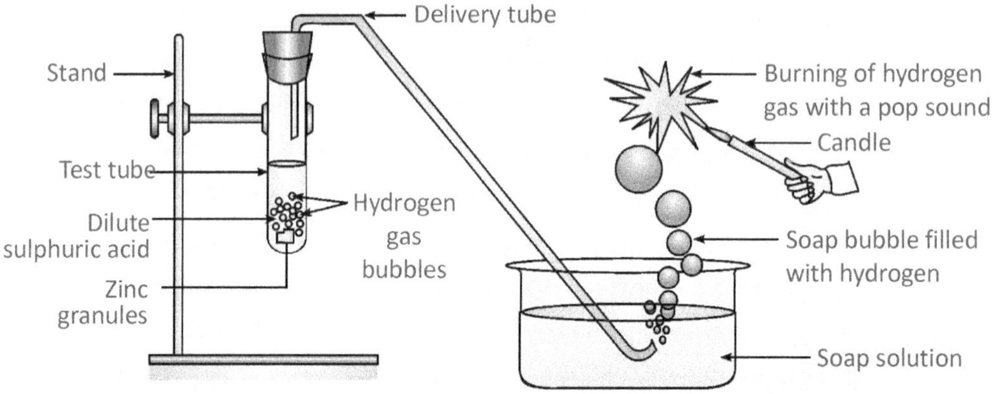

(b) The gas evolved is hydrogen.

$H_2SO_4 + Zn \longrightarrow ZnSO_4 + H_2(g)$ 1

(c) **We can test** for the hydrogen gas by passing it through soap solution and then bringing a burning candle near the soap bubbles filled with gas. Hydrogen gas will burn with pop sound. 2

28. (a) The myopic person may have a normal near point, *i.e.*, about 25 cm (or even less). In order to read a book with the spectacles, such a person must keep the book at a distance greater than 25 cm so that the image of the book by the concave lens is produced no closer than 25 cm. The angular size of the book (or its image) at the greater distance is evidently less than the angular size when the book is placed at 25 cm and no spectacles are needed. Hence, the person prefers to remove the spectacles while reading. 2½

(b) A hypermetropic person does not need spectacles to see distant objects as he has the far point at infinity. He cannot see nearby objects clearly while he can see distant objects clearly as his near point is more than 25 cm. Therefore, his far point will be infinity (here, sky), so his eye can easily focus the image of the sky on the retina. So, there is no need to wear spectacles at that time. 2½

OR

Power of a lens is defined by

$$D = \frac{1}{f}$$

where

f = focal length of the lens in meters. 1

(a) $D = -5.5$ dioptre

$$D = \frac{1}{f}$$

$$f = \frac{1}{D} = -\frac{1}{5.5} \text{ m}$$

$$= -\frac{100}{5.5} \text{ cm} = -0.1818\text{m}$$

$$= -18.18 \text{ cm}$$

Hence, for distant vision the person need the concave lens (negative focal length) of 18.18cm. **2**

(b) $D = 1.5$ dioptre

$$D = \frac{1}{f}$$

$$f = \frac{1}{D} = \frac{1}{1.5} \text{ m}$$

$$= 0.6666\text{m} = 66.66 \text{ cm}$$

Hence, for near vision the person need the convex lens (positive focal length) of 66.66 cm. **2**

29. **(a) Fertilisation**: The fusion of male gamete with a female gamete to form a zygote is known as fertilisation. **1**

(b) Menstruation: The breakdown and removal of the inner, thick and soft lining of the uterus along with its blood vessels in the form of vaginal bleeding when the egg is not fertilised is known as menstruation. It lasts for about two to eight days. **1**

(c) Binary Fission: Binary fission in an asexual mode of reproduction in which parent organism splits to form two new organisms. It can be seen in Amoeba. **1**

(d) Vegetative Propagation: In vegetative propagation, new plants are obtained from the parts of old plants like the root, stem or leaves etc., without the help of any reproductive organ. It can be seen in Bryophyllum **1**

(e) Regeneration: When body of an organism cuts into any number of pieces and each piece grows into a complete organism it is known as regeneration. It can be seen in Hydra and Planaria. **1**

OR

(a)

S.No.	Gamete	Zygote
1.	The germ cells that are fused during sexual reproduction are called gametes, e.g., sperm (male) and Ova (female).	It is product of fusion of male gamete and female gamete during sexual reproduction.
2.	Gametes are unfertilized reproductive cells.	Zygote is fertilized egg or fertilized Ovum.
3.	Being the product of meiosis, gamete are always haploid cells.	Since zygote is product of fusion of haploid male and female gamete, it is a diploid structure.

1 × 3 = 3

(b) Importance of gametes and zygote in sexual reproduction:

- Gametes are product of meiosis and hence carry half the chromosome number as that of parent cells.
- This chromosome number is restored during fertilization and zygote formation.
- Hence, gamete and zygote are the two phases of sexually reproducing organisms that help maintain the constant chromosome number in each species. **2**

30. **(a)** When two or more resistors are joined end to end, they are said to be connected in series combination. When two or more resistances are connected in series, then:

- The <u>current</u> through the circuit and also through <u>each resistor</u> <u>remains the same</u>.
- The <u>potential difference</u> becomes <u>sum of the individual potential difference across each resistor</u>.

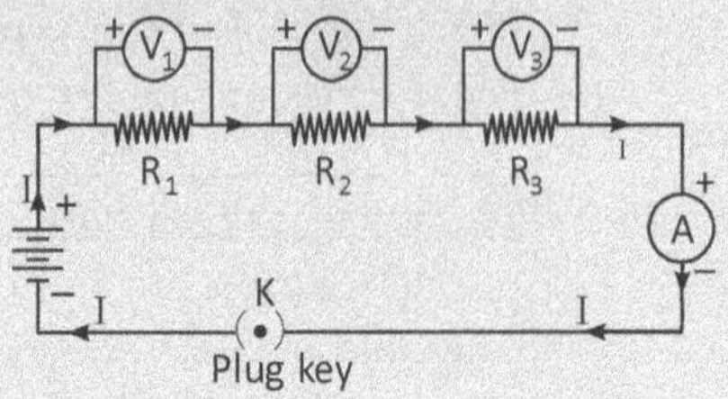

Total Voltage

= Sum of voltage drops

$$V = V_1 + V_2 + V_3$$

Voltage across each resistor

We know that

$$V = IR.$$

Therefore, $V_1 = IR_1$, $V_2 = IR_2$ and $V_3 = IR_3$

$$V = V_1 + V_2 + V_3$$
$$IR = IR_1 + IR_2 + IR_3$$
$$R = R_1 + R_2 + R_3$$

Thus we can say that <u>Equivalent resistance of the circuit is the sum of the individual resistances</u>. **3**

(b) R_1 =2W, R_2 = 3W and R_3 = 6W

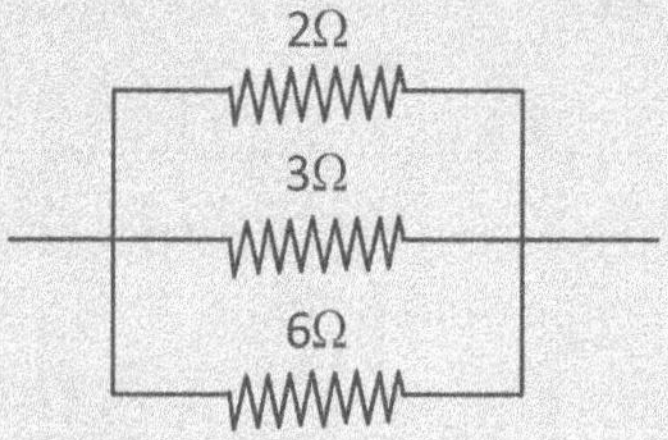

Equivalent resistance would be

$$\frac{1}{R} = \frac{1}{R_1} + \frac{1}{R_2} + \frac{1}{R_3} = \frac{1}{2} + \frac{1}{3} + \frac{1}{6}$$

$R = 1\Omega$ **2**

SAMPLE PAPER 8

CBSE - Class 10

SCIENCE

Time Allowed: 3 Hours | *Maximum Marks: 80*

General Instructions:

i. The question paper comprises three sections – A, B and C. Attempt all the sections.
ii. All questions are compulsory.
iii. Internal choice is given in each section.
iv. All questions in Section A are one-mark questions comprising MCQ, VSA type and assertion-reason type questions. They are to be answered in one word or in one sentence.
v. All questions in Section B are three-mark, short-answer type questions. These are to be answered in about 50 - 60 words each.
vi. All questions in Section C are five-mark, long-answer type questions. These are to be answered in about 80 - 90 words each.
vii. This question paper consists of a total of 30 questions.

SECTION - A

1. What will be the formula and electron dot structure of cyclopentane? **1**

2. Rays from sun converge at a point 15 cm in front of a concave mirror. Where should an object be placed so that size of its image is equal to the size of the object? **1**

3. **Answer question numbers 3(a)-3(d) on the basis of your understanding of the following paragraph and the related studied concepts.**

The space surrounding a magnet in which magnetic force is exerted, is called a magnetic field. The direction of magnetic field lines at a place can be determined by using a compass needle. A compass needle placed near a magnet gets deflected due to the magnetic force exerted by the magnet. The north end of the needle of the compass indicates the direction of magnetic field at the point where it is placed. When the magnet shown in the diagram below is moving towards the coil, the galvanometer gives a reading to the right.

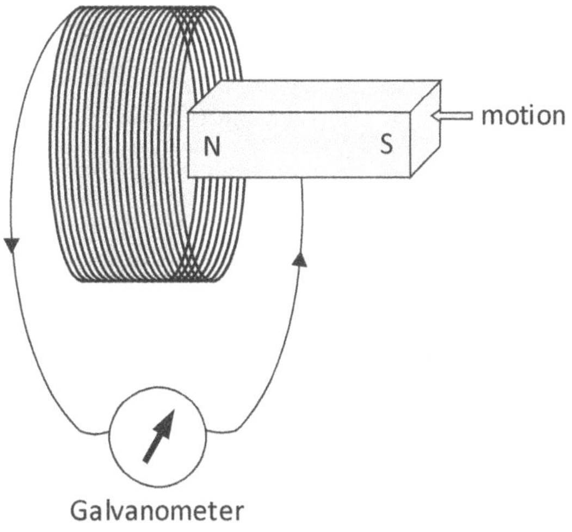

3(a) What is the name of the effect being produced by the moving magnet? **1**

3(b) State what happens to the needle shown on the galvanometer when the magnet is moving away from the coil. **1**

3(c) If the magnet is moved towards the coil at a great speed, state two changes that you would notice in the galvanometer. **1**

3(d) List three sources of magnetic fields. **1**

4. Analyse the following table given below and answer the questions that follow:

The hemoglobin level is expressed as the amount of hemoglobin in grams (gm) per deciliter (dL) of whole blood, a deciliter being 100 milliliters. The normal ranges for hemoglobin depend on the age and, beginning in adolescence, the gender of the person. The normal ranges are:

Age Group	Hemoglobin count (gm/dl)
Normal hemoglobin levels in new-born babies	17 - 22
Normal hemoglobin levels in children	11 - 13
Normal hemoglobin levels in Adults (Male)	14 - 18
Normal hemoglobin levels in Adults (Female)	12 - 16
Normal hemoglobin levels in Elderly (Male)	12.4 - 14.9
Normal hemoglobin levels in Elderly (Female)	11.7-13.8

Based on the above table answer the following questions

4(a) What does a low hemoglobin level mean? **1**

4(b) How is oxygen transported in human beings? **1**

4(c) Respiratory pigment in human body is

(i) Chlorophyll **(ii)** Water

(iii) Blood **(iv)** Haemoglobin **1**

4(d) Which of the following is an important component of haemoglobin?

(i) Iron **(ii)** Sodium

(iii) Calcium **(iv)** None **1**

5. From the list given below, select the character which can be acquired but not inherited:

(i) Colour of eye **(ii)** Colour of skin

(iii) Size of body **(iv)** Nature of hair **1**

6. The element with atomic number 14 is hard and forms acidic oxide and a covalent halide. To which of the following categories does the element belong?

(i) Metal **(ii)** Metalloid

(iii) Non-metal **(iv)** Left-hand side element **1**

7. Which of the following is a non-renewable source of energy?

(i) Wood **(ii)** Sun

(iii) Fossil fuels **(iv)** Wind **1**

OR

Fuel used in thermal power plants is:

(i) Water **(ii)** Uranium

(iii) Biomass **(iv)** Fossil fuels **1**

8. The movement of shoot towards light is:
   (i) Geotropism (ii) Hydrotropism
   (iii) Chemotropism (iv) Phototropism 1

9. A sample of soil is mixed with water and allowed to settle. The clear supernatant solution turns the pH paper yellowish-orange. Which of the following would change the colour of this pH paper to greenish-blue:
   (i) Lemon juice (ii) Vinegar
   (iii) Common salt (iv) An antacid 1

10. In Spirogyra, asexual reproduction takes place by:
   (i) Breaking up of filaments into smaller bits
   (ii) Division of a cell into two cells
   (iii) Division of a cell into many cells
   (iv) Formation of young cells from older cells 1

OR

In Rhizopus, tubular thread-like structures bearing sporangia at their tips are called:
   (i) Filaments (ii) Hyphae
   (iii) Rhizoids (iv) Roots 1

11. To focus the image of a nearby object on the retina of an eye:
   (i) the distance between eye-lens and retina is increased
   (ii) the distance between eye-lens and retina is decreased
   (iii) the thickness of eye-lens is decreased
   (iv) the thickness of eye-lens is increased 1

12. 2 mL each of conc. HCl, HNO_3, and a mixture of conc. HCl. and conc. HNO_3, in the ratio of 3 : 1 were taken in test tubes labeled as A, B and C. A small piece of metal was put in each test tube. No change occurred in test tubes A and B but the metal got dissolved in test tube C. The metal could be:
   (i) Al (ii) Au
   (iii) Cu (iv) Pt 1

OR

During electrolytic refining of zinc, it gets:
   (i) Deposited on cathode
   (ii) Deposited on anode
   (iii) Deposited on cathode as well as anode
   (iv) Remains in the solution 1

For question numbers 13 and 14, two statements are given- one labeled Assertion (A) and the other labeled Reason (R). Select the correct answer to these questions from the codes (i), (ii), (iii) and (iv) as given below:
   (i) Both A and R are true and R is correct explanation of the assertion.
   (ii) Both A and R are true but R is not the correct explanation of the assertion.
   (iii) A is true but R is false.
   (iv) A is false but R is true.

13. **Assertion A** : A 200 W bulbs glows with more brightness then 100 W bulbs. 1
   Reason R : A 100 W bulb has more resistance than a 200 W bulb.

14. **Assertion A** : Nitrogen is a non-metal. **1**

Reason R : Nitrogen has 5 valence electrons.

SECTION - B

15. **(a)** Define the term isomers.

(b) Draw two possible isomers of the compound with molecular formula C_3H_6O and write their names. **3**

16. Name the property that causes tendril to circle around the object. Explain how it happens and how is plant benefitted by it? **3**

17. You are given kerosene, turpentine and water. In which of these does the light travel fastest? Use the information given in the table below:

Medium	Refractive index	Medium	Refractive index
Air	1.0003	Crown glass	1.52
Ice	1.31	Canada Balsam	1.53
Water	1.33	Rock salt	1.54
Alcohol	1.36	Carbon disulphide	1.63
Kerosene	1.44	Dense flint glass	1.65
Fused quartz	1.46	Ruby	1.71
Turpentine oil	1.47	Sapphire	1.77
Benzene	1.50	Diamond	2.42

OR

Which type of phenomenon (reflection or refraction) occurs when light falls on:

(a) a highly polished surface like a mirror and

(b) a transparent medium like glass or water

(c) Name the physical quantity which remains the same when light goes from one medium to another medium **3**

18. **(a)** What is meant by potential difference between two points?

(b) How much energy is given to each coulomb of charge passing through a 6 V battery? **3**

19. **(a)** What is meaning of neutralization reaction? Give one example.

(b) 10 ml of a solution of NaOH is found to be completely neutralized by 8 ml of a given solution of HCl. If we take 20 ml of the same solution of NaOH, what will be the amount of HCl solution (the same solution as before) required to neutralize it? **3**

OR

Name the acid present in ant sting and give its chemical formula. Also give the common method to get relief from the discomfort caused by the ant sting. **3**

20. Name, state and explain with an example the rule used to determine the direction of force experienced by a current carrying conductor placed in a uniform magnetic field. **3**

21. How is the equal genetic contribution of male and female parents ensured in the progeny? **3**

OR

What are analogous organs? Explain with the help of an example. **3**

22. Answer the following:

(a) Why do elements in a group show similar property?

(b) An element M is in the third group of the periodic table. Write the formulae of its chloride and oxide. **3**

23. What measures can be taken to reduce the consumption of fossil fuels? **3**

24. Despite of good rains, we are not able to meet the demand for water of all people. Explain why? **3**

SECTION - C

25. Write a balanced equation for the following chemical reactions:

(a) Hydrogen + Chloride ⟶ Hydrogen chloride

(b) Barium chloride + Aluminium Sulphate ⟶ Barium sulphate + Aluminum chloride

(c) Sodium + Water ⟶ Sodium hydroxide + Hydrogen

(d) Calcium hydroxide + Carbon dioxide ⟶ Calcium carbonate + Water

(e) Zinc + Silver nitrate ⟶ Zinc nitrate + Silver **5**

OR

Write down the balanced chemical equation for the following:

(a) Silver chloride is decomposed in presence of sunlight to give silver and chlorine gas.

(b) Calcium oxide reacts with water to give lime water.

(c) Sodium hydroxide reacts with hydrochloric acid to give sodium chloride and water.

(d) Dilute hydrochloric acid is added to copper oxide to give green coloured copper chloride and water.

(e) Solution of barium chloride and sodium sulphate in water reacts to give insoluble barium sulphate and solution of sodium chloride. **5**

26. **(a)** Name a sexually transmitted disease and a method to avoid it.

(b) Draw a neat diagram of human male reproductive system and label the parts performing the following functions:

(i) Production of sperms

(ii) Gland which provide fluid

(iii) Provides low temperature for the formation of sperms

(iv) Common passage for sperm and urine **5**

27. Define the following terms and give their values for a normal eye:

(a) Range of normal vision.

(b) Least distance of distinct vision.

(c) Near point of the eye.

(d) Far point of the eye.

(e) Power of accommodation. **5**

OR

Answer the following:

(a) Define dispersion of light. How does a prism disperse white light?

(b) Which colour bends the most and the least? **5**

28. Determine the following quantities for the circuits shown below:

(a) the equivalent resistance

(b) the total current from the power supply

(c) the current through each resistor

(d) the voltage drop across each resistor and

(e) the power dissipated in each resistor **5**

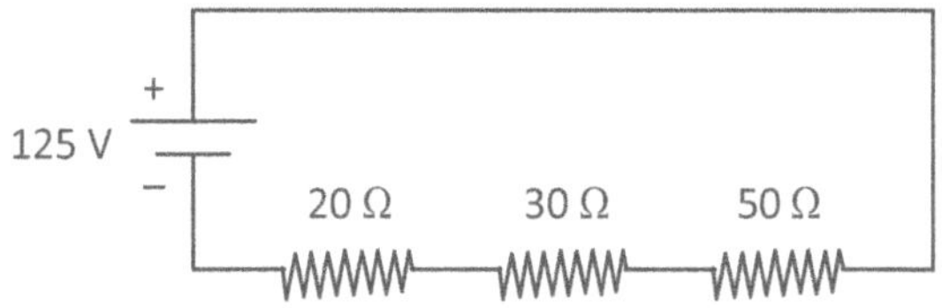

29. (a) Why does carbon form compounds by covalent bonding?

(b) An organic acid 'X' is a liquid which often freezes during winter time in cold countries. It has the molecular formula $C_2H_4O_2$. On warming with ethanol in the presence of a few drops of sulphuric acid, a compound `Y' with sweet smell is formed.

(i) Identify X and Y.

(ii) Write chemical equation for the reaction involved. **5**

30. Explain the process of nutrition in Amoeba. **5**

OR

How do carbohydrates, proteins and fats get digested in human beings? **5**

8

SOLUTION

CBSE - Class 10

SECTION - A

1. The formula for cyclopentane is C_5H_{10}.
Its electron dot structure is given below: **1**

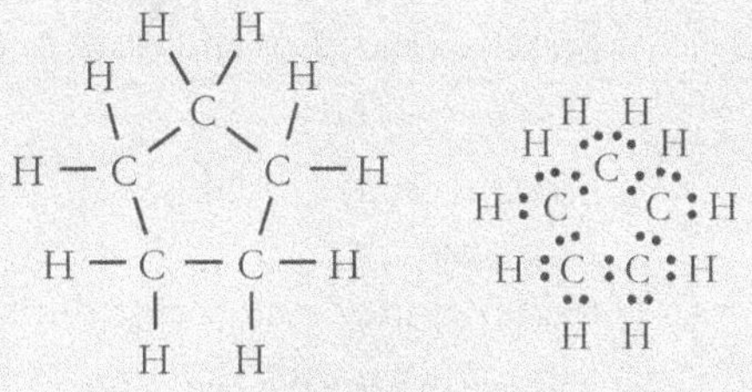

2. Sun is at infinite distance from the surface of the earth.
Now light rays from sun after reflection from concave mirror will converge at focus.
It is given that sunrays converge at 15 cm.
So, focal length of the mirror, $f = 15$ cm.
In case of a concave mirror, the size of image and object will be same if the object is placed at $2f$ or at centre of curvature.
Hence, in this case the object must be placed at $2f$ or $2 \times 15 = 30$ cm from the mirror. **1**

3. **(a)** Electromagnetic induction **1**

3. **(b)** When the magnet is moving away from the coil the galvanometer gives a deflection to the left. **1**

3. **(c)** If the magnet is moved towards the coil at a great speed, large deflection occurs to the right and that too more quickly. **1**

3. **(d)** Three sources of magnetic fields are Electromagnet, permanent magnet, wire carrying current. **1**

4. **(a)** A low hemoglobin level is referred to as anemia or low red blood count. A lower than normal number of red blood cells is referred to as anaemia and hemoglobin levels reflect this number. **1**

4. **(b)** **Transport of oxygen:** Haemoglobin present in the blood takes up the oxygen from the air in the lungs. It carries the oxygen to tissues which are deficient in oxygen before releasing it. **1**

4. **(c)** **(iv)** Haemoglobin **1**

Explanation: Respiratory pigment in human body is haemoglobin.

4. **(d)** **(i)** Iron **1**

Explanation: Iron is an important component of haemoglobin which is present in red blood cells. It carries oxygen from lungs to different parts of the body. Sources of iron include sunflower seeds, nuts, beef, beans, green leafy vegetables, tofu, amla, jaggery. Iron deficiency can lead to anaemia, that is a low count of haemoglobin as there is insufficient iron in the body to produce enough of haemoglobin.

5. **(iii)** Size of body **1**

Explanation: Environmentally determined traits are acquired. Size of body depends on nutritional status, health conditions etc.

6. **(ii)** Metalloid **1**

Explanation: Atomic number 14 is for Silicon element which is a metalloid and exhibit properties of both metals and non-metals. It has 4 electrons in its valence shell so tends to form covalent acidic oxide like non-metals.

7. **(iii)** Fossil fuels **1**

Explanation: Sources of energy which are present in limited amount and can't be recycled once used are known as non-renewable sources of energy. Fossil fuels are non-renewable source of energy.

OR

(iv) Fossil fuels **1**

Explanation: Large amount of fossil fuels are burnt every day in power stations to heat up water to produce steam which further runs the turbine to generate electricity.

8. **(iv)** Phototropism **1**

Explanation: Growth movement of plants in response to light is called as phototropism.

9. **(iv)** An antacid **1**

Explanation: pH paper gives greenish blue colour in weak alkaline medium so antacid ($Mg(OH)_2$) which is an alkaline compound will show greenish blue color on pH paper.

10. **(i)** Breaking up of filaments into smaller bits **1**

Explanation: Fragmentation is type of asexual reproduction in animals wherein parental body is broken down into pieces and each of these pieces develops into an individual animal.

OR

(ii) Hyphae **1**

Explanation: Thin branched filaments of fungi are called as hyphae.

11. **(iv)** the thickness of eye-lens is increased **1**

Explanation: The thickness of the eye lens is increased to focus the image of a nearby object on the retina of the eye.

12. **(ii)** and **(iv)** Au and Pt **1**

Explanation: A mixture of conc. HCl and conc. HNO_3 in the ratio of 3 : 1 forms aqua-regia which can dissolve gold (Au) and platinum (Pt).

OR

(i) Deposited on cathode **1**

Explanation: During electrolytic refining the pure zinc metal is deposited on cathode.

13. **(i)** Both assertion and reason are true and the reason is the correct explanation of the assertion. **1**

Explanation: The resistance,

$$R = \frac{V^2}{P}$$

i.e. $$R \propto \frac{1}{P}$$

This means that higher is the wattage of a bulb, lesser is the resistance and so it will glow bright.

14. **(i)** Both Assertion and Reason are true and Reason is the correct explanation of the assertion. **1**

SECTION - B

15. **(a)** **Isomers:** Compounds having same molecular formula but different molecular structures are known as isomers. **1**

(b) Isomers of the compound with molecular formula C_3H_6O can be :

- A ketone - Acetone

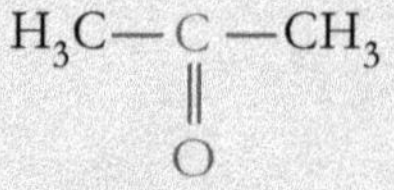

- An aldehyde - Propanal

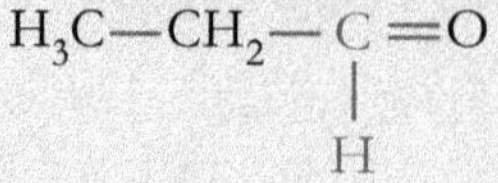

• An alcohol - Propenol

$H_2C{=}CH{-}CH_2{-}OH$ 2

16. The property of the plants that causes tendrils to circle around the support is called thigmotropism or Sensitivity to touch. 1

When tendril of a plant comes in contact with any object, the part of the tendril in contact with the object does not grow as rapidly as that part which is away from the object. This causes the tendril to circle around the object and in this manner tendrils coil around a support. It helps plant to climb against the support. 2

17. Speed of light in a medium is given by the relation for refractive index (n_m). Refractive index of a medium n_m is given by :

$$n_m = \frac{\text{Speed of light in vacuum}}{\text{Speed of light in the medium}}$$

$$= \frac{c}{v}$$

$$v = \frac{c}{n_m}$$

It can be inferred from the relation that speed of light is inversely proportional to the refractive index of the medium. So, we can say that light will travel the slowest in the material which has the highest refractive index and travel the fastest in the material which has the lowest refractive index.

It can be observed from table 10.3 that the refractive indices of kerosene, turpentine, and water are 1.44, 1.47, and 1.33 respectively. Therefore, light travels the fastest in water as water has the lowest refractive index. 3

OR

(a) When light falls on a highly polished surface like mirror, reflection occurs. 1

(b) Refraction of light occurs when light falls on a transparent medium like glass or water. When there is difference in the density of the medium, a ray tends to bend towards or away from the normal at the interface of media. 1

(c) Frequency of light remains the same when light goes from one medium to another medium. 1

18. **(a)** **Potential difference between two points:** Electric potential difference between two points in an electric circuit carrying some current can be defined as the work done to move a unit charge from one point to the other. It is represented by 'V'

Potential difference (V) between two

$$\text{points} = \frac{\text{Work done (W)}}{\text{Charge (Q)}}$$

Or $$V = \frac{W}{Q}$$ 1

(b) Here according to question, Charge

= 1 C and Potential difference

= 6 V

So, Work done

= 6 × 1 = 6 J

Therefore, 6J of energy is given to each Coulomb of charge passing through a battery of 6 V. 2

19. **(a)** When an acid reacts with a base to form salt and water, it is called neutralization reaction.

$$\underset{\text{Sodium hydroxide}}{NaOH} + \underset{\text{Hydrochloric acid}}{HCl} \longrightarrow \underset{\text{Sodium chloride}}{NaCl} + \underset{\text{Water}}{H_2O}$$

1½

(b) If we take double the amount of the same NaOH solution, the amount of the same HCl solution required to neutralize it is also double.

Since 10 mL of NaOH solution requires 8 mL of HCl solution

Therefore, 20 mL of NaOH solution will require 8 × 2 = 16 mL of HCl solution 1½

OR

Acid present in ant sting is formic acid which is also named as Methanoic acid. 1

Chemical formula for formic acid is HCOOH. **1**

It is acidic in nature, so an alkaline compound like wet baking soda can be used to neutralize its effect to get relief from discomfort. **1**

20. Fleming's left-hand rule is used to determine the direction of force experienced by a current carrying conductor placed in a uniform magnetic field. **1**

Fleming's left-hand rule states that: stretch the thumb, fore finger and middle finger of the left hand such that they are mutually perpendicular. If the first finger points in the direction of magnetic field and the second finger in the direction of current, then the thumb will point in the direction of motion or the force acting on the conductor. **1**

Example: When an electron enters a magnetic field at right angles, the direction of force on electron is perpendicular to the direction of magnetic field and current according to this rule. **1**

21. In human beings, equal genetic contribution of male and female parents is ensured in the progeny through inheritance of equal number of chromosomes from both parents. There are 23 pairs of chromosomes All human chromosomes are not paired. Out of these 23 pairs, the first 22 pairs are known as autosomes and the remaining one pair is known as sex chromosomes represented as X and Y. Females have a perfect pair of two X sex chromosomes and males have a mismatched pair of one X and one Y sex chromosome.

During the course of reproduction, as fertilization process takes place, the male gamete (haploid) fuses with the female gamete (haploid) resulting in formation of the diploid zygote. The zygote in the progeny receives an equal contribution of genetic material from the parents. Out of 23 pairs of chromosomes in progeny, male parent contributes 22 autosomes and one X or Y chromosome and female parent contributes 22 autosomes and one X chromosome. **3**

OR

Analogous organs: The organs which are developmentally and structurally very different that is they have a different ancestor, but perform the same function are called analogous organs.

Example: Analogous wings of a bird and an insect. **2**

The wings of a bird and an insect perform the same function of flying. The wings of a bird have a support of skeleton, flesh and feathers but insects have a fold of membrane as wings and a few muscles associated with it. Thus, wings of a bird and an insect are developmentally and structurally very different. So, they are analogous organs. **1**

22. **(a)** All the elements present in a group have same electronic configuration of the atoms. The physical and chemical properties of elements depend on the number of valence electrons. Elements present in the same group have the same number of valence electrons. Therefore, elements present in the same group have similar physical and chemical properties **1½**

(b) Element M is in the third group, therefore it will have a valency of 3. Its chloride and oxide are MCl_3 and M_2O_3 respectively. ($\because$ O and Cl have valencies of –2 and –1 respectively). **1½**

23. It is not possible to completely reduce the consumption of fossil fuels. However, some measures can be taken to reduce energy consumption such as:

(a) Fossil fuels should be used with care and caution to derive maximum benefit out of them.

(b) Fuel saving devices such as pressure cookers etc. should be used.

(c) Efficiency of energy sources should be maintained by getting them regularly serviced.

(d) Usage should be done wisely and wastage should be avoided.

(e) Public transport system with mass transit must be adopted on a large scale. **3**

24. Despite of good rains, we are not able to meet the demand for water of all people because

(a) Our population is increasing rapidly.

(b) The high yielding crops require much more water for irrigation.

(c) The changing lifestyle of people, especially in urban areas, is consuming more water.

(d) Discharge of untreated sewage and industrial wastes into rivers and lakes reduces the availability of usable water.

(e) Only a little rain water seeps into the ground and gets stored as ground water. **3**

SECTION - C

25. (a) Hydrogen + Chloride $\longrightarrow$ Hydrogen chloride

$H_2 + Cl_2 \longrightarrow 2HCl$ **1**

(b) Barium chloride + Aluminium sulphate $\longrightarrow$ Barium sulphate + Aluminum chloride

$3BaCl_2 + Al_2(SO_4)_3 \longrightarrow 2AlCl_3 + 3BaSO_4$ **1**

(c) Sodium + Water $\longrightarrow$ Sodium hydroxide + Hydrogen

$2Na + 2H_2O \longrightarrow 2NaOH + H_2$ **1**

(d) Calcium hydroxide + Carbon dioxide $\longrightarrow$ Calcium carbonate + Water

$2Ca(OH)_2 + 2CO_2 \longrightarrow 2CaCO_3 + 2H_2O$ **1**

(e) Zinc + Silver nitrate $\longrightarrow$ Zinc nitrate + Silver

$Zn + 2AgNO_3 \longrightarrow Zn(NO_3)_2 + 2Ag$ **1**

OR

(a) Silver chloride is decomposed in presence of sunlight to give silver and chlorine gas.

$2AgCl(s) \xrightarrow{\text{Sunlight}} 2Ag(s) + Cl_2(g)$ **1**

(b) Calcium oxide reacts with water to give lime water.

$CaO(s) + H_2O(l) \longrightarrow Ca(OH)_2$ **1**

(c) Sodium hydroxide reacts with hydrochloric acid to give sodium chloride and water.

$NaOH(s) + HCl(aq) \longrightarrow NaCl(aq) + H_2O(l)$ **1**

(d) Dil. hydrochloric acid is added to copper oxide to give green coloured copper chloride and water.

$CuO + 2HCl\ (dil.) \longrightarrow CuCl_2 + H_2O$ **1**

(e) Solution of barium chloride and sodium sulphate in water reacts to give insoluble barium sulphate and solution of sodium chloride.

$BaCl_2(aq) + Na_2SO_4 \longrightarrow BaSO_4 + 2NaCl(aq)$ **1**

26. (a) A disease which can be transmitted through sexual contact is called sexually transmitted disease or STD. These include warts or syphilis or HIV-AIDS.

They can be prevented by using condoms during sexual intercourse. **1**

(b) The parts of human male reproductive system performing the following functions:

(i) Production of sperms: Testis

(ii) Gland which provide fluid: Prostate gland

(iii) Provides low temperature for the formation of sperms: Scrotum

(iv) Common passage for sperm and urine: Urethra 2

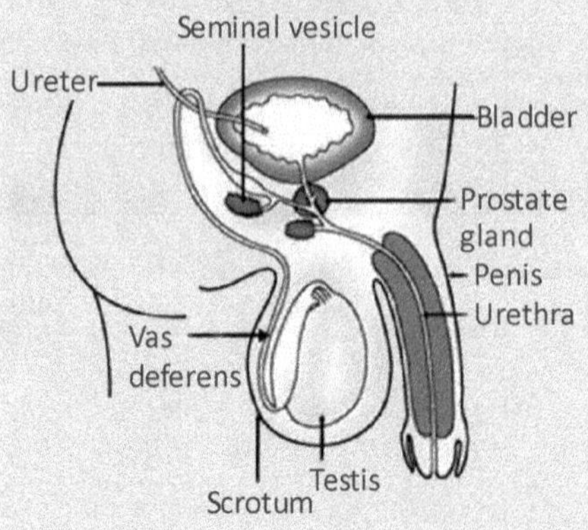

2

Human Male Reproductive System

27. (a) **Range of normal vision:** A normal eye can clearly see the objects situated anywhere between infinity and 25 cm from it. The range of vision is due to accommodation property of the eyelens. At distances less than 25 cm, the ciliary muscles cannot bulge the eye lens any more. So, the object cannot be focused on the retina and it appears blurred. The distance between infinity and 25 cm point is called the range of normal vision. 1

(b) **Least distance of distinct vision:** The minimum distance from the eye, at which the eye can see the objects clearly and distinctly without any strain is called the least distance of distinct vision. It is denoted by the letter D. For a normal eye, least distance of distinct vision is 25 cm. 1

(c) **Near point:** The nearest point from the eye, at which an object can be seen, clearly is called its near point. The near point of a normal eye is at a distance of 25 cm. 1

(d) **Far point:** The farthest point from the eye, at which an object can be seen, clearly is called the far point of the eye. For a normal eye, the far point is at infinity. 1

(e) **Power of accommodation:** The power of accommodation of the eye is the ability of the eye lens to adjust its focal length to focus on near and far (distant) objects. For a normal eye, the power of accommodation is about four dioptres. 1

OR

(a) **Dispersion of Light** can be defined as the splitting of white light when it passes through a glass prism into its constituent spectrum of colors (i.e. violet, indigo, blue, green, yellow, orange and red). 1

The colour sequence can be remembered by the acronym VIBGYOR.

The red colour (longer wavelength) is deviated the least while the violet colour (shorter wavelength) is deviated the most.

The pattern of the coloured bands obtained on the screen is called spectrum.

Sir Isaac Newton was the first to use a glass prism to obtain the spectrum of sunlight. 1

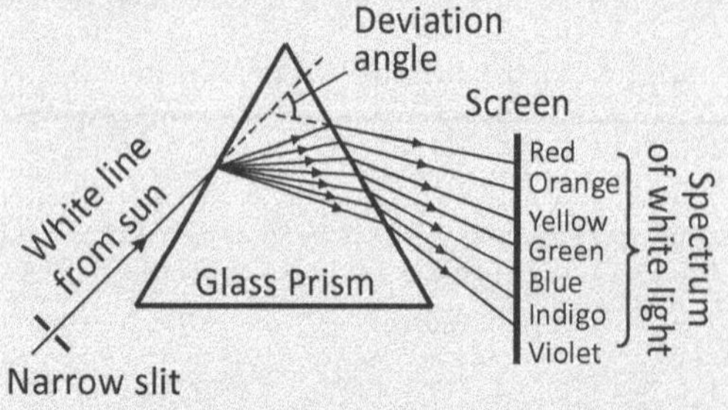

2

(b) The Violet colour bends the most and red colour bends the least. 1

28.

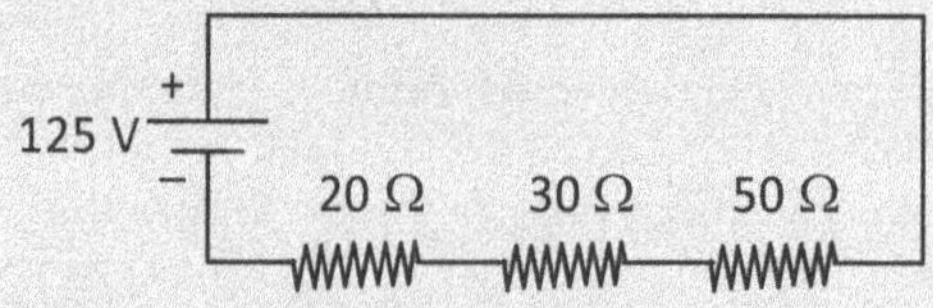

Given circuit diagram:

(a) Equivalent resistance:

Resistances in series add up.

$$R = R_1 + R_2 + R_3$$
$$= 20\Omega + 30\Omega + 50\Omega$$
$$= 100\Omega$$ 1

(b) Total current from the power supply: Total current is determined by the voltage of the power supply and the equivalent resistance of the circuit.

$$I = \frac{V}{R} = \frac{125}{100} = 1.25 \text{ A}$$ **1**

(c) Current through each resistor: Current is constant through resistors connected in series. **1**

(d) Voltage drop across each resistor

$V_1 = IR_1 = 1.25A \times 20\ \Omega = 25$ V

$V_2 = IR_2 = 1.25A \times 30\ \Omega = 37.5$ V

$V_3 = IR_3 = 1.25A \times 50\ \Omega = 62.5$ V

In a series circuit they should equal the voltage increase of the power supply.

$V_{total} = V_1 + V_2 + V_3$

125 V = 25 V + 37.5 V + 62.5 V

125 V = 125 V **1**

(e) The power dissipated in each resistor

$P_1 = V_1 \times I_1$

$= 25V \times 1.25A$

$= 31.250$ W

$P_2 = V_2 \times I_2$

$= 37.5V \times 1.25A$

$= 46.875$ W

$P_3 = V_3 \times I_3$

$= 62.5V \times 1.25A$

$= 78.125$ W

In a series circuit, the element with the greatest resistance consumes the most power. **1**

29. **(a)** Carbon forms a large number of organic compounds due to the self linking property known as catenation. **1**

(b) **(i)** Since X reacts with ethanol in presence of sulphuric acid and gives a compounds Y with sweet smell, so Y must be ester and hence X must be a carboxylic acid.. **1**

Since X is made of 2 C-atoms, so it is ethanoic acid CH_3COOH. **1**

Compound Y is ethyl ethanoate $CH_3COOCH_2CH_3$. **1**

(ii) The complete reaction is

$$CH_3COOH + CH_3CH_2OH \longrightarrow CH_3COOCH_2CH_3 + H_2O$$ **1**

30. **Nutrition in Amoeba:** The different processes involved in the nutrition of amoeba are:

(a) Ingestion: Ingestion is the process of taking food in the body. Amoeba is a unicellular animal, so it does not have a mouth for ingestion of food. Amoeba ingests the food by encircling it by forming pseudopodia. When the food is completely encircled, the food is engulfed in the form of a bag called food vacuole.

(b) Digestion: Digestion is the process of breaking the large and insoluble molecules in small and water soluble molecules. In amoeba, several digestive enzymes react on the food present in the food vacuoles and break it down into simple and soluble molecules.

(c) Absorption: The food digested by digestive enzymes is then absorbed in the cytoplasm by the process of diffusion. While the undigested food remains in the food vacuole. If amoeba absorbs a large amount of food, the excess food is stored in the cytoplasm in the form of glycogen and lipids.

(d) Assimilation: During the step the food is absorbed by the cytoplasm is used to obtain energy, growth and repair. This process of utilizing absorbed food for obtaining energy, repair and growth is called assimilation.

(e) Egestion: When sufficient amount of undigested food gets collected in the food vacuole, it is thrown out of the body by rupturing cell membrane. The process of removal of undigested food from the body is called egestion. **5**

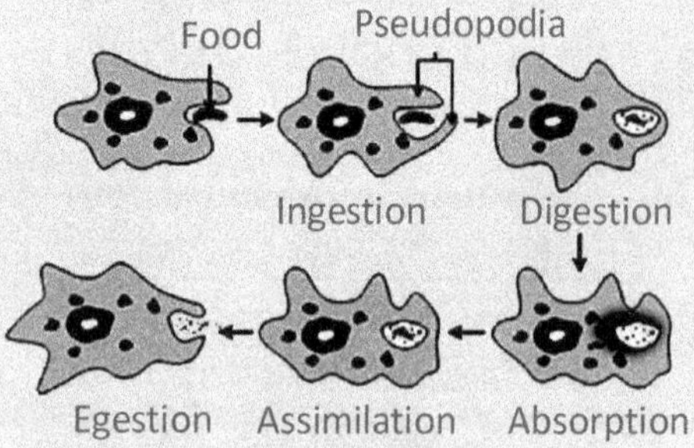

Steps Involved in Nutrition in Amoeba

OR

Digestion of carbohydrates: in mouth and small intestine

Mouth: Salivary amylase present in saliva breaks down starch into maltose.

Starch + Salivary Amylase ⟶ Sucrose 1

Small intestine:

- Pancreatic amylase presents in pancreatic juice breakdown the remaining starch into maltose.
- Maltase of intestinal juice breakdown maltose into glucose units.

Maltose + Maltase ⟶ Glucose

Lactose + Lactase ⟶ Glucose + Galactose 1

Digestion of Proteins: in stomach and small intestine.

Partial digestion of protein takes place in the stomach by gastric enzyme pepsin. Further digestion of protein happens in the small intestine.

Stomach: Pepsin is a protein digesting enzyme secreted by chief cells of stomach wall in its inactive form called as pepsinogen which in turn is converted into active pepsin upon exposure to HCl. Pepsin starts protein digestion into small polypeptides.

Protein + Pepsin ⟶ Polypeptides 1

Small intestine: Pancreatic juice secretes 'Trypsin' which digests polypeptides into peptides.

Polypeptides + Trypsin ⟶ Peptides

Erepsin of intestinal juice digests the peptides into amino acids.

Peptides + Erepsin ⟶ Amino acids 1

Digestion of Fats: done in small intestine.

Fat is at first emulsified by bile and then its digestion happens in the small intestine. Pancreatic lipase digests the emulsified fat globules into glycerol and fatty acids. Glycerol and fatty acids enter the villi cells where they are rejoined and packaged as lipoprotein droplets before entering the lacteals.

Fat + Lipase ⟶ Fatty acids + Glycerol 1

SAMPLE PAPER

9

CBSE - Class 10

SCIENCE

Time Allowed: 3 Hours *Maximum Marks: 80*

General Instructions:

i. The question paper comprises three sections – A, B and C. Attempt all the sections.
ii. All questions are compulsory.
iii. Internal choice is given in each section.
iv. All questions in Section A are one-mark questions comprising MCQ, VSA type and assertion-reason type questions. They are to be answered in one word or in one sentence.
v. All questions in Section B are three-mark, short-answer type questions. These are to be answered in about 50 - 60 words each.
vi. All questions in Section C are five-mark, long-answer type questions. These are to be answered in about 80 - 90 words each.
vii. This question paper consists of a total of 30 questions.

SECTION - A

1. What is Synapse? **1**

2. Name the simplest ketone. Also draw its structure. **1**

3. **Answer question numbers 3(a)-3(d) on the basis of your understanding of the following paragraph and the related studied concepts.**

Series or organisms taking part at various biotic levels form a food chain. Each step or level of the food chain forms a trophic level. The autotrophs or the producers are at the first trophic level. They fix up the solar energy and make it available for heterotrophs or the consumers. The herbivores or the primary consumers come at the second, small carnivores or the secondary consumers at the third and larger carnivores or the tertiary consumers form the fourth trophic level. The interactions among various components of the environment involve flow of energy from one component of the system to another.

3(a) What are trophic levels? **1**

3(b) Give an example of a food chain. **1**

3(c) What is the role of decomposers in the ecosystem? **1**

3(d) Explain why the number of trophic levels in a food chain is limited? **1**

4. **Analyse the following table given below and answer the questions that follow:**

The atomic radii of the element of second period are given below:

Second period element	B	Be	O	N	Li	F	C
Atomic Radii (pm)	88	111	66	74	152	64	77

4(a) Arrange these elements in decreasing order of their atomic radii. **1**

4(b) Why does atomic radius decreases as we move from left to right in a period? **1**

4(c) Which is not true about the noble gases?

(i) They are non metallic in nature **(ii)** They exist in atomic form

(iii) They are radioactive in nature **(iv)** Xenon is the most reactive among these **1**

4(d) Which of the following is the outermost shell for elements of period 2?

(i) K shell **(ii)** L shell

(iii) M shell **(iv)** N shell **1**

5. Which of the following is not attracted by a magnet:

(i) Steel **(ii)** Cobalt

(iii) Brass **(iv)** Nickel **1**

OR

The magnetic field lines:

(i) intersect at right angles to one another

(ii) interest at an angle 45° to each another

(iii) do not cross one another

(iv) cross at an angle of 60° to one another **1**

6. A trait in an organism is influenced by:

(i) Paternal DNA only **(ii)** Maternal DNA only

(iii) Both maternal and paternal DNA **(iv)** Neither by paternal nor by maternal DNA **1**

7. Figure shows a ray of light as it travels from medium A to medium B. Refractive index of the medium B relative to medium A is:

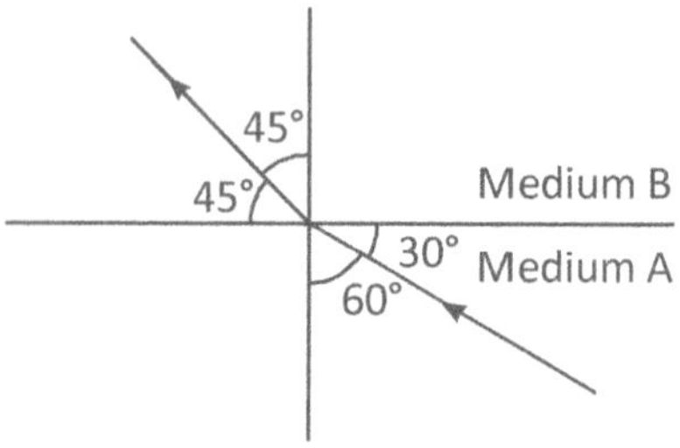

(i) $\frac{\sqrt{3}}{2}$ **(ii)** $\frac{\sqrt{2}}{\sqrt{3}}$

(iii) $\frac{1}{\sqrt{2}}$ **(iv)** $\sqrt{2}$ **1**

8. Which of the following gives the correct increasing order of acid strength?

(i) Water < acetic acid < hydrochloric acid

(ii) Water < hydrochloric acid < acetic acid

(iii) Acetic acid < water < hydrochloric acid

(iv) Hydrochloric acid < water < acetic acid **1**

OR

Which of the following statements is correct about an aqueous solution of an acid and a base?

(a) Higher the pH, stronger the acid

(b) Higher the pH, weaker the acid

(c) Lower the pH, stronger the base

(d) Lower the pH, weaker the base

(i) (a) and (c) **(ii)** (b) and (c)

(iii) (b) and (d) **(iv)** (b) and (d) **1**

9. If salivary amylase is lacking in the saliva, which of the following events in the mouth cavity will be affected?

(i) Proteins breaking down into amino acids

(ii) Starch breaking down into sugars

(iii) Fats breaking down into fatty acids and glycerol

(iv) Absorption of vitamins **1**

OR

In the list of organisms given below, those that reproduce by the asexual method are:

(a) Banana **(c)** Dog

(c) Yeast **(d)** Amoeba

(i) (b) and (d) **(ii)** (a), (c) and (d)

(iii) (a) and (d) **(iv)** (b), (c) and (d) **1**

10. Which one of the following best describes the function of the umbilical cord?

(i) feeds the embryo with digested substances

(ii) conveys nutrients and wastes to and from the embryo respectively

(iii) removes waste matter from the embryo to the mother's blood

(iv) supplies oxygenated blood from the mother to the embryo **1**

11. A student carries out an experiment and plots the V-I graph of three samples of nichrome wire with resistances R_1, R_2 and R_3 respectively as shown in figure. Which of the following is true?

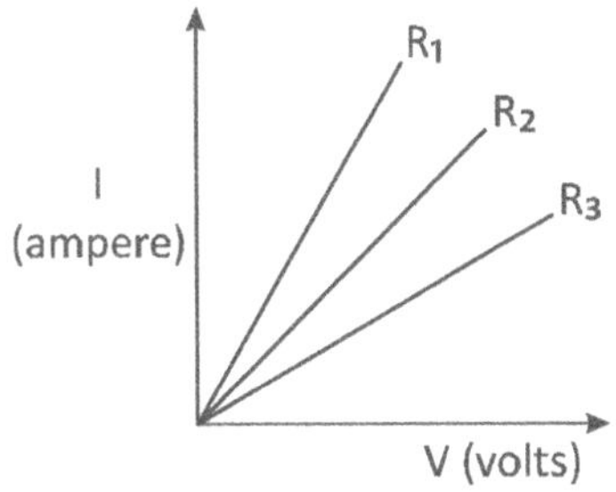

(i) $R_1 = R_2 = R_3$ **(ii)** $R_1 > R_2 > R_3$

(iii) $R_3 > R_2 > R_1$ **(iv)** $R_2 > R_3 > R_1$ **1**

12. Alloys are homogeneous mixtures of a metal with a metal or non-metal. Which among the following alloys contain non-metal as one of its constituents?

(i) Brass **(ii)** Bronze

(iii) Amalgam **(iv)** Steel **1**

For question numbers 13 and 14, two statements are given-one labeled Assertion (A) and the other labeled Reason (R). Select the correct answer to these questions from the codes (i), (ii), (iii) and (iv) as given below:

(i) Both A and R are true and R is correct explanation of the assertion.

(ii) Both A and R are true but R is not the correct explanation of the assertion.

(iii) A is true but R is false.

(iv) A is false but R is true.

13. **Assertion A** : Pupil is black in colour.

Reason R : Pupil is black in colour as no light is reflected in it. 1

14. **Assertion A** : The opening and closing of the pore is a function of the guard cells.

Reason R : Stomatal pores are the site for exchange of gases by diffusion. 1

SECTION - B

15. Resistance of a metal wire of length 1 metre is 26 ohms. If the radius of the wire is 0.15 mm, calculate the resistivity of the material. 3

OR

Answer the following:

(a) Why ammeter is always connected in series?

(b) Five dry cells each of 1.5 volt have internal resistance of 0.2, 0.3, 0.4, 0.5 and 1.2 ohms. When connected in series, what current will leave these five cells furnish through 10 ohm resistance? 3

16. **(a)** Under what condition does a farmer need to treat the soil on his field with quick lime or slaked lime or chalk?

(b) You are given two solutions A and B and their pH is 6 and 8 respectively. Answer the following:

(i) Which of the two solutions have more hydrogen ion concentration?

(ii) Which is acidic and which is basic? 3

OR

Equal lengths of magnesium ribbons are taken in test tubes A and B. Hydrochloric acid (HCl) is added to test tube A, while acetic acid (CH_3COOH) is added to test tube B. In which test tube will the fizzing occur more vigorously and why? 3

17. If accidentally we step on something sharp at once we move our foot away. What is this type of response known as? Also State how it is controlled. 3

OR

Answer the following:

(a) Which hormone is responsible for the changes noticed in females at puberty?

(b) Dwarfism results due to deficiency of which hormone?

(c) Blood sugar level rises due to deficiency of which hormone? 3

18. What is a group in a periodic table? In what part of a group would you separately expect the elements to have:

(a) the greatest metallic character

(b) the largest atomic size 3

19. You are given a strong bar magnet and a magnet compass needle. Describe an activity by which the magnetic field lines due to the bar magnet can be drawn. **3**

20. What are trophic levels? Give an example of a food chain and state the different trophic levels in it. **3**

21. What are esters? How are they prepared? **3**

22. What are Mendel's laws of inheritance? **3**

23. Draw a ray diagram showing the path of rays of light when it enters with oblique incidence:

(a) from air into water

(b) from water into air **3**

24. What are the disadvantages of using fossil fuels? **3**

SECTION - C

25. Answer the following:

(a) Define oxidizing agent.

(b) Translate the following statements into chemical equations and balance them.

(i) Hydrogen gas combines with nitrogen to form ammonia.

(ii) Hydrogen sulphide gas burns in air to give water and sulphur dioxide.

(iii) Barium chloride reacts with aluminium sulphate to give Aluminium chloride and a precipitate of barium sulphate.

(iv) Potassium metal reacts with water to give potassium hydroxide and Hydrogen gas. **5**

26. Draw the diagram of alimentary canal of man and label the following parts:

- Mouth
- Oesophagus
- Stomach
- Intestine **5**

OR

Draw the diagram of human respiratory system and label the following parts:

- Larynx
- Trachea
- Lungs
- Bronchi **5**

27. **(a)** What are the advantages of connecting electrical devices in parallel with the battery instead of connecting them in series?

(b) Two resistors of 20Ω and 40Ω are connected in parallel in an electric circuit. How does the current passing through the two resistors compare? **5**

OR

(a) What is meant by the series combination and parallel combination of resistances?

(b) In the circuit diagram given below five resistances of 5Ω, 20Ω, 15Ω, 20Ω and 10Ω, are connected as given in figure to a 6 V battery:

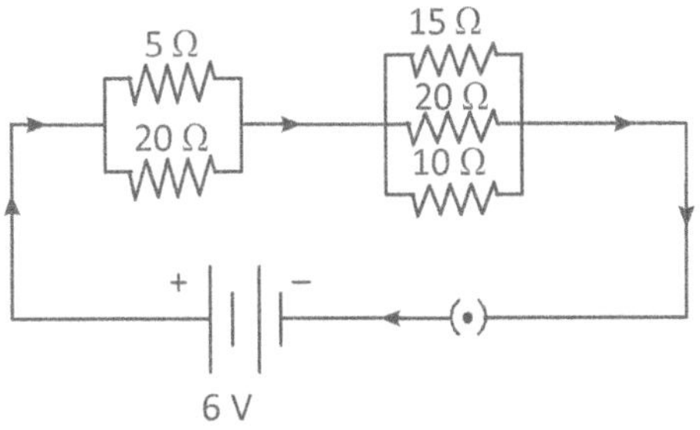

Calculate total resistance in the circuit. **5**

28. Give the structure of diamond. State its two important properties and two uses. **5**

OR

(a) What are hydrocarbons? Give examples.

(b) Give the structural differences between saturated and unsaturated hydrocarbons with two examples each.

(c) What is functional group? Give examples of four different functional groups. **5**

29. **(a)** Identify A, B, C and D in the given diagram and write their names.

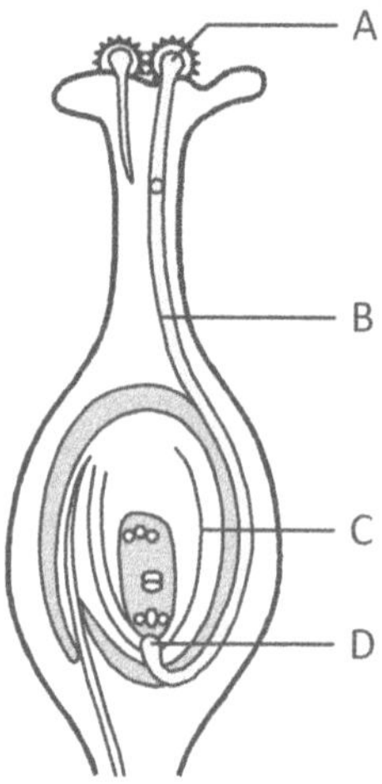

(b) What is pollination? Name the different types of pollination.

(c) Explain the process of fertilization in flowers. **5**

30. **(a)** List three common refractive defects of vision. Suggest the ways of correcting these defects.

(b) We see advertisement for eye donation on TV and newspaper. Write the importance of these advertisements. **5**

SOLUTION

9

CBSE - Class 10

SECTION - A

1. **Synapse:** A microscopic gap between a pair of adjacent neurons over which nerve impulses pass when going from one neuron to the next is called a synapse. They connect neurons. 1

2. The simplest Ketone is **Propanone** (commonly known as **Acetone**).The structure of ketone is CH_3COCH_3

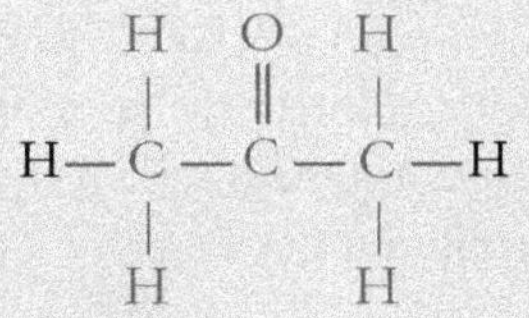

1

3. **(a)** The various levels or steps in a food chain are called trophic levels. They represent the successive stages of nourishment like primary producer, primary consumer, secondary consumer, tertiary consumer etc. 1

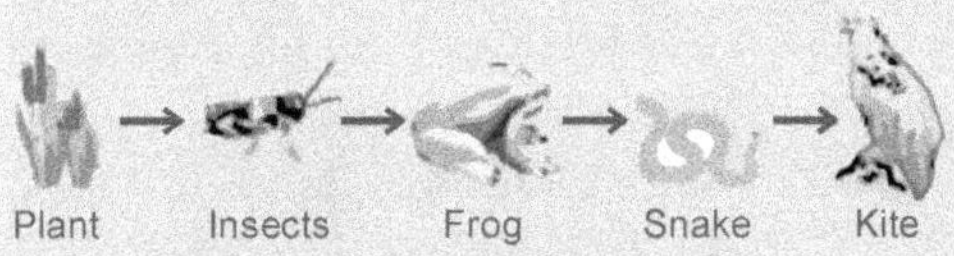

3. **(b)** Below is an example of food chain. In this example, an insect (example: grasshopper) eats plants. Insect is then eaten by the frog which is in turn eaten by the snake. The snake is then eaten by the kite. 1

3. **(c)** Decomposers are microorganisms which breakdown complex organic substances into simple inorganic substances and help in recycling of nutrients. They feed on the dead and decaying bodies of plants and animals. They return the nutrients back to the soil and thus help in making this ecosystem stable. 1

3. **(d)** Only 10% of the energy gets transferred from one trophic level to the next. So after 3 or 4 trophic levels, the energy available for passing on is too less to support another trophic level. Very little usable energy remains after 4 trophic levels. Hence the number of trophic levels in a food chain is limited. 1

4. **(a)** Elements in decreasing order of their atomic radii

Li	Be	B	C	N	O	F
152	111	88	77	74	66	64

1

4. **(b)** Atomic radius decreases from left to right in a period. This is due to increase in nuclear charge which tends to pull the electrons closer to the nucleus and hence the atomic size decreases. 1

4. **(c)** **(iii)** They are radioactive in nature. 1

Explanation: Noble gases are inert and are not radioactive in nature.

4. **(d)** **(ii)** L shell 1

Explanation: The elements of 2nd period contain two shells; K and d L shell.

5. **(iii)** Brass 1

Explanation: Brass is not a magnetic material.

OR

(iii) do not cross one another 1

Explanation: The magnetic field lines do not cross one another because the resultant force at any point on the north pole can only be in one direction. This is impossible if the lines intersect.

6. (iii) Both maternal and paternal DNA 1

Explanation: An organism develops from zygote which in turn is product of fusion of male and female gamete.

7. (i) $\frac{\sqrt{3}}{2}$ 1

Explanation: Here, angle of incidence = i = 60°

Angle of refraction = r = 45°

Refractive index of the medium B relative to A

$$n_{BA} = \frac{\sin i}{\sin r} = \frac{\sin 60°}{\sin 45°}$$

$$= \frac{\left(\frac{\sqrt{3}}{2}\right)}{\left(\frac{1}{\sqrt{2}}\right)} = \frac{\sqrt{3}}{\sqrt{2}}$$

8. (i) Water < acetic acid < hydrochloric acid 1

Explanation: Water is a natural substance, hydrochloric acid is a strong acid as it ionizes completely in water, whereas acetic acid ionizes only partially in water; hence, it is a weak acid.

OR

(iv) (b) and (d) 1

Explanation: The pH values lie between 0 to 14 in which 0 to 7 is acidic medium and 7 to 14 is alkaline or basic medium.

9. (ii) Starch breaking down into sugars 1

Explanation: Amylase is the enzyme which helps in primary digestion of starch only. Digestion of starch by salivary amylase into maltose starts in mouth. Oesophagus then pushes the food into stomach. It does not carry out digestion at all. Pancreatic amylase also digests remaining starch into maltose sugars. Intestinal maltase carries out final chemical digestion of maltose into glucose molecules.

OR

(ii) (a), (c) and (d)

Explanation: Among the given options, Amoeba (binary fission), Yeast (budding) and banana (vegetative propagule) reproduce by asexual reproduction whereas dogs reproduce by sexual method. 1

10. (ii) conveys nutrients and wastes to and from the embryo, respectively. 1

Explanation: The exchange of nutrients, oxygen and waste products between the embryo and the mother's body takes place through the umbilical cord.

11. (iii) $R_3 > R_2 > R_1$ 1

Explanation: Slope of V-I graph is proportional to 1/ Resistance.

It means when slope will be maximum, then resistance will be minimum.

From the figure, we can see that, slope of R_1 is maximum; hence its resistance will be minimum.

Slope of R_3 is minimum, so it's resistance will be maximum.

Therefore, $R_3 > R_2 > R_1$

12. (iv) Steel 1

Explanation: As it contains carbon which is a non metal.

- Brass-Copper and zinc
- Bronze-Copper and tin
- Amalgam-Mercury with other metals
- Steel-Iron with carbon

13. (i) Both assertion and reason are true and the reason is the correct explanation of the assertion.

Explanation: Pupil is black in colour as no light is reflected in it. 1

14. (ii) Both A and R are true but R is not the correct explanation of the assertion.

Explanation: Both statements are correct but REASON does not explain how guard cells open and close stomatal pores. 1

SECTION - B

15. Given: $l = 1$ m

$r = 0.15$ mm $= 1.5 \times 10^{-4}$ m

$A = pr^2 = 3.14 \times 2.25 \times 10^{-8}$

$= 7.065 \times 10^{-8}$ m^2

Now, resistivity $r = R \times \frac{A}{l}$

$= 26 \times \frac{7.065 \times 10^{-8}}{1}$

$= 183.69 \times 10^{-8}$ Ωm

Thus, the resistivity of the metal wire is 183.69×10^{-8} Ωm. **3**

OR

(a) An ammeter is used to measure the current flowing through a circuit. We know that current remains same in series connection. Also the resistance of an ammeter is very small due to which it doesn't affect the current to be measured. So, an ammeter is always connected in series to measure current. **1**

(b) Total voltage produced by the batteries

$V = 5 \times 1.5 = 7.5$ V

Total resistance

$R = (0.2 + 0.3 + 0.4 + 0.5 + 1.2) + 10$

$= 12.6\ \Omega$

Therefore,

current $I = \frac{V}{R} = \frac{7.5}{12.6} = 0.595$ A. **2**

16. (a) For healthy growth of plants, the soil should be neither alkaline nor highly acidic. If the soil that is on the field is too acidic then the farmer should treat the soil with quicklime or slaked lime or chalk as they are all alkaline substances and adding them to the soil will neutralize the acidic nature of soil. **1**

(b) pH of solution A = 6

pH of solution B = 8

(i) We know that the pH of any solution is inversely proportional to the hydrogen ion concentration. This means that the solution that has lower pH number will have the higher hydrogen ion concentration. So it means solution A will have the higher hydrogen ion concentration. **1**

(ii) Also Solution A is acidic and solution B is basic because H^+ ion concentration is higher in acidic solutions. **1**

OR

Equal lengths of magnesium ribbons are taken in test tubes A and B. Hydrochloric acid (HCl) is added to test tube A, while acetic acid (CH_3COOH) is added to test tube B.

In both cases, hydrogen gas is evolved. When metal reacts with acid it forms salt and hydrogen gas.

Metal + Acid ⟶ Salt + Hydrogen gas **1**

Fizzing will occur more vigorously in test tube A containing hydrochloric acid. This is because hydrochloric acid is stronger acid than acetic acid and reaction between magnesium ribbon and HCl is faster in test tube A than the reaction between Magnesium and acetic acid in test tube B. **2**

17. When a person steps upon a pointed object, he immediately removes his feet as he feels a sharp pricking pain under his feet. This happens due to reflex action. **1**

The nerve receptors present under the feet become active when the person steps on the pebble. The receptor sends impulse that is transported by the neurons to the spinal cord. The reflex action sends message via motor nerves to remove the feet. The nerves carry that impulse to the sense receptors present inside the skin under the feet. As a result the person moves his feet away from the pebble. This to and fro movement of impulses happens within a blink of our eyes. **2**

OR

(a) Oestrogen is responsible for development of secondary sexual characters in females at puberty. **1**

(b) Growth hormone promotes growth and development of the body. **1**

(c) Insulin controls blood sugar level by stimulating oxidation of glucose and absorption of glucose by liver and muscle cells. **1**

18. Group is a vertical column in the periodic table. The elements placed in a vertical column in the periodic table are said to belong to the same group. **1**

(a) As the metallic character increases on going down a group, the greatest metallic character is expected to be shown by the elements in the lowest part of a group. **1**

(b) Atomic size increases on moving down a group. So, element at the bottom of a group would be of largest size in that group. **1**

19. The magnetic field lines of a bar magnet can be mapped using a magnetic compass. The compass can be moved from one pole of the bar magnet to another and we can trace the field lines by moving the compass gradually and drawing the corresponding line which the compass would trace while following a particular line of force. **1**

Activity:

- Place the bar magnet on a sheet of white paper fixed on a drawing board. Mark the boundary of the magnet.
- Place the magnetic compass near the north pole of the given magnet.
- Mark the position of two ends of the needle. Now move the needle to a new position such that its south pole occupies the position previously occupied by its north pole.
- In this way proceed step by step till you reach the south pole of the given magnet.
- Join the points marked on the paper by a smooth curve. This curve represents a field line. Repeat the above steps for new positions of compass needle. **2**

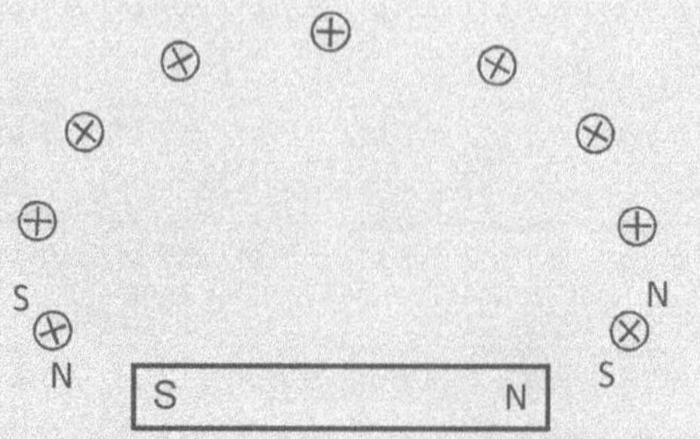

20. The various steps in a food chain at which the transfer of food(or energy) takes place are called trophic levels. In a food chain, each step representing an organism forms a trophic level. **1**

The four trophic levels are:

(i) Autotrophs are at the primary level which fix the sunlight and produce their own food,

(ii) Primary consumers or herbivores come at the second level

(iii) Secondary consumers or small carnivores come at the third level and

(iv) Tertiary consumers or the large carnivores come at the last level

The above is an example of food chain.

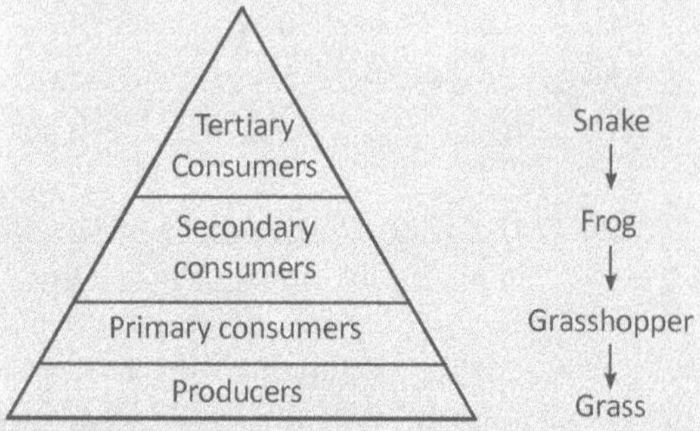

2

21. **Esters:** Esters are sweet smelling compounds of general formula RCOOR′. **1**

They are formed by the reaction of carboxylic acids with an alcohol in the presence of conc. sulphuric acid.

$$RCOOH + R'OH \xrightarrow{\text{Conc. } H_2SO_4} RCOOR' \text{ (ester)} + H_2O$$

Reaction of ethanoic acid with ethyl alcohol produces ethyl acetate.

Formation of ethyl acetate (ester) indicates sweet smell.

$$CH_3COOH + C_2H_5OH \xrightarrow{\text{Conc. } H_2SO_4} CH_3COOC_2H_5 + H_2O$$

This reaction between a carboxylic acid and an alcohol to form an ester is called the esterification reaction. **2**

22. Mendel's Laws of inheritance are:

(i) Law of dominance: When two homozygous individuals with one or more sets of contrasting characters are crossed the characters that appear in the F1 hybrids are dominant characters.

(ii) Law of segregation: The characteristics of an organism are determined by internal factors which occur in pairs. Only one of a pair of such factors can be present in a single gamete.

(iii) Law of independent assortment: In the inheritance of more than one pair of contrasting characters in a cross simultaneously, the factors responsible for each pair of traits are distributed independently to the gametes. **3**

23. (a) From air into water: When ray of light enters with oblique incidence from air into water, then it goes from optical rarer medium to optical denser medium and velocity of light decreases which in turn bends the incident light towards the normal. Here $i > r$

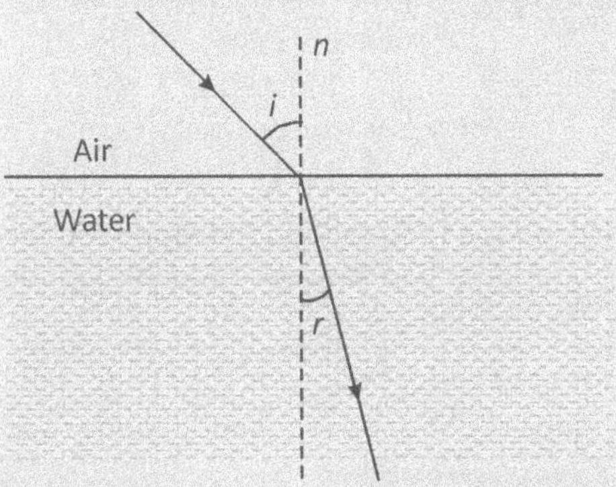

1½

(b) From water into air: When ray of light enters with oblique incidence from water into air, then it goes from optical denser medium to optical rarer medium and velocity of light increases which in turn bends the incident light away from the normal. Here $i < r$.

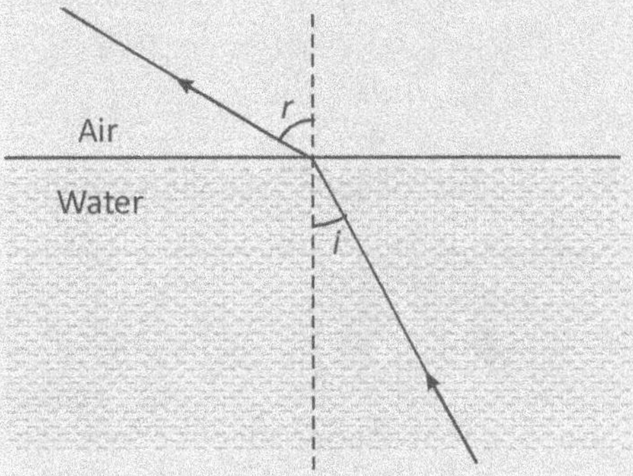

1½

24. Disadvantages of using Fossil fuels:

(i) Air pollution: Burning of fossil fuels generate a lot of chemicals like oxides of sulphur, carbon and nitrogen and release them into the atmosphere.

(ii) Acid Rains: On burning they produce acidic gases like CO_2, SO_2, SO_3, NO_2. These gases such as SO_2, SO_3, and NO_2 causes acid rains, which affect our water and soil resources

(iii) Greenhouse Effect and Global warming: Burning of fossil fuels release gases like carbon-dioxide which trap the heat in the atmosphere without releasing it and causing temperatures to increase steadily. Excess of CO_2 gas contributes to the global warming due to its greenhouse effect.

(iv) They are non-renewable sources of energy. **3**

SECTION - C

25. **(a)** Oxidizing agent: is a substance which gives oxygen or gains hydrogen.
For example in the given reaction:
$CuO + H_2 \longrightarrow Cu + H_2O$
CuO has given oxygen, hence it is oxidizing agent. **1**

(b) **(i)** Hydrogen gas combines with nitrogen to form ammonia.
$H_2 + N_2 \longrightarrow NH_3$
Balanced:
$3H_2 + N_2 \longrightarrow 2NH_3$ **1**

(ii) Hydrogen sulphide gas burns in air to give water and sulpur dioxide.
$H_2S + O_2 \longrightarrow H_2O + SO_2$
Balanced:
$2H_2S + 3O_2 \longrightarrow 2H_2O + 2SO_2$ **1**

(iii) Barium chloride reacts with aluminium sulphate to give aluminium chloride and a precipitate of barium sulphate.
$BaCl_2 + Al_2(SO_4)_3 \longrightarrow AlCl_3 + BaSO_4$
Balanced:
$3BaCl_2 + Al_2(SO_4)_3 \longrightarrow 2AlCl_3 + 3BaSO_4$ **1**

(iv) Potassium metal reacts with water to give potassium hydroxide and hydrogen gas.
$K + H_2O \longrightarrow KOH + H_2$
Balanced:
$2K + 2H_2O \longrightarrow 2KOH + H_2$ **1**

26. Alimentary canal of man:
Mouth Oesophagus Stomach Intestine

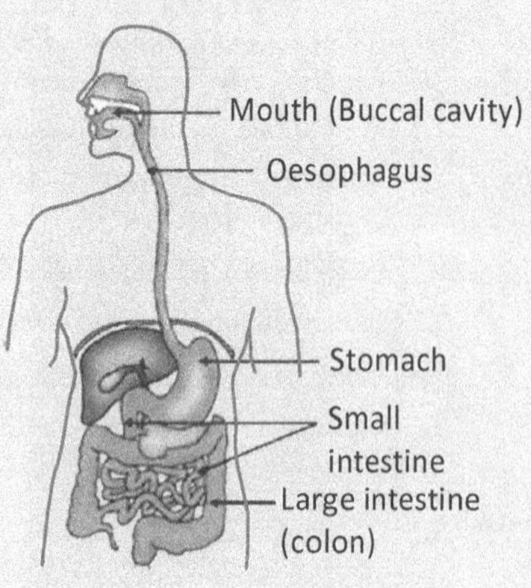

Alimentary Canal of Man **5**

OR

Human respiratory system:
Larynx Trachea Lungs Bronchi **5**

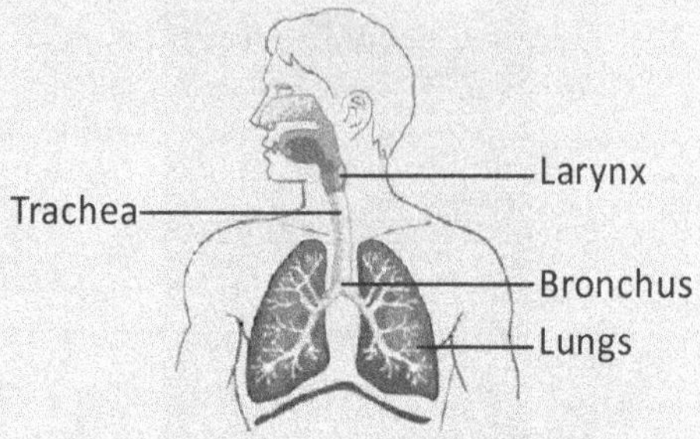

Human Respiratory System

27. **(a)** **Advantages of connecting electrical devices in parallel are:**

(i) There is no division of voltage among the appliances when connected in parallel. The potential difference across each appliance is equal to the supplied voltage.

(ii) The total effective resistance of the circuit can be reduced by connecting electrical appliances in parallel.

(iii) If one appliance fails to work, others will continue to work properly if they are connected in parallel combination. **3**

(b) Here, for parallel combination the potential difference will be same.
Let the potential difference =V
Then the current passing through the resistance 20 ohm will be,
$I_1 = V/20.$
The current passing through the resistance 40 ohm will be,
$I_2 = V/40$
Clearly we see that,
$I_1 = 2I_2$
Hence current in 20W is double as compared to the current in 40W resistor. **2**

OR

(a) **Resistors connected in series:** In a series combination of resistors the current is the same in every part of the circuit or the same current flows through each resistor, *i.e.*, there is only one path for the flow of current.

When several resistors are joined in series, the resultant resistance of the combination R_S equals the sum of their individual resistances, R_1, R_2, R_3.

$$R_S = R_1 + R_2 + R_3$$

Parallel Combination of resistors: In a parallel circuit each resistor is placed in its own separate branch. A parallel circuit provides multiple paths for the current to flow.

The reciprocal of the equivalent resistance of a group of resistances joined in parallel is equal to the sum of the reciprocals of the individual resistances.

$$\frac{1}{R_p} = \frac{1}{R_1} + \frac{1}{R_2} + \frac{1}{R_3}$$ 2

(b) To find total resistance in the circuit.

Let R_A be the value of total resistance in first combination *i.e.* 5Ω and 20Ω.

Then $$\frac{1}{R_A} = \frac{1}{R_1} + \frac{1}{R_2}$$

$$\frac{1}{R_A} = \frac{1}{5} + \frac{1}{20}$$

$$\frac{1}{R_A} = \frac{4+1}{20} = \frac{5}{20}$$

or $R_A = 4\ \Omega$ 1

Let R_B be the value of resistance in this combination. Then,

$$\frac{1}{R_B} = \frac{1}{R_3} + \frac{1}{R_4} + \frac{1}{R_5}$$

$$\frac{1}{R_B} = \frac{1}{15} + \frac{1}{20} + \frac{1}{10}$$

$$\frac{1}{R_B} = \frac{4+3+6}{60} = \frac{13}{60}$$

or $R_B = \frac{60}{13}\Omega$ 1

Total resistance across the circuit will be:

$$R_A + R_B = 4\ \Omega + \frac{60}{13}\Omega = 8.6\ \Omega$$ 1

28. Structure of diamond: In diamond each carbon atom is tetrahedrally bonded to four other carbon atoms through four strong covalent bonds. Thus no free electrons on carbon are left. It occurs in all shapes and sizes. Even though it is a sparkling material it is made up of carbon which is black. The shine in diamond is based on its definite crystalline arrangement. This strong covalent bonding in its structure makes it hardest natural substance and a non-conductor of electricity. 1

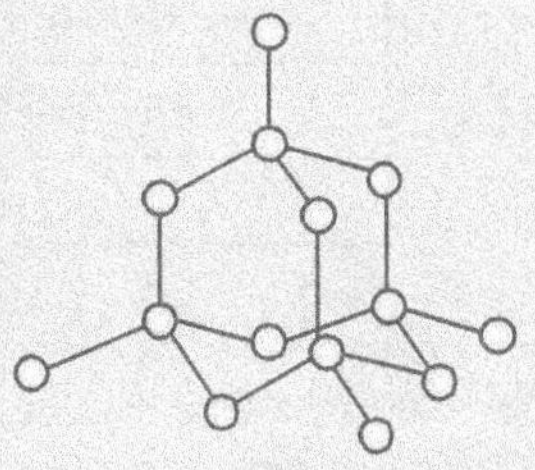

Properties of Diamond:

- Due to the presence of large 3-D network of C-C covalent bonds, diamond is very hard and have high melting point.
- It is a non-conductor of heat. It is a poor conductor of electricity as all the 4 electrons are utilized in making covalent bonds, leaving no free electrons to conduct electricity. 2

Uses of Diamond:

- Due to its brilliant shine, it is used in making jewellery.
- Due to its hardness, it is used in making, cutting and drilling tools and is used to cut glass.
- It is also used in surgical instruments to remove cataract from the eyes. 2

OR

(a) Compounds which are formed from carbon and hydrogen atoms are called as hydrocarbons. Some common examples of hydrocarbons are methane (CH_4), ethane (C_2H_6), ethene ($CH_2{=}CH_2$), ethyne (C_2H_2), cyclohexane (C_6H_{12}) and benzene (C_6H_6). 1

(b) Saturated hydrocarbons have only C-C bonds means all carbon atoms are bonded with single covalent bonds. The unsaturated hydrocarbons have multiple bonds (double or triple covalent bonds) between carbon atoms.

Examples of saturated hydrocarbons: Methane (CH_4), Ethane (CH_3—CH_3)

Examples of unsaturated hydrocarbons: Ethene ($H_2C = CH_2$), Ethyne (HC CH) **2**

(c) An atom or group of atoms that is responsible for characteristics physical and chemical properties for organic compound is found is called as functional group.

Examples of four functional groups are:

Name of functional group	Formula of functional group
Alcohol	% OH
Carboxylic acid	COOH
Aldehyde	CHO
Ketone	>C=O

2

29. **(a)** A represents the pollen grain

B represents the pollen tube

C represents the ovary

D represents the female germ cell

½ × 4 = 2

(b) The transfer of pollen grains from the anther to the stigma of a flower is known as pollination. It is of two types:

Self-pollination: It is the transfer of pollen grains from the anther to the stigma of the same flower or another flower on the same plant.

Cross-pollination: It is the transfer of pollen grains from the anther to the stigma of the flower present on two different plants. **1**

(c) Fertilisation occurs when the male gamete present in a pollen grain joins with the female gamete or egg present in ovule. When the pollen grain falls on the stigma of the carpel, it bursts open and grows a pollen tube downward through the style towards the female gamete in the ovary. Here, zygote is formed which later grows into embryo. Zygote divides repeatedly to form an embryo within the ovule. Ovule develops a thick coat & gradually forms seed. Ovary of flowers develops and becomes a fruit. **2**

30. **(a)** The three common refractive defects of vision are:

- **Myopia** (or short sightedness) It is corrected by using concave lenses of appropriate power.
- **Hypermetropia** (or far sightedness) It is corrected by using convex lenses of appropriate power.
- **Presbyopia** It is corrected by using bifocal lenses of appropriate power in which the upper part consists of a concave lens (to correct myopia) and lower part consists of convex lens (to correct hypermetropia). **3**

(b) Eye donation advertisements are important as they make people aware about donation of organs after their death. Eyes of a dead person can be donated to the person having corneal blindness; it will help him/her to see the world. We can also register ourselves and encourage others also to register to eye donation camps that can preserve our eyes after our death and donate them to the needy. **2**

SAMPLE PAPER 10

CBSE - Class 10

SCIENCE

Time Allowed: 3 Hours *Maximum Marks: 80*

General Instructions:

i. The question paper comprises three sections – A, B and C. Attempt all the sections.
ii. All questions are compulsory.
iii. Internal choice is given in each section.
iv. All questions in Section A are one-mark questions comprising MCQ, VSA type and assertion-reason type questions. They are to be answered in one word or in one sentence.
v. All questions in Section B are three-mark, short-answer type questions. These are to be answered in about 50 - 60 words each.
vi. All questions in Section C are five-mark, long-answer type questions. These are to be answered in about 80 - 90 words each.
vii. This question paper consists of a total of 30 questions.

SECTION - A

1. What happens when a mature Spirogyra filament attains considerable length? **1**

2. Under what condition in an arrangement of two plane mirrors, incident ray and reflected ray will always be parallel to each other, whatever may be angle of incidence? **1**

3. **Answer question numbers 3(a)-3(d) on the basis of your understanding of the following paragraph and the related studied concepts.**

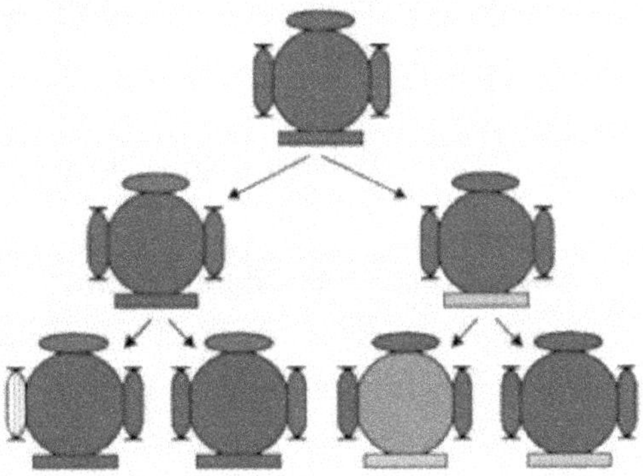

Inheritance from the previous generation provides both a common basic body design, and subtle changes in it, for the next generation. The original organism at the top will give rise to two individuals, similar in body design, but with subtle differences. Each of them, in turn, will give rise to two individuals in the next generation. Each of the four individuals in the bottom row will be different from each other. While some of these differences will be unique, others will be inherited from their respective parents, who were different from each other. Selection of variants by environmental factors forms the basis for evolutionary processes.

3(a) If a trait A exists in 10% of a population of an asexually reproducing species and a trait B exists in 60% of the same population, which trait is likely to have arisen earlier? **1**

3(b) How does the creation of variations in a species promote survival? **1**

3(c) Give any 1 factor that could lead to the rise of a new species? **1**

3(d) Which of the processes, sexual reproduction or asexual reproduction, brings about maximum variations in the offsprings? **1**

4. Analyse the following reactivity series given below and answer the questions that follow:

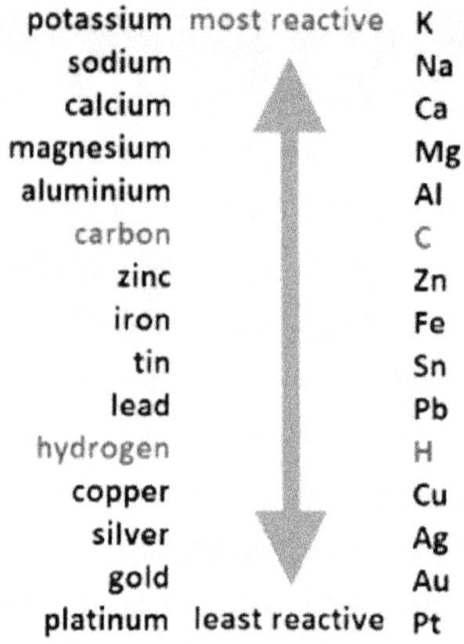

4(a) Which of the two metals is more reactive: copper or silver? **1**

4(b) What will happen if a strip of zinc is immersed in a solution of copper sulphate? **1**

4(c) If copper is kept open in air, it slowly loses its shining brown surface and gains a green coating. It is due to the formation of

(i) $CuSO_4$ **(ii)** $CuCO_3$

(iii) $Cu(NO_3)_2$ **(iv)** CuO **1**

4(d) Which one of the following four metals would be displaced from the solution of its salts by other three metals?

(i) Mg **(ii)** Ag

(iii) Zn **(iv)** Cu **1**

5. The shape of the earth's magnetic field resembles that of an imaginary:

(i) U-shaped magnet

(ii) Straight conductor carrying current

(iii) Current-carrying circular coil

(iv) Bar magnet **1**

6. New species may be formed if:

(a) DNA undergoes significant changes in germ cells.

(b) Chromosome number changes in the gamete.

(c) There is no change in the genetic material

(d) Mating does not take place

(i) (a) and (b) **(ii)** (a) and (c)

(iii) (b), (c) and (d) **(iv)** (a), (b) and (c) **1**

7. The most appropriate definition of a natural resource is that it is a substance/commodity that is:

(i) present only on land
(ii) a gift of nature which is very useful to mankind
(iii) a man-made substance placed in nature
(iv) available only in the forest 1

OR

The three R's that will help us to conserve natural resources for long term use are:

(i) recycle, regenerate, reuse
(ii) reduce, regenerate, resuse
(iii) reduce, reuse, redistribute
(iv) reduce, recycle, reuse 1

8. Which of the following is not a physical change?

(i) Boiling of water to give water vapour
(ii) Melting of ice to give water
(iii) Dissolution of salt in water
(iv) Combustion of Liquefied Petroleum Gas (LPG) 1

OR

Which of the following is (are) an endothermic process(es)?

(a) Dilution of sulphuric acid
(b) Sublimation of dry ice
(c) Condensation of water vapours
(d) Evaporation of water

(i) Both (a) and (c) (ii) Only (b)
(iii) Only (c) (iv) Both (b) and (d) 1

9. In which part of the alimentary canal food is finally digested?

(i) Stomach (ii) Mouth cavity
(iii) Large intestine (iv) Small intestine 1

10. The image formed by a plane mirror is:

(i) virtual, behind the mirror and enlarged
(ii) virtual, behind the mirror and of the same size as the object
(iii) real, at the surface of the mirror and enlarged
(iv) real, behind the mirror and of the same size as the object 1

OR

A ray of light strikes a plane mirror PQ at an angle of incidence of 30°, is reflected from the plane mirror and then strikes a second plane mirror QR placed at right angles to the first mirror. The angle of reflection at the second mirror is:

(i) 30° (ii) 45°
(iii) 60° (iv) 90° 1

11. If the key in the arrangement as shown below is taken out (the circuit is made open) and magnetic field lines are drawn over the horizontal plane ABCD, the lines are:

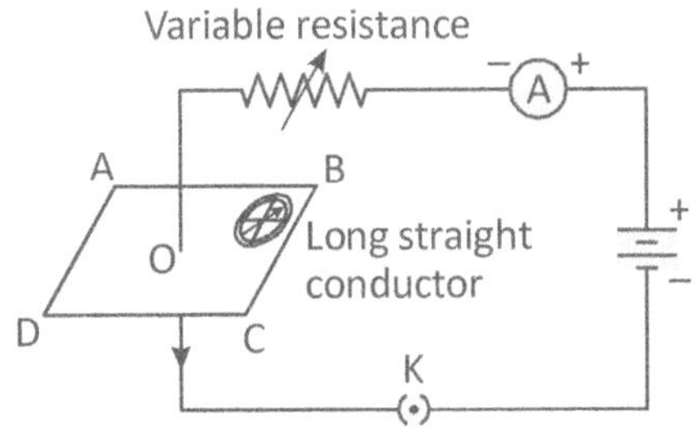

(i) Concentric circles
(ii) Elliptical in shape
(iii) Straight lines parallel to each other
(iv) Concentric circles near the point O but of elliptical shapes as we go away from it **1**

12. Carbon exists in the atmosphere in the form of:

(i) Only carbon monoxide
(ii) Carbon monoxide in traces and carbon dioxide
(iii) Only carbon dioxide
(iv) Coal **1**

For question numbers 13 and 14, two statements are given- one labeled Assertion (A) and the other labeled Reason (R). Select the correct answer to these questions from the codes (i), (ii), (iii) and (iv) as given below:

(i) Both A and R are true and R is correct explanation of the assertion.
(ii) Both A and R are true but R is not the correct explanation of the assertion.
(iii) A is true but R is false.
(iv) A is false but R is true.

13. Assertion A : Fuse wire must have high resistance and low melting point.
Reason R : Fuse is used for small current flow only. **1**

14. Assertion A : Though the same current flows through the line wires and the filament of the bulb but heat produced in the filament is much higher than that in line wires.
Reason R : The filament of bulbs is made of a material of high resistance and high melting point **1**

SECTION - B

15. List the limitations of Newlands' Law of Octaves? **3**

16. Write the balanced chemical equation for the following reactions and identify the type of reaction in each case:

(a) In Thermite reaction, iron (III) oxide reacts with aluminium and gives molten iron and aluminium oxide.
(b) Magnesium ribbon is burnt in an atmosphere of nitrogen gas to form solid magnesium nitride.
(c) Chlorine gas is passed in an aqueous potassium iodide solution to form potassium chloride solution and solid iodine. **3**

OR

Give the characteristic tests for the following gases:

(a) CO_2 (b) SO_2 (c) H_2 **3**

17. Size of image of an object by a mirror having a focal length of 20 cm is observed to be reduced to $1/3^{rd}$ to its size. At what distance, the object has been placed from the mirror? What is the nature of the image and the mirror? **3**

OR

A student is given three mirrors of equal size—concave, convex and plane. How will he identify them without touching their surfaces. **3**

18. List the properties of magnetic field lines? **3**

19. When a metal X is treated with cold water, it gives a basic salt Y with molecular formula XOH (molecular mass = 40) and liberates a gas Z which easily catches fire. Identify X, Y and Z and also write the reaction involved. **3**

20. A student constructed a box type solar cooker. He found that it did not work efficiently. What could this be due to? Give any four possible mistakes in the construction and operation of the solar cooker. What maximum temperature can ordinarily be reached inside a solar cooker? **3**

21. A red haired woman marries a brown haired man, and all the children are brown haired. Explain this genetically. **3**

22. Four resistors of 2Ω each are joined end to end to form a square ABCD. Calculate the equivalent resistance of the combination between any two adjacent corners. **3**

23. What is biological magnification? Will the levels of this magnification be different at different levels of the ecosystem? **3**

24. Explain how DNA copying is an essential part of the process of reproduction? What are the advantages of sexual reproduction over asexual reproduction? **3**

OR

Answer the following:

(a) Name any 2 plants that reproduce by grafting.

(b) List any two benefits to an organism that reproduces through spores. **3**

SECTION - C

25. Look at figure and answer the following questions:

(a) What change would you observe in the calcium hydroxide solution taken in tube B?

(b) Write the reaction involved in test tubes A and B respectively.

(c) If ethanol is given instead of ethanoic acid, would you expect the same change?

(d) How can a solution of lime water be prepared in the laboratory?

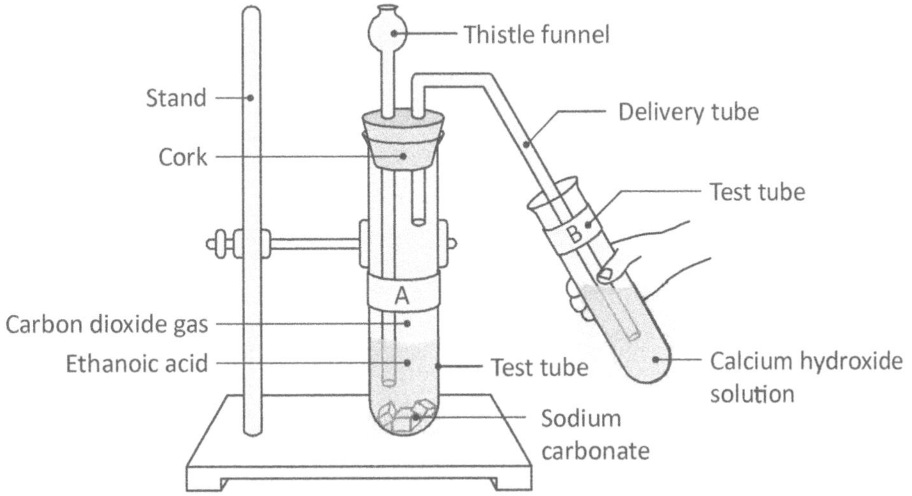

5

OR

Give reasons:

(a) Why is pure ethanoic acid known as glacial acetic acid?

(b) Why is ethanol used as antifreeze?

(c) Why is ethanol mixed with methanol known as denatured alcohol?

(d) Why is oxyacetylene flame used for welding purposes?

(e) What is gasol? **5**

26. Define reflex arc. Explain the pathway followed during a reflex action. Draw flowchart showing the sequence of events which occur during sneezing. **5**

27. For making cake, baking powder is taken. If at home your mother uses baking soda instead of baking powder in cake.

(a) How will it affect the taste of the cake and why?

(b) How can baking soda be converted into baking powder?

(c) What is the role of tartaric acid added to baking soda? **5**

28. Explain the refraction of light through a triangular glass prism using a labeled ray diagram. Hence, define the angle of deviation. **5**

OR

Make a diagram to show how hypermetropia is corrected. The near point of a hypermetropic eye is 1 m. What is the power of the lens required to correct this defect? Assume that the near point of the normal eye is 25 cm. **5**

29. Draw and explain the sectional view of human female reproductive system and label the parts. **5**

30. What is Joule's heating effect? How can it be demonstrated experimentally? List its four applications in daily life. **5**

OR

Determine the following quantities for each of the two circuits shown below...

the equivalent resistance,

the total current from the power supply,

the current through each resistor,

the voltage drop across each resistor, and

the power dissipated in each resistor.

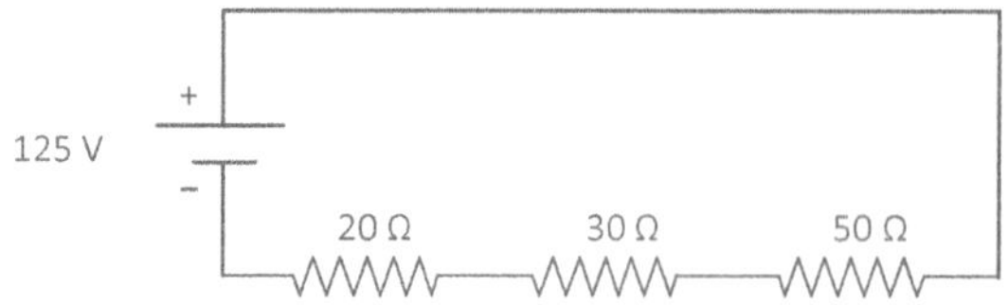

5

10

SOLUTION

CBSE - Class 10

SECTION - A

1. When a mature spirogyra filament attains considerable length, it breaks up into smaller fragments or pieces, and each fragment grows into a new filament or individual. **1**

2. When two plane mirrors are placed at right angle with each other, then the incident ray and reflected ray will always be parallel to each other, irrespective of the angle of incidence. **1**

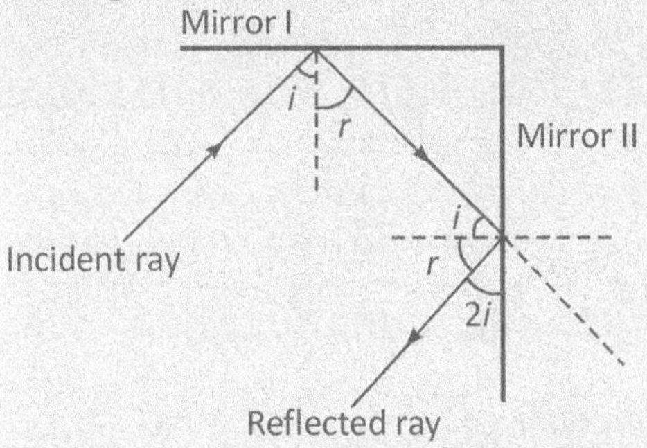

3. **(a)** Trait B is likely to have arisen earlier because in asexual reproduction traits are carried from parents to offspring with least variations so since trait B has higher percentage it is likely to have arisen earlier. **1**

3. **(b)** The variations provide stability to the population of various species by preventing them from getting wiped out during adverse conditions. The natural environment also changes, and variations in species which become suited to the environment help it to survive. **1**

3. **(c)** The factors could lead to the rise of a new species are :
   (1) Natural Selection
   (2) Method of Genetic Drift
   (3) Gene Variation on Mutation
   (4) Geographical and environmental factors **1**

3. **(d)** Sexual Reproduction **1**

4. **(a)** Copper **1**

4. **(b)** When a strip of zinc metal is put in copper sulphate solution, then the blue colour of copper sulphate solution fades gradually and red brown coating of copper is deposited on zinc strip.

$$\underset{\text{Zinc}}{Zn} + \underset{\text{Copper Sulphate}}{CuSO_4} \longrightarrow \underset{\text{Zinc Sulphate}}{ZnSO_4} + \underset{\text{Copper}}{Cu}$$ **1**

4. **(c)** **(ii)** $CuCO_3$ **1**

   Explanation: Copper reacts with moist carbon dioxide in the air and form green colour basic copper carbonate.

4. **(d)** **(ii)** Ag **1**

   Explanation: Least reactive metal can be displaced from its solution by other three metals. Silver is least reactive out of given four metals.

5. **(iv)** Bar magnet **1**

   Explanation: The shape of the earth's magnetic field resembles that of an imaginary bar magnet.

6. **(i)** (a) and (b) **1**

   Explanation: Change in genetic material leads to reproductive isolation of population into a new species.

7. **(ii)** a gift of nature which is very useful to mankind **1**

Explanation: Resources that occur naturally within environment are called as natural resources.

OR

(iv) reduce, recycle, reuse **1**

Explanation: Reduce, recycle and reuse can conserve the natural resources.

8. **(iv)** Combustion of Liquefied Petroleum Gas (LPG) **1**

Explanation: A physical change involves only change in physical state whereas a chemical change results in the formation of new substances. Boiling of water, melting of ice and dissolution of salt are physical changes as no new products are formed.

OR

(iv) Both (b) and (d). **1**

Explanation: An endothermic process involves absorption of heat such as sublimation and evaporation needs heat energy.

9. **(iv)** Small intestine **1**

Explanation: Digestion of food starts in mouth by salivary amylase. From here it enters into the stomach via oesophagus. Gastric juice of stomach digests the protein part of food. Pancreatic amylase, trypsin and lipase as well as intestinal peptidases and maltase carry out the final chemical digestion of food in small intestine. The simpler substances formed by chemical digestion are then absorbed by small intestinal villi.

10. **(ii)** Virtual, behind the mirror and of the same size as the object **1**

Explanation: The image formed by a plane mirror is virtual, behind the mirror and of the same size because it cannot be projected on a screen.

OR

(iii) 60° **1**

Explanation:

Here, $\angle ABN = \angle NBC$

as (angle of incidence = angle of reflection)

$\angle BCO = \angle NBC$

(alternate angles)

$\angle MCB = 90° - \angle BCO = 60°$

($\angle MCB$ = angle of incidence for mirror QR)

Now, $\angle MCB = \angle MCD = 60°$

($\angle MCD$ = angle of reflection from mirror QR and angle of incidence = angle of reflection)

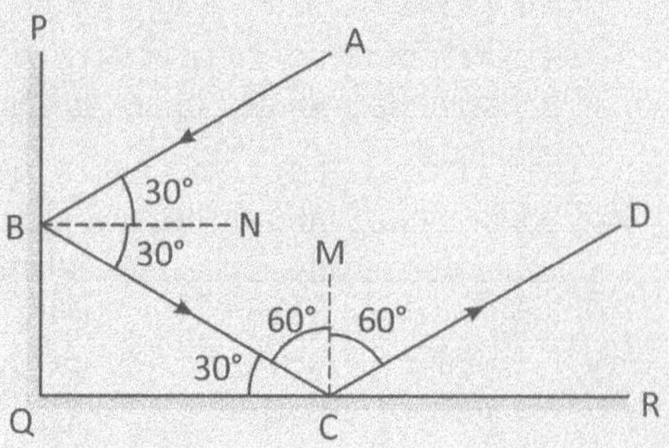

11. **(iii)** Straight lines parallel to each other **1**

Explanation: If key is taken out then current will stop and no magnetic field exists due to the conductor. The only magnetic field is due to Earth's magnetic field and is straight lines parallel to each other, whose horizontal component is directed from geographical South to geographical North on the horizontal plane ABCD. Therefore at the point O, there will be earth's magnetic field and they will be straight lines parallel to each other.

12. **(iii)** only carbon dioxide **1**

Explanation: Carbon exists only in the form of carbon dioxide gas (CO_2) in air.

13. **(iii)** Assertion is true but reason is false. **1**

Explanation: Fuse wire must have high resistance because in series current remains same, therefore according to Joule's law

$$H = i^2Rt$$

That is heat produced is high if R is high.

The melting point must be low so that wire may melt with increase in temperature. As the current equal to maximum safe value, flows through the fuse wire, it heats up, melts and break the circuit.

14. **(i)** Both assertion and reason are true and the reason is the correct explanation of the assertion **1**

Explanation: Filament of bulb and line wire are connected in series, hence current through both of them is same. We know that $H=i^2Rt$ and resistance of the filament of the bulb is much higher than that of line wires, hence heat produced in the filament is much higher than that in line wires.

SECTION - B

15. Limitations of Newlands' Law of Octaves:

(a) It was not applicable throughout the arrangement. It was applicable only till calcium, as after calcium every eighth element did not possess properties similar to that of the first.

(b) It was assumed by Newlands that only 56 elements existed in nature and no more elements would be discovered in the future. But, later on, several new elements were discovered, whose properties did not fit into the Law of Octaves.

(c) The position of cobalt and nickel in the group of halogens with the elements fluorine and chlorine (F, Cl) which have different properties could not be explained.

(d) Placing of iron far away from cobalt and nickel, which have similar properties as iron, could also not be explained.

Thus, Newlands' Law of Octaves worked well with lighter elements only. **3**

16. **(a)** Thermite reaction, iron (III) oxide reacts with aluminium and gives molten iron and aluminium oxide.

$$\underset{\text{[Iron (III) oxide]}}{Fe_2O_3(s)} + 2Al(s) \longrightarrow \underset{\text{(Iron)}}{2Fe(l)} + \underset{\text{(Aluminium oxide)}}{Al_2O_3(s)} + \text{Heat} + \text{Light}$$

It is an exothermic redox reaction as well as displacement reaction because aluminium displaces iron from iron (III) oxide. **1**

(b) Magnesium ribbon is burnt in an atmosphere of nitrogen gas to form solid magnesium nitride.

$$3Mg + N_2 \longrightarrow 2Mg_3N_2$$

It is a combination reaction as well as redox reaction. **1**

(c) Chlorine gas is passed in an aqueous potassium iodide solution to form potassium chloride solution and solid iodine.

$$2KI + Cl_2 \longrightarrow 2KCl + I_2$$

It is a displacement as well as redox reaction. **1**

OR

Characteristic tests for the following gases:

(a) **CO_2** gas: When CO_2 gas is passed through lime water; it forms insoluble calcium carbonate which turns the solution milky. This is called as lime water test.

$$Ca(OH)_2 + CO_2 \longrightarrow CaCO_3 + H_2O$$

The solution becomes clear in excess of CO_2 because of formation of soluble calcium bicarbonate.

$$CO_2 + H_2O + CaCO_3 \longrightarrow Ca(HCO_3)_2$$ **1**

(b) **SO_2 gas:** Due to acidic nature, sulphur dioxide gas turns moist litmus paper from blue to red. It also changes the orange colour of acidified potassium dichromate solution to green.

$$K_2Cr_2O_7(aq) + 3SO_2(g) + H_2SO_4(aq) \longrightarrow Cr_2(SO_4)_3(aq) + K_2SO_4(aq) + H_2O(l)$$ **1**

(c) H_2 gas: In the presence of atmospheric oxygen, hydrogen gas burns with a pop sound. **1**

17. Here, it is not given whether the mirror is concave of convex. So, we will do calculations for both types of mirror.

For concave mirror:

Focal length, $f =$ 20 cm;

Magnification, $m = -\frac{1}{3}$

Since, magnification, $m = -\frac{v}{u}$

Magnification, $m = -\frac{1}{3} = -\frac{v}{u}$

$v = \frac{u}{3}$

Using mirror formula, we have

$\frac{1}{v} + \frac{1}{u} = \frac{1}{f} = \frac{1}{u} + \frac{3}{u} = \frac{4}{u}$

$u = 4f = -80$ cm

The object should be placed at a distance 80 cm from the concave mirror to form real and inverted image. **1½**

For convex mirror:

Focal length, $f = +$ 20cm;

Magnification, $m = +\frac{1}{3}$

Magnification, $m = \frac{1}{3} = -\frac{v}{u}$

$v = -\frac{u}{3}$

Using mirror formula, we have

$\frac{1}{v} + \frac{1}{u} = \frac{1}{f}$

$\frac{1}{f} = \frac{1}{u} - \frac{3}{u} = -\frac{2}{u}$

$u = -2f = -40$ cm

The object should be placed at a distance 40 cm from the convex mirror to form virtual, erect and diminished image. **1½**

OR

Identification of mirror: The student is given three mirrors. He will see his face in each mirror, turn by turn. Initially, keep the face close to the mirror but, slowly move away from the mirror.

(a) If the image formed on the mirror is of the same size as our face but laterally inverted (*i.e.* left face looks right and vice-versa) for all positions, then it is a plane mirror.

(b) If the image formed is erect and enlarged initially but gets inverted as the face is moved away, then it is a concave mirror.

(c) If the image formed is erect and smaller in size for all positions, then it is a convex mirror. **3**

18. Properties of Magnetic field lines:

(i) Magnetic field is a quantity that has both direction and magnitude.

(ii) They emerge from the north pole of a magnet and enter at the south pole of the magnet.

(iii) Inside the magnet, the direction of field lines is from south pole to its north pole. Hence, magnetic field lines are closed curves.

(iv) The relative strength of the magnetic field is shown by the degree of closeness of the field lines. Crowded field lines represent the strong magnetic field.

(v) The magnetic field at any point is represented by the tangent at that point. No two field lines intersect each other. If they intersect, it would mean that at point of intersection there would be two field directions, which is not possible.

(vi) They are dense close to the poles and sparse away from them. It means magnetic field is strongest around poles of the magnet.

½ × 6 = 3

19. Given, molecular formula of Y = XOH and molecular mass of Y = 40

So, atomic mass of metal X would be,

M + 16 + 1 = 40

M = 40 – 17 = 23

Metal with atomic mass 23 is sodium(Na) and reaction of it with cold water will form the base sodium hydroxide (NaOH) and liberates H_2 gas which easily catches fire.

$2Na + 2H_2O \text{ (Cold)} \longrightarrow 2NaOH + H_2$- **1**

X = Sodium (Na)
Y = Sodium hydroxide (NaOH)
Z = Hydrogen gas (H_2) **2**

20. The student must have made the following mistakes:

(i) He might be using a plastic cover instead of glass cover.

(ii) Reflector mirror might have not been properly adjusted.

(iii) He might not have used black containers or box is not fully insulated.

(iv) He might have not blackened the interior of the solar cooker.

½ × 4 = 2

Maximum temperature attained in a solar cooker is about 140°C. **1**

21. A red haired woman marries a brown haired man, and all the children are brown haired. The brown hair colour genes are dominant to the red hair colour genes. When there was exchange of gametes in male and female the dominant character was brown hair and recessive character was red hair. That is why the children were having brown coloured hairs. **2**

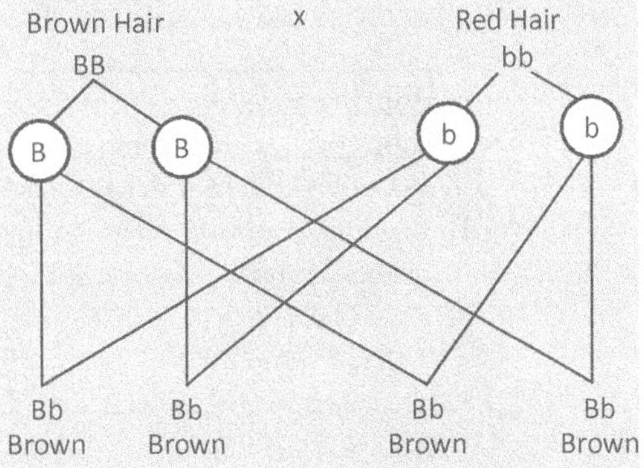

1

22. The circuit diagram will be:

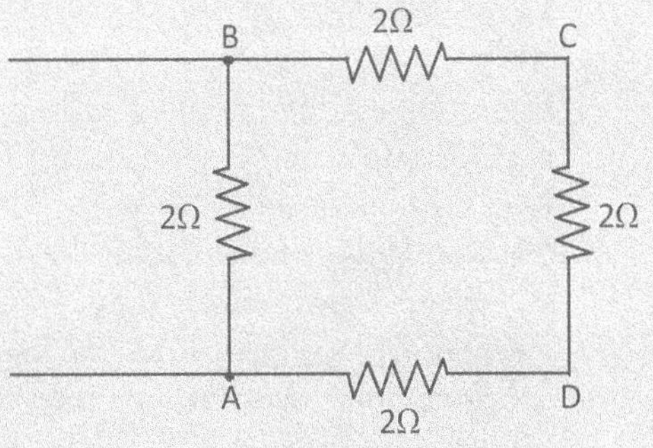

1

Let us consider the equivalent resistance between points A and B.

Here, three resistances R_2(BC), R_3(CD), R_4(DA) of 2 ohm each are in series, and this combination is connected in parallel across the resistor R_1 of 2 ohm(AB) (R_1 = 2 ohm)

Equivalent resistance of the three series resistors,

$$R' = R_2 + R_3 + R_4$$
$$= 2 + 2 + 2 = 6 \text{ ohms}$$

Thus, required equivalent resistance (R)

$$\frac{1}{R} = \frac{1}{R_1} + \frac{1}{R'} = \frac{1}{2} + \frac{1}{6} = \frac{4}{6}$$

R = 1.5 ohm. **2**

23. **Biological magnification:** The increase in concentration of harmful chemical substances like pesticides in the body of living organisms at each trophic level of a food chain is called Biological magnification. **1**

Several pesticides and harmful chemicals enter our body through food chain and remain there without being decomposed. The accumulation of these harmful chemicals increases towards the higher side of the food chain that is the level or concentration of the harmful chemicals increases with increasing trophic level. So, it is different at different levels of the ecosystem. Humans which perhaps occupy the highest point in the food chain will face highest accumulation. **2**

24. DNA copying is an essential part of the process of reproduction because it makes possible the transmission of genetic information from parents to offspring in the next generation. DNA contains information for the inheritance of characteristics from the parents to the next generation. **1**

Advantages of sexual reproduction over asexual reproduction:

(i) In sexual reproduction, more variations are produced. Thus, it ensures survival of species in a population.

(ii) The new formed individual has characteristics of both the parents.

(iii) Variations are more viable in sexual mode than in asexual one. This is because in asexual reproduction, DNA has to function inside the inherited cellular apparatus. **2**

OR

(a) Two plants that reproduce by grafting are apple and peach. **1**

(b) Benefits to an organism that reproduces through spores:

(i) Large numbers of spores are reproduced in one sporangium.

(ii) Spores are distributed easily by air to far-off places to avoid competition at one place

(iii) Spores are covered by thick walls which enables them to survive under unfavorable conditions.

(iv) By surviving under adverse conditions, the spores make these plants live forever. **2**

SECTION - C

25. **(a)** Calcium hydroxide solution in test tube B will react with carbon dioxide gas and turns milky due to the formation of insoluble calcium carbonate ($CaCO_3$). **1**

(b) Test tube A:

$Na_2CO_3 + 2CH_3COOH \longrightarrow 2CH_3COONa + CO_2 + H_2O$

Test tube B:

$Ca(OH)_2 + CO_2 \longrightarrow CaCO_3 + H_2O$ **2**

(c) If ethanol is given instead of ethanoic acid, no change will occur because ethanol is a very weak acid and cannot decompose Na_2CO_3 to give CO_2 gas.

$Na_2CO_3 + CH_3CH_2OH \longrightarrow$ No reaction **1**

(d) Lime water (calcium hydroxide) is usually prepared by the reaction of calcium oxide (quick lime) with water. Some of it will dissolve to form calcium hydroxide (lime water) while majority of it will remain suspended. Filter the solution. The clear solution thus obtained is called lime water.

$CaO + H_2O \longrightarrow$ Suspension $\xrightarrow{\text{Filter}} Ca(OH)_2$ **1**

OR

(a) When pure ethanoic acid is cooled, it freezes forming glacier like crystals. Therefore, 100% acetic acid, obtained by melting these crystals is called glacial acetic acid. **1**

(b) Ethanol has a freezing point below 0°C. Thus when mixed with water it serves to depress the freezing point of water below zero degrees Celsius (32 Fahrenheit). **1**

(c) The alcohol to be used in industry is subjected to lower exercise duty whereas the alcoholic beverages are subjected to high exercise duty. To prevent its misuse for drinking purposes, the industrial alcohol is denatured *i.e.* is made unfit for drinking by adding certain poisonous substances such as methanol. Such an alcohol is known as denatured alcohol. **1**

(d) Welding purposes need to melt the metals which require a lot of heat. Oxyacetylene burns to produce a large amount of heat which is sufficient to melt metals and so it is used for welding. **1**

(e) Gasol denotes a gas mixture typically consisting of 95% propane and 5% butane. **1**

26. **Reflex arc:** The pathway through which nerve impulses pass during reflex action is called reflex arc. **1**

Reflex arc involves:

- Receptors- receive the message from external environment.
- Sensory neuron- carries the message from the receptor to the central nervous system.

- Central nervous system- processes the message and sends impulses to the concerned part of the body in the form of response.
- Motor neuron- carries the message from the central nervous system to the effector.
- Effector- responses against the stimulus. 2

Sneezing occurs when a foreign particle (irritant) irritates the nasal passage. The sequence of events that take place during sneezing are as follows:

Nerve endings located in the nasal passage identifies the irritant entered in the nose

↓

Receptor sends the information or nerve impulse to the sneezing centre located in brain stem

↓

Brain stem in return sends instructions to the lungs or diaphragm for response

↓

Diaphragm moves abruptly, chest muscles contract in response to the instructions received

↓

Air blows out from nose and mouth instantly and rapidly

↓

Sneezing occurs in response to the irritant

2

27. **(a)** Baking soda is sodium hydrogen carbonate ($NaHCO_3$). It decomposes to sodium carbonate, water and carbon dioxide on heating.

$$2\,NaHCO_3 \longrightarrow Na_2CO_3 + H_2O + CO_2\uparrow$$

Baking powder is a mixture of sodium hydrogen carbonate ($NaHCO_3$) with tartaric acid. It readily reacts with sodium carbonate and neutralizes it.

Therefore use of baking soda will give a bitter taste to cake due to the presence of sodium carbonate. 2

(b) Baking powder is formed by addition of tartaric acid to baking soda. 1

(c) Presence of tartaric acid in baking powder neutralizes the effect of sodium carbonate formed during decomposition of baking soda. Tartaric acid is added to neutralize the bitterness produced by the baking powder. Also when baking powder mixes with water, then the sodium hydrogen carbonate reacts with tartaric acid to evolve carbon dioxide gas which gets trapped in the wet dough and bubbles out slowly making the cake to rise and hence 'soft and spongy' thus endowing them with a light, fluffy texture. The equation which takes place can be shown as:

$$NaHCO_3 + H^+ \longrightarrow Na^+ + CO_2 + H_2O$$ 2

28. When a ray of light is incident on a glass prism, it refracts bending towards the normal. When this refracted ray is incident on the second side of the prism, it refracts and moves away from the normal. Thus the emergent ray has deviated from its original path.

The angle by which the emergent ray has bent away from the incident ray is called the angle of deviation. 1

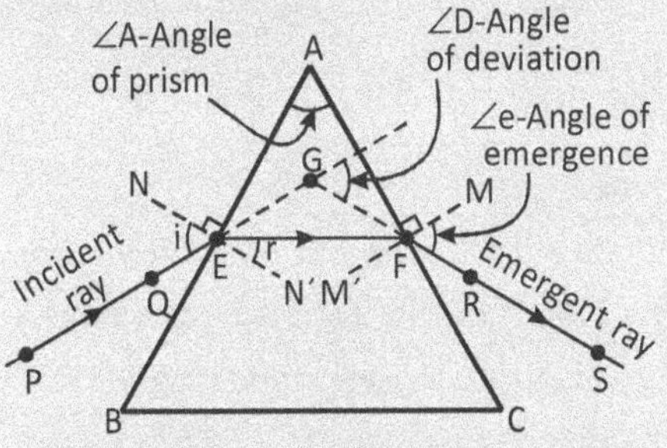

2

The light ray PE enters from air to glass (rarer to denser medium) at surface AB and therefore, bends towards the normal. The refracted ray EF now exits from glass and enters air (from denser to rarer medium) and therefore, bends away from the normal. 2

OR

Below are the diagrams of how hypermetropia is corrected. If a person is suffering from hypermetropia and unable to see the objects which are nearer to 1 metre. It means near point of hypermetropic eye is 1 m. This is shown in figure (a) 1

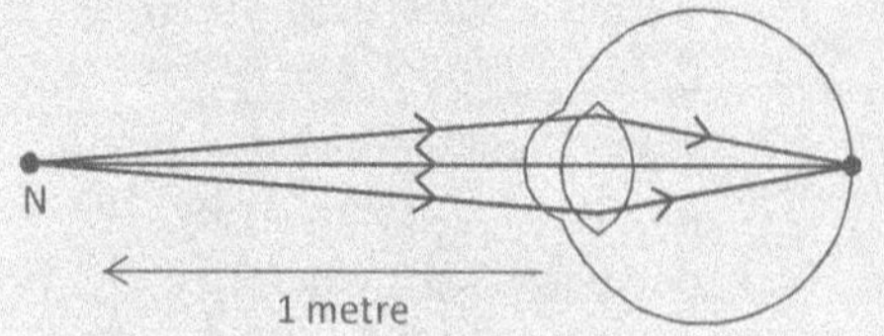

Fig. (a) Nearpoint of a Hypermetropic eye

The image of any object which is nearer than 1 metre forms after the retina, hence the person is unable to see nearby objects. This is shown in figure (b) 1

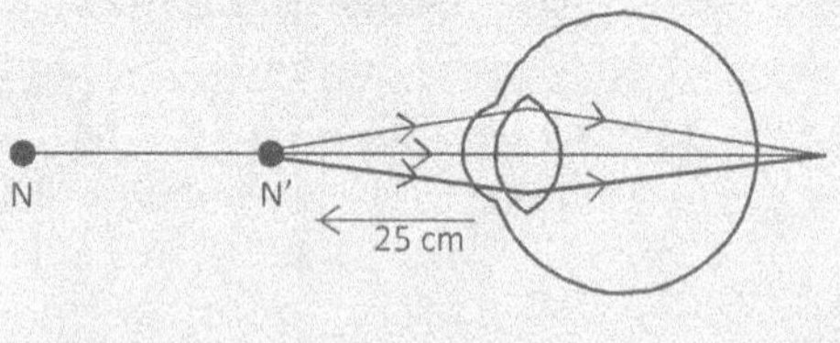

Fig. (b) Hypermetropic eye

If we choose a convex lens of the appropriate focal length such that it makes the image of the nearby object at 1 metre, the hypermetropic eye may able to see the object. This is shown in figure (c). 1

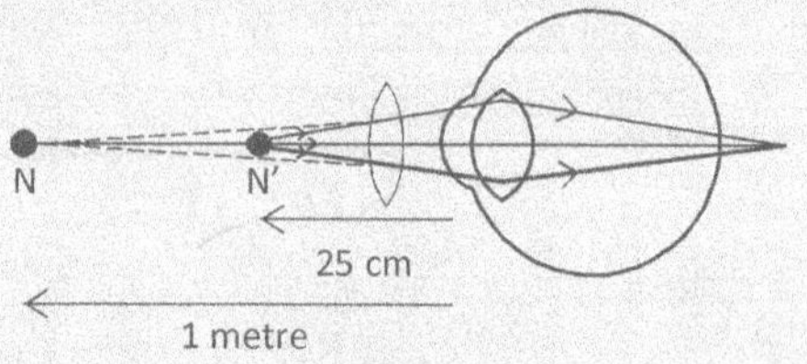

Fig. (c) Correction of Hypermetropic eye

Now find the focal length of this convex lens:

$$u = -25 \text{ cm}$$

$$v = -1 \text{ metre} = -100\text{cm}$$

For lens, $\frac{1}{v} - \frac{1}{u} = \frac{1}{f}$

$$-\frac{1}{100} - \left(-\frac{1}{25}\right) = \frac{1}{f}$$

$$-\frac{1}{100} + \frac{1}{25} = \frac{1}{f}$$

$$\frac{1}{f} = \frac{-1+4}{100} = \frac{3}{100} \text{ cm}$$

$$f = \frac{100}{3} \text{ cm}$$

$$\text{or } \frac{1}{3} \text{ m}$$

power of the lens $= \frac{1}{f}$

focal length is in metres.

$$P = \frac{3}{1} = +3.0 \text{ D}$$

Power is positive means it is a convex lens.

So, power of the required convex lens is +3.0 D. 2

29. **Human female reproductive system:** Female reproductive system consists of the following parts:

- A pair of Ovaries
  - ❖ One on each side of uterus
  - ❖ Produce female sex cell (ovum/ova)
  - ❖ Secrete female hormones estrogen & progesterone

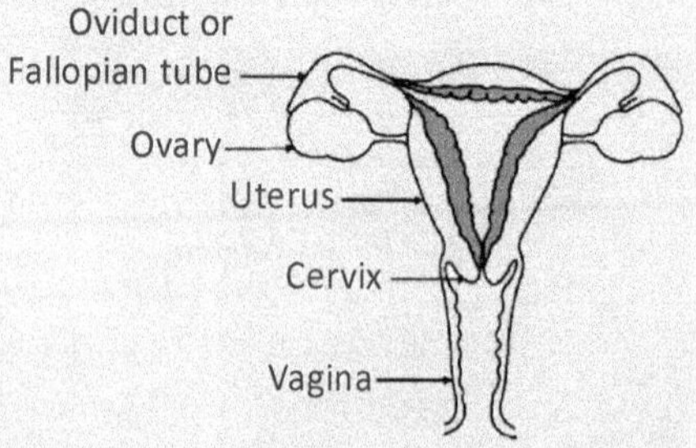

Labelling 2

- Fallopian tube
  - ❖ Exist in pairs, originating from uterus extending up to each ovary
  - ❖ Receives ovum from ovary
- Uterus
  - ❖ Pear-shaped muscular hollow structure
  - ❖ Foetus develops here
- Cervix
  - ❖ Narrow lower part of uterus
- Vagina
  - ❖ Tube like structure
  - ❖ Sperm discharge occurs here
  - ❖ Acts as birth canal 2

30. **Joule's heating effect:** When an electric current is passed through a high resistance metallic wire, like nichrome wire, the resistance wire becomes very hot and produces heat. This effect is known as heating effect of current or Joule's heating effect. **1**

Joule's law of heating states that the heat H produced in a conductor of resistance R due to current flowing through it for time t is $H = I^2Rt$ **1**

A simple experiment to demonstrate heating effect of current is that if we switch on the bulb for a long period of time then it will become hot. This shows that when electric current flows through a metallic conductor, heat is produced in it. **1**

Applications of Joule's heating effect in daily life are:

i. Electric fuse is a safety circuit devices work on this principle. Electric fuse in the electric circuit melts when large current flows in the circuit.

ii. Electric iron, electric heater and water heater etc. works on the principle of heating effect of current.

iii. Electric bulb glows when electric current flows through the filament of the bulb. **2**

OR

Resistances in series add up.

$$R = R_1 + R_2 + R_3$$
$$= 20\ \Omega + 30\ \Omega + 50\ \Omega$$
$$= 100\ \Omega$$ **1**

Total current is determined by the voltage of the power supply and the equivalent resistance of the circuit.

$$I = V/R = 125V/100\Omega$$
$$= 1.25\ A$$ **1**

Current is constant through resistors connected in series. **1**

Voltage drop across each resistor

$V_1 = IR_1 = 1.25A \times 20\ \Omega = 25\ V$

$V_2 = IR_2 = 1.25A \times 30\ \Omega = 37.5\ V$

$V_3 = IR_3 = 1.25A \times 50\ \Omega = 62.5\ V$ **1**

On a series circuit they should equal the voltage increase of the power supply.

$V_{total} = V_1 + V_2 + V_3$

$125\ V = 25\ V + 37.5\ V + 62.5\ V$

$125\ V = 125\ V$

the power dissipated in each resistor.

$P_1 = V_1 \times I_1$

$P_1 = 25V \times 1.25A = 31.250\ \Omega$

$P_2 = V_2 \times I_2$

$P_2 = 37.5V \times 1.25A = 46.875\ \Omega$

$P_3 = V_3 \times I_3$

$P_1 = 62.5V \times 1.25A = 78.125\ \Omega$ **1**

In a series circuit, the element with the greatest resistance consumes the most power.

11

SAMPLE PAPER
(SELF ASSESSMENT)
CBSE - Class 10

SCIENCE

Time Allowed: 3 Hours *Maximum Marks: 80*

General Instructions:

i. The question paper comprises three sections – A, B and C. Attempt all the sections.
ii. All questions are compulsory.
iii. Internal choice is given in each section.
iv. All questions in Section A are one-mark questions comprising MCQ, VSA type and assertion-reason type questions. They are to be answered in one word or in one sentence.
v. All questions in Section B are three-mark, short-answer type questions. These are to be answered in about 50 - 60 words each.
vi. All questions in Section C are five-mark, long-answer type questions. These are to be answered in about 80 - 90 words each.
vii. This question paper consists of a total of 30 questions.

SECTION - A

1. What is the function of petal in a flower? **1**

2. Draw the electron dot structure of chlorine molecule. **1**

3. **Answer question numbers 3(a)-3(d) on the basis of your understanding of the following paragraph and the related studied concepts.**

We use a lot of acidic food in our everyday life. Some of these are beneficial while some others are harmful directly or indirectly. For example, oranges contain citric acid, apples contain malic acid, tomatoes contain oxalic acid, curd contains lactic acid and so on. Wine, beer, coffee etc. are acidic and harmful. Spicy food causes acidity. Sweets produce a lot of acid in the mouth and cause tooth decay. Curd attacks copper vessel forming toxic compounds and makes it unfit for consumption.

Now answer the following questions:

3(a) A person has taken spicy food and is feeling uncomfortable. What do you suggest he should do? **1**

3(b) If we eat sweets, it is suggested that we should brush our teeth. What quality of tooth paste would you suggest? **1**

3(c) In naturopathy, it is suggested that in the morning, we should drink water kept in a copper vessel overnight. However, copper vessel gets tarnished after a few days. Why does they get tarnished? **1**

3(d) What method do you suggest to clean it so that it begins to shine again? **1**

4. The following table gives the value of resistivity of some materials:

Material	A	B	C	D
Resistivity (W-m)	1.63×10^{28}	6.43×10^{28}	9.63×10^{28}	10.03×10^{28}

4(a) Which one is the best conductor of electricity out of them? Give reason for your answer.

(i) A **(ii)** B

(iii) C **(iv)** D **1**

4(b) The resistivity does not change if:

(i) the material is changed

(ii) the temperature is changed

(iii) the shape of the resistor is changed

(iv) both material and temperature are changed **1**

4(c) Which material would you suggest to be used in electric heating devices? Give reason for your choice. **1**

4(d) You have two wires of identical dimensions made of materials A and C. If the resistance of wire made of C is 60Ω. What is the resistance of the other wire made of material A? **1**

5. A plotting compass is placed near the south pole of a bar magnet. The pointer of plotting compass will:

(i) point away from the south pole **(ii)** point parallel to the south pole

(iii) point towards the south pole **(iv)** point at right angles to the south pole **1**

OR

The strength of the magnetic field between the poles of an electromagnet would be unchanged if:

(i) current in the electromagnet winding were doubled

(ii) direction of current in electromagnet winding were reversed

(iii) distance between the poles of electromagnet were doubled

(iv) material of the core of electromagnet were changed **1**

6. When two parents are crossed, the offspring are referred to as:

(i) Recessives **(ii)** test cross

(iii) F1 generation **(iv)** F2 generation **1**

7. The atomic particle whose number in the atoms of an element always remains the same and which forms the real basis for the modern classification of elements is:

(i) Electron **(ii)** proton

(iii) neutron **(iv)** meson **1**

OR

Which of the following statements is not a correct statement about the trends when going from left to right across the periods of the periodic table?

(i) The elements become less metallic in nature

(ii) The number of valence electrons increases

(iii) The atoms lose their electrons more easily

(iv) The oxides become more acidic **1**

8. Rays from sun converge at a point 15 cm in front of a concave mirror. Where should an object be placed so that size of its image is equal to the size of the object?

(i) 15 cm in front of the mirror

(ii) 30 cm in front of the mirror

(iii) Between 15 cm and 30 cm in front of the mirror

(iv) More than 30 cm in front of the mirror **1**

9. Given below are a few statements related to biodiversity. Pick those that correctly describe the concept of biodiversity:

(a) Biodiversity refers to the different species of flora and fauna present in an area

(b) Biodiversity refers to only the flora of a given area

(c) Biodiversity is greater in a forest

(d) Biodiversity refers to the total number of individuals of a particular species living in an area

(i) (a) and (b) **(ii)** (b) and (d)

(iii) (a) and (c) **(iv)** (b) and (c) **1**

10. Solid calcium oxide reacts vigorously with water to form calcium hydroxide accompanied by liberation of heat. This process is called slaking of lime. Calcium hydroxide dissolves in water to form its solution called lime water. Which among the following is are true about slaking of lime and the solution formed?

(a) It is an endothermic reaction

(b) It is exothermic reaction

(c) The pH of the resulting solution will be more than seven

(d) The pH of the resulting solution will be less than seven

(i) (a) and (b) **(ii)** (b) and (c)

(iii) (a) and (d) **(iv)** (c) and (d) **1**

11. A big tree falls in a forest but its roots are still in contact with the soil. The branches of this fallen tree grow straight up (vertically). This happens in response to:

(i) water and light **(ii)** water and minerals

(iii) gravity and water **(iv)** light and gravity **1**

OR

Select the mis-matched pair

(i) Adrenaline—Pituitary gland **(ii)** Testosterone—Testes

(iii) Estrogen—Ovary **(iv)** Thyroxin—Thyroid gland **1**

12. As light from a far off star comes down towards the earth:

(i) it bends away from the normal **(ii)** it bends towards the normal

(iii) it does not bend at all **(iv)** it is reflected back **1**

For question numbers 13 and 14, two statements are given- one labeled Assertion (A) and the other labeled Reason (R). Select the correct answer to these questions from the codes (i), (ii), (iii) and (iv) as given below:

(i) Both A and R are true and R is correct explanation of the assertion.

(ii) Both A and R are true but R is not the correct explanation of the assertion.

(iii) A is true but R is false.

(iv) A is false but R is true.

13. **Assertion A** : In the given circuit if lamp B or C fuses then light emitted by lamp A decreases. **1**

Reason R : Voltage in A decreases.

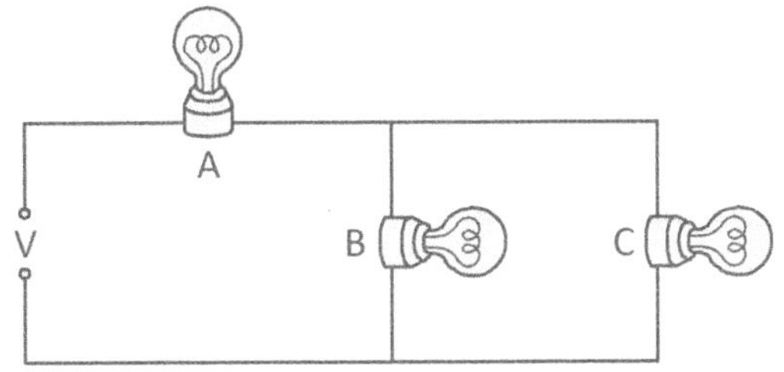

14. **Assertion A** : Human, frog and bird have a common ancestor. **1**

Reason R : Limbs of human, frog and bird are homologous.

SECTION - B

15. On heating blue coloured powder of copper (II) nitrate in a boiling tube, copper oxide (black), oxygen gas and a brown gas X is formed.

(a) Write a balanced chemical equation of the reaction.

(b) Identify the brown gas X evolved.

(c) Identify the type of reaction.

(d) What could be the pH range of aqueous solution of the gas X? **3**

OR

On adding a drop of barium chloride solution to an aqueous solution of sodium sulphite, white precipitate is obtained.

(a) Write a balanced chemical equation of the reaction involved.

(b) What other name can be given to this precipitation reaction?

(c) On adding dilute hydrochloric acid to the reaction mixture, white precipitate disappears. Why? **3**

16. "Hydrogen occupies a unique position in Modern Periodic Table". Justify the statement. **3**

17. Name three different glands associated with the digestive system in humans. Also name their secretions. **3**

OR

What are the differences between the transport of materials in xylem and phloem? **3**

18. With the help of a diagram, show asexual reproduction in Rhizopus. **3**

19. One-half of a convex lens is covered with a black paper. Will this lens produce a complete image of the object? Verify your answer experimentally. Explain your observations. **3**

20. What are the constituents of solder alloy? Which property of solder makes it suitable for welding electrical wires? **3**

21. What causes the wind to blow? Explain the principle of working of a windmill. State two advantages of using wind energy. **3**

OR

Answer the following:

(a) What is the role of decomposers in the ecosystem?

(b) Suggest one word for each of the following statement/definitions:

(i) The physical and biological world where we live in

(ii) Each level of food chain where transfer of energy takes place

(iii) The physical factors like temperature, rainfall, wind and soil of an ecosystem

(iv) Organisms which depend on the producers either directly or indirectly for food **3**

22. AB is a current carrying conductor in the plane of the paper as shown in figure. What are the directions of magnetic fields produced by it at points P and Q? Given $r_1 > r_2$, where will the strength of the magnetic field be larger?

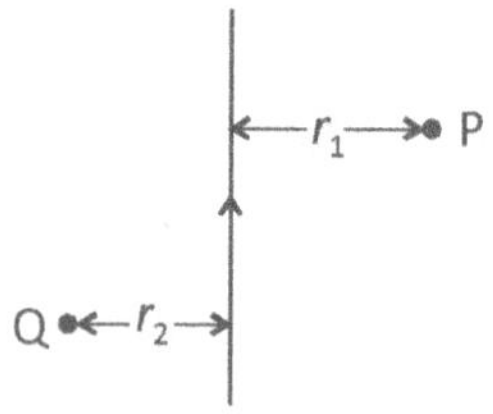

3

23. What will happen if we kill all the organisms in one trophic level? **3**

24. A woman has only daughters. Analyze the situation genetically and provide a suitable explanation. **3**

SECTION - C

25. Answer the following:

(a) What is saponification? Write the reactions involved in this process.

(b) Why detergents are better cleansing agents than soaps? Explain. **5**

OR

Answer the following:

(a) Write a chemical equation for each of the following types of chemical reactions of organic compounds:

(i) Oxidation reaction (ii) Addition reaction (iii) Substitution reaction

(b) Write the structural formula of ethanol. What happens when it is heated with excess of conc. H_2SO_4 at 443 K? Write the chemical equation for the reaction stating the role of conc. H_2SO_4 in this reaction. **5**

26. (a) Label the parts (a), (b), (c) and (d) and show the direction of flow of electrical signals in the given figure.

(b) Write the functions of (a) and (d).

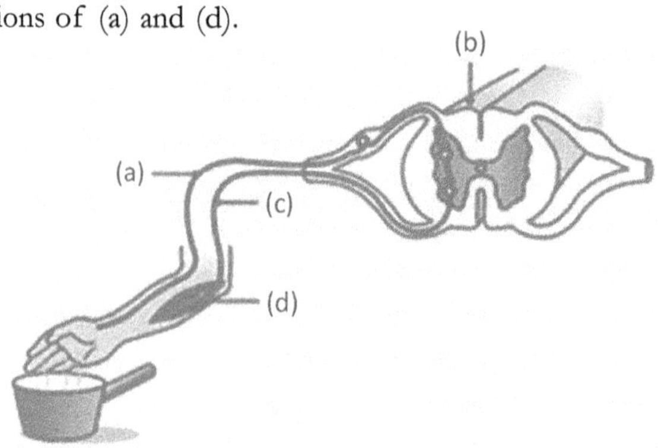

5

OR

What are the major parts of the brain? Mention the function of different parts. **5**

27. Distinguish between a gamete and zygote. Explain their roles in sexual reproduction. **5**

28. A non-metal A which is the largest constituent of air, when heated with H_2 in 1:3 ratio in the presence of catalyst (Fe) gives a gas B. On heating with O_2 it gives an oxide C. If this oxide is passed into water in the presence of air, it gives an acid D which acts as a strong oxidising agent.

(a) Identify A, B, C and D.

(b) To which group of the periodic table does this non-metal belongs? **5**

29. A person is able to see objects clearly only when these are lying at distances between 50 cm and 300 cm from his eye.

(a) What kind of defects of vision he is suffering from?

(b) What kind of lenses will be required to increase his range of vision from 25 cm to infinity? Explain briefly.

(c) The far point of a myopic person is 150 cm. What is the nature and the power of lens required to correct the defect? **5**

30. What does an electric circuit mean? Draw a schematic diagram of an electric circuit. Name a device that helps to maintain a potential difference across a conductor in a circuit. When do we say that the potential difference across a conductor is 1 volt? Calculate the amount of work done in shifting a charge of 2 coulombs from a point A to B having potentials +10 V and –5 V respectively. **5**

OR

Give reason for the following:

(a) An electric bulb is not filled with air but is filled with argon or nitrogen.

(b) The filament type electric bulbs are not power efficient.

(c) The coils of heating devices are made of alloys rather than pure metals.

(d) Copper and aluminium wires are usually used for electricity transmission.

(e) The current that makes the heater element red hot only slightly warms the connecting wire leading to the heater. **5**

12

SAMPLE PAPER
(SELF ASSESSMENT)

CBSE - Class 10

SCIENCE

Time Allowed: 3 Hours *Maximum Marks: 80*

General Instructions:

i. The question paper comprises three sections – A, B and C. Attempt all the sections.
ii. All questions are compulsory.
iii. Internal choice is given in each section.
iv. All questions in Section A are one-mark questions comprising MCQ, VSA type and assertion-reason type questions. They are to be answered in one word or in one sentence.
v. All questions in Section B are three-mark, short-answer type questions. These are to be answered in about 50 - 60 words each.
vi. All questions in Section C are five-mark, long-answer type questions. These are to be answered in about 80 - 90 words each.
vii. This question paper consists of a total of 30 questions.

SECTION - A

1. Name the two ways in which glucose is oxidized to provide energy in various organisms. **1**

2. How does the metallic character vary across the period? Explain. **1**

3. Answer question numbers 3(a) - 3(d) on the basis of your understanding of the following paragraph and the related studied concepts.

The element radium was discovered by Madame Curie. She was successful in isolating 0.2 g of the element from the mineral pitchblende. For this work, she was awarded the Nobel Prize in Chemistry in 1911. In her honour, UNESCO declared the year 2011 as the International year of Chemistry. The discovery of radium opened a new field of radioactivity and thereafter many new radioactive elements have either been isolated from natural sources or have been prepared artificially in the laboratory by nuclear reactions. Radioactive materials are extensively being used for power generation and in the diagnosis and treatment of many fatal diseases.

Inspite of these benefits, radiation leakage from nuclear plants causes severe health problems to the mankind. Further, atomic bomb and other weapons of mass destruction use radioactive materials.

Now answer the following questions:

3(a) Which is the process used to harness nuclear energy these days? **1**

3(b) What is the major problem in harnessing nuclear energy? **1**

3(c) What is nuclear fission? Explain with an example. 1

3(d) Give any one advantage of nuclear energy? 1

4. The following chart explains the dihybrid cross in detail between one pea plant with round and green seeds and the other pea plant having wrinkled and yellow seeds. Analyse it and answer the following questions:

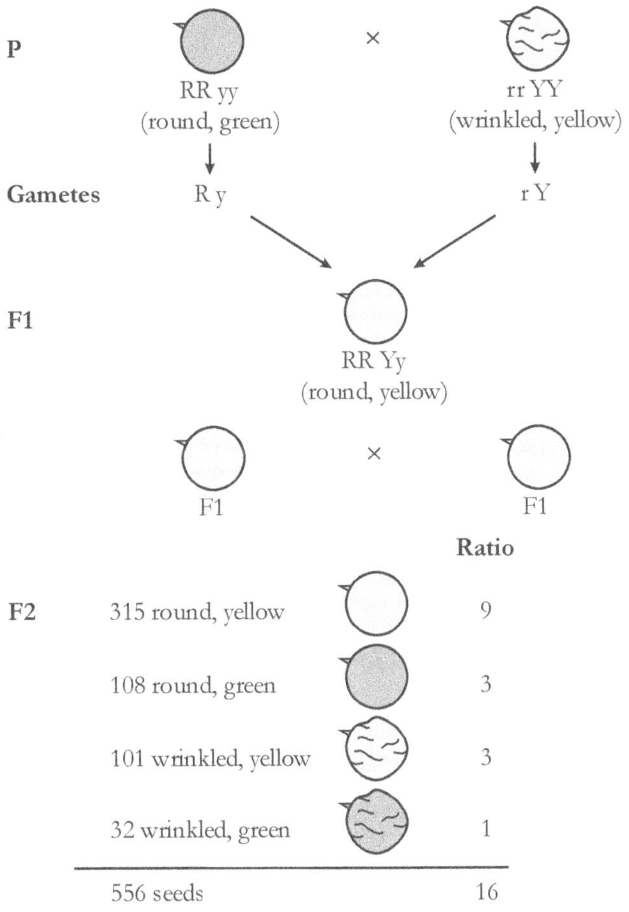

4(a) In the F2 generation of a cross, progeny having different traits are produced in the ratio 3 : 1. State whether it is a monohybrid cross or a dihybrid cross? Give one example of such a cross. 1

4(b) Why did Mendel choose pea plant for his experiments? Give any one reason. 1

4(c) Exchange of genetic material takes place in:

(i) Vegetative reproduction **(ii)** Asexual reproduction

(iii) Sexual reproduction **(iv)** Budding 1

4(d) A cross between a tall plant (TT) and short pea plant (tt) resulted in progeny that were all tall plants because:

(i) Tallness is the dominant trait

(ii) Shortness is the dominant trait

(iii) Tallness is the recessive trait

(iv) Height of pea plant is not governed by gene 'T' or 't' 1

5. The rechargeable battery used in a mobile phone hand set is usually:

(i) lead ion battery **(ii)** sodium ion battery

(iii) hydrogen ion battery **(iv)** lithium ion battery 1

6. Which of the following ray diagrams is correct for the ray of light incident on a concave mirror as shown in figure?

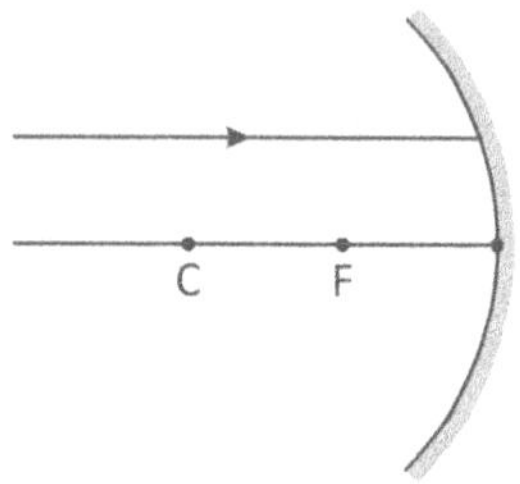

(i)

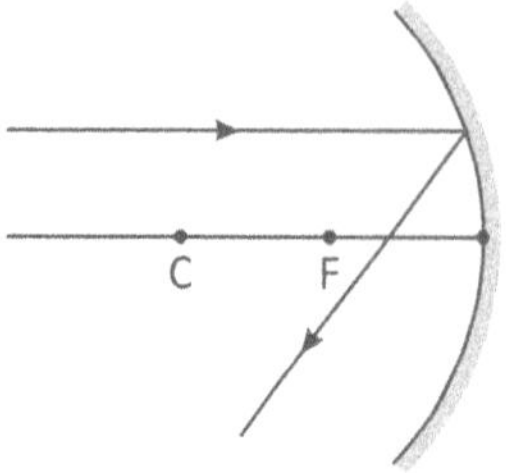

(ii)

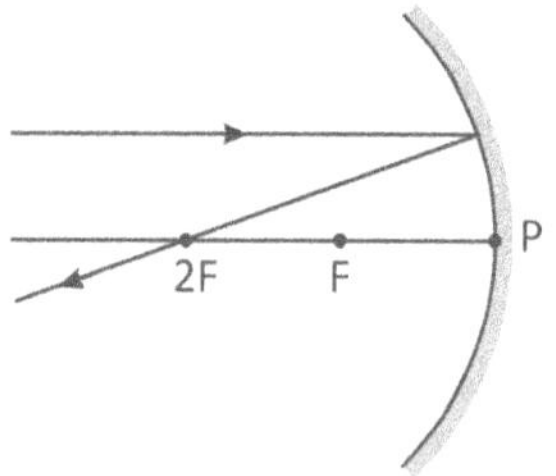

(iii)

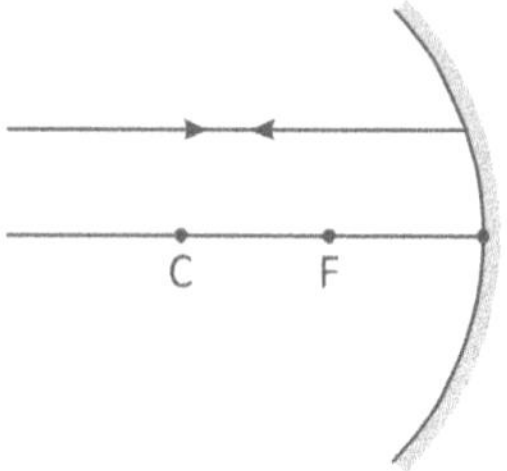

(iv)

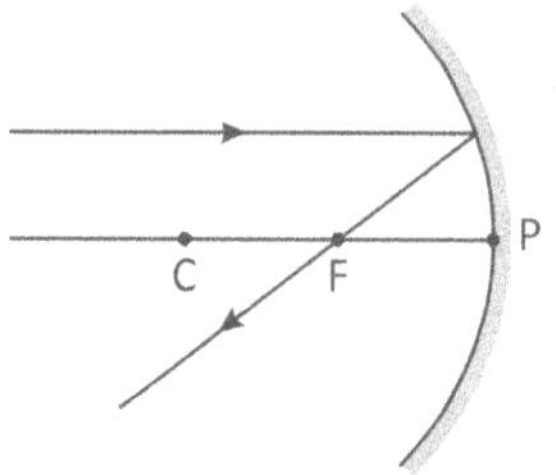

1

7. When air is blown from mouth into a test-tube containing lime water, the lime water turned milky due to the presence of:

(i) Oxygen | **(ii)** Carbon dioxide

(iii) Nitrogen | **(iv)** Water vapour | 1

OR

If salivary amylase is lacking in the saliva, which of the following events in the mouth cavity will be affected?

(i) Proteins breaking down into amino acids

(ii) Starch breaking down into sugars

(iii) Fats breaking down into fatty acids and glycerol

(iv) Absorption of vitamins | 1

8. When hydrogen sulphide gas is passed through a blue solution of copper sulphate, a black precipitate of copper sulphate is obtained and the sulphuric acid so formed remains in the solution. The reaction is an example of:

(i) combination reaction | **(ii)** displacement reaction

(iii) decomposition reaction | **(iv)** double decomposition reaction | 1

OR

When copper turning are added to silver nitrate solution, a blue coloured solution is formed after some time. It is because copper:

(i) Displaces silver from the solution | **(ii)** Forms a blue colored complex with $AgNO_3$

(iii) Is oxidized to Cu^{2+} | **(iv)** Is reduced to Cu^{2+} | 1

9. The characteristics transmitted from parents to offspring are present in:

(i) Cytoplasm | **(ii)** Ribosome

(iii) golgi bodies | **(iv)** genes | 1

10. The red colour of the sun at the time of sunrise and sunset is because:

(i) red colour is least scattered **(ii)** blue colour is least scattered

(iii) red colour is most scattered **(iv)** blue colour is most scattered 1

11. If the resistance of a certain copper wire is 1 Ω, then the resistance of a similar nichrome wire will be about:

(i) 25 Ω **(ii)** 30 Ω

(iii) 60 Ω **(iv)** 45 Ω 1

OR

The resistivity of a certain material is 0.6 Ωm. The material is most likely to be:

(i) an insulator **(ii)** a superconductor

(iii) a conductor **(iv)** a semiconductor 1

12. In which of the following compounds —OH is the functional group?

(i) Butanone **(ii)** Butanol

(iii) Butanoic **(iv)** Butanal 1

For question numbers 13 and 14, two statements are given- one labeled Assertion (A) and the other labeled Reason (R). Select the correct answer to these questions from the codes (i), (ii), (iii) and (iv) as given below:

(i) Both A and R are true and R is correct explanation of the assertion.

(ii) Both A and R are true but R is not the correct explanation of the assertion.

(iii) A is true but R is false.

(iv) A is false but R is true.

13. **Assertion A:** Generally, the colour of indicators changes in particular pH range.

Reason R: Indicators are weak acids or weak base and exhibit different colours in molecular form and ionic form. 1

14. **Assertion A:** The stars twinkle while the planets do not.

Reason R: The stars are much bigger in size than the planets. 1

SECTION - B

15. **(a)** A lens has a power of –4D. What is its focal length?

(b) An object is kept at a distance of 100 cm from the above lens. Calculate the image distance and the magnification. 3

16. Two resistors with resistance 5 Ohm and 10 Ohm respectively are to be connected to a battery of 6V so as to obtain:

(a) Minimum current flowing

(b) Maximum current flowing

(i) How will you connect the resistors in each case?

(ii) Calculate the strength of total current in the circuit in the two cases. 3

17. Two conducting wires of the same material and of equal lengths and equal diameters are first connected in series and then in parallel in a circuit across the same potential difference. Find the ratio of heat produced in series and parallel combination. 3

OR

(a) State Ohm's law.

(b) A piece of wire of resistance 20 Ohms is drawn out so that its length is increased to twice of its original length. Calculate the resistance of the wire in the new situation. 3

18. Red beetles live in a bush with green beetles. Eventually the number of green beetles increases as compared to red beetles.

(a) Give reason for the increased number of green beetles.

(b) State two advantages of variation.

(c) List the factors that could lead to the rise of a new species. **3**

19. Answer the following:

(a) Explain how auxins help in bending of plant stem towards light.

(b) Distinguish between cerebrum and spinal cord. **3**

OR

Answer the following:

(a) What is the difference between reflex action and walking?

(b) Mention the significance of reflex action.

(c) Name the part of the brain which controls the posture and balance of the body. **3**

20. Answer the following:

(a) Mention the adaptations of leaf for photosynthesis.

(b) Why does absorption of digested food occur mainly in small intestine? **3**

21. Why is damage to the ozone layer a cause for concern? What steps are being taken to limit this damage? **3**

22. Answer the following:

(a) Name any three halogens.

(b) Mention the group to which they belong and their valency.

(c) What type of compounds will they form with elements of group 1? **3**

23. Explain the action of dilute hydrochloric acid on the following with balanced chemical equations and observations for the reactions:

(a) Magnesium ribbon **(b)** Sodium hydroxide **(c)** Crushed egg shells **3**

24. Answer the following:

(a) How is tooth decay related to pH? How can it be prevented?

(b) What is the change in colour of pH paper dipped in a solution having a pH = 13? **3**

OR

What is the effect of following on acetic acid?

(a) litmus test.

(b) addition of a pinch of baking soda. **3**

SECTION - C

25. Answer the following:

(a) Two ores A and B of a moderately reactive metal were taken. On heating ore A gives CO_2 whereas Ore B gives SO_2. What steps will you take to convert them into metals? Write balanced chemical equations for the reactions involved.

(b) How does the property of iron change when small quantity of Chromium and Nickel is mixed with it?

(c) Can we stir silver nitrate solution with a copper spoon? Why or why not? **5**

26. An organic compound A is a constituent of cough syrups. This compound on heating with alkaline $KMnO_4$ forms another organic compound B, which turns blue litmus to red. Compound A and B combine in the presence of concentrated sulphuric acid to give a sweet smelling compound C.

(a) Identify the compounds A, B and C.

(b) Write the chemical equation of the reaction that takes place to form the compound C and name the reaction.

(c) Draw the electron dot structure of A.

(d) Write equation for reaction of A with sodium. **5**

OR

(a) Draw a labeled diagram of a micelle. How is micelle formation helpful in cleaning clothes having oily spots?

(b) Why are detergents better cleaning agents than soaps? **5**

27. Answer the following:

(a) Give an example of bisexual flower. What is its female reproductive part known as?

(b) Draw a diagram of its longitudinal section showing the process of germination of pollen on stigma and label the following on it:

(i) Male germ cell **(ii)** Female germ cell

(iii) Ovary **(iv)** Pollen tube

(c) Pollination may occur without fertilization but fertilization will not take place without pollination. Give reasons. **5**

OR

(a) What is the importance of DNA copying in reproduction?

(b) Draw a labelled diagram of the longitudinal section of a flower. **5**

28. Answer the following:

(a) Construction of dams over rivers affects the ecological balance. Comment.

(b) As far as strategies go, reuse is considered better than recycling. Why?

(c) Mention any two advantages of ground water.

(d) Name the traditional water harvesting structures in:

(i) Rajasthan **(ii)** Himachal Pradesh **5**

29. Answer the following:

(a) Give the function of iris in human eye.

(b) A student is unable to read clearly the words written on the board, placed at a distance of 4 m from him. Name the defect of vision the boy is suffering from. Explain how this defect can be corrected. Draw the ray diagram to show the correction of this defect. **5**

30. How does a solenoid behave like a magnet? Can you determine the north and south poles of a current–carrying solenoid with the help of a bar magnet? Explain. **5**

OR

(a) Distinguish between overloading and short-circuiting in a domestic circuit.

(b) What is a fuse wire? Give its characteristics and advantages? **5**

13

SAMPLE PAPER
(SELF ASSESSMENT)
CBSE - Class 10

SCIENCE

Time Allowed: 3 Hours *Maximum Marks: 80*

General Instructions:

i. The question paper comprises three sections – A, B and C. Attempt all the sections.
ii. All questions are compulsory.
iii. Internal choice is given in each section.
iv. All questions in Section A are one-mark questions comprising MCQ, VSA type and assertion-reason type questions. They are to be answered in one word or in one sentence.
v. All questions in Section B are three-mark, short-answer type questions. These are to be answered in about 50 - 60 words each.
vi. All questions in Section C are five-mark, long-answer type questions. These are to be answered in about 80 - 90 words each.
vii. This question paper consists of a total of 30 questions.

SECTION - A

1. "Cell division is a type of reproduction in unicellular organism". Justify. **1**

2. What is a tropic movement? Explain with an example. **1**

3. **Answer question numbers 3(a)-3(d) on the basis of your understanding of the following paragraph and the related studied concepts.**

A chemistry student placed a strip of blue litmus paper and a strip of pink litmus paper in a glass dish. Then she added a drop of dilute sulfuric acid to each strip of litmus paper. She observed that the blue litmus paper turned pink, but the pink litmus paper did not change color. Next she placed a drop of sodium hydroxide (NaOH) on other strips of blue and pink litmus paper. This time, the pink litmus paper turned blue, but the blue litmus paper did not change. Finally, she put a drop of distilled water on strips of blue and pink litmus paper. Neither strip changed color. She repeated the tests several times with the same results. The student concluded that acids turn blue litmus paper pink; bases, such as sodium hydroxide, turn pink litmus paper blue. As water did not affect either pink or blue litmus paper, she reasoned that water was not an acid or a base, but a neutral substance.

Keeping these results in mind, the student poured a little sodium hydroxide into a beaker containing pink and blue litmus paper. Then she added hydrochloric acid (HCl) drop by drop until the solution became neutral. She determined that a new, neutral substance had formed in the beaker. The substance was table salt, or sodium chloride (NaCl), which is one of many salts formed from an acid and a base.

3(a) If a drop of an unknown substance turns blue litmus paper pink, but does not change pink litmus paper, what will be the substance - an acid or a base? **1**

3(b) When strips of blue and pink litmus paper are put in a beaker filled with a clear solution, neither litmus paper changes color. What can you say about the solution? **1**

3(c) Based on the results of this experiment, when would a salt be formed? **1**

3(d) What happens when nitric acid is added to egg shell? **1**

4. The following table given below shows the resistivity of three materials X, Y and Z. Analyse the table and answer the following questions:

Samples	X	Y	Z
Resistivity	3×10^{-9}	11.1×0^{-6}	18×10^{-17}

4(a) Arrange the samples in increasing order of conductivity. **1**

4(b) Which of these is best conductor? **1**

4(c) Which are these is best insulator?

(i) X **(ii)** Y

(iii) Z **(iv)** None of these **1**

4(d) Electrical resistivity of a given metallic wire depends upon:

(i) Its length **(ii)** Its thickness

(iii) Its shape **(iv)** Nature of the material **1**

5. One of the following does not inject an acidic liquid into the skin through its sting. This is:

(i) honey bee **(ii)** ant

(iii) wasp **(iv)** nettle leaf hair **1**

6. The refractive index of four substance P, Q, R and S are 1.50, 1.36, 1.77 and 1.31 respectively. The speed of light is the maximum in the substance:

(i) P **(ii)** Q

(iii) R **(iv)** S **1**

7. Which of the following statement(s) is/are true about heart?

(a) Left atrium receives oxygenated blood from different parts of body while right atrium receives deoxygenated blood from lungs

(b) Left ventricle pumps oxygenated blood to different body parts while right ventricle pumps deoxygenated blood to lungs

(c) Left atrium transfers oxygenated blood to right ventricle which sends it to different body parts

(d) Right atrium receives deoxygenated blood from different parts of the body while left ventricle pumps oxygenated blood to different parts of the body

(i) (a) **(ii)** (b)

(iii) (b) and (d) **(iv)** (a) and (c) **1**

8. The major problem in harnessing nuclear energy is how to:

(i) split nuclei **(ii)** sustain the reaction

(iii) dispose of spent fuel safely **(iv)** convert nuclear energy into electrical energy **1**

OR

Which part of the solar cooker is responsible for greenhouse effect?

(i) Coating with black colour inside the box

(ii) Mirror

(iii) Glass sheet

(iv) Outer cover of the solar cooker **1**

9. The following reaction is used for the preparation of oxygen gas in the laboratory:

$$2KClO_3(s) \xrightarrow[\text{Catalyst}]{\text{Heat}} 2KCl(s) + 3O_2(g)$$

Which of the following statement(s) is/are correct about the reaction?

(i) It is a decomposition reaction and endothermic in nature

(ii) It is a combination reaction

(iii) It is a decomposition reaction and accompanied by release of heat

(iv) It is a photochemical decomposition reaction and exothermic in nature **1**

OR

Which of the following are combination reactions?

(a) $KClO_3 \xrightarrow{\text{Heat}} 2KCl + 3O_2$

(b) $MgO + H_2O \longrightarrow Mg(OH)_2$

(c) $4Al + 3O_2 \longrightarrow 2Al_2O_3$

(d) $Zn + FeSO_4 \longrightarrow ZnSO_4 + Fe$

(i) Both (a) and (c) **(ii)** Both (c) and (d)

(iii) Both (b) and (d) **(iv)** Both (b) and (c) **1**

10. Which of the following statements are true for flowers?

(a) Flowers are always bisexual

(b) They are the sexual reproductive organs

(c) They are produced in all groups of plants

(d) After fertilization they give rise to fruits

(i) (a) and (d) **(ii)** (b) and (c)

(iii) (a) and (c) **(iv)** (b) and (d) **1**

OR

Characters that are transmitted from parents to offspring during reproduction show:

(i) Only similarities with parents

(ii) Only variations with parents

(iii) Both similarities and variations with parents

(iv) Neither similarities nor variations **1**

11. To focus the image of a nearby object on the retina of an eye:

(i) the distance between eye-lens and retina is increased

(ii) the distance between eye-lens and retina is decreased

(iii) the thickness of eye-lens is decreased

(iv) the thickness of eye-lens is increased **1**

12. Which of the following are correct structural isomers of C_4H_{10}?

(a) 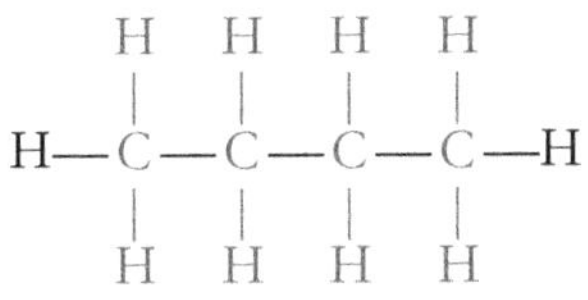

(b) 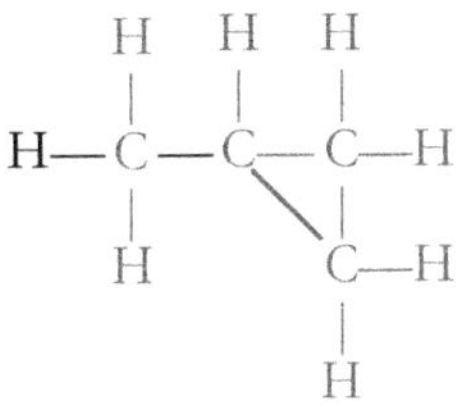

(c) 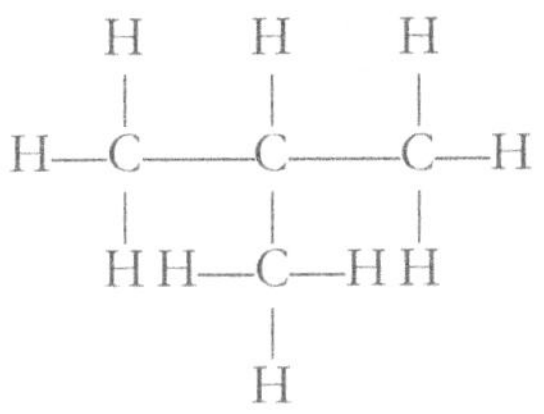

(d) 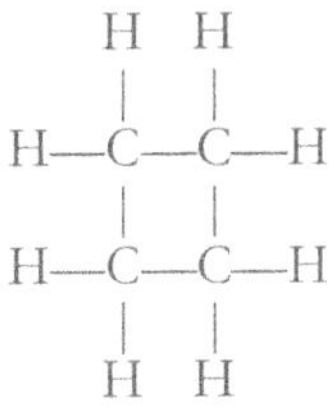

(i) (a) and (c)
(ii) (b) and (d)
(iii) (a) and (b)
(iv) (c) and (d) **1**

For question numbers 13 and 14, two statements are given- one labeled Assertion (A) and the other labeled Reason (R). Select the correct answer to these questions from the codes (i), (ii), (iii) and (iv) as given below:

(i) Both A and R are true and R is correct explanation of the assertion.
(ii) Both A and R are true but R is not the correct explanation of the assertion.
(iii) A is true but R is false.
(iv) A is false but R is true.

13. **Assertion A :** The energy of charged particle moving in a uniform magnetic field does not change. **1**
Reason R : Work done by magnetic field on the charge is zero.

14. **Assertion A :** Acquired traits cannot be passed from one generation to next generation. **1**
Reason R : Inaccuracy during DNA copying of acquired trait is minimum.

SECTION - B

15. Define a chemical reaction. State four observations that help us to determine whether a chemical reaction has taken place or not? Write one example of each. **3**

OR

(a) Explain the term "corrosion" with an example. Write a chemical equation to show the process of corrosion of iron.
(b) What special name is given to the corrosion of iron?
(c) What type of chemical reaction is involved in the corrosion of iron?
(d) Name any three objects (or structures) which are gradually damaged by the corrosion of iron and steel. **3**

16. A child is standing in front of a magic mirror. She finds the image of her head bigger, the middle portion of her body of the same size and that of the legs smaller. What will be the order of combinations for the magic mirror from the top? **3**

17. Compare and contrast bio-mass and hydro electricity as a source of energy. **3**

OR

What is the main constituent of biogas? How is biogas obtained from biomass? Write any two advantages of using this gas. **3**

18. Answer the following:

(a) What is a clone? Why do offspring formed by asexual reproduction exhibit remarkable similarity?

(b) Explain how offspring and parents of organisms reproducing sexually have the same number of chromosomes? **3**

OR

Answer the following:

(a) Rahul observes bread mould grow profusely on a moist slice of bread rather than on a dry slice of bread. Explain the observation briefly.

(b) Colonies of yeast fail to multiply in water, but multiply in sugar solution. Give reason. **3**

19. Define electric power. An electric motor is rated at 2kW. Calculate the cost of using it for 2 hours daily for the month of September if each unit costs INR 6. **3**

20. P, Q and R are 3 elements which undergo chemical reactions according to the following equations:

(i) $P_2O_3 + 2Q \longrightarrow Q_2O_3 + 2P$

(ii) $3RSO_4 + 2Q \longrightarrow Q_2(SO4)_3 + 3R$

(iii) $3RO + 2P \longrightarrow P_2O_3 + 3R$

Answer the following:

(a) Which element is most reactive?

(b) Which element is least reactive?

(c) State the type of reaction listed above. **3**

21. Answer the following:

(a) Define hormones.

(b) Label the endocrine gland in the figure given below:

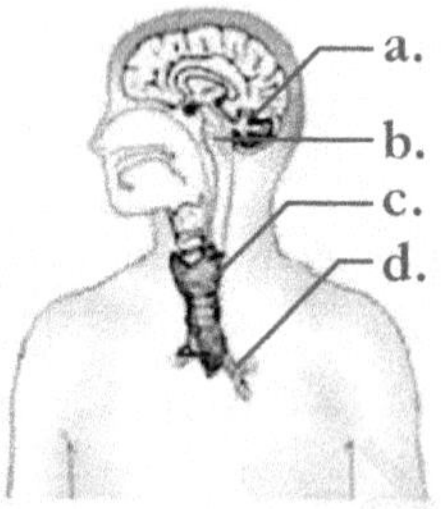

3

22. Under what conditions permanent electromagnet is obtained if a current carrying solenoid is used? Support your answer with the help of a labeled circuit diagram. **3**

23. Answer the following questions:

(a) Combustion of coke is a combination reaction. CO_2 is not a pollutant. Then why is combustion of coke harmful?

(b) Which decomposition reaction followed by two combination reactions is involved in white wash of walls?

(c) Give one use of tin plating in daily life? **3**

24. List some of the steps that can be taken to conserve energy sources like coal and petroleum. **3**

SECTION - C

25. Answer the following:

(a) Why is blood circulation in human heart called double circulation?

(b) Draw a diagram of cross section of the human heart and label its parts. **5**

OR

Answer the following:

(a) Explain why the rate of photosynthesis in plants is low both at lower and higher temperatures.

(b) Is green light most or least useful in photosynthesis and why?

(c) Draw the diagram to show open stomatal pore of a leaf and label guard cells and chloroplast on it. **5**

26. What is atmospheric refraction? Use this phenomenon to explain the advanced sunrise and delayed sunset. **5**

OR

Draw a labeled diagram to explain the formation of rainbow in the sky. **5**

27. Answer the following:

(a) Mention the pH range within which our body works. Explain how antacids give relief from acidity. Write the name of one such antacid.

(b) Fresh milk has a pH of 6. How will the pH change as it turns to curd? Explain your answer.

(c) A milkman adds very small amount of baking soda to fresh milk. Why does this milk take longer time to set as curd?

(d) Mention the nature of tooth pastes. How do they prevent tooth decay? **5**

28. Answer the following:

(a) How would you bring about the following conversions? Name the process and write the reaction involved.

(i) Ethanol to ethene **(ii)** Propanol to propanoic acid

(b) Give a test that can differentiate between butter and cooking oil? **5**

OR

(a) Explain the term 'isomers'. Give one example of isomers.

(b) Write (i) structural formula, and (ii) electron-dot structure, of any one isomer of n-heptane

(c) Write the IUPAC name of the compound having the formula n-C_4H_{10}.

(d) Write the IUPAC names for the following:

(i) 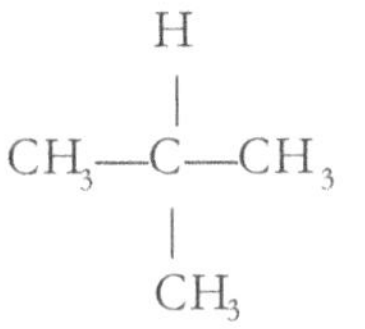

(ii) 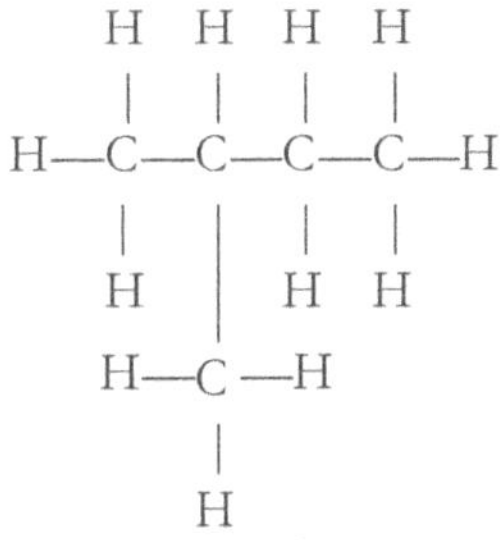

(iii) 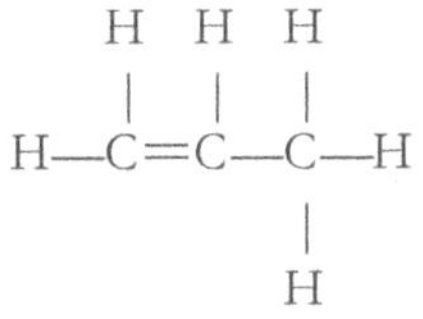

(iv) 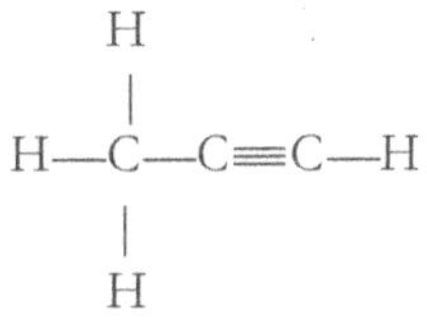 **5**

29. Study the following current time graphs from two different sources:

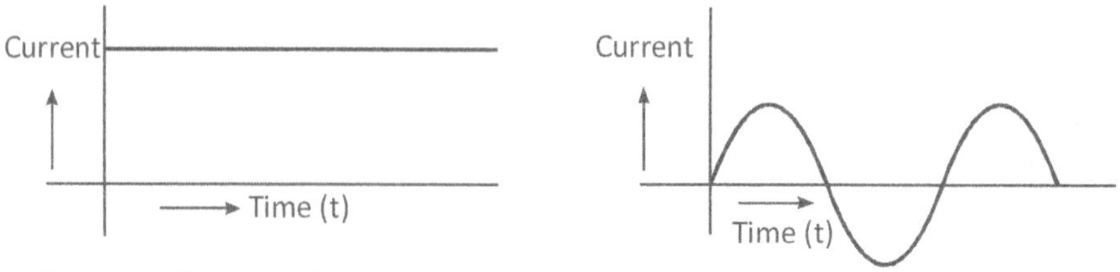

(a) Name the type of current in two cases.
(b) Identify any one source for each type of these currents.
(c) What is the frequency of current in case II in India?
(d) Use above graphs to write two differences between the current in two cases. **5**

30. Define evolution. How does it occur? Describe how fossils provide us evidences in support of evolution. **5**

SOLUTIONS

Available on
www.educart.net

14

SAMPLE PAPER
(SELF ASSESSMENT)

CBSE - Class 10

SCIENCE

Time Allowed: 3 Hours *Maximum Marks: 80*

General Instructions:

i. The question paper comprises three sections – A, B and C. Attempt all the sections.
ii. All questions are compulsory.
iii. Internal choice is given in each section.
iv. All questions in Section A are one-mark questions comprising MCQ, VSA type and assertion-reason type questions. They are to be answered in one word or in one sentence.
v. All questions in Section B are three-mark, short-answer type questions. These are to be answered in about 50 - 60 words each.
vi. All questions in Section C are five-mark, long-answer type questions. These are to be answered in about 80 - 90 words each.
vii. This question paper consists of a total of 30 questions.

SECTION - A

1. What is meant by the term regeneration? 1

2. Define parasitic nutrition. Name an organism having parasitic mode of nutrition. 1

3. **Answer question numbers 3(a)-3(d) on the basis of your understanding of the following paragraph and the related studied concepts.**

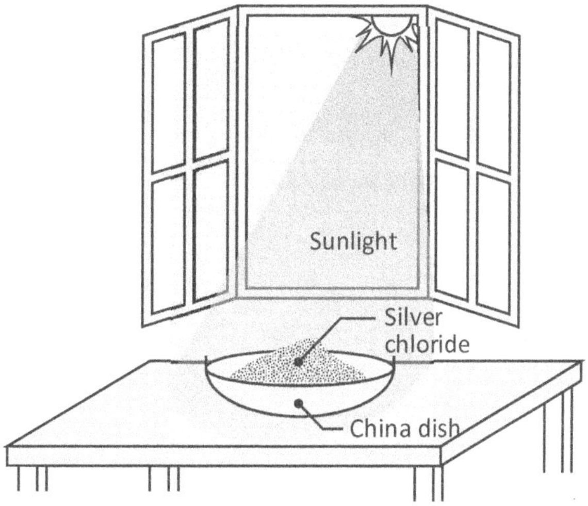

During a chemical reaction atoms of one element do not change into those of another element. Nor do atoms disappear from the mixture or appear from elsewhere. Actually, chemical reactions involve the breaking and making of bonds between atoms to produce new substances. To demonstrate a reaction, 2 g of silver chloride is taken in a china dish and placed in sunlight.

Answer the following questions based on the above activity:

3(a) What will you observe after some time? **1**

3(b) What is this reaction known as? **1**

3(c) Write the balanced chemical equation for this reaction. **1**

3(d) Give reasons for the observations. **1**

4. The following table given below shows the information about two heaters A and B. Analyse the table and answers the following questions:

	Power	Voltage	Resistance	Current
Heater A	100W	220V	?	?
Heater B	150W	220V	?	?

4(a) Which Heater has high resistance? **1**

4(b) If 1KWH is priced at 30 paise, which heater will be costlier if they run for 1 hours each? **1**

4(c) Unit of electric power may also be expressed as **1**

(i) volt ampere **(ii)** kilowatt hour

(iii) watt second **(iv)** joule second **1**

4(d) The rate of flow of an electric charge is known as:

(i) Electric potential **(ii)** Electric conductance

(iii) Electric current **(iv)** None of these **1**

5. Single circulation, *i.e.*, blood flows through the heart only once during one cycle of passage through the body, is exhibited by:

(i) Labeo, Chameleon, Salamander **(ii)** Hippocampus, Exocoetus, Anabas

(iii) Hyla, Rana, Draco **(iv)** whale, dolphin, turtle **1**

6. The human species has genetic roots in:

(i) America **(ii)** Africa

(iii) Australia **(iv)** Antarctica **1**

7. Which of the following is the valence shell for the elements of second period of the modern periodic table?

(i) M shell **(ii)** K shell

(iii) L shell **(iv)** N shell **1**

8. Which of the following represents 'X' in the given figure?

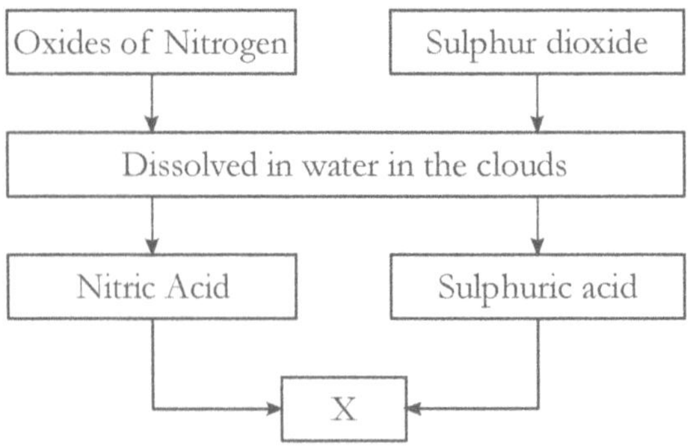

(i) Air pollutant | (ii) Smog
(iii) Acid rain | (iv) Salts 1

9. Which one of the following materials cannot be used to make a lens?

(i) Water **(ii)** Glass

(iii) Plastic **(iv)** Clay 1

OR

A small bulb is placed at the focal point of a converging lens. When the bulb is switched on, the lens produces:

(i) a convergent beam of light **(ii)** a divergent beam of light

(iii) a parallel beam of light **(iv)** a patch of coloured light 1

10. One of the following does not happen during a chemical reaction. This is:

(i) Breaking of old chemical bonds and formation of new chemical bonds

(ii) Formation of new substances with entirely different properties

(iii) Atoms of one element change into those of another element to form new products

(iv) A rearrangement of atoms takes place to form new products 1

OR

You are given the solution of lead nitrate. In order to obtain a yellow precipitate you should mix with it a solution of:

(i) potassium chloride **(ii)** potassium nitride

(iii) potassium sulphide **(iv)** potassium iodide 1

11. During adolescence, several changes occur in the human body. Mark one change from the following associated with sexual maturation in boys:

(i) loss of milk teeth **(ii)** increase in height

(iii) cracking of voice **(iv)** weight gain 1

OR

Characters transmitted from parents to offspring are present in:

(i) Cytoplasm **(ii)** Ribosome

(iii) Golgi bodies **(iv)** Genes 1

12. Which of the following changes occur when you walk out of bright sunshine into a poorly lit room?

(i) the pupil becomes larger **(ii)** the lens becomes thicker

(iii) the ciliary muscle relaxes **(iv)** the pupil becomes smaller 1

For question numbers 13 and 14, two statements are given- one labeled Assertion (A) and the other labeled Reason (R). Select the correct answer to these questions from the codes (a), (b), (c) and (d) as given below

(a) Both A and R are true and R is correct explanation of the assertion.

(b) Both A and R are true but R is not the correct explanation of the assertion.

(c) A is true but R is false.

(d) A is false but R is true.

13. **Assertion A** : Acetic acid is monobasic acid.

Reason R : Acetic acid is a weak acid and produces less concentration of H+ ions.

14. **Assertion A** : Chemical properties of the elements belonging to the same group are the same. 1

Reason R : Elements belonging to the same group possess the same number of valence electrons. 1

SECTION - B

15. Is the chromosome number of zygote, embryonal cells and adult of a particular organism always constant? How is the constancy maintained in these three stages? **3**

16. Draw ray diagrams showing the image formation by a convex mirror when an object is placed:

(a) at infinity

(b) at finite distance from the mirror **3**

OR

Answer the following:

(a) Why does the ray passing through the centre of curvature of a concave mirror retraces its path?

(b) Draw the given diagram in your answer book and complete it for the path of a ray of light after passing through the lens.

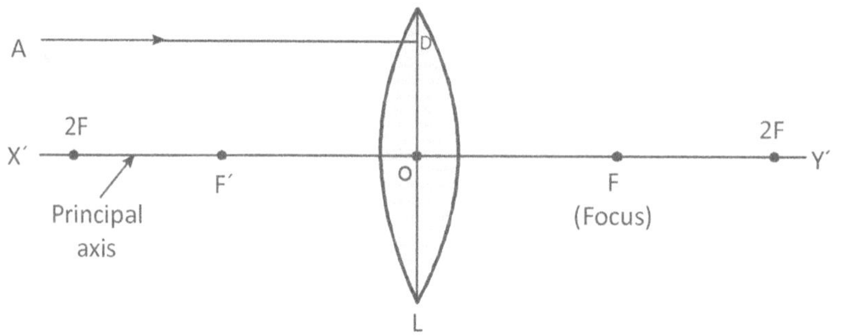

3

17. The person A has only B chromosomes in all its gametes. On the other hand, another person C has chromosome D in half of gametes and chromosome E in another half of gametes. When chromosomes B and D combine during fertilization, a female zygote results. On the other hand, combination of B and E chromosomes produces a male zygote.

(a) What are chromosomes **(i)** B **(ii)** D **(iii)** E?

(b) Out of B, D and E, which 2 chromosomes are of the same type?

(c) Which chromosome is smaller in size?

(d) What is the general name of chromosomes such as B and E?

(e) Out of the two persons A and C, which one is male and female? **3**

18. The values of current I flowing in a given resistor for the corresponding values of potential difference V across the resistor are given below:

I (Amperes)	0.5	1.0	2.0	3.0	4.0
V (volts)	1.6	3.4	6.7	10.2	13.2

Plot a graph between V and I and also calculate the resistance of that resistor. **3**

19. Answer the following:

(a) Why do fire flies glow at night?

(b) Grapes hanging on the plant do not ferment but after being plucked from the plant can be fermented. Under what conditions do these grapes ferment? Is it a chemical or a physical change? **3**

20. Why is alternating current preferred over direct current? List any three reasons. **3**

21. Explain the terms analogous and homologous organs with examples. **3**

22. Nitrogen (atomic number 7) and phosphorus (atomic number 15) belong to group 15 of the Periodic Table. Write the electronic configuration of these two elements. Which of these will be more electronegative? Why? **3**

23. Answer the following:

(a) What would happen if all the green plants disappear from the earth?

(b) If a plant is releasing carbon dioxide and taking in oxygen during the day, does it mean that there is no photosynthesis occurring? Justify your answer. **3**

OR

Answer the following:

(a) What will happen to a plant if its xylem is removed?

(b) Given below is the diagram of a stomatal apparatus. Label the parts A, B, C and D. **3**

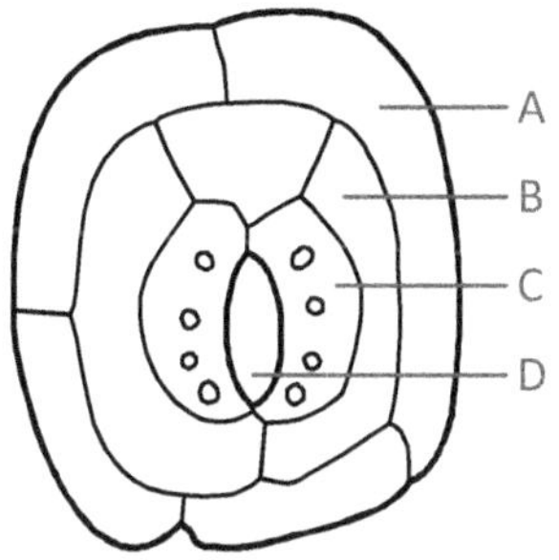

24. **(a)** Dry pellets of a base 'X' when kept in open absorbs moisture and turns sticky. The compound is also formed by chloralkali process. Write the chemical name and formula of X. Describe chloralkali process with balanced chemical equation. Name the type of reaction that occurs when X is treated with dilute hydrochloric acid. Write the chemical equation. **3**

(b) While diluting an acid, why is it recommended that the acid should be added to water and not water to acid? **3**

OR

2 g of ferrous sulphate crystals are heated in a dry boiling tube:

(a) List any two observations.

(b) Name the type of chemical reaction taking place.

(c) Write the chemical equation for the reaction.

(d) Name the products obtained. **3**

SECTION - C

25. What are the major parts of the brain? Mention the function of each part. **5**

OR

Answer the following:

(a) What is meant by 'tropisms' (or tropic movements)? Explain with an example.

(b) What are the different types of tropisms? Define each type of tropism. Write the name of stimulus in each case. **5**

26. List six differences in the physical properties of metals and non-metals. **5**

OR

State five uses each of metals and non-metals. **5**

27. **(a)** Name the condition that results due to the eye lens becoming cloudy. Suggest any one way by which its defect is rectified.

(b) A person uses a lens of power -1.0 D for correcting his distant vision and for correcting his near vision he uses a lens of power + 2.0 D. Calculate the focal length of the lenses required to correct these defects.

(c) Explain why a normal eye is not able to see clearly the objects placed closer than the near points. **5**

OR

The radius of curvature of a convex mirror used as a rear view mirror in a moving car is 2.0 m. The truck is coming from behind it at a distance of 3.5m. Calculate (a) position (b) size of the image relative to the size of truck. What will be the nature of the image? **5**

28. A student fixes a sheet of white paper on a drawing board. He places a bar magnet in the centre of it. He sprinkles some iron filings uniformly around the bar magnet. Then he taps the board gently and observes that the iron filings arrange themselves in a particular pattern.

(a) Why do the iron filings arrange in a pattern?

(b) What do the lines along which the iron filings align represent?

(c) What does the crowding of iron filings at the end of the magnet indicate?

(d) List the properties of magnetic field lines. **5**

29. **(a)** Complete the following equation:

$$CH_3—COOH + NaHCO_3 \longrightarrow \_\_\_\_\_ + \_\_\_\_\_ + \_\_\_\_\_$$

(b) What is the cause of the hardness of water? Why soap do not form lather with hard water? Mention the disadvantage of cleaning clothes with soap in hard water. **5**

30. What are the three R's to save the environment? Explain with one example of each. **5**

CPSIA information can be obtained
at www.ICGtesting.com
Printed in the USA
LVHW061431231120
672396LV00032B/1960

9 789387 279827